Paul's Narrative Thought World

The
TAPESTRY
of
TRAGEDY and TRIUMPH

Ben Witherington, III

Westminster/John Knox Press
Louisville, Kentucky

Book and cover design by Susan E. Jackson

Cover illustration: Photograph by Ben Witherington, III. Detail from the John Piper tapestry, Chichester Cathedral, Chichester, England. The three central panels of the tapestry shown here represent the Trinity.

First edition

Published by Westminster/John Knox Press
Louisville, Kentucky

This book is printed on acid-free paper that meets the American National Standards Institute Z39.48 standard. ∞

PRINTED IN THE UNITED STATES OF AMERICA

9   8   7   6   5   4   3

Library of Congress Cataloging-in-Publication Data

Witherington, Ben, 1951–
    Paul's narrative thought world : the tapestry of tragedy and triumph / Ben Witherington, III. — 1st ed.
        p.   cm.
    Includes bibliographical references and indexes.
    ISBN 0-664-25433-0 (alk. paper)
    1. Bible. N.T. Epistles of Paul—Criticism, Narrative.   2. Narration in the Bible.   I. Title.
BS2650.2.W57   1994
227'.06—dc20   93-39391

ginitive   Cf   parousia
polemics (135)   ff   parenetic
Corpus (136) hcdr of the J   Sapiential
          Q   Redaction (P. 105)

Paul's Narrative Thought World

Ishmael vs Isaac
Hagar vs Sara

Covenants
below the mtn on the mtn – 10 Command

74 I Can't have it – I want it

Christ ⭢ Christians (Similarities ⭢ differences)

Paul: If J is alive then he must be God – after all
if He lives after the death on a cross
that was reserved to humiliate ... etc

*To my friends
Richard Hays and Tom Wright,
fellow followers of the Story,
fellow diggers in the communal plot.*

*To those who taught me Pauline theology—
Andrew Lincoln and Kingsley Barrett.*

*May we always follow Bengel's dictum:
"Apply the whole of yourself to the text;
apply the whole of the text to yourself."*

We look at life from the back of the tapestry,
seeing the loose ends and the knots.
But occasionally the light is bright enough
to shine through the fabric,
and we discern the beautiful design
of both dark and light colors
on the other side.

—Paraphrase of a quotation attributed
to John Muir (1838–1914), naturalist

Contents

Acknowledgments   ix
Introduction   1

PART 1
The Darkened Horizon

1. Paradise Lost   11
2. The Human Malaise   21
3. Flashback: Shades and Shadows in the Vale of Tears   29

PART 2
Keeping the Faith and Laying Down the Law:
From Abraham to Moses and Beyond

4. The First Face of Faith: Abraham   40
5. The Glorious Guardian and the Leader Who Laid
   Down the Law   51
6. True Jews, Torah, and the Future of Ethnic Israel   57
7. Synopsis: The Story Thus Far   73

PART 3

The Surprising Story of the Crucified Conqueror

8. The Origins of a Symbolic Universe   86
9. The Redeemer Stoops to Conquer   94

PART 4

The Omega Man: His Identity, Ministry, and Majesty

10. The Christ: God's Anointed and Appointed One   131
11. A Human Being and the Eschatological Adam   138
12. The *Koinonia* of Jesus and Paul   147

PART 5

The Power and the Glory: The End and Beyond

13. All Roads Lead to the Cross   160
14. First Up from the Dead: Firstfruits of the Harvest   169
15. Therefore God Has Given Him the Name "Lord"   181
16. The Royal Return   186
17. Flashback: A Twofold Trip from Heaven to Earth   205

PART 6

"A Good Likeness": The Story of Christians

18. Saul Searching   215
19. The Christening of the Believer: The Story of Life
    in Christ and Life in the Spirit   245
20. Synopsis of the Plot: The Story of the Christian   338

Epilogue: The Tapestry Complete   352
Scripture Index   357
Author Index   371

Acknowledgments

Grateful acknowledgment is made to the following for permission to reproduce copyrighted material.

Scripture quotations from the Revised Standard Version of the Bible are copyright 1946, 1952, © 1971, 1973 by the Division of Christian Education of the National Council of the Churches of Christ in the U.S.A. and are used by permission.

Scripture quotations from the New Revised Standard Version of the Bible are copyright © 1989 by the Division of Christian Education of the National Council of the Churches of Christ in the U.S.A. and are used by permission.

Augsburg Fortress, for material adapted and reprinted from *Jesus the Sage*, by Ben Witherington, III, copyright © 1994 Augsburg Fortress.

Harcourt Brace & Company, for excerpts from "As the Ruin Falls," in *Poems*, by C. S. Lewis, copyright © 1964 by the Executors of the Estate of C. S. Lewis and renewed 1992 by C. S. Lewis Pte. Ltd.

Macmillan Publishing Company, for excerpts from *The Poems of W. B. Yeats: A New Edition*, edited by Richard J. Finneran. Copyright 1924 by Macmillan Publishing Company, renewed 1952 by Bertha Georgie Yeats.

Oxford University Press, for excerpts from *The Poems of Gerard Manley Hopkins*, copyright © 1967 by The Society of Jesus.

Every effort has been made to obtain permission for the use of poetry not in the public domain and to comply with the requirements of copyright holders. If any rights have been inadvertently infringed upon and this is brought to the publisher's attention, proper acknowledgment will be made in subsequent printings.

Introduction

TAPESTRIES are complex and colorful human creations requiring hours and hours of hard work if done by hand. One can appreciate the stitchery only if time is taken to look very closely at small portions of the work, and even then one may have to look at its back to get a sense of the labor and technique involved. If, however, this is the only way one looks at a tapestry, it is possible to miss the overall pattern or picture that the tapestry is attempting to convey. It is possible to miss the drama for the details. On the other hand, if by stepping back and reflecting on the whole tapestry one gains a clear sense of the nature of the overall drama portrayed on the tapestry, it is much easier to understand the character and function of its individual panels and details.

Sometimes studying Paul's thought world is rather like studying such a tapestry. One quite naturally gets caught up in fascinating portions, details, and even matters of technique and local color. Although one has a suspicion there is some purpose or design binding the whole together, which each part is helping to express, from such close range it is not at all clear what that purpose might be. Some suggest, "We must examine each thread carefully, and once we have exhaustively considered each separate panel of the tapestry, only then can we attempt to reconstruct the whole." Others say, "Let us look at the earliest part of the tapestry sewn, and we will be able to see how it has developed from there." Still others urge, "Let us consider what is central to the tapestry and read its more contingent or secondary elements in that light." To all these voices one is tempted to answer, "But why not step back once more and try again to look at the *whole*, which is much more than the

1

sum of its parts, even the dominant and colorful ones?" This book is an attempt to do just that with Paul's narrative thought world.

On the surface of things, it might seem an exercise in frustration to talk about Paul's narrative thought world. Approaching Paul's thought from the point of view of narrative, one could argue, is rather like going to a philosophical debate and expecting a story to break out. After all, Paul's letters are full of practical advice and theological ideas, not stories. If one wants narratives, one turns to the Gospels or Acts or the Hebrew scriptures, but surely not to Paul. I suspect that this sort of impression has been created in part because we all read Paul in the ways we have been trained to read him since at least the time of Luther, which entails a focus not only on Pauline ideas such as justification through faith but also on post-Enlightenment assumptions about distinctions between being and doing, ideas and action, propositional truth and narratives. Yet when one actually reads Paul, not only does one discover within his letters narratives about Christ (e.g., Phil. 2:6–11; 1 Cor. 15:20–28), about himself (2 Cor. 11:30–12:30; Gal. 1:11–2:21), about Israel (Rom. 9—11; 1 Cor. 10:1–5; Gal. 4:22–31), about the origins of the Christian community (1 Cor. 15:1–11), and about the world outside the community of faith (Rom. 1:18–32), but one continually discovers that Paul is always alluding to larger narratives by means of brief phrases or quotations of narratives, especially those found in the Hebrew scriptures. It is because of this that I have become convinced that *all* Paul's ideas, all his arguments, all his practical advice, all his social arrangements are ultimately grounded in a story, a great deal of which is told in the Hebrew scriptures, but some of which is oral tradition reflecting developments that happened after Old Testament times. Paul's thought, including both theology and ethics, is grounded in a grand narrative and in a story that has continued to develop out of that narrative.[1]

This Story is a tale as large as the universe and yet as small as an individual human being. It is, however, not a Story about everything, not even about all of human history. It is a Story that focuses on God's relationship to humankind, from the beginning of the human race in Adam to its climax in the eschatological Adam, and beyond. It is a Story about creation and creature and their redemption by, in, and through Jesus Christ. It is a Story about a community of faith created out of the midst of fallen humanity. It involves both tragedy and triumph, both the lost and the saved, both the first and the last. Its focus is repeatedly on divine and human actions on the stage of human history. It is out of this Story, which Paul sees as involving both history and His story (i.e., Christ's), that he argues, urges, encourages, debates, promises, and threatens.

It is not true that this Story amounts simply to Paul's appropriating the narratives or even the nonnarrative portions of the Hebrew scriptures.[2] Although these scriptures are in many ways the primary source of, and resource for, this Story,[3] it also involves elements from other traditions (Jewish, Greco-Roman, Christian), elements of logic (e.g., the syllogism in 1 Cor. 15:13ff.), and perhaps most important, elements drawn from Paul's own and other Christians' experiences of God in Christ. It is because of what Paul believes and has experienced to be true about Jesus that he reads the Hebrew scriptures, other traditions, and his own life as he does. For Paul, Christ is the central and most crucial character in the human drama, and everything Paul says about all other aspects of the Story is colored and affected by this conviction.[4] This becomes obvious even in unexpected ways and places. For instance, 1 Cor. 10:4 reveals not only that Paul reads the story of Israel in the light of his Christian faith but also that he believes Christ was already part of that story even during the Exodus-Sinai events. Indeed, Paul believes the one he calls Christ was already present and active before the human story began, even active in the creation of the universe (cf. 1 Cor. 8:6; Col. 1:15–17).[5] In Paul's view, one is always in danger of saying too little about Jesus Christ, not too much.

As has recently been stressed in the important volumes now emerging out of the Society of Biblical Literature Pauline Theology Seminar, there is a need to do detailed exegetical work to build up a picture of the theology or theologies that arise from individual Pauline letters, as well as a need to try to compare and even synthesize insights from these separate inquiries in order to develop a sense of Paul's theology writ large.[6] I have spent the last thirteen years exegeting and teaching Paul's letters and Paul's theology, and I appreciate both the need for and difficulty of such a task. Such inductive approaches are always helpful, though there is always a danger of missing the larger shape of the forest while appreciating the character of particular trees in it. There are, however, at least two additional problems with this approach.

First, it can lead to the assumption that Paul's thought arises out of, and only in response to, particular situations in his congregations. I would suggest that this is essentially incorrect. The situations Paul addresses cause him to articulate his thoughts in one way or another, but those thoughts have *arisen* as a result of his deep and ongoing reflection on the narrative that molds all of his thoughts.[7]

One must always bear in mind that we have in all Paul's letters the words of a mature Christian person who, even in the case of the earliest letter we have, has had at least ten years to reflect on the Christian faith. Whatever development Paul's thought has undergone seems to have taken place almost entirely before any of these letters were written.[8] Even in regard to the crucial subject of Christology, there is precious little evidence of new developments in Paul's later letters.[9] The contingent situations affect how Paul articulates his thoughts, but those thoughts are basically not ad hoc in character. Thus it is incorrect to talk about a coherent core of Paul's thought that is surrounded by a contingent fringe of his thought. Contingency has to do by and large with the mode of expression, not the matter expressed. As N. R. Petersen has said: "Paul integrates his social instructions within a symbolic universe rather than a social one, for the consequences of compliance or non-compliance are not determined socially, that is by social actors, but eschatologically by the Lord. In this respect, therefore the force of Paul's instructions is derived from the symbolic universe which makes them non-negotiable and gives them the status of commands."[10] But this is true not only about Paul's ethical instructions but also about his theology, for as Petersen stresses, "Theology is a form of systematic reflection upon prior knowledge."[11]

Second, the inductive approach, if it is ever to arrive at the stage of discussing "Pauline theology" and not just the theology in a particular letter, must undertake a constructive task, deciding how to order and interrelate and synthesize the various pieces of information one has derived from detailed exegesis. Up to this point, this task has almost always been undertaken by building an artificial framework on which to hang the pieces of information. For example, the famous *ordo salutis* (the order of salvation—justification, then sanctification, then glorification)[12] has been used to arrange discussions of Pauline theology even though it was known that this deals only with soteriology, not with Paul's whole thought world. Such an approach is problematic because it treats Paul's theology not as reflections on his narrative thought world, but as if it were a collection of topics in a history-of-ideas discussion, which simply needs to be arranged in a logical order.

As an alternative to treating Paul's thought in a history-of-ideas manner, I would suggest that Paul has already provided us with hints and sometimes clear expressions of a fundamental Story out of which all his discourse arises.[13] What is needed is to connect the exegetical details to the corresponding places in the plot they comment on or come from. Then one will have a *Pauline* context for interpreting individual texts and details. Of course, it is also very important to be sensitive to the responsive and rhetorical dimensions of the text that cause it to be framed in one way rather than another as Paul addresses different situations and audiences. One must ask questions like these: Is this said for rhetorical effect? Is this statement part of a polemical passage? Does Paul deemphasize this spiritual gift because of problems in Corinth? Nevertheless, Paul is articulating his understanding of the fundamental Story he believes is true in all these specific contexts.

As I see it, Paul refers to four interrelated stories comprising one larger drama: (1) the story of a world gone wrong; (2) the story of Israel in that world; (3) the story of Christ, which arises out of the story of Israel and humankind on the human side of things, but in a larger sense arises out of the very story of God as creator and redeemer; and (4) the story of Christians, including Paul himself, which arises out of all three of these previous stories and is the first full installment of the story of a world set right again. Christ's story is the hinge, crucial turning point, and climax of the entire larger drama, which more than anything else affects how *the* Story will ultimately turn out.[14] The Story contracts to Christ, the seed of Abraham, and then once again expands to include Christ's many followers. Paul reads the entire Story not only in light of the story of Christ but also in light of the story of Christians, and particularly in light of how he believes the drama will ultimately be concluded by Christ and for his followers.

Because we must examine both the presupposed Story and how Paul has reflected on the story in various ways, this work is to some extent a study of both the narrative that generates Paul's worldview, and that worldview itself, including theology and ethics, among other things. Because it must be both, it presupposes a great deal of preparatory exegesis that I am not able to include here due to the exigencies of space. Some of this exegesis may be found in several of my other works.[15] It is time now, however, to embark on a journey through a Story as old as time itself and as recent as ourselves. I have written this in good faith because for me His story is not merely history, not merely part of Israel's or humanity's story, but in a real sense my story as well. I must tell it not only to understand Paul or Paul's redeemer but also to understand myself and my savior as well.

Pentecost 1993

NOTES TO INTRODUCTION

1. In this study I maintain a slightly different distinction from that found in R. B. Hays, *The Faith of Jesus Christ* (Chico, Calif.: Scholars Press, 1983), 17ff., between narrative, which has to do with a story in a text, and story, which is also a narrating of events but in oral form. For convenience sake I will use the term *Story* with a capital S to refer to the whole of the drama Paul reflects on, both in and beyond the text of scripture.

2. It will be seen that my approach in this book differs somewhat from those seeking "echoes" of texts and contexts from the Hebrew scriptures in that it is somewhat broader. I am interested in the underlying story, or narrative, pattern that is sometimes alluded to or evinced in the course of handling the Old Testament, but also comes to light in other places and ways.

3. See R. B. Hays, *Echoes of Scripture in the Letters of Paul* (New Haven: Yale University Press, 1989), passim.

4. Thus E. P. Sanders, *Paul and Palestinian Judaism* (London: SCM Press, 1977), 442ff., is quite right that Paul thinks from "solution" to "plight," from life in Christ to what must be true about life outside Christ and Christ's body. This important insight, although certainly helping us understand *how* Paul thinks about things and where he starts, does not, however, adequately help us understand the relationship between solution and plight or the points where they fit in the narrative plot and why.

5. I believe it very likely that Paul wrote Colossians and also 2 Thessalonians, and that Ephesians is at the very least a development of Paul's thought congenial to his own views by one of his close associates, if not actually written by him. I am also unconvinced by the arguments for the second-century date of the Pastoral Epistles. Nevertheless, the real basis for this study is the so-called capital Paulines, to which I add Colossians and 2 Thessalonians. Ephesians and the Pastoral Epistles will be treated as later developments in the Pauline tradition, whether by Paul (which I would not rule out) or a later Paulinist. Because arguing for the Pauline character of Ephesians and the Pastorals is a necessity in view of the majority of scholars doubting their authenticity, and because this is not the place or time to engage in such an argument, none of the major conclusions of this study are based on the data in Ephesians or the pastorals; but we will mention from time to time how they further spin out certain aspects of Paul's narrative thought.

6. See J. M. Bassler, ed., *Pauline Theology*, vol. 1: *Thessalonians, Philippians, Galatians, Philemon* (Minneapolis: Fortress Press, 1991).

7. I would distinguish between (1) Paul's symbolic universe, which entails those things that Paul takes to be inherently true and real, the fixed stars in Paul's mental sky; (2) Paul's narrative thought world, which is Paul's reflections on his symbolic universe in terms of the grand Story. This undergirds (3) Paul's articulation of his theology, ethics, and so forth, in response to the situations he must address. When one is talking about (3), one will need to talk about the relationship between coherence and contingency, as J. C. Beker puts it (cf. esp. his *Paul the Apostle: The Triumph of God in Life and Thought* [Philadelphia: Fortress Press, 1980]), and be concerned with all sorts of exegetical details. This is less the case when one's focus is on (2), which is the subject of this book.

8. See C. K. Barrett, *From First Adam to Last* (New York: Charles Scribner's Sons, 1962), 3: "We know how Paul understood him in the forties, fifties, and sixties of the first century and, we may add, in the thirties too, for there is no indication whatever that Paul radically changed his views of Jesus between his conversion and the beginning of his letter writing; rather the contrary."

9. The chronology of Paul's letters affects how one views the development of Paul's thought; but even following the widely received notions that Thessalonians is early, Corinthians and Romans in the middle, and Philippians and Colossians probably later, the most one usually comes up with is that cosmic Christology is more developed in Colossians (and in Ephesians) than in the earlier letters. It is not, however, entirely absent from these earlier letters.

10. N. R. Petersen, *Rediscovering Paul: Philemon and the Sociology of Paul's Narrative World* (Philadelphia: Fortress Press, 1985), 135.

11. Petersen, *Rediscovering Paul*, 202. He underscores this point. I am indebted to Petersen, Hays, N. T. Wright, *The New Testament and the People of God* (Minneapolis: Fortress Press, 1992), and S. Fowl, *The Story of Christ in the Ethics of Paul* (Sheffield, Eng.: JSOT Press, 1990), to mention only a few, for helping me to crystallize my reflections about Paul's narrative thought world.

12. Cf., e.g., H. Ridderbos, *Paul: An Outline of His Theology* (Grand Rapids: Wm. B. Eerdmans, 1975), or D.E.H. Whiteley, *The Theology of St. Paul* (Philadelphia: Fortress Press, 1964).

13. See Wright, *The New Testament*, 405: "It is arguable that we can only understand the more limited narrative worlds of the different letters if we locate them at their appropriate points within this overall story-world, and indeed within the symbolic universe that accompanies it."

14. Here I take an approach somewhat different from that of N. T. Wright, who argues that "Paul is telling again and again the whole story of God, Israel, and the world as now compressed into the story of Jesus" (*The New Testament*, 79). Christ is nowhere identified as Israel in Paul's thought, neither as the Israel according to the flesh nor as the "Israel of God." Furthermore, too much of the story of humankind lies outside the story of Christ, including the portion about humanity's fall and fallenness. That Christ's story causes a rereading and realignment of these larger stories is true, but they cannot simply be compressed into the story of Jesus. What can be said is that the story of Christians in some sense takes place in Christ and is modeled on Christ's story.

15. For example, in my *Jesus, Paul, and the End of the World* (Downers Grove, Ill.: I-V Press, 1992) for discussions of Pauline eschatology; in commentary form in my *Conflict and Community in Corinth: A socio-Rhetorical Commentary on 1 and 2 Corinthians* (Grand Rapids: Wm. B. Eerdmans, 1994); and in my socio-rhetorical Philippians commentary, forthcoming from Trinity Press International in 1994.

PART 1
The Darkened Horizon

Things fall apart; the centre can not hold;
Mere anarchy is loosed upon the world,
The blood-dimmed tide is loosed, and everywhere
The ceremony of innocence is drowned;
The best lack all conviction, while the worst
Are full of passionate intensity.

—William Butler Yeats
"The Second Coming"[1]

COMMENTATORS have often noted how very little Paul has to say about creation or creatures prior to the Fall. Even when Adam and Eve are briefly brought into the picture, it is almost always as part of the explanation of where sin and death have come from, or of what it means to be tempted and deceived (cf. Rom. 5:12–21; 2 Cor. 11:3). Furthermore, when Paul talks about creation, he is speaking of creation as it now exists, groaning under the burden of futility to which the Fall subjected it. When Paul reflects on the world, he is almost always reflecting on a world gone wrong or a world the form of which is passing away (1 Cor. 7:31). We hardly ever hear him "sighing for Eden";[2] nor does he speak of human origins like William Wordsworth: "But trailing clouds of glory do we come / From God, who is our home: / Heaven lies about us in our infancy!"[3]

When Paul thinks of human origins, he is never lost in reverie. If his speech is not ominous, it is usually very matter of fact: we began in Adam as creatures of dust and with a merely physical life principle (1 Cor.

15:47–48); or we were created in God's image (1 Cor. 11:7), with woman originally coming forth from Adam, but ever since all have come forth from women (11:8, 12). This scant attention to original innocence, or life before the darkened horizon, is not a result of Paul's being an early Gnostic rejecting the material world as inherently evil and the spirit as good. Paul simply does not believe we *live* in that Edenic world any longer. The shadow of disease, decay, and death, the influence of evil and the powers of darkness must ever be reckoned with in the world in which Paul and his converts live. Paul could never have been an early advocate of Transactional Analysis, intoning "I'm OK, and you're OK." For him that would have been a serious misreading of the human story.

In Paul's view, the cosmos and all that is in it have been subjected to the futility of fallenness. Although humanity was created in God's good image, ever since the primeval parents committed a fateful and fatal transgression, that image has been marred though not obliterated. The mirror has been broken though not entirely shattered. Glimpses of God-likeness still may be seen when one examines the human story, but it is also true that fallenness has touched every aspect of human nature—mind, body, spirit. For Paul, humankind has fallen, and it cannot get up by its own power or strength. This is why, when Paul expresses or alludes to the fundamental human story, he speaks of a need for a radical resuscitation of the dying, a freeing of the enslaved, and other like metaphors.

For Paul, salvation is not a human self-improvement scheme that can be accomplished by a mere increase of information about self, world, and God. Though humankind is not beyond redemption, nor even as bad as it might be, it is nonetheless past the point of being able to save itself. Salvation, in Paul's understanding of the story, thus requires two things: (1) a savior figure who comes from beyond the darkened horizon; (2) salvation that must effect a radical transformation of those it touches.

It is time now, however, to reflect in more depth on the dark backdrop to the story of salvation. In a sense, Paul paints this story much like a Rembrandt picture of the Last Supper. The deepening dark serves to set off the intense light. But we must consider the darkness first—the story of the world, the flesh, and the Devil.

1

Paradise Lost

> Of man's first disobedience, and the fruit
> Of that forbidden tree, whose mortal taste
> Brought death into the world and all our woe,
> With loss of Eden, till one greater Man
> Restore us, and regain the blissful seat
> Sing heavenly Muse . . .
>
> —*John Milton*
> Paradise Lost *1.1–6*[4]

ADAM AND EVE

THE story of the human world begins, in Paul's thought, with Adam and Eve.[5] What is most critical for Paul is not who Adam or Eve were so far as their own experience of life in the garden is concerned but the effect of their actions on the human race as its progenitors and representative heads.[6] It is interesting that Paul, unlike some of his later misinterpreters, does not seem to hold Eve mainly responsible for the Fall even though he knows the story says she was deceived by the serpent (2 Cor. 11:2). Rather, it is by Adam that death came into the world (cf. Rom. 5:12; 1 Cor. 15:21–22). When it comes time to assign blame, Paul places the burden of it on the man, not the woman.

Paul does not see gender distinctions, nor some gender-distinctive roles, nor even some apparel meant to reflect creation-order distinctions as a result of the Fall. Rather, gender distinctions and distinctiveness are seen

11

as good manifestations of the way God began the human story, the way
God created man and woman, the way God intended humankind to be.
This is clear from Paul's argument in 1 Cor. 11:2–16. Paul, however, goes
on to suggest that when the creation is redeemed and renewed in Christ,
although gender distinctions are still important he does not believe that
biology necessarily dictates destiny in regard to religious roles. Women,
like men, may pray and prophesy so long as they both manifest the tokens
of their gender distinctiveness. It is important to stress this at the outset of
our reading of Paul's narrative thought world, for not only does salvation
presuppose human fallenness in Paul's telling of the Story, but it is creation
that is being redeemed and renewed, not obliterated, in Christ. This
becomes most evident in Paul's discussions of things like the new creation
(2 Cor. 5), the resurrection body of believers (1 Cor. 15), the renewal of the
material world (Rom. 8), and other related matters. One must be clear on
the big picture—the general contours of the relationship of creation, Fall,
and redemption as Paul envisions the tale—if one is to make sense of the
individual acts in the drama.

Paul certainly was aware that "Adam," before it ever might be
considered a personal name, meant human being or earth creature (one
derived from the earth). As human beings created in God's image, Adam
and Eve alike had the capacity to make moral judgments about good and
evil, at least insofar as they knew it was wrong to disobey an explicit
command of their Maker. So it is that Paul does not couch his discussion of
the original transgression by using phrases like "an accident" or "a slip." In
Paul's understanding of the story, Adam and Eve were guilty of an
intentional and blameworthy error—indeed, of an act of willful rebellion
or revolt. In sum, Paul believes that the primal parents didn't fall—they
jumped!

One might then assume that this is just a story of *human* tragedy, but it
is not so. The effect of the original revolt was felt not only by the
descendants of Adam and Eve but by all of creation. The bondage of sin
and decay descended upon the whole cosmos (Rom. 8:21a); thus redemption, if it is to be adequate, must be cosmic in scope. Hence Paul says that
all of creation stands on tiptoes waiting eagerly for the resurrection day
when the liberation of humankind is completed, because the rest of
creation will also obtain "the freedom of the glory of the children of God"
(Rom. 8:21b). Shakespeare understood well the scope of the tragedy.

> When I do count the clock that tells the time,
> And see the brave day sunk in hideous night;
> When I behold the violet past its prime,
> And sable curls all silver'd o'er with white; . . .

Then of thy beauty do I question make
That thou among the wastes of time must go,
Since sweets and beauties do themselves forsake,
And die as fast as they see others grow;
And nothing 'gainst Time's scythe can make defence
Save breed to brave him when he takes thee hence.

—*William Shakespeare*
Sonnet 12[7]

Adam and Eve's story, however, is more than primeval; it is also in a sense representative. The charter of human existence was to be inferior to God but superior to the rest of creation.[8] Adam and Eve were to be creators and rulers on a smaller scale but similar to the one in whose image humanity was made. Instead, because of the revolt, humankind became subject to idolatry, immorality, abuse of personhood, abuse of power. By attempting to become more than they were, Adam and Eve became less than they ought to be. By listening to the serpent they broke the chain of the creation order, submitting to those they were supposed to rule over.

> The total result of Adam's revolt is that [humankind] suffers grievous misfortune. In himself, he is deprived of privileges and attributes which originally he enjoyed. He is mortal, not immortal; he is subjected to unhappiness, being the victim of fear, pain, and death; he is deprived of abilities, physical and mental, which were formerly his. Moreover, he finds himself in a world in which the sovereign authority of the beneficent God is manifestly denied. Evil powers are at large in the universe.[9]

Idolatry is by definition the worshiping or obeying of something as God that is in fact less than God. Seeking to be as gods, Adam and Eve became more like the lesser creatures in several ways: (1) the human story, like that of other sentient beings, becomes red in tooth and claw, an endless struggle for survival, an endless competition for superiority; (2) the human story, like that of other creatures, becomes a story of the sort of moral promiscuity common among the lesser animals; (3) the human story even degenerates into the worship of parts of creation (animals, natural forces, even human beings) as if they were the Creator. This is the ugly legacy left behind by those primeval parents.

But this is not all. Adam and Eve not only did these deeds for humankind as our representatives. They also passed on the inclination—indeed, the determination—to "go and do likewise" ever since. Another early Jew puts it this way: "Each of us has been the Adam of his [or her] own soul" (2 Bar. 54:19). Paul concludes, "Therefore, just as sin came into

the world through one man, and death came through sin, . . . so death
spread to all *because all have sinned*" (Rom. 5:12). Like father, like son; like
mother, like daughter.

In one of his most creative moves, Paul in Rom. 7:7–13 retells the story
of the Fall[10] in the midst of his discussion of the Law and its effect on fallen
human beings. To understand this passage one must recognize three
things: (1) Paul believes that Moses wrote the Pentateuch, including
Genesis; (2) the "law" in Moses' books includes more than simply the Law
that the historical Moses conveyed to God's people. It can even include the
very first commandment not to eat of the fruit of the tree of the knowledge
of good and evil. Indeed, some even saw God's original commandment to
Adam and Eve as a form of one of the ten given to Moses on Sinai. (3) It
appears that Paul understood the original sin to be a violation of the Tenth
Commandment against "coveting," the desiring of something more and
other than one ought to desire, in this case, coveting the fruit from the one
prohibited tree. In Rom. 7:7–13 Paul is dealing with the paradox that
although God's commandments are all good, yet human beings would not
know what sin is had there not been any commandments. "I would not
have known what it is to covet if the law had not said, 'You shall not
covet.' "

Paul tells again the tale of Adam in the first person, and with personification of Sin.[11] One could just as easily read Rom. 7:8–11 as follows: "But
the serpent [sin], seizing an opportunity in the commandment, produced in
me all kinds of covetousness. . . . But I [Adam] was once alive apart from the
law, but when the commandment came, sin sprang to life and I died, and
the very commandment that promised life proved to be death to me. For
sin [the serpent], seizing an opportunity in the commandment, deceived
me and through it killed me." Here is the familiar primeval tale of life apart
from sin, a commandment, deception, disobedience, and ensuing death.

In favor of this interpretation are the following factors: (1) Notice in v.
7 there is reference to one specific commandment against coveting, or
desire. (2) In v. 8 there is further reference to *the commandment* singular,
which can hardly be a reference to the Mosaic law in general but rather to
one specific directive. (3) Verse 9 says, "I was living once without or apart
from the law." Surely the only persons Paul ever thought were alive before
or without the law were Adam and Eve.[12] (4) In v. 11 sin is clearly
personified as though it was a living thing: "Sin took opportunity through
the commandment and deceived me." This was precisely what happened
when the serpent used the commandment to deceive Eve (and Adam) in the
garden. (5) Paul uses the same verb (*exepatesen*) here as he does in 2 Cor.
11:3 to speak of the deception in the garden.[13] (6) The punishment for this
first sin was ultimately physical death. But as Cain and Abel's story shows,

spiritual death happened first, and it is probably the latter Paul has in mind here. (7) In v. 7 Paul says sin was not *known* (*egnon*) except through the commandment. This verb could mean "have experimental knowledge of," perhaps on analogy with v. 5. This condition would only properly be the case with Adam. After the Fall, everyone has experience of sin with or without the law.[14] This is most naturally taken as a description of Adam's awakening consciousness of the possibility of sin when the first prohibition was given. The view that best explains all the details of the text, including the past tense verbs, is that Paul is here reflecting back on the experience of Adam. This is a perfect example of how Paul does theology by reflecting back on the grand narrative that undergirds all his thought.[15] This discussion about Adam must also be seen in light of what Paul says about all fallen humanity's being in Adam—and sinning and dying (Rom. 5:12–21). In Rom. 7:7–13, Adam stands only for himself, but vv. 14–25 seem, as we will see, to be about all fallen humanity who follow in Adam's footsteps, and can therefore be said to be *in Adam*.

A few final comments on this critical passage in Rom. 7:7–13 are in order. Verse 12 introduces the conclusion about the Law, which has been Paul's primary subject for discussion since at least 7:1. The Law is holy, just, and good. It in itself did not produce sin or death in the father or mother of the race. Sin, *or rather evil personified* (*the serpent*), which in early Jewish thinking often was understood to refer to the Satan, used the Law to this end. The exceeding wickedness of evil is revealed in that it will even take a good thing, the Law, and twist it to produce an evil end—death—which the Law was not really intended to produce.

Paul does not believe that evil is some abstract force, like fate, that occasionally and blindly strikes humans down. Paul believes that evil happens according to the directions and malignant intentions of a personal Evil One, a dark lord whom Paul is even willing to call "the god of this world." This Evil One deliberately seeks to blind the minds of unbelievers so they may not see salvation's light (2 Cor. 4:4). We have already seen hints from the discussion of Adam and Eve that there are other conspirators in the story of human demise, and we must consider them now.

THE DEVIL AND HIS MINIONS

THE POWERS OF DARKNESS AND THEIR EVIL AGE

Paul does not attempt formally to explain how evil entered the world, though he assumes that sin enters the picture with Adam and Eve. He seems to have believed both that God created all things in a state of moral goodness, but also that personal and purposeful evil was already present in the garden prior to the revolt of Adam and Eve. It is not human structures that are the ultimate source of evil,[16] nor is it that the natural world is inherently evil or malevolent by its very nature. For Paul, evil is personal both on a human and supernatural level. He seems to see evil forces being directed by an ultimate personal cosmic source.

> The scale of evil about which the Pauline writers speak is in one sense much smaller than the political realm: personal immorality, weakness, bondage, fear, and suffering, and the peculiar problem of the relation between Jews and gentiles. In another sense the scale is much broader: Satan, the god of this world, cosmic alienation and reconciliation, the end of this age. It is striking that so little is said about solutions or explanations for any of the ordinary evils that plague everybody. Pauline Christianity seems, at least in the extant letters, to offer no general theodicy. Rather, attention is paid only to factors that arise for the first time because the readers have become Christians.[17]

This evaluation somewhat underplays the fact that Paul *does* believe that the powers of darkness use good things that are given to humans by God, such as the law and human governments (cf. Rom. 13:1–2; 2 Thess. 2:13ff.), to serve their malign ends. It is true, however, that Paul's focus is mainly on personal or cosmic evil, not the evil that is transpersonal but less than supernatural. We must accordingly first examine Paul's view of the supernatural and cosmic evil in the world.

Many suggest one key phrase is *stoicheia tou kosmou* (Gal. 4:3). This particular phrase is found nowhere else in all Greek literature except here and in Gal. 4:8–9, so far as material antedating or contemporary with this text is concerned. The term *stoicheia* by itself in Greek literature (both pagan and Jewish) seems sometimes to mean the elements that make up the material world.[18] Paul, however, is hardly talking about earth, air, fire, and water in Gal. 4:3. The cognate verbal form *stoichein* is found in Phil. 3:16, where it means to keep in line with some principles. In pagan literature *stoicheion* often means the elements or fundamental principles of learning.[19] A use of *stoicheia* (without *kosmou*) is found in Heb. 5:12; 6:1, where it refers to the basic Christian teachings on fundamental matters (cf. 6:2).

Is Paul talking about heavenly bodies or the elemental spirits that were thought to control or reside on, or be synonymous with, these stars? Through astrology it was thought one could learn one's fate as controlled by these elemental spirits, or star gods. In favor of this view seems to be Gal. 4:8–9, where Paul speaks of the *stoicheia* that are by nature not gods. Possibly the reference to angels' having delivered the Law in Gal. 3:19–20 suggests a connection between supernatural beings and the Law.[20]

I have suggested elsewhere that at numerous points the author of Hebrews seems to be drawing on the Pauline corpus, particularly Galatians and 1 Corinthians, and using it in his own way.[21] This being so, Heb. 5–6 may reflect the earliest non-Pauline interpretation of what Paul meant in Gal. 4:8–9. Paul could certainly be referring to the elementary teaching or religious principles of the universe, which would include both the Law of Moses and Gentile principles (cf. 4:4). In Gal. 4 and also in Col. 2:8, the context has to do with being enslaved to the law or some principles that involve a rigid legalism. In Col. 2:8, the phrase "according to the traditions of humanity," parallels "according to the elementary principles of the world," and in vv. 20–22 Paul lists some of these regulations. Submitting to the *stoicheia* means obeying regulations such as "do not handle," "do not touch," which Paul calls the teachings of human beings. Colossians 2:23 indicates that these regulations include some sort of asceticism, which does not keep in check "the flesh."[22] Finally, the Greek text of Gal. 4:8 omits a word and reads "the ____ which are not by nature gods." One may as easily insert the word "things" in the blank as the word "beings." I conclude that Paul is not referring to "elemental spirits of the universe" when he speaks of the *stoicheia*, though the powers of darkness may use the Law or human traditions to enslave people. Paul's heavens are not emptied of demons and angels by this conclusion about *stoicheia tou kosmou.*

For Paul there is a great difference between what is true of those in Christ and what is true for those who are "in the world." In order to understand the exceeding darkness of the dark, we must contrast it with what is true for those who are in the light. Those in Christ are freed from bondage either to the Law or to any other sort of elementary principles. These become weak and beggarly elements once one is saved by the powerful Christ. Galatians 4:9 may suggest that Paul is not talking about the Old Testament law, for elsewhere he calls it holy, just, and good, not beggarly. Nor have the Gentiles turned back to the Mosaic law, for they were not under it previously (cf. Rom. 2:12–16). Paul, however, does want to say that bondage to any sort of legalism, either pagan or Jewish, foisted upon one by dark powers in order to enslave one, is something Christians should have outgrown. Galatians 4:3 suggests that to remain under the Law is to remain as a child. We will discuss this further when we come to the point in the story where Moses and Israel appear on the stage.

When Paul actually wants to discuss supernatural or cosmic beings, whether angels or the Devil's minions, he uses terms other than *stoicheia*. For example, in Rom. 8:38 we are told of beings or forces that will not separate believers from Christ's love, including angels, *archai* (rulers), and powers. If these beings were all on God's side, Paul would surely not speak of them as possible sources of separation of believers from the love of God in Christ. Paul clearly distrusts all such supernatural powers and forces. Though *archai* can refer in other contexts to civil magistrates, here it is linked to angels and probably denotes supernatural beings. Barrett suggests that *archai* refers to the princes of these apparently evil angels (cf. 1 Cor. 15:24; Col. 1:16; 2:10, 15).[23] Normally, *archai* are associated in Paul with *exousiae* (authorities—cf. 1 Cor. 15:24; Eph. 1:21; 3:10; 6:12; Col. 1:16; 2:10, 15), or *dunameis* (powers) as in Rom. 8:38 and Eph. 1:21, 1 Cor. 15:24, or *kuriotetes* (dominions—Col. 1:16; Eph. 1:21). All of these names were current in Judaism for angelic powers of various sorts.[24]

Christ won the decisive battle over these spirits or angelic beings and has exposed them for what they are, making a public example of them by his death on the cross (Col. 2:14, 15).[25] They have not yet been destroyed, however, and they continue rearguard action trying to fight back (Eph. 6:12). Even after Christ's decisive victory on the cross, believers must combat them. They are seen as the real source of many problems and sufferings. First Corinthians 15:24 indicates that the complete subjugation of these dark forces happens only after the return of Christ and at the end of history. Meanwhile, they have been disarmed in the sense that they have no power over Christians to force them to do things against their will. Paul's essential position is that Christians are safe in Christ, however, should they go back to their old ways or to new legalistic and nonfaith ways, they can again be enslaved or endangered by supernatural evil.[26]

For Christians to resubmit themselves to such powerless powers was foolishness and bondage all over again, from which Christ came to set them free. Paul points out that believers will judge fallen angels (1 Cor. 6:3). Although 1 Cor. 11:10 may refer to protection from evil "peeping Tom" angels (cf. Gen. 6:1–4), it more likely alludes to good angels as the guardians of the proper order of things in creation and in worship.[27]

It is striking how seldom, in comparison to the Synoptic Gospels, Paul speaks about "demons" (1 Cor. 10:20–21). This is likely in part because he believes Christ has objectively triumphed over such beings on the cross, and in part because he believes that faithful believers cannot be possessed by such beings, for the Holy Spirit and Christ are in some manner subjectively dwelling within believers' bodies as in a temple.

This sort of protection and liberation is not, however, to be found in the lives of those who dwell in darkness. In Paul's view, ever since the Fall humans are in bondage to sin (Rom. 1); they are still enticed and led astray to idols (1 Cor. 12:2), which must be completely turned from and rejected if one is to serve a living and true God (1 Thess. 1:9). Paul believes that the world outside of Christ and Christ's community is a very dark place, not least because of the Adversary, the Satan.[28]

SATAN AND THE DEVIL OF A TIME

> So farewell hope, and with hope farewell fear,
> Farewell remorse! All good to me is lost;
> Evil be thou my good; by thee at least
> Divided empire with heaven's king I hold
> By thee, and more than half perhaps will govern;
> As man ere long, and this new world shall know.
>
> —*John Milton*
> *Satan's soliloquy*, Paradise Lost, *4:109–113*[29]

Paul has a clearly formed notion of the Satan, who is the ruler not only over all the wicked heavenly hosts but is even said to be the god of this age and the one who destroys the flesh (cf. 1 Cor. 5:5). In 1 Cor. 5:5, "flesh" may mean the sinful attitudes or inclinations, but perhaps it is more likely that Paul means physical flesh here, because Paul sees death as the enemy that is apparently in Satan's hands (cf. 1 Cor. 15:24–26).

Satan is the one who tempts a person to do evil (1 Cor. 7:5), as an individual, but also he attempts to gain advantage over the body of Christ by sowing seeds of discord and disunity into the body (cf. 2 Cor. 2:11). Satan is very deceptive, for he disguises himself as an angel of light (2 Cor. 11:14) and can send physical or spiritual problems, called messengers by Paul, to plague people (2 Cor. 12:7). Satan can "block" Paul from coming and being with his fellow believers (1 Thess. 2:18). It is Satan who promotes lawlessness and chaos in the world, and it is not until Christ returns that Satan is finally dealt with once and for all (cf. 2 Thess. 2:8–12). This last text indicates that Satan is also capable of producing pretend signs and wonders with all power.

This Dark One is by no means powerless even in the Christian era, and believers alone cannot dispose of or dispossess him from his place in this world. It is God alone who will truly crush Satan under believers' feet (Rom. 16:20). Crucifixion, resurrection, exaltation to the right hand of power all represent decisive though not final victories over Satan. Paul does not, like the Fourth Gospel, talk about Satan as the ruler of this world (cf. John 12:31; 16:11), but he does use a similar phrase, "the god of this world" (2 Cor. 4:4). Clearly, he sees Satan as a powerful figure who has been judged by Christ. It is precisely this external and supernatural cosmic evil in the universe that makes it impossible for us to reduce Paul's gospel to an existentialist program of self-improvement to rid ourselves of sin.[30]

There are both external and internal forces that lead to sin and evil in humanity and in the world. Internally, Christians have been renewed and given sufficient grace to withstand the onslaughts of Satan if they will do so and rely on Christ. But externally, the world is still a dark place, and Satan is able, if he has a willing subject, to lead even a believer astray (cf. 1 Cor. 12:1–3; Gal. 3:1; 1 Tim 5:14–15).

Thus far we have dealt with the Devil and his cohorts. Yet one further aspect of the world needs to be explored—Paul's description of it as "this present evil age" (Gal. 1:4) This seems to be a reference not to a particular age of history, but every age of history since the Fall. It is the age all fallen people have always lived in. This sort of terminology is found elsewhere in Jewish literature (1 Q.Hab.5.7f.). Deliverance for the Christian is not out of the material world but rather from its ethical wickedness and fallen worldviews. In short, Christ came to set people free from the evil in the world, not from the world itself. Christians are those who are not to be conformed to "this age" (Rom. 12:2), that is, to its ruling orientation and lifestyle. Christians are those upon whom the ends of this present evil age and all the ages of history have come (cf. 1 Cor. 10:11). Those who remain in Christ are in some sense preserved and protected from the age's power until Christ returns.

The phrase "this age" (cf. 1 Cor. 1:20) stands in contrast not to previous ages of history, but to the age to come. It is often noted that Paul in the so-called capital Paulines never talks about the age to come and that he adopted this framework from Judaism. Both are true statements. However, Paul has altered the Jewish framework to include a Messiah who has broken into history *during* this present evil age; therefore, there are already present in this age some elements of the age to come.[31] The tension between the already and the not yet, between what is already true in the believer, in the body of Christ, and even in the world, and what is yet to come in Paul's thought seems to be reflected in his use of the age language.

2

The Human Malaise

WE are now in the position to ask what is true personally of the individual outside of Christ, whether Jew or Greek. We will have occasion to explain later that Christians experience the tension between flesh and spirit, not that between old person and new person. Sin in the Christian cannot be explained as the old person dragging him down inevitably. For Paul, holiness, not sin, was to be expected of the Christian, and sinful behavior and temptation were assumed to be avoidable or escapable by the help of God (cf. 1 Cor. 10:12–13). The more profound riddle for Paul is why there is sin in a new creation in Christ at all, not how there can be a new creation in the midst of this present evil age.

The chief context for our remaining discussion in this chapter must be Rom. 1–7. Paul's exposition in Rom. 1:18 begins with a discussion of the Gentiles' state outside of Christ. They are seen as wicked and idolators. They deliberately suppress the truth and have engaged in worship of images of parts of the creation, rather than worshiping the creator. Paul insists that they knew God, by which he means they knew God's power and deity as revealed in creation, but they refused to honor God or give thanks for what they knew of God. Instead, they became futile in their thinking, and the result of their rebellion was that their minds were further darkened. This is simply another way of saying that "the god of this world [is] blinding the minds of the unbelievers" (2 Cor. 4:4). The "god of this world" is a bold metaphor for Satan and shows how powerful Paul thought him to be in regard to unbelievers. Satan is god of this world in that in its falseness the world reflects his character and lordship; sin, death, and evil seem to reign.

21

Yet it is also true according to Romans 1 that unbelievers choose to be or remain those who acknowledge the "god of this world," not the true God. They are thus not exonerated because Satan has deceived them. They were willing to be deceived, choosing darkness and not what they knew of God's power and deity, and so they are responsible for willfully choosing to do otherwise (cf. 2 Thess. 2:9, 10). Gentile nonbelievers exchanged truth for a lie and creator for creature (Rom. 1:25), so God gave them up to debauchery. Paul would include under this rubric all sorts of sexual behavior prohibited in the Hebrew scriptures, including homosexual behavior and bestiality.[32]

What is most important about this material in Romans 1 is the clear link made between belief and behavior. In Paul's view, a base mind leads to base and wicked conduct. At Rom. 1:29–31, Paul makes clear the full extent of what giving oneself up to false religions and wicked ways of life can lead to in one's conduct. For such as these there will be judgment without mercy according to the works they have done (Rom. 2:6–8). Paul clearly believed that those who reject God, and in particular God in Christ, must be numbered among the perishing (2 Cor. 4:3).

Thus far, Paul sounds rather like many other early Jewish preachers holding forth against Gentile wickedness and idolatry. However, at Rom. 2:9 Paul goes on to say that, as the Hebrew prophets said, judgment for sin begins with the household of God, to the Jew first then to the Gentile. God shows no partiality, and Jews will not be exempted simply because they are Jews.

Beginning at Rom. 2:12, Paul indicates that judgment will be universal outside of Christ. All who have sinned with or without the Law will perish.[33] The Law will be used to judge those who are under the Law, and those not under the Law will be judged by what they do know, by what is clear about God from the creation.[34] At Rom. 2:15, Paul insists that God has written in all human hearts, even Gentiles, what the Law basically requires, and God has also given to all a conscience. This can accuse or excuse one's thoughts or conduct. The image of God has not been totally obliterated even in the most fallen of creatures. We should likely see Rom. 2:15 as a foreshadowing of Rom. 7:14–25. In Paul's view, whatever the advantages of being a Jew, and they are many (cf. Rom. 9:1–5), Jews are no better off in regard to the judgment of God, because "all, both Jews and Gentiles, are under the power of sin'" (Rom. 3:9), all have sinned and fallen short of God's grace (3:23).

At Rom. 5:12 Paul goes on to explain in terms of the Genesis story that not only did sin enter the world through Adam, but that all his progeny also went on to sin as well. Thus death, the wages of sin (Rom. 5:12), came upon all both because of the sin of Adam, but also because of our own sin.

All deserved the death penalty with and like Adam. Sin and death came to reign over all humankind (5:17). Romans 5:21 says sin reigned *in* death. Romans 6:17 makes clear that those outside Christ are "slaves to sin," unable to avoid sin or to free themselves from sin's bondage (6:20). All of this discussion in Romans 5 and especially in Romans 6 prepares us for Paul's most profound discourse on human lostness outside Christ. This discourse is found in Rom. 7:14–25, and to it we must give careful attention now.

Certainly the most controverted of all the chapters in the whole of the Pauline corpus is Romans 7. On this chapter hinges whole theories of what the normal Christian life is or isn't like.[35] There are at least seven or eight theories of whom Paul is talking about in 7:14–25. The first thing to notice about the context is that Romans 7 is not an isolated excursus, but a continuation of the discussion of the Law, and in fact of the general discussion in Rom. 1–6. Furthermore, if read carefully, the text also seems to flow quite naturally into the discussion in Romans 8. It will be necessary to compare and contrast Romans 7 and 8 at a couple of crucial points in order to discern whom Paul is talking about in 7:14–25.

Romans 7:5–6 seems to be a preview of the drift of the following argument. Notice that Paul in these two verses first states what believers *were* (imperfect tense verb) in the flesh, and in v. 6 we hear of what "we" (believers) now have been made. Believers have been released from the Law. Cranfield's view that Paul means here "set free from the law's condemnation" has to be read into the text.[36] Rather, the analogy with the death of the husband in 7:1–4 suggests a total release from this law, for when the husband is dead the wife is totally free from being subordinate to, being bound to obey, or bound to the deceased husband in any real way. It is natural then to assume that Paul will go on to contrast the believer's condition before and after the point of release, which must surely refer to conversion.

As even Cranfield has to admit, in 7:6 as in 8:8, 9, Paul uses the phrase *en sarki* ("in the flesh") to denote a condition that for the Christian now belongs to the past. This seems to me an admission that must prove fatal to his argument. On the one hand he wants to say that "we no longer have the basic direction of our lives controlled and determined by the flesh."[37] On the other hand, by referring 7:14–25 to the Christian as a description of the normal, even the best, Christian life, Cranfield insists that when Paul says that "we are fleshly" (*sarkinos*) sold under sin in v. 14, this is not a contradiction to the assertion that "we have been released from being in the flesh" in a moral sense. Surely this is a case of trying to have it both ways.

Due attention in this passage must be carefully paid to the change in tenses. In vv. 7–13 we have past tenses, whereas in vv. 14–25 we have present tenses. This strongly suggests to most commentators that either Paul is changing the subject somewhat in the second half of the material, or he is changing the time frame in which he is viewing the one subject. I would suggest that the subject is Adam in vv. 7–13, and then in vv. 14–25 those who are *in Adam*. Adam is seen as Exhibit A of what happens when humans submit to temptation. Then Paul explains how Adam's legacy has been continued, how the effect of his sin has caused bondage for all, and thus how all fallen creatures inevitably perpetuate Adam's error again and again.

Cranfield provides the most exhaustive list of options for whom the "I" may refer to in 7:14–25, to which we will add one more at the end: (1) the *ego* in these verses is autobiographical, referring to Paul's present experience as a Christian; (2) the *ego* is autobiographical, referring to Paul's past experience before his conversion, as he viewed it *then*; (3) is the same as (2), except that *ego* refers to Paul's Christian view of his pre-Christian state; (4) *ego* refers to the experience of the non-Christian Jew as he or she views it; (5) the passage presents the non-Christian Jew as seen through Christian eyes; (6) it presents the experience of the so-called carnal Christian, one living at a level he or she should not and trying to fight the battle against sin on his or her own steam; (7) it presents the experience of Christians, generally including the very best and most mature; (8) it refers to someone under the conviction of sin, having heard the Law preached, who is in the process of conversion. On this last view Rom. 7:14–25 and Rom. 8:1–17 record a sort of psychological transcript of a conversion going from conviction of sin and recognition of sin's bondage to deliverance.

Some commentators, such as E. Käsemann, have combined several views, arguing for instance that vv. 14–20 refers to the experience of the pious person represented by the Jew; and then in vv. 21–25 the reference is to all of fallen humanity.[38] It is fair to say that perhaps a majority of commentators now think that Paul could not possibly be describing how the Jew felt about his or her *own* experience. Many, following E. P. Sanders,[39] also think these verses must be dealing with a Christian view of some sort of pre-Christian condition.

If Paul is capable of using the "I" in vv. 7–13 to refer to someone other than himself, he is perfectly capable of continuing this trend in these verses as well. Without some indication of a change in technique, one should presume that Paul is continuing to use the "I" rhetorically. Against the view that Paul is referring to his present experience must be what K. Stendahl has pointed out at length.[40] Not only does Paul believe he is successfully working out his own salvation with fear and trembling and pressing on to the goal to which God has called him (Phil. 3:12–16), but as Stendahl shows, Paul almost never speaks of repentance or forgiveness in a

Christian context. In short, Paul manifests a robust conscience, not a sin-laden one. His anxieties are basically about and for his fellow Christians and Jews, *not* about his own spiritual condition, so far as we can tell. One would be hard-pressed to find in any of his letters any evidence of Paul apologizing for or confessing *sin* (not to be confused with weakness) that he committed *as* a Christian, much less any indication that he felt he was a slave to sin and bound in its clutches.

The first option mentioned above then must be rejected. It has arisen because of the enormous influence of Luther (and before him Augustine), Calvin, and in our own era Barth, Cranfield, and others. It has arisen because Romans 7 has not been read as Paul's reflection on Genesis 3 and its sequel—on what it means first to have been Adam, and second to be Adam's children.[41] Everywhere else, when Paul talks about those in Adam and those in Christ he quite properly contrasts the two states (cf. 1 Cor. 15:21–22; Rom. 5:12–15). Redemption for Paul means a great deal more than just a change of position in relationship to God or even a change of opinions about God; it means a real subjective change affecting the human will, mind, and emotions (cf., e.g., 2 Cor. 5:17; Rom. 8:2–9; 12:2). It is only the human body and the inclinations or desires that the fallen body stimulates that Paul sees as largely untouched by redemption as of yet. "Though the body is dead because of sin, the Spirit is life because of righteousness" (Rom. 8:10), and so the believer by the Spirit's power can put to death the fallen deeds prompted by the body (8:13). Greater is the One who is in the believer than either the urges of the fallen body or any force that confronts the believer in the world.

The second option mentioned above can be quickly dismissed in light of Phil. 3:6b and Gal. 1:14. What is not quite clear is whether this *was* Paul's view of his state when he was a Jew or whether it is now his view—probably the former.[42] Certainly, Paul's sense of the inadequacy of the position even of the pious Jew is quite clear in Rom. 2—3 and 9—11. This suggests that we must rule out option four as well. There is no reason to think, if Paul did not feel like the Romans 7 person while a Jew, that other Jews did or do.

In regard to views five through eight, we will now turn to more detailed exegesis to sort these out. The present tenses in this section must be taken with absolute seriousness. Paul is describing a condition that is *now* true of someone or some group in his own day. Paul begins v. 14 by using his customary "for we know" phrase, a formula he often uses when he is drawing on common or shared knowledge among Christians (cf. 8:22; 2 Cor. 5:1).

What Paul is about to say is connected to what precedes, for he is continuing to talk about the law. Here we have a basic contrast—the law is spiritual, but the "I" Paul has in mind is fleshly, sold under sin. It is very difficult *not* to relate this back to Rom. 7:5–6. According to those verses, there is a group of people, namely Christians, who *were* in the flesh, but now he is talking about an individual or group that *is* in that condition. Paul says clearly to his Christian audience in 8:9: "*You are not in the flesh*"(the crucial *en sarki* again). Further, he says of Christians in 8:2 that the law of the spirit of life has freed them from the law of sin and death. The verb "freed" is in the aorist referring to the punctiliar event of past conversion. In light of this context with 7:5–6 and 8:1–9 on either side of our passage, it is very difficult to see how 7:14–25 could be Paul's description of the normal, much less the superlative, Christian life. Who then is in view?

There seem to be basically two options. Paul could be referring to the Jew who knows and strives to obey the Law, but the Jew as seen now with the twenty-twenty hindsight of the Christian. This person does know that the Law is good and recognizes in his mind its goodness, but his fallen nature leads him to do what his mind condemns.[43] The other possibility is that Paul is referring more broadly to all those who are still in Adam, still under the bondage to sin, but who have seen through the law, God's law, the error of their ways and as a result are under the conviction of sin, perhaps indeed on the point of conversion.

It must be remembered that Paul has earlier said that even in the case of Gentiles who are "apart from the law," what the law requires is nonetheless written on their hearts, and they may seek to do instinctively what it requires (Rom. 2:14–15). It is thus not necessary to conclude that Paul is *just* speaking of non-Christian Jews in 7:14–25. Indeed, it must count in favor of our interpretation that the law of God in vv. 7–13 and 14–25 must surely refer to the same thing, both being part of one discussion.[44]

The view that Paul is describing a carnal Christian here seems almost impossible in light of what follows in chapter 8 when Paul describes the condition of his *whole* audience as being free from the law of sin and death, not in bondage to it. Also, Paul is not here discussing apostasy, the rejection of the faith by one once a believer, but rather the general condition of those outside Christ. As 8:7 says succinctly, the person whose mind is set "on the flesh" cannot submit to God's law, which is the precise condition of the person described in 7:14–25[45] and is not the condition of the Christian who has been set free by the Spirit from the "law," or rule of sin and death (8:2).[46]

The bottom line for Cranfield and others who follow Luther's intro-spective interpretation of Romans 7 is that what new creation means is *not* sanctification and empowerment of the will to resist sin and have victory over it, but apparently only the renewal of the mind, or of one's views. Cranfield says repeatedly that believers become increasingly aware of their sin as sanctification proceeds. This is true as far as it goes, but if one stops there one has an inadequate understanding of how Paul viewed the power of God's Spirit in the Christian life. Paul believes that the Spirit really can and does set one free from *bondage* to sin, not simply make one more aware of one's sin. The spirit of slavery has been supplanted by the Spirit of adoption (8:15), and what the Christian is prompted to cry is not, "Who will deliver me from the body of this death or from bondage to sin?"[47] but, "Abba Father!" (cf. 7:24–8:15).

Lest Paul be misunderstood, he is certainly not saying Christians do not still have inclinations to sin. As long as Christians have a fallen body, that will still be true, but the believer is made capable by the power of the Spirit to resist these inclinations and also temptations from without. The point is not that Christians never sin, but that this is not inevitable. Nor is it that Christians are already perfect; even Paul repudiated such a claim (Phil. 3:12–16). The point is that the Spirit has renovated the human will to the point where sin can be resisted. Sin does not make the believer an offer he or she cannot refuse (1 Cor. 10:12–13). Luther's famous theological motto *simul justus et peccator*, "always the sinner and yet justified," when predicated of the Christian amounts to a very inadequate understanding of Paul's view of the work of the Spirit in sanctification insofar as it affects not just the mind but the will.

Once and for all, who then is the person who does not understand his behavior and deeds, who is the one who hates what he does, who wills one thing and practices another? Certainly not the Paul who boasts of his deeds for Christ and is willing to boast of the deeds of various of his converts such as the Philippians.

Käsemann's view that a pious Jew is in view up to v. 20 is based on understanding *nomos* in v. 14 as a reference to the Mosaic law.[48] However, if *nomos* in vv. 6–13 could refer to the original commandment to Adam, as reflected, of course, through Mosaic language, then there is no reason why in v. 14 *nomos* could not continue to refer to the original prohibition of God to Adam, which then encompasses all of fallen humanity in Adam. It is easier to see vv. 14–20 as a general description of fallen humanity outside Christ, but as seen from a Christian point of view, not as the sinner sees him- or herself. If Paul is trying to describe the anatomy of conversion in Rom. 7—8, then Paul may have a particular subcategory of Adam's kin in view in vv. 14–25, namely, those under conviction of sin and on the brink of conversion to Christ.

At 7:21 and also in 8:2 Paul seems to use the term "*nomos*" in a different sense to mean a principle, a fundamental rule. Paul is saying, "I find it to be a fundamental principle (of the fallen individual) . . . ," and again in 8:2 he is saying, "The principle (or rule) of the Spirit of life has set me free from the principle (and power) of sin and death." If this is correct, Paul is not talking in this context about the law that Moses himself bequeathed to his people per se, and thus he is not likely talking about Jews in particular, those "under the Mosaic law."

Romans 7:25a is most naturally seen as an anticipation of what Paul is going to say in Romans 8 about the normal Christian life, for he knows who already has set believers free and what the true condition of the Christian already is—set free from the principle of sin and death. Sin remains, but in the Christian it does not reign. The Christian is no longer in bondage. This is what Paul celebrates here, in advance. Romans 7:25b then is a return to the main theme of Romans 7, a sort of summing up before turning to the good news of the next chapter, and should not be seen as a displaced verse. The chapter then concludes with a statement about the conflict that exists within the individual in question, whose mind is a servant to God's law but whose flesh is a slave to the law of sin. This cannot be the same person described in 8:2, or else contrasts and grammar have no meaning.

This whole discussion in Romans 7 clearly is a Christian insight into the human condition, not one that comes generally to fallen humanity, and it is doubtful that Paul here is reflecting on his own conversion experience. Rather, as with the rest of the chapter, the discussion is generally referring first to the condition of Adam, then to the condition of those in Adam, and perhaps particularly to the one at the point of becoming in Christ.

The problem with the most common Protestant reading of this passage is that it involves interpreting the passage in light of the wrong story. Instead of reading it in the light of Luther's own anguished pilgrimage, which led him to see himself in Rom. 7:14–25, we should have been reading it in the light of the story Paul alludes to here—the story of Adam (vv. 7–13) and his fallen descendants outside of Christ (vv. 14–25).

3

Flashback

*Shades and Shadows
in the Vale of Tears*

THERE are three universals that Paul believes all experience. *All* live in this present age and are subject to its spiritual and even supernatural wickedness and problems; even the creation itself experiences the Fall (Rom. 8:19ff.). *All* are in bondage to sin, both Jew and Gentile, so none can be justified by their works (Rom. 3:23–25). *All* are subject to death. Paul believes that outside of Christ one experiences the true lordship of the world, the flesh, and the Devil over one's existence. Thus, outside Christ there is only lostness and a complete inability to save oneself.

One may come to understand that one is lost, as the tale in Rom. 7:14–25 suggests, perhaps by hearing God's Word or perhaps by reflecting on the substance of the law that resides in every human heart. But one cannot do anything about this lostness on one's own save cry out against it. The Welsh poet Dylan Thomas once wrote, "Do not go gentle into that good night, . . . Rage, rage against the dying of the light." The person in Rom. 7:14–25 is raging, but can be delivered only by an outside force, a deliverer from beyond the darkened horizon, one who is not tainted in like fashion by the soot of fallenness.

The world that Paul describes, though not as bad as it might be, is a world in which darkness has touched every aspect of life and existence in the material world. It is a world in which one must cry out, "Who will deliver me from the body of this death?" Yet Paul does not believe that God has simply left humankind to its own evil machinations. He does not believe that God would leave the world bereft of hope. Paul believes that God always had a plan of redemption, always meant to send a new light

29

into the heart of the darkness, always had a means of salvation to be worked out through a particular people—Abraham and his descendants—to whom we must now turn.

NOTES TO PART 1

The Darkened Horizon

1. From *The Collected Poems of W. B. Yeats* (New York: Macmillan Co., 1959), 184–85.

2. I borrow a phrase from the title of W. Willimon's helpful study on human fallenness, *Sighing for Eden* (Nashville: Abingdon, 1985).

3. From "Ode: Intimations of Immortality from Recollections of Early Childhood," in W. Heath, ed., *Major British Poets of the Romantic Period* (New York: Macmillan & Co., 1973), 258. Nor does he sound like G. M. Hopkins, who rhapsodizes: "The world is charged with the grandeur of God. It will flame out, like shining from shook foil." From *The Poems of Gerard Manley Hopkins*, ed. W .H. Gardner and N. H. MacKenzie (London: Oxford University Press, 1967), 66.

4. I am following the edition of J. Hollander and F. Kermode, eds., *The Literature of Renaissance England* (Oxford: Oxford University Press, 1973), 760.

5. We are concerned in this study to understand Paul's thought and the story that undergirds it. There is neither time nor space to debate the historical substance of this story here. It must be stressed, however, that not only does Paul believe the story of Adam and Eve to be theologically profound, but it seems clear from texts like Romans 5 and 1 Corinthians 15 that he also believes it to be historically true. He does not think that he is dealing with "cleverly devised myths," for he consistently bases his statements about the eschatological Adam, Christ, on the assumption that the first Adam really was the first created human being, who along with Eve really did commit the first sin (cf. 1 Cor. 15:45–49; 2 Cor. 11:3), causing the mess humanity has found itself in ever since. This is also evident from the way Paul treats death—not as a natural closure to human life, but as the enemy (1 Cor. 15:26), as something brought into the world by the first human transgression (1 Cor. 15:21). The story of Christ in Paul's thought presupposes this larger Story, and the former cannot be understood fully without the latter.

6. C. K. Barrett, *From First Adam to Last* (New York: Charles Scribner's Sons, 1962), 5: "Paul sees history gathering at nodal points, and crystallizing upon outstanding figures—men who are notable in themselves as individual persons, but even more notable as representative figures. These men as it were incorporate the human race, or sections of it, within themselves, and the dealings they have with God they have representatively on behalf of their fellows. Not that each member of the race may not and does not have his own relation with God; but these fall into a pattern which may be described under a few names." This work was written long before the present appropriate concern for using more inclusive language when speaking of human beings.

7. From *The Sonnets of William Shakespeare*, ed. L. Fox (Norwich, Eng.: Jarrold & Sons, n.d.), 12.

8. So Barrett, *From First Adam*, 17.

9. Ibid., 8–9. Again, the masculine pronouns and modifiers in this quotation were originally intended to be gender inclusive.

10. See S. Lyonnet, "L'histoire du salut selon le ch. 7 de l'épitre aux Romains," *Biblica* 43 (1962): 117–51; J. A. Zeisler, *Paul's Letter to the Romans* (Philadelphia: Trinity Press International, 1989), 182–83. I do not think Zeisler's suggestion that Adam is the model, but Paul the subject, the "I" here, will work. Paul does not speak of Adam as prototype, but as founder and representative head of the human race, his actions affect his descendants. One of the keys to understanding this passage is to note the change in verb tenses between 7:7–13 and 7:14ff., the latter of which is largely told in the present tense and speaks of Adam's present descendants locked in the bonds of sin, unless freed by Christ. In 7:7–13 we have aorists and imperfects referring to some critical events in the past.

11. Paul is perfectly capable of using a wide range of rhetorical devices, so there is no reason that here he could not have used an important technique of Greco-Roman rhetoric, namely, the use of "I" to speak dramatically not of self but of some other significant person of relevance for his audience. In this case that someone is Adam. On Paul's skillful use of rhetoric, see my *Conflict and Community in Corinth: A Socio-Rhetorical Commentary on 1 and 2 Corinthians* (Grand Rapids: Wm. B. Eerdmans, 1994), 25ff.

12. The attempt to refer this to the idea of the Bar Mitzvah, Paul referring to his condition before he came of age and took the yoke of the law upon his shoulders at age twelve or thirteen, although not impossible seems very unlikely. Even one who was not yet a "son or daughter of the commandments" was still in a general sense expected to obey at least portions of the Mosaic law, such as honoring father, mother, and God.

13. See also 1 Tim. 2:14.

14. It is also possible that by *egnon* Paul means "recognize." "I did not see sin for what it was except through the law." If this is right, then the point is that sin is revealed to be sin by the law. But can fallen humanity really say, "I would not have known desire if the law hadn't prohibited something?" In light of Romans 1, 5, and 6, it seems doubtful Paul could mean this here.

15. Perhaps one problem for the Adam view might seem to be the verb *anezesen* in v. 9b. Many translate this as "renewed," "live anew," but notice the contrast between "I was living" in v. 9a and "sin was living" or "coming to life" in v. 9b. C.E.B. Cranfield, *Romans I* (Edinburgh: T. & T. Clark, 1975), 352, rightly says the meaning here of this verb must be "sprang to life," "came to life." Though the commandment was intended for life, (indeed, if Adam had obeyed the commandment, he could even have eaten of the tree of life), instead it turned out to be death for Adam. Spiritual death is in view here. Sin deceived and spiritually killed the founder of the race.

16. Reference is to structures such as governments, though they too may reflect and express that evil in which fallen humanity is involved. See Eph. 6:12.

17. W. A. Meeks, *The First Urban Christians* (New Haven: Yale University Press, 1983), 189.

18. Cf. Plutarch *Moralia* 875C; Wisd. Sol. 7:17, 19:18; 4 Macc. 12:13.

19. Isocrates *Ant.* 2.16; Plutarch *Lib. Educ.* 16.2; Xenephon *Mem.* 2.1.1.

20. See J. A. Zeisler, *Pauline Christianity*, rev. ed. (Oxford: Oxford University Press, 1990), 83.

21. Cf. my article "The Influence of Galatians on Hebrews," *New Testament Studies* 37 (1991): 146–52.

22. Although Paul certainly has nothing against fasting and praying or sexual abstinence for the sake of prayer (cf. 1 Cor. 7:5); he is nevertheless critical of a certain sort of understanding of the benefits of asceticism. One must not confuse punishing the physical body with mortifying the sinful attitudes and inclinations humans have. These are distinguishable behaviors.

23. C. K. Barrett, *The Epistle to the Romans* (New York: Harper & Brothers, 1957), 174.

24. Cranfield, *Romans I*, 442: "In the NT epistles they seem to be applied both to angelic beings which are thought of as obediently fulfilling their divinely appointed roles in the ordering of the universe and in the affairs of [humankind] and also to spiritual forces of evil which have to be resisted by Christians (cf., e.g., Eph. 6:12). What Paul is here concerned to say is simply that there is no spiritual cosmic power, whether benevolent or malevolent, which will be able to separate us from God's love in Christ. And this he can say with confidence, because he knows that Christ has once and for all won the decisive battle against the rebellious powers (cf. Col. 2:15; also Eph. 1:21, 22a; 1 Pet. 3:22), so that their effectiveness has been drastically curtailed and their final complete subjection assured."

25. P. T. O'Brien, *Colossians, Philemon* (Waco, Tex.: Word, 1982), 133, explains Col. 2:15 as follows: "He stripped the principalities and powers, who had kept us in their grip through their possession of this document, divesting them of their dignity and might. God exposed to the universe their utter helplessness leading them in Christ in his triumphal procession. He paraded these powerless 'powers and principalities' so that all the world might see the magnitude of his victory. But these spiritual powers had not been annihilated. In that triumphal procession they were visible. They continue to exist, inimical to [humankind] and his interests (Rom. 8:38, 39). Nevertheless, they are powerless figures unable to harm the Christian who lives under the lordship of Christ. How foolish is it then for the Colossians to think, as the false teachers want them to, that they needed to grovel before these weak and beggarly elements as though they controlled the lines of communication between God and [humanity]."

26. Sometimes Paul seems to speak of a positive role angels could play; they were intermediaries delivering the law to God's people (Gal. 3:19, cf. 4:14).

27. See my discussion of this passage in *Conflict and Community in Corinth*, ad loc.

28. The Hebrew *Ha Satan* is not a proper name in the Old Testament, but means the Adversary. In Job 1–2 he plays the role of the prosecuting attorney wanting to place Job on trial. Cf. my *Jesus the Sage and the Pilgrimage of Wisdom* (Minneapolis: Fortress Press, 1994), chap. 1.

29. Hollander and Kermode, eds., *The Literature of Renaissance England*, 794.

30. See Barrett, *From First Adam*, 114ff.

31. In the later Pauline letters (cf. Eph. 1:20), the phrase "the age to come" is used and seems to imply that the age is not yet here. This is one reason commentators have often suspected that Ephesians is by a later understudy of Paul and not by Paul himself. But for Paul, Christ's coming and its benefits were just a foretaste of the age to come, just as the Spirit was a down payment, not the full installment of the age to come. It cannot be ruled out, however, that the reason Paul does not talk of the age to come (apart from in Ephesians) is that he saw it as in some sense already come. The question is, In what sense?

32. Paul's view of both male and female homosexual behavior is much the same as that of other early Jews. Cf. the important article by R. B. Hays, "Relations Natural and Unnatural: A Response to John Boswell's Exegesis of Romans 1," *Journal of Religious Ethics* 14 (1986): 184–215. Paul knows nothing of the modern debate of whether this sort of behavior is a result of nature or nurture, heredity or social conditioning.

33. Paul speaks very little about hell or eternal damnation, though verses like the one just discussed show well enough he believed in such things. Paul was no universalist; it is those who are in Christ who will be saved.

34. Though there is a natural theology here, it does not save the Gentiles to know this, because this knowledge does not transform them. Rather, Romans 1 says that they reject what they know is right. However, Paul never says that anyone is condemned because they have not heard of Christ. Romans 1 suggests that people are judged on the basis of what they *do* with what they *know* of God. One must distinguish in Paul's thought between a willful ignoring and rejecting of God, and ignorance of Christ because one has not yet been within earshot of the preaching (cf. Rom. 10:14).

35. All too often, when discussions of Paul's anthropology have been attempted, Romans 7 has been the chief battleground. Asking what it tells us about Paul's view of human nature or even Christian nature has often obscured the fact that the context for the discussion in Romans 7 is the Law, or more specifically, the effect of the Law on fallen human beings.

36. Cranfield, *Romans I*, 337–38.

37. Ibid.

38. E. Käsemann, *Commentary on Romans* (Grand Rapids: Wm. B. Eerdmans, 1980), 198–211.

39. See E. P. Sanders, *Paul and Palestinian Judaism* (London: SCM Press, 1977), 474ff.

40. See K. Stendahl's famous article "The Apostle Paul and the Introspective Consciousness of the West," *Harvard Theological Review* 56 (1963): 199–215.

41. See N. T. Wright, *The Climax of the Covenant* (Edinburgh: T. & T. Clark, 1991), 227–28, who suggests that there are various allusions in 7:14–25 to the story of Cain, though he thinks the primary reference in these verses is to Israel under the Law. He is surely right that "the thought of this passage is very close to that of 2:17–24; 3:19–20; 4:15; 5:20; and 7:1–6; but now it is given the sharp edge of an analysis . . . by means of the rhetorically vivid 'I.' " He may well be right about the reference to Israel here as well.

42. See Zeisler, *Paul's Letter to the Romans*, 183.

43. Romans 7:22 gives us some clue to Paul's anthropology, though the verse should not be overpsychologized. He says the person in question rejoices in the law of God "in his inner being." What is this "inner self"? Cranfield equates it with the "mind" of vv. 23 and 25, and 12:2. At this point 2 Cor. 4:16 may be compared. Cranfield insists that Paul means by inner person the person as renewed by the Holy Spirit—the human personality insofar as it has been renovated. In short, he argues that it amounts to the new creation. If this is the case, Paul is here talking about a Christian. Against this understanding, if one looks at 2 Cor. 4:16 carefully, there the inner person does not equal the new creation; for Paul says that this inner person is *being* renewed, whereas outer bodies or forms are wasting away. The inner person must first *exist before it can be renewed.* Paul is not likely talking about something that exists only in believers. All human beings have a sort of dualism between body and human spirit or body and mind. Paul clearly believes that the mind exists prior to conversion; thus, if indeed there is a parallel between mind and inner person here, the text does not necessarily have to imply a renewed mind. Verse 22 then means no more than that this person rejoices in God's Law in his inner being.

44. In 7:13 Paul speaks of *the* commandment. In v. 14 he says the law is spiritual, and it is in his innermost being and mind (vv. 22–23), just as is seen in Rom. 2:15. Without further explanation, the hearer would surely assume that the law referred to in 7:13 was the same as that referred to in 7:14. Notice also the inner conflict referred to in Rom. 2:15, where the conscience reflecting on the substance of the law written in one's heart may accuse or excuse, just as is seen in 7:21–23.

45. Philosophers may indeed want to debate what it means to say a person wills one thing and does another, for surely the willing is the agency through which doing happens. What Paul seems to mean is that this person intends with his mind to do one thing, but there is another force at work in his personality that actually controls his willing and doing. Paul is not talking about the Christian who tries hard, but whose deeds do not quite measure up to his or her intentions. The point here is not the falling short or even the imperfection of Christian good deeds, but the exceeding sinfulness of sinful deeds. The person Paul has in mind has sin dwelling in him or her (v. 17). Later Paul is to say that sin dwells in this person's members, which suggests that the physical aspect of one's being is the point of contact for sin to enter in and lead one into sin. The person Paul has in mind is a slave to sin, having been taken over by sin almost as a *habitus.* Verse 18 says that "*no good dwells in my flesh.*" Again we must compare the exact same phrase in 7:6. This person intends to do good but is simply unable to carry out such an intention. Is v. 20 an attempt to exculpate the individual or group in question because they cannot help themselves, being taken over by sin? Probably not, for the point Paul is driving at here is the bondage of the will, not the excuse making or excusability of the sinner's behavior.

46. As we will see in due course, it is not impossible for a person who has been a Christian to apostasize and even to return to sin's bondage, like the person described in 7:14–25. But Paul wants to stress that such behavior in a Christian is neither acceptable nor inevitable; therefore it is not a legitimate option, much less

a legitimate excuse for sin in the Christian life. Those in Christ can and must reject living "according to the flesh," according to the sinful inclinations (8:5–15).

47. Cranfield's attempt (*Romans I*, 365ff.) to see the Christian as the one in anguish and in bondage here is forced. There is significant debate as to whether v. 24 should be read as "this body of death" or "the body of this death." The *touto* could modify either noun grammatically. Cranfield insists that what Paul has in mind here is a cry to die, to be delivered from the condition of life in the body. This makes little sense in view of what follows in Romans 8. There Paul talks about not liberation *from* the body but liberation *in* the body—spiritual liberation. This in turn suggests that the term "body" in 7:24 means not the physical body; instead, the term is used in light of the *oikousa*, the sin that is dwelling in this person (vv. 17, 23). Paul is talking about the *habitus* of sin and death that has taken up residence in the individual, not the physical body per se or even the physical body under the dominion of sin. It may be of some relevance here that in 2 Cor. 4—5 Paul does not say his first preference is to be absent from the body, but rather for the body to be further clothed with a resurrection one.

48. Käsemann, *Commentary on Romans*, 199ff.

PART 2

Keeping the Faith
and Laying Down the Law

From Abraham to Moses
and Beyond

Ring out the old, ring in the new, . . .
Ring out the false, ring in the true.

Ring out the grief that saps the mind,
For those that here we see no more;
Ring out the feud of rich and poor,
Ring in redress to all mankind. . . .

Ring out the want, the care, the sin,
The faithless coldness of the times;
Ring out, ring out my mournful rhymes,
But ring the fuller minstrel in. . . .

Ring in the valiant man and free,
The larger heart, the kindlier hand;
Ring out the darkness of the land,
Ring in the Christ that is to be.

—*Alfred, Lord Tennyson*
"In Memoriam"[1]

WHENEVER a Jew thought of the beginnings of the story of a chosen people, he or she thought of the story of Abraham. It was in this story that one could begin to hear the death knell of the old hostility toward God and the ringing in of a new positive relationship. It was in the life of Abraham that God began the process of retrieval of a people set apart from the masses of fallen humanity. When Paul thinks of the human beginnings of paradise regained, he thinks of that first great example of faith. Paul does not believe that there are several stories of God's redeeming work; there is essentially only one that leads from Abraham to Christ and beyond. When he wants to reflect on matters such as a right relationship with God, faith being reckoned as righteousness, and the ultimate human origins of the redeemer, he does not think of law courts or judicial decisions, but of the story of God's gracious choice of Abraham and Abraham's grateful trusting response. One of the keys to a proper Pauline reading of large portions of Galatians, Romans, and also some of the Corinthian letters is a proper reading of the story of Abraham and his descendants and of the relationship of Abraham's story to the story of Moses, and a proper understanding that both stories are being read in the light of Christ.

Before we reflect on this first stage in the story of redemption, it is important to recall *how* Paul reads the Hebrew scriptures in general. He reads them from first to last as a prophetic book all of which has relevance in various ways for the followers of Christ. In a revealing remark, he cites the story of Israel as an example for his converts. He says, "These things occurred as examples *for us,* so that we might not desire evil as they did" (1 Cor. 10:6), and even more tellingly in 10:11: "These things happened to them to serve as an example, *and they were written down to instruct us, on whom the ends of the ages have come.*" In Paul's view it is not only that in Christ all of God's promises in scripture come to full fruition (2 Cor. 1:20), but that for Christians, living in the eschatological age, all of the scriptures have unique relevance. The scriptures themselves, and not just God's salvation plan, are seen as teleological in character and thus are written especially for that last and eschatological community of God's people.[2] This also means that "the gospel is the fulfillment, not the negation of God's word to Israel."[3]

For Paul there is one Holy Writ for all God's people and one continuous people of God from Abraham through Moses to Christ and beyond. Because there is always only one true Israel, which is never simply identical with "the Israel according to the flesh" (Rom. 9:6, 7), there is also only one group to whom the scriptures always and everywhere apply. Jew and Gentile united in Christ are seen by Paul as the continuation of the true Israel that began with Abraham, indeed, as the fulfillment of the double promise to Abraham of seed and of being a blessing to all nations.

In Paul's hermeneutic, scripture sometimes simply serves as analogy or to provide historical examples for the purpose of warning or encouragement. Sometimes it serves to provide the true story of the origins of God in Christ, sin, Fall, salvation, and the community of faith. Sometimes it is literally reapplied, and sometimes it is metaphorically reapplied (1 Cor. 9:9). Sometimes one or another part of it is seen to have been fulfilled in Christ in such a way that it has come to an end, in particular in the case of much of the Mosaic law. In the latter case it is no longer literally applicable, though it still may be used to provide theological, spiritual, ethical, or metaphorical (again 1 Cor. 9:9) grounding for the story of Christian faith that Paul seeks to tell. Or again, Paul may use even Mosaic material that is seen to be literally defunct to answer such questions as these: What is God's character like? What are human beings like? What should the relationship between God and humankind be like? Bearing these things in mind, we will be better prepared for the *tour de force* argument that Paul uses to relate Abraham to Christ and to his followers.

4

The First Face of Faith

Abraham

C. K. BARRETT, in reflecting on the place of Abraham in Paul's narrative thought world, suggests:

> Viewed in himself, Abraham could be the last term in the series that began with Adam. Adam sought to establish his own security at God's expense, and lost it. Abraham was content to leave his security to God, in faith, trusting in the power of God to bring life out of death. So far, this was a reversal of Adam's fall. It is also true that Abraham's faith may be imitated and repeated. Yet Abraham is not the end of the story.[4]

It comes as something of a surprise that Paul, the former Pharisee, devotes a whole chapter (Romans 4) to the example of Abraham, then discusses him and his immediate descendants again in Rom. 9:6–15, and finally stresses that he himself is a descendant of Abraham (11:1). Moses scarcely comes into the discussion at all (see Rom. 10:5). Also in Galatians, when Paul wants to present an example of faith and faithfulness, he appeals at length to Abraham (3:6–18) and returns again to discuss at length Abraham's two sons, had by Hagar and Sarah, in the famous "allegory" in Gal. 4:21–31.

It is not as if Paul does not appreciate the glorious aspects of Moses' career (2 Cor. 3) or that he denies that the Law that came through Moses was holy, just, and good (cf. Rom. 7:7, 12; 9:4). For Paul, the experience of Abraham is critical, indeed, *the* critical example of faith prior to Christ himself, for as he says in Gal. 3:8: "And the scripture, foreseeing that God would justify the Gentiles by faith, declared the gospel beforehand to Abraham." Abraham is the prototype of Christian faith because he heard

40

the first preaching of the Good News and responded appropriately. It is for this reason, above any others, that Paul stresses that Abraham is the ancestor in the faith of both Jews and Gentiles. He is "*our* ancestor." Even Gentiles share the faith of Abraham (Rom. 4:16).

As with all the other stories he draws on from the Hebrew scriptures, Paul looks at the story of Abraham through his christological and ecclesiological glasses. Thus the elements he stresses are those that are most relevant to his discussion of Christian faith and its bases.[5] Nevertheless, this Christian hermeneutic does not negate either the likelihood that these stories had played a large role in Paul's own faith development long before he encountered Christ on Damascus road, or the fact that Paul felt compelled to read the story of Christ and Christians in the light of the narratives of Hebrew scriptures. The oral gospel tradition had to make sense in light of God's Word, even if some very creative readings of the Old Testament were required. — *at Paul's time O7*   *NT*

At this juncture it is critical to ask which elements of the story of Abraham ground Paul's thought and provide the wider context or matrix out of which it arises. It is easy to become too preoccupied with some aspects of the story of Abraham that in fact Paul makes little or nothing of. For example, the whole discussion in Genesis 22 of the attempted sacrifice of Isaac as a basis for Paul's thoughts on the sacrifice of Christ deserves only passing mention. The most one can say is that there is a possible allusion in Rom. 8:32 to Gen. 22:16 (LXX), but that Paul makes very little of it. For Paul, "the outstanding example of Abraham's faith was not his willingness to sacrifice his son but his confident belief that God would give himself and his wife a child, notwithstanding their great age."[6] What Paul omits from his discussions and allusions, such as Abram's encounter with Melchizedek (Gen. 14) or the Sodom and Gomorrah episode (Gen. 19), is in some ways as significant as what he includes.

One must carefully read through Gen. 12—22 both to catch the echoes in Paul's discussions in Rom. 4, 9 and Gal. 3—4 and to understand their larger significance. Certainly one of the most important points for Paul is the chronology of the story of Abraham. It is critical not only that Abram is *already* promised in Gen. 12:2–3 that he will have many offspring and be a blessing to all the families of the earth, but that God's covenant with Abram is already initiated in Genesis 15. Then, in 15:6 we have the crucial statement "And he believed the Lord; and the Lord reckoned it to him as righteousness." All of this transpires *prior* to any discussion of circumcision as a covenant sign, which comes in Genesis 17.[7] Genesis 15:6 also comes prior to the discussion of Hagar and Ishmael (Gen. 16; 21:8–21) and Sarah and Isaac (Gen. 18; 21). This is critical for Paul, for it allows him to appeal to God's original dealings with Abraham over against any later institution of circumcision, whether with Abraham or in connection with the Mosaic covenant.

For example, in Rom. 4:11–12 Paul interprets Abraham's circumcision as the seal of a righteousness he already had obtained by faith while still uncircumcised. The purpose of this was not simply so that Abraham's relationship with God would be based on faith, but so that he could be the ancestor of those who believe without circumcision (i.e., Gentiles) as well as of those who believe following Abraham's example and are also circumcised. Like many early Jews, he seems to operate with the principle that the earlier remarks have higher authority and deserve priority. Paul's reading of Gen. 12—22 in Rom. 4, 9 and Gal. 3—4 is illumined by recognizing not only the echoes of the larger contexts in Hebrew scriptures but how the flow and chronology of those narratives affects the discussion.

We will begin with the material in Romans because it is not found in a polemical context where forensic rhetoric is being used, as is the case in Gal. 3—4.[8] Romans 4:1 has long been a verse that scholars have found difficult to interpret. How could Abraham be said to be the father according to the flesh of Gentiles as well as Jews? The verse stands in the midst of a discussion not merely about the basis of human relationship with God, though that is clearly in view (cf. 3:21–24), but whether or not the basis of that relationship to God differs for Jews and Gentiles. Paul's most fundamental premise in this argument is that because God is one and is the God of both Jews and Gentiles, God justifies all on the same basis— namely, faith, "apart from works of the Law" (3:28–30). That Paul is not talking about faithfulness but rather faith seems clear enough from 3:28. Paul differs dramatically from the Jew who wrote Jub. 23:10 and argued there that Abraham was the model of one who kept the Law even before it was given, and thus that Gen. 15:6 refers to Abraham's faithfulness, not his faith. Paul also differs from the author of 1 Macc. 2:51–52, who linked Gen. 15:6 with Abraham's later willingness (Gen. 22) obediently to offer Isaac as a sacrifice. Compared with these writers, Paul is a stickler for accurately chronicling the events of Abraham's life in the proper order.

Some have seen the introduction of Abraham in Rom. 4:1 as abrupt. This is not so if one reads Rom. 3:21–4:25 in light of Gen. 15—17, where the subject of faith being reckoned as righteousness also arises. The more difficult issue is how we are to read the structure of Rom. 4:1. Is Paul talking about what Abraham "gained" by faith, or is he talking about something he and other believers have found out about Abraham from reading the scriptures carefully? I would suggest it is the latter, and following R. B. Hays I think Rom. 4:1 should be read as follows: "What then shall we say? Have we found [by reading Gen. 15—17 properly] Abraham to be our forefather according to the flesh?"[9] In favor of this reading are the following factors: (1) There are clear structural parallels in Romans to this use of two rhetorical questions, the first being "What then shall we say?" (cf. Rom. 6:1; 7:7; 9:14; 9:30). (2) The phrase "according to the flesh" can hardly modify the verb "found," and this latter verb is never used in Paul or in the rest of the New Testament to mean "gain" or "acquire." It must be remembered that Genesis 15 says nothing about Abraham looking for or seeking justification, it simply says in 15:6 that he believed God's word. (3) As Hays points out, in Rom. 7:10 and 7:21 Paul uses precisely this term "find" to refer to the results of an inquiry or discussion.[10] (4) Were Paul talking about something Abraham found, we would expect Paul to have used the aorist infinitive, not the perfect *heurekenai* of "find" as we have in 4:1.[11]

The assumed answer to Paul's second rhetorical question ("Is Abraham our forefather according to the flesh?") is the same as the explicit answer given to the second rhetorical question in Rom. 6:1, 7:7, and 9:14—"Certainly not!" Thus, in vv. 2–3 Paul states plainly the truth that Abraham cannot be the ancestor of all of us according to the flesh; rather, he is our ancestor according to faith because the scripture (Gen. 15:6) says plainly, "He believed God and it was reckoned to him as righteousness." Paul puts it somewhat differently in Rom. 9:6–7, but the effect is the same: Not all Abraham's physical descendants are true Israelites, for it is not the children of the flesh but the children of promise who are Abraham's true descendants. The issue in Romans 4 is more the human side of the equation (faith) and in Romans 9 the divine side (election), but the principle of Abraham being counted "our forefather" or believers being counted his descendants is the same in each case. Justification comes by God's electing grace and only through faith, not through works of the Law.

The issue in Rom. 3—4 is not just *how* Abraham or his true descendants were reckoned as righteous, but *whether* Jews and Gentiles would *both* be reckoned to have such a status *on the same basis*. The answer to the how question is faith, and so the answer to the whether question is an emphatic yes. The reason things have turned out in this way is that Paul presupposes the dark story of human fallenness in his reading of both the Abraham story and the story of his spiritual descendants. In the matter of justification, "there is no distinction [between Jew and Gentile], since *all* have sinned and fallen short of God's glory" (3:23) and since, as already mentioned, God is one, the only God of both Jews and Gentiles.[12]

Paul clearly sees Abraham as Exhibit A of relating to God on the proper eschatological basis, and thus as a paradigm for all true believers. Romans 4:23–24 makes this clear: "Now the words, 'it was reckoned to him,' were written not for his sake alone, but for ours also. It will be reckoned to us who believe in him who raised Jesus our Lord from the dead." Just as

Abraham, despite the fact that his body was as good as dead (4:19), hoped against hope and believed God's promise that he would produce a miracle child out of a situation where no new life seemed possible, so also Christians have believed in new life out of death in the case of Jesus, and it was reckoned to believers as righteousness.[13] Here we have what S. Fowl calls the use of an *exemplar*. Abraham is not merely analogous to the Christian but provides a sort of paradigm for Christians to follow, because the story of Abraham is scriptural and serves as "a concrete formulation which is normative for a particular community."[14] The assumption is not just that imitation of Abraham's behavior is possible but that God deals with him as God deals with those in Christ.

A few words about this "reckoning" are in order. The Abraham story does not suggest the idea of imputed righteousness, but rather something counting in the place of righteousness. Zeisler puts it this way: " 'It was reckoned to him as righteousness' . . . probably does not mean that his faith (or his faithfulness) was to be regarded as equivalent to or as constituting righteousness, but rather that it was to be counted in lieu of righteousness, instead of it."[15] In both Rom. 4:3 and Gal. 3:6, the most salient Pauline passages where the idea of imputed righteousness is generally thought to be present, Paul is discoursing on Gen. 15:6 and thus on what was true in Abraham's case, and by analogy what is also true in the case of Christian believers.

Not even his christological hermeneutic leads Paul to suggest that the righteousness being discussed in Gen. 15:6 is the righteousness that Christ possessed, which is being exchanged with Abraham's faith. Indeed, in Rom. 3:21 and especially in 3:25 the subject is not Christ's righteousness but rather God's, which is revealed subjectively through faith in Christ and objectively through Christ's atoning sacrificial death. Thus, if the subject was divine righteousness, it would not be Christ's but God's according to both the context in Romans and in Genesis.

However, yet another and better interpretation lies nearer at hand. The parallel between works and righteousness in Rom. 4:4–5 suggests that the issue is Abraham's *own* righteousness. Abraham's faith is credited as righteousness instead of his works producing and earning him the status of righteousness. If there is exchange here, it would be between Abraham's deeds and his faith, and in view of the clear paralleling of Abraham and the believer in 4:23–24, Paul seems to assume that the same is true with Christians. This is especially so because Paul says Gen. 15:6 was written for Christians as well as for Abraham. A careful reading of Paul's handling of the Abraham story in light of the larger context in Genesis 15—17 helps us avoid jumping to wrong conclusions.[16] The "righteousness of faith" (Rom.

4:13) is the righteousness that is reckoned because one has faith, not the righteousness of someone else that comes to the believer through faith.

At this point we must turn to that greatest of all repositories of Pauline scripture citation and allusion—Romans 9—11—where Paul discusses the present and future of ethnic Israel. About one third of these three chapters is devoted to scripture citation, and about 40 percent of that one third involves citations from Isaiah, seen as the great commentary on the future of Israel. As R. B. Hays has argued:

> [Romans 9—11] is most fruitfully understood when it is read as an intertextual conversation between Paul and the voice of Scripture. . . . Scripture broods over this letter, calls Paul to account, speaks through him; Paul, groping to give voice to his gospel, finds in Scripture the language to say what must be said, labors to win the blessing of Moses and the prophets. . . . The insistent echoing voice of Scripture in and behind Paul's letter presses home a single theme relentlessly: the gospel is the fulfillment, not the negation of God's word to Israel.[17]

Because we have commented at length on the general character and scholarly discussion of this passage elsewhere,[18] we will confine ourselves to a few remarks on Abraham's role in this incredible revisioning of salvation history and its character. Abraham is seen in this material as the patriarch par excellence, as the one Paul is most proud to be even a physical descendant of (11:1), and perhaps also as the "root" discussed in Rom. 11:16–18.

What Paul sets out to do, after the introduction in Rom. 9:1–5, is to provide a history lesson of sorts. It is meant to show that because God has always worked by the principle of election, which also involves selection within the elect group, and because there has always been a righteous remnant, a true Israel, not merely an Israel after the flesh, God's word and promises to Jews have not failed. The issue of God's own character is raised by the Jews' lack of response to the preaching and Paul's insistence that Jesus Christ is the one means through whom the benefits of the promises to Abraham are realized.[19]

Abraham fits into this argument in several ways. First, Paul's argument moves in two directions at once: (1) not all of Abraham's physical descendants are true Israel and (2) not all of true Israel is made up of Abraham's physical descendants.

> The striking thing about the way Paul's argument proceeds is that he is not merely arguing that God has the right to choose only some, but that even among the elect God had the right to break some of them off and include others. Election . . . does not necessarily entail the guarantee of

salvation for particular individual Israelites. . . . Paul here is interested in the current and future historical fate of non-Christian Jews, not their eternal destiny.[20]

Second, Paul in Rom. 9:8, in similar fashion to the argument in Rom. 2:28–29, argues that Abraham's "seed" is constituted not by his children who are born in the course of nature but those who come by the promise and are because of this counted as Abraham's true descendants. This argument shows again how crucial Gen. 15:6 is for Paul's understanding, not only of Abraham's story, but also for understanding the story of his true descendants—Jews and Gentiles united in Christ. In Paul's view, the true descendants of Abraham, his seed, are also those who relate to God on the basis of faith in the promises. This in turn leads to the argument that the "righteous remnant" of Jews are Jewish Christians who relate to God in the way Abraham did, other Jews being temporarily broken off from the people of God so that, and until, the full number of Gentiles may be grafted into this people.

The use of the term "seed" in Rom. 9:7 to mean Abraham's physical descendants, in particular the progeny "in" and including Isaac, is important and differs from the way Paul uses the term in Gal. 3:16. Here "seed" is a category that includes but is not synonymous with children.[21] It is only "in Isaac" that Abraham's seed will be acknowledged (9:7b).[22] In Gal. 3:16 Christ is said to be *the* seed (again *sperma*) of Abraham. Romans 9:7b is a quotation of Gen. 21:12, showing that the controlling context in Genesis is the discussion of election through Isaac and not through Ishmael, whereas in Gal. 3:15–16 it appears certain that Gen. 17:6–7 lies in the background. Genesis 17:6–7 reads: "I will make you exceedingly fruitful; and I will make nations of you, *and kings shall come from you.* I will establish my covenant between me and *you, and your offspring* after you throughout their generations, for an *everlasting covenant,* to be God to you and to your offspring after you." The key to the different uses of the term *sperma* is to be found in the larger contexts of each respective text.

The text alluded to in Galatians is not about selection within election, as in the Genesis 21 text, but about an everlasting covenant that involves the promise of royalty coming from Abraham. Paul makes much of the singular "offspring" in Galatians, knowing very well, as Rom. 9:6–7 shows, that a literal reading of the term would require it to be understood as a collective noun. He does so because the larger context of Genesis 17 has provided him a basis for discussing *the king,* the anointed one whom Israel has longed for and dreamed of, and the everlasting covenant, and perhaps also because he views Christ as an inclusive personality—Christians become heirs of Abraham "in Christ."[23]

A failure to pick up the intertextual echo here has led many commentators astray in their interpretations of Gal. 3:16. This in turn has often led to charges that Paul in desperation is resorting to legerdemain in order to pull his exegetical Christ out of Abraham's hat. But it is not so. Paul truly believed, as did various other early Jews, that the messianic king would be a true, indeed the truest, descendant of Abraham, the one who would establish or at least renew the everlasting covenant. Furthermore, Paul was utterly convinced that in Christ all the promises of offspring, kings, everlasting covenant to Abraham come to fruition. Equally important, he believed that both Jewish and Gentile Christians were in some way "in Christ" so that what is given to him is given to them. If he is the seed of Abraham, so are they by way of Christ, and therefore "seed" still has a collective sense in Gal. 3:16, though in an indirect manner.

The new covenant is but the consummation of the one begun with Abraham in ever so many ways: (1) The basis for obtaining the benefits of the Abrahamic and new covenant is faith in God's promises. (2) Both involve not only the circumcised but the uncircumcised. In Paul's view, circumcision is not seen as the essential thing that establishes the covenant with Abraham, for Genesis 15 precedes Genesis 17. (3) Both involve children given by God. (4) Both involve an everlasting covenant. (5) Both involve a promise of world, not merely of land, for *in* Abraham all the families of humankind were to be blessed, *from* Abraham were to come many nations (Gen. 17:6), and *through* his ultimate descendant—Christ, the seed of Abraham—they also become one family of God, both circumcised and uncircumcised.[24] I thus conclude that in Paul's mind the new covenant in Christ is but the completion or fulfillment of the Abrahamic one.

This is hardly a surprising conclusion for one who also elsewhere argued that in Christ "every one of God's promises is a 'Yes'" (2 Cor. 1:20), and for Paul "promises" are almost always associated with Abraham (cf. Rom. 9:4, 9). Still thinking of Genesis 17 in 2 Corinthians 1, Paul goes on to argue that believers have been sealed in the covenant, indeed christened, not by circumcision like Abraham (cf. Rom. 4:11 to Gen. 17:10ff.), but by God's greater eschatological gift to his believing people— the Holy Spirit. There are thus elements of continuity and discontinuity between the Abrahamic covenant and the new covenant in Paul's mind, but he chooses to stress the continuity, realizing that in the eschatological age signs are often replaced by the things they signify.[25]

The cost of this linkage of Abraham and Christ, of the Abrahamic and the new covenant, will prove to be high. It means that the Mosaic covenant must be seen as a parenthesis, an interim, and thus a temporary arrangement between the promises given to and in Abraham and the promises fulfilled to and in Christ. This by no means suggests that the Law is a bad thing, only a temporary one, given as a guardian to keep God's Jewish people in line until the messiah should come (cf. below).

We must now turn to Gal. 3–4.[26] Here matters are complicated because Paul is comparing and contrasting two covenants—the Abrahamic one (particularly in its stage of fulfillment and completion in Christ) and the Mosaic one. In light of Gal. 3:15, it is clear that Paul sees the call and promise of blessing of Abram in Genesis 12 as the original establishing of the covenant with him, a covenant established on the basis of faith in God's promise of seed. Paul will contrast this with the Mosaic covenant, which came later and was "added because of transgressions" (3:19), but only until Christ came to fulfill the promise given to Abraham. The Mosaic covenant did not annul the Abrahamic one (3:17), nor is the law opposed to the promises (3:21); it is simply that the two were given for different purposes and function on different bases.

When Paul thinks of the character of the Mosaic covenant, several texts are critical for him: (1) Deut. 27:26 cited in Gal. 3:10; (2) Lev. 18:5 cited not only in Gal. 3:12 but also in Rom. 10:5; and (3) Deut. 21:23 cited in Gal. 3:13. The latter is seen to refer to the Law's judgment on one who is crucified—namely, that he is cursed by God. The middle of these citations speaks of the ongoing basis of living or life in the Mosaic covenant— namely, works of the Law. The first speaks of the obligation to obey not just a part but the whole of the Law, and the consequences of failure— namely, one is cursed by the Law. Those who relate to God as Abraham did are children of promise; those who relate on the basis of the Mosaic covenant's requirements for works are said to be under a curse (3:10).

This surprising result happens because, although the Law could tell persons what they ought to do, it could not enable them to do it. The Law could not make one alive (3:21b)—understood to mean both the power and the will to live in a particular way pleasing to God. The problem is that the Law is given to fallen human beings, but it does not enable them to keep it. Thus its *effect* is death dealing, not life giving, whereas its intention was to make sin known and in fact to guard, even imprison, Israel until the redeemer came (3:23).

Because Paul sees all of the Hebrew scriptures as prophetic in character, he is able to say in Gal. 3:8–9: "And the scripture, foreseeing that God would justify the nations by faith, declared the gospel beforehand to Abraham, saying, 'All nations will be blessed in you.' For this reason, those who believe are blessed with Abraham who believed." Here again Paul appeals to the beginnings of the story of Abraham, quoting Gen. 12:3 about the nations being blessed in him and understanding the term *nations* to refer to Gentiles, as was common. How very different this is from Ben

Sira's reading of the story, who in effect reads the story backward from Genesis 22 to Genesis 17 to Genesis 15 to Genesis 12 and so argues: "Abraham was the great father of a multitude of nations, and no one has been found like him in glory. He kept the law of the Most High, and entered into a covenant with him; he certified the covenant in his flesh, and when he was tested he proved faithful. *Therefore the Lord assured him* with an oath that the nations would be blessed through his offspring" (Sir. 44:19–21). Here Abraham's faithfulness, his keeping of the (Mosaic) law even before Moses, is seen as the basis of the promise of blessing. It may be that Paul's opponents in Galatia argued in fashion similar to what we find in Sirach.[27] They stressed the Mosaic covenant, circumcision, and proper connections with the earthly Jerusalem. To this Paul responds with his typology about Hagar and Sarah and their offspring, Ishmael and Isaac.

Unfortunately, the material in 4:21–31 has sometimes been read as follows: Hagar equals the old covenant, Sarah the new; Hagar the earthly Jerusalem, Sarah the heavenly one, and finally, Hagar represents Judaism, whereas Sarah represents Christianity.[28] Against this I must stress that Paul is engaging in an intramural debate with Jewish Christians, not non-Christian Jews, over the character of the gospel. Romans 9—11 and 2 Corinthians 3 show that Paul is fully able to defend the benefits of being a Jew in general, and even some aspects of Moses' story, to its cultured detractors. One must not forget the polemical context in which Gal. 4:21–31 is given.[29]

The reading of H. D. Betz of Gal. 3—4, that Hagar simply represents the old covenant, is, I believe, wrong. Rather, she represents the Mosaic covenant, whereas Sarah represents the Abrahamic one and its fulfillment in Christ. The typology in Gal. 4:21–31 presupposes the earlier lengthy discussion about the importance and validity of the Abrahamic covenant and how the promises to Abraham are not annulled by the Mosaic covenant but rather are fulfilled in Christ, the "Seed." Thus, although it is true that Paul is stressing that the new covenant supercedes the Mosaic one as the basis of both Gentile and Jewish Christians relating to God, Paul is not simply arguing that Christianity replaces Judaism. The argument is about which form of Judaism is the legitimate one—the Christian form with its link to the Abrahamic covenant, or the Mosaic form as maintained by the Judaizers and elsewhere by non-Christian Jews.[30] Before we conclude this discussion, W. D. Davies' judicious summary deserves to be quoted at some length:

In accepting the Jew, Jesus, as the Messiah, Paul did not think in terms of moving into a new religion but of having found the final expression and intent of the Jewish tradition within which he himself had been born. For him the gospel was according to the Scriptures; it was not an alien importation into Judaism but the true development of it, its highest point, although in its judgment on the centrality which some Jews had given to a particular interpretation of the law it showed a radicalism which amounted to a new creation.[31]

When Paul thinks about Abraham's story, he thinks especially about that initial encounter recorded in Genesis 12, and, more important, the initial act of covenanting between God and Abraham in Genesis 15. In Paul's view, Genesis 17 and the discussion of circumcision must be seen as a later development that does not annul what was said in Genesis 15. Abraham is at once for Paul the forefather of all true believers—Jew and Gentile alike—and the paradigm for all true believers of how they ought to relate to God. The story of faith being reckoned as righteousness does not begin with Christ but with Abraham. Furthermore, the story of Abraham and Sarah and their offspring provides an example of how God has always worked out God's plan of election, and selection within election, on the basis of promises, faith, and grace.

A careful reading of the intertextual echoes that resound through Rom. 4, 9—11, and Gal. 3—4 shows that Paul's narrative thought world, which is grounded in the Hebrew scriptures but goes beyond it to include the story of Jesus Christ and his followers,[32] is generating most of Paul's discussion and arguments. His use of the Hebrew scriptures as a gigantic prophetic textbook allows him to use widely differing texts for similar purposes, applying his christological and ecclesiological hermeneutic in various ways. In all cases, a careful rereading of the Old Testament texts Paul cites or alludes to provides a larger and clearer context in which to understand what he is trying to say.

The story of Abraham does not, however, stand alone. It is incomplete, for Abraham did not live to see all the promises made to him fulfilled. For Paul, the completion and fulfillment of the story comes in the story of Christ and those who are in Christ. This all important connecting of the Abrahamic and new covenants, this reading of the Abrahamic story as revealing that God had always had a gospel plan—indeed, the gospel had been proclaimed to Abraham first—required a very different sort of reading of the story of Moses. It is time to sojourn in the Sinai for a while.

5

The Glorious Guardian
and the Leader
Who Laid Down the Law

PAUL gives some brief reflections on Christ as the Christian's passover—
which should lead to a moral housecleaning in the Christian community (1
Cor. 5:7)[33] and to the tale of the Red Sea crossing and the miracle of manna
in the wilderness in 1 Corinthians 10.[34] However, when Paul thinks of
Moses, for him the heart of the story is the tale of Moses ascending Sinai to
receive the Ten Commandments and the larger Mosaic covenant that
resulted. Just as sin is the one word that encapsulates the story of Adam, and
faith that of Abraham, the phrase "the Law" best summarizes Paul's understanding of the significance of the drama in which Moses was caught up.[35]

Before we examine the key retelling in 2 Corinthians 3 of Moses on the
mount, a few words about the typology in 1 Corinthians 10, which draws
on the story of the Exodus and wilderness wanderings, are in order.[36] As
with the typology in Galatians 4, Paul's handling of the Old Testament
narrative would no doubt have surprised some, for in both cases Paul's
Christian rereading and retelling of the tale give it certain fresh and
unexpected twists and turns. For example, few would have expected anyone
to claim that Christ *was* the rock in the wilderness that provided God's
people with water. Despite J.D.G. Dunn's protests,[37] Paul is not simply
doing a typological allegory of *present* Christian spiritual realities. The
order of the day in 1 Corinthians 10 is drawing a close analogy between
what actually happened to the Israelites in the desert and from whence
their help came, and what could happen to the Corinthians who have the
same source of aid. As 1 Cor. 10:4, particularly the verb tense, and 10:9
suggest, Paul believes that Christ was already present and involved in the

liberating of Jews from bondage in Egypt and providing sustenance for them as they journeyed toward the Promised Land.

As we will discuss more fully in the next chapter, the narrative out of which Paul envisions the "first half" of the story of Christ is the narrative of personified Wisdom as it is found in Prov. 3, 8—9, and particularly in Wisd. Sol. 7—11. In Wisdom of Solomon 11, it is Wisdom who guides Israel through the wilderness and provides water from the rock, a role that Paul now predicates of Christ, for in 1 Cor. 1:30 Paul identifies Christ as Wisdom sent from God. Just as Abraham had the gospel preached to him in advance, so the Israelites had help from Christ in advance as well.

Paul's vision of the oneness of God, of God's people, and of God's plan of salvation throughout all time leads him to these sorts of analogies, not as intriguing exercises in fanciful exegesis but because he really believes God's salvation plan already began in Abraham and already involved the preexistent Christ long before he "took on the form of a servant." It is this sort of vision of the narrative of salvation that leads to the treating of all the Hebrew scriptures, including the later ones like Wisdom of Solomon, as (1) prophetic in character, (2) meant to be interpreted by means of a christological and ecclesiological hermeneutic, and (3) addressed not only to their original audiences but also especially to the ultimate community of God gathered in the eschatological age, who were finally in a position and condition to understand the fuller sense of the scriptures.

In 2 Corinthians 3, Paul is offering a tale of the two ministries of two called servants of God, Moses and the apostle himself. In that context Paul has things to say about two covenants, the Mosaic one and the new one.[38] This tale is clearly *not* about the Hebrew scriptures, nor is Paul offering here an endorsement of spiritual vs. literal interpretation of the text of the Old Testament, nor is he pitting the written Word against the Spirit.[39] He is comparing and contrasting ministries and the covenants on behalf of which these ministries are undertaken.

Moses went up the mountain, received the Ten Words, and came back down trailing clouds of glory. Paul does not doubt even for an instant that the revelation to Moses and the effect of the encounter of God with Moses were glorious. Nor does he doubt that Moses came back down clutching God's true Word. The Law, says Paul, is holy, just, and good, and indeed even spiritual (Rom. 7:12, 14). Paul's entire argument is misread unless the story in 2 Corinthians 3 is seen in light of the larger Pauline narrative thought world, which allows Paul to put the Moses story into its proper perspective.

Paul is using a salvation-historical argument that goes as follows: "No one disputes that the Mosaic covenant came attended with splendor. The fact is, however, that its glory or splendor has been eclipsed by the greater splendor of the new covenant, and so not only the glory on Moses' face but the Mosaic covenant itself is being annulled" (2 Cor. 3:11). Unfortunately, the effect of the glorious Mosaic covenant on fallen human beings is death, not life (see vv. 6–7), because the Mosaic law cannot empower or enliven its recipients so they might obey it. Thus the ministry of Moses stands in contrast to the ministry of the new covenant in that only the latter brings life by means of the Holy Spirit.[40]

How very different is Paul's view from what we find in the Jewish commentary Exodus Rab. 41.1 (on Ex. 31:18), which reads: "While Israel stood below engraving idols to provoke their Creator to anger . . . God sat on high engraving tablets which would give them life."

Several aspects of the story require further comment. In 3:13 the veil clearly refers to that which Moses literally placed over his face. The glory on his face had come, as Ex. 34:29 puts it, from Moses' having talked with God. Taking 2 Cor. 3:14a and v. 15 together, they suggest that the other veil Paul refers to is *not* over the written Law, but over the hearts of the Israelites who hear it, which is just another way of saying that their hearts/minds have been hardened. One should compare the similar argument about the hardening of the Israelites in Rom. 11:7 and v. 25 at this juncture. This suggests that Paul had already formulated what he thought about non-Christian Jews well before he ever wrote Romans and had formulated it in part by meditating on the story of Moses' shining countenance in Ex. 34:29–35 and its implications now that the more glorious covenant had come.

Paul believes that Christ or the Spirit is the one who takes away the veil, revealing that Moses' covenant has a temporary glory, now eclipsed by the light radiating from the face of Christ, which is reflected in the heart of the believer (4:6). It is this glorious revelation and light that Paul says is "the light of the gospel of the glory of Christ, who is the image of God." Here again Paul is retelling the story of Christ in light of his narrative thought world, in this case reflecting not just on Exodus 34, but on what is said about Wisdom in Wisd. Sol. 7:26: "For she is a reflection of eternal light, a spotless mirror of the working of God, and an image of God's goodness." The author had already said she was a pure emanation of the glory of the Almighty (7:25). Paul, of course, means more than this, for he is talking about a person, not a personified attribute of God, but the indebtedness seems clear enough.

The verb *katargeo*, used in 2 Cor. 3:7, 11, 13, 14 in various forms, is critical. In its New Testament usage, it is mainly found in the Pauline corpus (21 of 27 uses), and *always* elsewhere in Paul it refers to something replaced, invalidated, or abolished, not merely something faded.[41] The contrast between the ministry that brings life and the one that brings death strongly suggests that it has the same sense in 2 Corinthians 3. The coming of Christ has put even former goods in the shade and in effect made them obsolescent. The argument is not about human attitudes toward the Law, nor about approaches to the Law; nor even is Paul suggesting that the Law was defective in character—only inadequate to accomplish what fallen humans needed done to them. The implications are drawn in regard to the *effect* of the Law on fallen humans as opposed to the *effect* of the Spirit. Because of this, the ministry of Moses, including the Mosaic Law and covenant, which in Paul's mind *is* the old covenant, must be and has been annulled. The coming of Christ has brought it to an end (Rom. 10:4).

It is this same salvation-historical perspective that undergirds the entire discussion in Gal. 3–4 as well and leads Paul to see the Mosaic covenant and its Law as having a temporal and temporary purpose in God's larger salvation plan. What Gal. 3:19, 23, 24 indicates is that the age of Mosaic law was a parenthesis between promise and fulfillment, and that believers are now beyond that era in the salvation history timetable. Galatians 3:19 says it clearly: "The Law was until (*achris*) Christ came." Before he came, "we were confined under law" (v. 23). In v. 24 Paul draws an analogy between a *paidagogos* and the law.

A *paidagogos* was a slave who was the personal attendant of a freeborn rich boy. The *paidagogos* accompanied the boy wherever he went. The slave's job was not to be the boy's educator per se, but rather to teach him good manners, using the rod if necessary, to take him to school and walk him home, and to help him with his homework, making him recite what he learned. Thus the *paidagogos* was basically a guardian, disciplinarian, and custodian who imposed restraint on a young boy until he came of age. He was not basically an educator;[42] he was rather more like a male nanny or babysitter. Thus we should not translate here "the law was our instructor until Christ came" (v. 24). Rather, the point is that the Law attempted to define sin and confine sinners, keeping them under supervision until Christ came.

The analogy with the *paidagogos* also implies clearly that when Christ came, the Law was no longer necessary, so far as its role as confiner and its intended purposes are concerned. Verse 25 indicates that believers are no longer under the Law because they are all children of God through faith in Christ. Galatians 4:1–3 says the same thing in another way. Until the time was fully come, they were like children under a guardian and in that sense no freer than a slave. But when "Christ came we were redeemed out from under the Law." This does not mean that the Law or its giving was sin[43]—merely that its effect on fallen and sinful people was condemnation and a curse, not salvation and blessing. Humankind needed to be freed from the curse and condemnation as well as its cause—sin.

Galatians 3:19 says clearly that the Law was added because of transgressions. Paul stresses that the Law rests on works.[44] At 4:21–31 in his "allegory" Paul makes clear that those who desire to go back and place themselves under the Mosaic covenant are going back into bondage, confinement, indeed a form of slavery. "Mount Sinai bears children for slavery, but we are called to be descendants of Abraham, not by way of the slave girl and Ishmael, but by way of the free woman, Sarah and Isaac" (i.e., by way of the Abrahamic covenant, not the Mosaic one).[45] The association of Hagar and Ishmael with the Law is a twist in the tale the audience surely would not have expected, but then Paul is a creative storyteller.

Paul thus comes to a climax at Gal. 5:1: "For freedom Christ has set us free. Stand firm, therefore, and do not submit again to a yoke of slavery." No Pharisee would call the Law a yoke of slavery, but in light of Christ, Paul did. For him, to seek to be justified before God by way of the Law was to fall away from grace. This was what the Judaizers had done and were teaching the Galatian Gentiles to do by insisting they accept circumcision and Jewish ways in order to become full Christians. For Paul there could be only one way of salvation. If it was by faith in Christ, then obedience to the Law, no matter how sincere, could not accomplish it.

At 2 Cor. 3:6 Paul insists he is a minister of a new covenant and is made competent to be so by the Spirit, not the written code, for "the written code kills, but the Spirit gives life." Verse 7 shows that this is a reference to the Mosaic law, even that part carved in stone, the Ten Commandments. The effect of the Law was negative on fallen human beings, regardless of how splendid it was in itself.

It is clear enough that Paul did not come to these sorts of conclusions simply by rereading his Hebrew scriptures. Rather, they are the result of rereading the text with a new perspective; or, to use a metaphor, he reexamined the map of salvation history with a new key, which led him to look at the Mosaic covenant in the light of the one Christ brought to fulfillment, and so to look at Moses' glory in light of Christ's.[46]

No doubt there were some probing questions Paul must have asked himself, such as, If what I believe about salvation by grace through faith in the crucified and risen Jesus is true, what must be true about Moses and the Law? Even this sort of question, which required a radical renovation of his understanding on many things, did not lead Paul to reject the narrative thought world grounded in the Hebrew scriptures he had inherited as a Jew. Not for a moment does Paul suppose that because what he believes about Jesus is true, the scriptures must be wrong. Rather, he concluded that as a Pharisee he had greatly misunderstood what Messiah, salvation, faith, faithfulness to God, and the revelation of the scriptures amounted to. Furthermore, Paul's assigning the Mosaic covenant and Law to obsolescence does not lead him to take a general antinomian approach to his Christian faith. Yes, the Law of Moses has been superceded, but by two things—the faith of Jesus Christ and the Law of Christ, to which Paul has become "in-lawed" (1 Cor. 9:21). The means of initial right relationship with God is faith in Paul's schema, but Paul does affirm a sort of "covenantal nomism" that supercedes the sort of required response of obedience in the Mosaic covenant. Paul says bluntly, that Christians are not "under the Mosaic law" (1 Cor. 9:20), but he also expects various imperatives for all the churches to be obeyed. Paul does not believe obedience to God and God's Word is optional for those who are Christians, nor is faith simply seen as a substitute for obedience after conversion in Paul's vision of things. We will say more about this when we discuss the story of Christians.

For now, it is sufficient to say that Paul believes that the Mosaic law cannot have a positive soteriological function for the very good reason that it does not give the life or power necessary to allow one to keep all its stipulations, nor can it sustain life without the Holy Spirit. Because of this impotence, the Law leads to curse and condemnation of humans who try to use it as a means of obtaining right-standing with God. Barrett argues:

> Christ, says Paul (Rom. 10:4), is the end of the law with a view to effecting righteousness for everyone who believes . . . because with him came the new age, whereas the law belonged to the old age. Righteousness is now realized by a new divine gift, accepted in faith; *but this does not mean that the law as such is wrong, or that it is a misleading account of what God requires from [humankind], or of his relations with [human beings].*[47]

Where then for Paul does this leave the people who are still under the Law? How does Paul view the present and future of the "Israel according to the flesh"? What is the condition of Jews who still look to Sinai, now that Christ has come? Does the law still have a meaningful function for non-Christian Jews? To answer these sorts of questions we must return once more to Paul's fullest discussion of election and selection in Rom. 9—11, with side glances elsewhere.

6

True Jews, Torah, and the Future of Ethnic Israel

The early chapters of Romans testify that Paul regards the present as a time out of joint, an age riddled with anomalies: despite the revelation of the righteousness of God, human beings live in a state of rebellion and sin, and Israel stands skeptical of its appointed Messiah. Under such circumstances, God's justice is mysteriously hidden and the people of God are exposed to ridicule and suffering, as Israel learned during the period of the exile. Paul's pastoral task thus entails not only formulating theological answers to doubts about God's righteousness but also interpreting the suffering that the faithful community encounters during this anomalous interlude.[48]

As early as Romans 2, Paul reminds his audience that if they are going to be sticklers about preaching the Law they too are called to obey it all. The Law and circumcision are of no value if one does not obey God's commandments. At v. 29 Paul gives his essential definition of a Jew. Being a Jew and real circumcision are a matter of the heart and of one's mind or spiritual condition (cf. Rom. 9:6ff.). If as Paul says, real circumcision is a matter of the heart and a matter of one's spiritual condition, not ethnic heritage, then an uncircumcised Gentile could fit into this category. He or she is a Jew (i.e., God's chosen person) who is so inwardly.

Paul argues in Romans 9 that the adoption and promises do belong to Israel according to the flesh, but that not all Israel *is* true Israel. There has always been a process of selection within the broader context of the corporate election of Israel. This in practice means that the promises and adoption and other benefits are only efficacious for those who recognize

57

the Messiah who came forth from the patriarchs (9:5). It is Paul's claim that this has always been the way God works out his salvation-historical plan, and Paul will demonstrate that at some length in Rom. 9—11. As the allusion to Jeremiah 18 in Rom. 9:20–21 shows, what Paul is discussing here is the fate of Israel as a group; he is not offering reflections on the doctrine of predestination of individuals to salvation or damnation.[49] But it is not just the fate of Israel but also the faithfulness of God that is on the line in Paul's mind.

It is clear enough from the anguish expressed by Paul in Rom. 9—11 that he had not written off and would not have his audience write off non-Christian Jews. Yet on a superficial reading of Paul, one could get very conflicting impressions about his view of the present and future of ethnic Israel. On the one hand, to them belonged the sonship, the glory, the covenant(s), the giving of the Law, the worship, the promises, the patriarchs. "Of their race according to the flesh is the Christ" (Rom 9:4–5). At Rom. 3:2 Paul says, "To them were entrusted the oracles of God" (cf. Eph. 2:12). At Rom. 11:28 Paul says, "As regards election they are beloved, for the sake of their forefathers." He adds, "The gifts God gave Israel and the call are irrevocable" (v. 29). When answering if God's first chosen people had stumbled so as to fall *permanently*, Paul answers emphatically, "By no means!" (Rom. 11:11).

On the other hand, Paul asserts that in Christ "there is neither Jew nor Greek" (Gal. 3:28; cf. Col. 3:11), which suggests that categories do not count in the new economy of things. At Gal. 6:15 Paul says that circumcision counts for nothing; he goes on in the next verse to add peace on the "Israel of God." Although it is possible that Paul is referring to the faithful remnant of Jews in his day, vv. 16a and 16b refer to the same group. Furthermore, Paul has said that peace would be upon those who walk by the rules, including the rule that neither circumcision nor uncircumcision counts for anything—only a new creation![50] It is thus most likely that in Galatians 6 he is referring to Jews and Gentiles united in Christ as the Israel of God, which would seem to imply that the old Israel had been replaced or at least temporarily suspended.

Again, at 1 Thess. 2:14–16 Paul says the Jews killed the Lord and their prophets, drove them out, displeased God, and hindered Paul from preaching to the Gentiles that they may be saved, "so as always to fill up the measure of their sins." He adds, "But God's wrath has come upon them *eis telos*." There are some serious difficulties with taking this last phrase to mean "at last" or "finally," which would refer to a judgment that is imminent or here.[51] Some have assumed such a translation and argued that here Paul is referring to particular Jews who have opposed the work of Christ, not the Jews as a whole. This translation of this passage has led to the charge that Paul engaged in an anti-Semitic attitude after his conversion to Christ, which in turn has led some to argue that it is an interpolation into the text of 1 Thessalonians, an argument without objective textual support.[52]

The charge of anti-Semitism, however, is unwarranted, for elsewhere Paul says it is simply those who oppose the gospel, whoever they might be, and those who persecute Christians that face the wrath of God (Phil. 3:18f., 2 Thess. 1:5–9). It is clear in Rom. 9—11 that Paul holds out the hope that many Jews will be saved eventually. Indeed, at the beginning of Romans he says that the gospel is "the power of God for salvation to everyone who has faith, to the Jew first, and also to the Greek" (Rom. 1:16). Accordingly, I must insist that we should seek another translation of *eis telos* in 1 Thess. 2:16c.

J. Munck has pointed out that elsewhere this phrase means "until/unto the end" (cf. Matt. 10:22; Mark 13:13 = Matt. 24:13; Rev. 2:26; Hermas *Sim.* 9.27.3).[53] Further, translating the phrase as "finally" requires one to see the main verb as a prophetic aorist, something apparently not found anywhere else in the New Testament and certainly not found with the verb *ephthasen* ("come"). This verb surely refers to something that has already transpired. Taking "until the end" to modify "wrath" leads to the conclusion that Paul here is saying much the same thing that he says in Romans 11—that God's wrath has come upon non-Christian Jews temporarily until the end, until the final events in salvation history. In Romans 11 he will use the metaphor of their being temporarily broken off from the people of God until the full number of Gentiles has been grafted in. Paul then is not talking in 1 Thess. 2:16c about a final or fatal rejection of the Jews by God, a punishment of them with eternal judgment.

In Paul's scheme of things there can be temporal judgments by God that are not final. There can be election by God of people like a Cyrus or a Pharaoh to specific historical tasks that in no way implies the salvation or damnation of these individuals. In fact, it is Paul's view that even positive election is a corporate thing, either in Israel or in Christ, and as such, individuals within the corporate group may in the end find themselves on the outside. Not all Israel is *true* Israel.

The way Paul chooses to explain his somewhat complicated vision of things is by retelling in Rom. 9—11 the tale of salvation history. He begins with Abraham and works his way through the story of Ishmael, Isaac, Jacob, Esau, Moses, and Pharaoh. Then he turns to the prophets Hosea and Isaiah to support his argument about non-Christian Jews' currently being outside true Israel. Only in Romans 11 does he turn to the future of Israel and how he believes things will finally turn out. One must not read Romans 9 or 10 in isolation from Romans 11. Let us consider some details and the flow of the argument.

In Rom. 9—11 Paul is writing to an audience that is at least predominantly Gentile, and he is doing something of an *apologia* for his Jewish kin; but even more he is trying to justify the ways of God to himself and whoever else is listening. He attempts to answer certain questions these Gentile Christians might have and to warn them against presumption because they now have Christ and salvation and some Jews currently do not. In essence, Paul tries to answer the following questions: (1) Has God rejected his first chosen people once and for all? (2) Why did the Jews reject Jesus, if he was indeed the Jewish Messiah? (3) Is there any continuity between Israel and the *ekklesia* (Christian community), and between God's basis of dealing with each one? In Romans 11 Paul seeks to uphold and make clear God's character.

Paul could wish himself cut off from Christ if it would help his fellow Jews to come to Christ (Rom. 9:3). Despite all the preparation and benefits the Jews had from God and despite all Paul's apostolic labors, Israel by and large had rejected the gospel Paul preached and thereby, in Paul's view, had rejected their Messiah.

At Rom. 9:3–4 Paul calls the Jews only his human kin. He had another family he was now part of that was not based on flesh and blood relationships. At vv. 4–5 Paul rehearses the advantages and blessings of the Jews, and he seems to be thinking in a rather logical progression: (1) Israel was made God's sons (and daughters)[54] in the Exodus; (2) they saw God's glory in the pillars of fire and cloud; (3) God made a series of covenants with them, including especially the one at Sinai;[55] (4) this involved the setting up of the Law and of divine worship; (5) it also involved the promises that the patriarchs earlier got—progeny, promised land, to be God's covenant people. Mention of the promises causes Paul to remember the patriarchs and also perhaps the ultimate fact about Israel—from Israel came forth the Messiah. To Paul, although this is the preeminent fact, it is also the most ironic one as well, for most Jews had rejected Jesus.[56]

These considerations might lead to the conclusion that God's Word had failed, but Paul says not on the basis of the concept of (1) election and (2) the righteous remnant. As already mentioned, the argument moves in both directions: not all of Abraham's physical descendants are truly Israel, *and* not all of Israel is made up of Abraham's physical descendants. Paul wants to emphasize (Rom. 9:8) that "not the children of Abraham's flesh, born in the course of nature . . . but those who come by promise . . . are counted as Abraham's seed." This is shown not only by God's election of only some Israelites (i.e., through Isaac and not through Ishmael) but also later by God's election of Gentiles as well.

Paul, in vv. 6–13, carries the argument through two generations because of possible objections. That it was not heredity but God's promise that was determinative is shown by the fact that Isaac's birth took place in the context of sterility and old age. It could have been objected that Ishmael was not chosen simply because his mother was a slave woman and not a true Jew. However, Paul responds, "But look at the next generation. Jacob and Esau came from the same Jewish mother and father, in the same act of conception. They were born at the same time, and yet Jacob was chosen and Esau was not." This shows that it was God's divine election and mercy, not human circumstances, that determined the choice. The reasons God had for choosing Jacob, not Esau, Paul does not mention—though doubtless he thought God had reasons. Because God's choice is pure grace, God is free to have mercy on whomever God chooses.[57]

Paul adds several qualifying remarks. The promises do belong to Israel, but who is true Israel? Paul is arguing that the righteous remnant, the true Israel, had been reduced to one—Christ, by the time of his coming. The promises of God are "yes" in Him. The word "reckoned," "counted," arises here again at 9:8, and we have already seen its use at Rom. 4:3. It indicates that God creates righteous ones by reckoning it, counting faith as if it were righteousness, and by not counting sins against a person (Rom. 4:6, 8). Who is counted as righteous, who is a righteous remnant, is determined by the free grace and decision of God, not by works or heredity. God can raise up Israelites from stones if he wanted to, as John the Baptist said (Matt. 3:9; Luke 3:8).

The sentence "Jacob I loved but Esau I hated" is a quotation from Mal. 1:2f., and it likely means in the Hebrew "I preferred/chose Jacob over Esau." There was no fully adequate comparative mechanism in Hebrew or Aramaic, and so this was the best way to say "love more than" or "preferred over." Paul wants to stress God's freedom in calling out and choosing God's people, a freedom Paul will go on to stress God *still* has.[58]

We are talking here, however, about corporate election, with Christ as the Elect One. He was the chosen one, the promised sent one, the man of destiny. Believers are only elect in Christ (Gal. 3:29), through whom they become the descendants of Abraham and his heirs. The *means* by which Paul says any individual participates in Christ and his election is by exercising the gift of faith in him and in God's promises. Paul does not say in Rom. 9—11 that predestination is the means by which some individual or individuals *become* part of the elect.[59] Thus election is neither arbitrary nor fortuitous. It was in Israel before; it is in Christ now.

These verses intend to emphasize not just or even primarily God's freedom, but God's mercy. If God does anything for sinful humans, it is mercy. If God does not, God is not unjust, for fallen humans deserve nothing. Paul explains why God has done what God did with the Jews, *temporally and temporarily* hardening them, as God did with Pharaoh. It is

because God wanted to deal with all on the basis of mercy and grace, not
obligation and works. "It is because God is merciful that justification by
faith is possible. And God is determined to treat [people] on the basis of
mercy; indeed, if he treated them otherwise none would survive. But if his
dealings with them are to be governed by his mercy they cannot be
determined by [human] will, or earnest striving towards a goal."[60]

We cannot dwell on the example of Pharaoh at length except to note
that Pharaoh too was used to serve God's purposes of salvation and mercy.
Pharaoh supplied the occasion for God to demonstrate his power and
deliver his people, and proclaim his name throughout the earth. Even v. 18,
which speaks of God's hardening whomever he chooses to harden, does
not necessarily imply that Pharaoh was hardened eternally, but rather for a
time, so God could deliver Israel in dramatic fashion and manifest divine
glory and sovereignty. In a daring and even shocking move Paul transfers
the imagery of Pharaoh and his situation to Paul's own human kin, the
Jews. Israel now exists as hardened for the same purpose Pharaoh was
hardened before: (1) to provide the occasion for a divine act of God's
deliverance in which people are freed from the Law, sin, and death; (2) to
act so as to cause salvation to come to the Gentiles or so that God's
salvation will be proclaimed throughout the earth. God's ends are merciful; therefore, both Pharaoh's and Israel's self-will and hard-heartedness
are overruled and used for God's purposes.[61] It is part of the mystery of
God's plan and intention to create a people quite apart from what anyone
might expect involving Gentiles.

Romans 9:21–24 is especially difficult grammatically and otherwise.
Paul speaks of God, who "endured the vessels of wrath prepared for
destruction" (cf. Isa. 54:16). For Paul, the "vessels of mercy" are those Jews
and Gentiles God has now called out and into Christ. Paul says that God
for a long time was patient with these "vessels of wrath." Even then God
did not condemn or judge them immediately. The overarching explanation
is that God has done things in this fashion because the Almighty wished to
show mercy to those whom he called, both Jews and Gentiles. It also
intimates that God wanted to reveal both wrath against sin but also divine
saving power.

The phrase "vessels of wrath prepared for destruction" may apply to
Jews as well as Gentiles (vv. 27, 29). Did God prepare them for such?
Cranfield points out that there is a difference in the verbs applied to the
vessels of wrath and vessels of mercy. The verb used with the latter vessels
means prepared beforehand, whereas the former verb need not imply a
divine determination at all. Chrysostom and others of the early Fathers
took *katartidzein* ("prepare") to mean that these vessels prepared themselves for wrath. Cranfield suggests the translation "ready (or ripe) for

destruction" without any implication of anyone human or divine preparing them for it.[62] In fact, Paul does not even say they will go on to be destroyed, although they are "fit" for it. We thus do not likely have the idea here of predestination to damnation.

At 9:30–33 Paul argues that God has caused a partial rejection of some Israelites as well as the inclusion of some Gentiles in the believing community, but now he wants to explain, humanly speaking, why these things happened. The human reason why some Israelites were rejected and some Gentiles accepted is that the former pursued right-standing with God by works of the Law, the latter by faith in Christ. The Israelites were right to pursue righteousness, and the Law was a good thing, but to seek righteousness by virtue of the Law[63] in the end had to fail, for the Law could not give the life or power to fulfill it. Salvation came by grace through faith alone.[64]

Because Paul's relationship with and belief in Christ changed significantly his view of Israel, it would be only natural to expect that his view of the Law would change, for the two are so closely bound together. Before examining Romans 10, we must start with the background in the Hebrew scriptures and the various uses of the term *nomos* in Paul's letters.

The word *Torah* in Hebrew means instruction or teaching, not law per se. However, in the Greek translation of the Old Testament (the Septuagint, or LXX), *nomos*, which literally means "law," refers to Torah, even though elsewhere these words do not mean the same thing. We must bear in mind that the LXX was not an academic or scholarly document but an attempt to translate the Old Testament for those who could not read Hebrew. Thus, when a reader of the LXX reads *nomos* in the Old Testament, she or he was likely to understand it to mean law, not merely instruction. Barrett concludes from this that the translation of Torah as *nomos* helped foster a legalistic way of looking at the Old Testament instructions. Early Judaism was not purely legalistic, but in Barrett's view, that was a prominent if not dominant orientation, and Paul grew up with it. If so, for Paul the Old Testament was Law, and there was a strictness in it. One must obey it in order to be a good Jew. For the pre-Christian Paul, that required one's wholehearted obedience to the Law. Yet apparently some did this to obtain merit in God's sight.[65] Paul's use of the term *law* varies with the context and covers the whole gamut of meaning that both Torah and law as terms usually mean.

It is interesting that Paul only once uses the phrase "the Law of Moses" (at 1 Cor. 9:9), and there he is referring specifically to Deut. 25:4, not to the Holiness Code or the Ten Commandments. Probably the phrase "law of Moses" means for him the Pentateuch, or at least all the legal principles in the Pentateuch. There seem to be occasions when Paul can use the term *law* to mean the Old Testament, for instance at 1 Cor. 14:21, where Paul quotes Isa. 28:11–12, but calls it the law. This may be because Paul saw the whole Old Testament in light of and as an expansion of and explication of the Law given at Sinai, at least insofar as what came *after* the giving of the Mosaic law. Perhaps Paul thought of the prophets as prosecutors of the covenant lawsuit, bringing Israel to court and to account by means of the Mosaic law.

Paul can, however, also use the standard phrase "the law and the prophets" to mean the Old Testament in which "the law" means the Pentateuch (Rom. 3:21). It appears from Rom. 3:10–19 that Paul can call even the Psalms "the law." He also adds at 3:19 that the law is for a specific group of people; that is, it speaks only to those "under it" (cf. 1 Cor. 9:20). For Paul the law is a package deal, it stands or falls together. He does not distinguish between the moral precepts and the ceremonial parts. This is evident indirectly from the fact that Paul never speaks of "laws" plural. Whenever he uses the term *nomos* it is in the singular, *the* law, meaning the whole thing taken as a corporate unit. When Paul wants to talk about specific commandments or ordinances, he uses a different word—*entolai* (cf. Rom. 13:9; Eph. 2:15). We have already seen that Paul can use the term *nomos* to mean something more general—a principle. Romans 3:27 means "On what principle?" At Rom. 7:21a, Paul seems to use it in the Greek sense of what is customary or normal ("I find it to be normally the case," or "I find it to be a rule"). Romans 8:2 may mean "the principle of the Spirit." In the main, however, Paul means by Law, the Jewish law, given by God and found in the Old Testament with an emphasis on the demands or requirements of that Law. This includes ethical (Rom. 2:17–24; 7:7; 13:8–10) and cultic and ritual material (Gal. 2:11–21; 5:3; including circumcision).

We seem to have in Gal. 1:14 and Phil. 3:5–6 an indication of how Paul viewed the Law prior to his conversion. These texts reveal that Paul, being very strict as a Pharisee, was a zealot for the Law. This zeal even led him to persecute God's community and try to destroy the Christian faith (Gal. 1:23). Surely, one of the reasons Paul speaks of the incapacity and problems of the Law most vividly was that his zeal for the Law led him to oppose God's work and God's Messiah and God's new people. When after the Damascus road experience, Paul believed Jesus was the Messiah of God, this implied in itself a radically different way of looking at the Old Testament in general, Israel, and also the Law in particular.[66]

From our earlier discussion of Rom. 4, 7 and Gal. 3—4, we learned that the Law could not be a means of salvation for fallen people, for it could not give life. How much less could it be so for God's new creation in Christ?

Galatians 2:21 suggests that Paul's reasoning proceeds as follows: (1) Christ died for a purpose, so believers might have right-standing with God. (2) Because they have it through Christ, then it must *not* be available through the Law. (3) If it is not available through the Law, then the Law is powerless to give life or make anyone good, thus it cannot be a Christian's means of salvation.[67]

The Law failed to make humans good, not because of any inherent evil or flaws in the Law, but because its subjects, human beings, were fallen creatures, sold under sin. In theory the Law could have brought righteousness and life if its subjects were in some prefallen condition. Unfortunately, the effect of the Law on fallen humans was worse than failure. It even served as a goad to sin and wickedness, and placed human beings under a burden they could not bear, a bondage they could not free themselves from. These *effects* do not tell us, however, how Paul viewed the intended *purpose* of the Mosaic law.

Like his view of Israel, Paul's view of the Law is conditioned by the role he sees it playing in the broader story of God's salvation plan for humanity. Because of what he believes about Christ, Paul had come to believe that the Law had a special purpose for a specific period of time.[68] As Gal. 3—4 shows, Paul sees the Mosaic law serving as the guardian and confiner of God's people until they came of age, until Christ came. It thus has a temporary, not permanent, function as Law. This helps us understand why Paul says what he does in Rom. 10:4.

This text indicates that Christ has brought to an end the era in which the Law could even possibly be seen as a means of salvation or right-standing with God, or even be seen as a means of maintaining a proper relationship with God.[69] The idea of covenantal nomism may well represent how many early Jews viewed the role of the Law in their lives, that is, as a means of responding to God's gracious election.[70] Paul, however, would strongly point out that the believer is no longer under *that* Mosaic covenant; thus "doing the Mosaic law in order to continue to live" in fellowship with God was both an inadequate and, now that Christ has come, an inaccurate way to relate to God. The proof of this conclusion can be seen in Paul's exposition in Rom. 7:1–4.

Romans 7 begins with an analogy between obligation to the law and a wife's obligation to her husband. She is obligated to him as long as he lives, but when he dies she is free from the law that prohibits her marrying another man. Notice in 7:1–3 that Paul speaks about being bound both to the Law in general and to a particular law governing a particular case. At 7:4 he draws his analogy—"likewise we have died to the law" (i.e., believers are no longer obligated to it or bound by it). They belong to another—

Christ. It has often, and rightly, been pointed out that the central and directing role the Law played in Paul's life before his Damascus road experience is now played by Christ.

At 7:5 Paul says that sinful passions are aroused by the Law; that is, the Law lets one know what behavior is forbidden and therefore to a fallen creature what is desirable. But having been released from the Law, the fallen person is no longer held captive by it, believers serve not under the old written code but in or by means of the new life of the Spirit (7:6).

When Paul wants to speak about something Christians are obliged to obey, it is the Law of Christ, not the Mosaic law. This is not because Paul believes God has changed or that God has changed his mind about anything over the course of salvation history. God's character is seen as constant; hence the constant stress on God's faithfulness. Paul also believes, however, that God's plan has been *progressively revealed*, and one can judge the function of the earlier covenants only in light of Christ and his fulfillment of the Abrahamic covenant.[71] The clearer, more complete, indeed final revelation of God's character and plan is seen in Christ. In terms of Rom. 9—11, what this means is that Paul is trying to show that God delays justice in order to show mercy. Even God's hardening of Jews is temporary and in order to show mercy on Gentiles.

Love, grace, and mercy then say something more fundamental about God's character than Law does. Paul could never have called love an interim arrangement of God; indeed, 1 Corinthians 13 makes evident that love is the one quality, even more than faith and hope, that will outlast this age and exist in the age to come. Law is a necessary expression of God's holiness, but if Paul were to describe God in a short phrase, it would be as holy Love, not sporadically loving Holiness (cf. 1 John 4:8). Grace was sent in the person of Jesus Christ because God, being God, could not stand by and let sin abound among the people of God. God looks not merely to be just, but to be the justifier of even the ungodly. Paul would not, however, want to suggest that holiness is peripheral to God's character. Indeed, it is so crucial that Christ had to die to reflect God's just and righteous character and meet God's just demands for the punishment of human sin. The cross shows that it is necessarily a case of both/and. In light of God's character as revealed in the scriptures and as rehearsed in Romans 9, what then does Paul want to stress about the future of Israel?

At 10:1–2 Paul makes no bones about his desire. His own prayer is that all Israel be saved, even if scripture does testify to a remnant concept. Paul says, you have to give them credit, they are pursuing the right goal (righteousness) with enthusiasm, in contrast to most Gentiles, who could not care less. Their problem is that they do not understand how the righteousness God wants, and wants to give, is obtained—through faith alone, faith in Christ. Christ is the end of the Law in the sense of law as a means of obtaining right-standing with God, so that a status of righteousness is available to all who believe.

Paul in vv. 5ff. is able to show that both kinds of righteousness were already spoken of in the Old Testament; indeed, both are referred to in "the law," that is, the Pentateuch. In vv. 7 and 9 we have free paraphrases of Deut. 30:13 and 30:14 respectively. Salvation comes by faith in, and confession of, Jesus as risen Lord. In the most essential matter there is no distinction between Jew and Gentile. Whoever calls upon the name of the Lord will be saved. He is Lord and Savior of both Jews and Gentiles. The result of belief with the whole heart is *dikaiosune*, righteousness, or right-standing with God. Here there is little difference between righteousness and salvation. To be in right-standing with God is to be saved.

In 10:14–21 Paul indicates how it came about that Gentiles were saved—through preaching. Faith in Christ is impossible if one has not heard of and about him. This not only means missionary work is absolutely necessary, but it makes clear that no one can be saved without first having heard of Christ. How this affects the Old Testament saints who also did not hear we are not told. People can call only on the one in whom they believe; they can believe only if they have heard; they can hear only if it is preached, if someone is sent by the Lord. Thus God is the beginning and end of the process.

At vv. 18ff. Paul prepares for what is to follow, and he forestalls an objection. It is not the case that Israel has not heard; they cannot use that as an excuse. The word of the gospel has already gone out sufficiently for them to have heard and understood. The Old Testament even foreshadows both paradoxes: both Israel's disobedience to what they heard about the Messiah, and the Gentiles' response of faith. The quotation of Deut. 32:21 at v. 19 also introduces another point. Israel will be put to shame by believing Gentiles and will also be provoked to jealousy.

Romans 11:1–10 is Paul's explanation of the situation of Israel using the concept of a righteous remnant. God has not cast off Israel as a whole, and Paul himself and other Jewish Christians are living proof. Paul then goes on to show that there was an Old Testament precedent for a small righteous remnant in the midst of a largely apostate Israel in the time of Elijah, who confronted the problems of Israelites aligning themselves with Baal. The situation now, says Paul, is no different. Now as then there is a righteous remnant of Jews who have done what God required and expected of them. This gives Paul reason for hope for Israel as a whole, not because God will deal with them on any basis but faith, but because he believes that the coming in of the Gentiles will finally, or at the end, provoke Israel to jealousy.

At vv. 4–5 there is a play on words. Verse 4 tells about those who God says are "left" (*katelipon*), so too now, says Paul, there is a leftover (*leimma*), that is, a remnant. Paul uses the verb *gegonen*, which may be translated "has come into being" or "has happened." The point then is not that there are some Jews who never were outside God's elect people, but that God has by his free grace raised up (cf. 11:6) a new righteous remnant from out of the midst of largely apostate Israel.

At 11:1–2 Israel as a whole is called "the people whom God foreknew," but quite clearly this foreknowledge did not prevent many from being apostate and responding improperly. God knew and loved them, even in advance of their response, but not all responded to this love. Individuals in the elect group can opt out, apostasize, or be broken off.[72]

What this seems to imply on first blush is that Israel outside of Christ is no longer chosen. In the era after the coming of Christ there are not two people of God, but one.[73] Various factors favor this view: (1) At Gal. 6:2 Paul uses "The Israel of God" to refer to the church. (2) Paul has a way of transferring other terminology as well, that once was used of Israel, to refer to the church. At Rom. 1:7 the church is God's beloved (cf. 1 Thess. 1:4; 2 Thess. 2:13; Col. 3:12; and Ex. 19:5); the church is a people (*laos*) of God's own possession (cf. Rom. 9:24–26, citing Hos. 2:23; 1:10; Titus 2:14); the church is the circumcision (Phil. 3:3).

At Rom. 11:11 Paul grants that the Jews, not counting the remnant, had stumbled and thus temporarily lost their place to the Gentiles. But though they have stumbled and are frequently out of the race, God has not disowned or disenfranchised them, because of his faithfulness to his word. Even their folly had a positive result.

> It was the failure of the mission to the Jews that led to the mission to the Gentiles (cf. Acts 13:46; 18:6; 28:28), who were thereby brought within the scope of salvation and through the Gospel received the assurance that in due time they would possess it 13:11–14.[74]

Beginning at v. 13, Paul addresses the Gentiles for a while, by way of a metaphor drawn from the Old Testament, in order to prevent Gentiles from boasting or being presumptuous. Paul stresses they were only grafted in by God's grace and only because some of the Israelites had apostasized. They are not the root,[75] but the branches grafted in later. Thus they should not boast. Also, they too, if unfaithful, can be broken off, as the Israelites were.[76]

Paul's hopes seem realistic at v. 14—to save some of his fellow Jews by provoking their jealousy through his preaching to Gentiles (cf. 1 Cor. 9:22). Those occasional individual conversions prefigure but do not inaugurate "all Israel being saved"; that only takes place when "the full number of Gentiles have come in." The full conversion of Israel stands only at the end of history as an eschatological event.

Beginning with v. 16 we have a series of images that seem to suggest an overlap between Israel and the church, and more continuity than we have thus far suspected. However, it must be kept in mind that the first believers in Jesus were all Jews brought into his community through Christ's own ministry or shortly thereafter, and no doubt they saw themselves as "true Israel."[77] However, with v. 16 the question becomes, Are both metaphors referring to the same thing? Some have seen here a reference to the holy patriarchs (cf. v. 28) and Israel, or alternatively, Jewish Christians and all Jews. Cranfield sees v. 16a referring to Jewish Christians and v. 16b to Jews. Barrett, however, is probably right that v. 16 is continuing the argument of v. 15, and so in each case the firstfruit and the root are Jewish Christians. Who then are the lump and the branches? It is usually assumed that it must be "all Israel," (i.e., "the nation," cf. v. 28 below). But if v. 16 prepares for v. 17, then it is also possible that the lump and the branches (both representing sizable groups) are the Gentiles who are part of the elect whole *with* the Jewish Christians (the firstfruits and the root) and *after* the Jewish Christians.

Paul, of course, knows (v. 24 shows it) that he is describing a process that is contrary to nature. You cannot graft wild olive branches into a domesticated olive tree. But this contrary-to-nature idea is precisely the point. The grafting in of the Gentiles is an act of grace and is contrary to nature. Paul wants his Gentiles to keep this in mind. He is not interested in being horticulturally accurate here, only theologically correct using the form or image from nature.

The image is an Old Testament one, from Jer. 11:16 and Hos. 14:6, where Israel is seen as an olive tree. Here then in Romans 11 Paul insists that Israel, at least true Israel, is the people of God. Christian Jews are *not* grafted into the church; rather, Gentile Christians are grafted into God's people, into God's Israel.

Verse 19 answers the objection—"But God broke off the Jews to graft me in; therefore, he must prefer me." This is not so, for God has not rejected Old Testament Israel, and Gentiles are only in on the basis of faith. God is always the same, not changing the divine mind or exchanging a Jewish people for a Gentile one. God's kindness or severity corresponds to faith or unfaith, not a whim to choose first Jews and then Gentiles. The only reason any Jews were broken off was unfaith, not a change in God's mind. Paul reminds the Gentiles that God's present kindness may be exchanged for severity if they give way to unfaith. Indeed, it is in some ways easier to receive back a Jew than to graft in a Gentile. "It will be easier—if

such things can be compared—to bring back to the holy people a Jew born
into the covenants of grace, endowed with the law (which did after all bear
witness to the manifestation of God's righteousness by grace through
faith—3:21), and instructed by the messianic prophecies, than to introduce
for the first time a Gentile whose only advantage was the dim vestige of
religion which warned him that the world of which he was part was not his
but God's (1:20)."[78] Ultimately, however, Paul means to suggest not that
Jews will come back in and supplant the present Gentiles who are in, but
will be added to them.

At 11:25–32 Paul states explicitly what the olive tree metaphor implies.
The eschatological secret is revealed, being something not obvious to
human eyes and logical deduction and ordinary scrutiny of the historical
process. It is revealed so Gentiles could come into God's people. This
secret makes understandable the otherwise inexplicable. The hardening
that has fallen on the Jews has only fallen on part of them,[79] and it will last
only until the full number of the Gentiles comes in. Probably the phrase
"the full number of the Gentiles" means the added number necessary to
make up the full complement of Gentiles among God's people. It is surely
unlikely he means "all Gentiles whoever lived."

The climax, or the fulfillment of this mystery, is referred to at v. 26c:
"and *houtos* (thus/in this manner) all Israel will be saved." Does this mean:
(1) when the full complement of Gentiles have been added in to the few
Jewish Christians, this will amount to all Israel? (2) that after all the
Gentiles are in, then "all Israel" will be saved? To accept (1) means "Israel"
is used differently in v. 26 than it was in v. 25, which is unlikely especially in
view of the ongoing contrast between Jews and Gentiles in vv. 11–32. View
(2) then is more likely, but what does *houtos* mean here, and what does "all
Israel" mean—every single individual Jew? In view of how steeped this
whole section is in Old Testament allusions and quotations, we may
compare 1 Sam. 7:5; 25:1; 1 Kings 12:1; 2 Chron. 12:1; Dan. 9:11; and M.
San. 10:1, where "all Israel" includes not absolutely all, but the corporate
whole with some exceptions who are in the minority.[80]

In regard to the meaning of *houtos* here, the *kai* ("and") that precedes it
could be translated "even so." This would comport with the theme of the
whole section in which Paul stresses that God deals with the Gentiles in the
same fashion that God deals with the Jews. In other words, just as the full
number of Gentiles will be brought in, even so "all Israel" will be saved *by
means of faith in Christ. Houtos* by itself can be either retrospective or
prospective. The problem with this view is that we do not have a *preceding
kathos* ("just as") to suggest such a comparison.

Dunn, however, suggests that following the temporal reference in *achri
ou* ("until when the . . ."), *kai houtos* (and so) may likewise have some

temporal sense, concluding that the bringing in of the Gentiles will be a means of provoking the Israelites to jealousy, and "in this manner all Israel will be saved."[81] Cranfield makes much the same point showing the difference between *kai houtos* and *houtos kai*. The former is translated "and thus" and means "and so (as a result)."[82] The end result of this view is much the same as Dunn's. These views seem nearest the mark and do not require us to translate *houtos* as "then,"[83] nor do they require us to envision that Paul thinks God in the end will deal with non-Christian Jews on any other basis than faith. The eschatological miracle foreseen is that when the full number of Gentiles come in, like a nuclear reaction reaching critical mass, this will *finally* provoke the Jews to jealousy and to belief in Christ in large numbers. This latter in turn will signal or correspond with life from the dead, the resurrection of believers, and thus with the return of Christ.

It is also possible to take *houtos* followed by *kathos* in a correlative sense[84] to mean "thus (in this manner or fashion) . . . just as it is written." This would closely link v. 26c to v. 27. I suspect that the latter possibility is less likely, even though it seems clear enough that v. 27 comments on and clarifies what precedes.

Verse 27 is meant to verify from the Hebrew scriptures that God intends to save Israel at the end and climax of history. Paul here quotes Isa. 59:20–21a and 27:9. The point of this is not only to stress that in the end God will save Israel,[85] but that God will do it in the same manner as he has saved Gentiles—by getting them to repent and have faith, by taking away their sins, and by turning away impiety from Jacob.[86] God does not go back on his grace and promises and the calling of his first chosen people, though in every age faith is the proper response, lest some individual think he or she could get in without it.[87]

But it is not just that God is always free and always merciful, it is that God always expects the people of God to respond as Abraham did—in faith and trust. So then for Paul, the salvation-history story actually involves the following:[88] (1) It has always been the case that God related to his people on the basis of mercy and expected faith. (2) It has always been true that not all Israel is true Israel; a righteous-remnant concept has always applied in the entire history of God's people. (3) Election has always been a matter of being part of the elect group, being in Israel according to the flesh, or being in Christ. It was and is possible with either group for other individuals to be grafted in or broken off from the group. (4) In Paul's view, at present Jewish Christians are the righteous remnant and Gentiles have been grafted into them. But in the future, by an eschatological miracle the Redeemer will come from Zion (here presumably heaven)[89] and will drive away impiety from ethnic Israel, and so many more will be saved. (5) There has always been only one true people of God. Christ as the seed of

Abraham and then the first Jewish Christians are the bridge between the Old Testament saints and the *ekklesia*, which is Jew and Gentile united in the body of Christ.

The implications of Rom. 9—11, written to put Gentile Christians in their place, are that even the salvation of the Gentiles is not just for their own sake but also for the sake and return of ethnic Israel to God. The Gentiles have no Messiah but the Jewish Messiah, no promises but the promises given to Abraham, no gospel but that which has always been for the Jew first and then the Gentiles (Rom 1:16). The *ekklesia* is not in and Israel out; rather, the *ekklesia* is the true development of Israel and is the means to spur on the "fleshly" Israel's envy and return. Only thus will God's people become one complete elect group with a full complement of Jew and Gentile, united as the body of the Jewish Messiah. Whether by Paul, as I think likely, or by a Paulinist, Paul's vision of the way things are and ought to be is beautifully expressed at Eph. 2:11–18, a passage much like the one we have just explored:

> So then, remember that at one time you Gentiles . . . that you were at that time without Christ, being aliens from the commonwealth of Israel, and strangers to the covenants of promise, having no hope and without God in the world. But now in Christ Jesus you who once were far off have been brought near by the blood of Christ. For he is our peace; in his flesh he has made both groups into one and has broken down the dividing wall, that is, the hostility between us. He has abolished the law with its commandments and ordinances, that he might create in himself one new humanity in place of the two, thus making peace, and might reconcile both groups to God in one body through the cross, thus putting to death that hostility through it. So he came and proclaimed peace to you who were far off and peace to those who were near; for through him both of us have access in one Spirit to the Father.[90]

7

Synopsis
The Story Thus Far

GOD made a perfect beginning of the human drama, but it was quickly spoiled by the first couple God created. The first sin brought disease, decay, death, suffering, sorrow, and bondage to sin into the world. That was not all, however, for there were also cosmic evil and powers of darkness, which goaded humans, even the first humans, into sin. Where these powers came from and how they came to be as they are are matters shrouded in darkness. The problems of the world were primarily, but by no means exclusively, human historical ones.

God, however, had a remedy in mind—the calling out and equipping of a people meant to bear witness to all and sundry of God's character and plan for salvation. The most critical subplot of human history is salvation history, and it is the focus of the Hebrew scriptures. God called out Abram, and Abram responded to God's call and promises with trust and obedience. His faith was reckoned as righteousness, thereby setting up the pattern by which the Almighty desired for all human creatures to relate to God. The Abrahamic covenant was meant to be an everlasting one, and the promises made to Abraham of seed, of nations, of kings, of being a blessing to all the world were irrevocable. God would always be faithful to the divine character and true to the word, the promises.

Somewhat unexpectedly there was a hiatus between the giving of the promises to Abraham and their fulfillment. During this interim period God's people—being still very fallen creatures, to which the Exodus-Sinai events bore abundant witness—needed to be kept in line and under restraint until the promises could be fulfilled, until the ultimate Seed

73

should come upon the human stage. For this purpose, provisionally to set apart God's people in both material and spiritual ways from others, the Mosaic law was given, which included the Ten Commandments. The Law was holy, just, and good, but it was also wholly incapable of enabling fallen humans to keep it. It could not give life nor free fallen ones from the bondage of sin. Indeed, quite contrary to its purpose, which was to reveal and limit sin, it even had the horrid effect of stimulating sin in some.

There was a sense in which the Law *in essence* had already been given to Adam. Adam and Eve could have kept it before the Fall, but chose to do otherwise. Ever since, the Law could not be wholly kept, and thus it shut up even God's people under condemnation and curse. The story of Adam's fall and the general fallenness of all those in Adam, including those given the Mosaic law, is retold in Romans 7, in the context of the discussion about the Law. Sin, death, and condemnation are associated with the Law because of the character of its recipients, not the character of the Law itself.

The world was a very dark place indeed, for even God's people endured the plight of blindness, caused by the "god of this age," who used creation and even God's good Law to further enhance the bondage of humanity. The world cried out, Who will deliver me from this bondage to sin, this body of death? Even Israel cried out for her messiah, yet strangely few recognized him when he came in the person of Jesus of Nazareth.

Yet this development did not catch God by surprise. Indeed, God was using it to do some surprising things, such as save the full number of Gentiles first before the full number of Jews! Ethnic Israel, who had rejected Christ, was only temporarily broken off from the people of God, so that Gentiles might be grafted into that community of the saved. God would yet produce an eschatological miracle, and when the Redeemer came again he would turn away the impiety of Jacob, as the prophets had foretold. They too would once again relate to God as their forefather Abraham had—on the basis of faith.

But this is in some measure getting ahead of the story. One cannot fully understand a grand return without first hearing about the grand entrance of the Seed of Abraham, who was also Seed of David. Where did he come from? What was his mission? What did he accomplish? What did it matter to Jews or Gentiles? To the story of the Christ we must now turn, for therein lies the heart of the matter. Into the heart of darkness came a very great light.

> This day, when my soul's form bends towards the east,
> There I should see a sun, by rising set,
> And by that setting endless day beget;

But that Christ on this Cross, did rise and fall,
Sin had eternally benighted all.

—*John Donne*
"Good Friday, 1613. Riding Westward"[91]

NOTES TO PART 2

Keeping the Faith and Laying Down the Law

1. From *The Poetic and Dramatic Works of Alfred Lord Tennyson* (Boston: Houghton Mifflin, 1899), 251.

2. See N. T. Wright, *The Climax of the Covenant* (Edinburgh: T. & T. Clark, 1991), 264: "I suggest that Paul saw scripture as story and prophecy, *not* in the abstract sense of mere typological prefigurement between one event and another . . . but in the sense of a very specific story functioning in a very specific way. For Paul, the story was always moving toward a climax; it contained within it . . . advance warnings and promises about that climax (the story of Isaac, of the Exodus, and so forth); and most importantly, it was a story whose climax, Paul believed, *had now arrived.*"

3. R. B. Hays, *Echoes of Scripture in the Letters of Paul* (New Haven, Conn., 1989), 34.

4. C. K. Barrett, *From First Adam to Last* (New York: Charles Scribner's Sons, 1962), 45.

5. In fact, one can say that to some degree there is a sort of symbiotic relationship between Paul's reading of the Hebrew scriptures and his understanding of the story of Christ. The direction of influence is not simply one way. Barrett, *From First Adam*, 30, argues that "Paul was not in the habit of taking over ready-made ideas and thought forms, even when these bore a real affinity with his own thought. He preferred to work out his own material on first principles, and pick out Old Testament characters for development on the basis of their intrinsic significance." I would suggest that this is basically correct; however, it underplays the extent to which the narratives in the Hebrew scriptures undergird and provide the fertile soil for Paul's thought. To say he uses a christological hermeneutic in handling the Old Testament is one thing. To say that he simply starts with his own experience and the Christian gospel and then in piecemeal fashion picks out parts of the Old Testament for development is not wholly accurate. Even in the case of Paul's understanding of the story of Christ, he envisions that story in light of the story of Wisdom as found in Prov. 8, Wisd. Sol. 7—9, and elsewhere (cf. below pp. 89ff.) Only when he discusses the death, resurrection, and return of Christ is it evident that the starting point is the Christian message and not the Hebrew scriptures.

6. Barrett, *From First Adam to Last*, 29, who critiques the views on the sacrifice of Isaac often espoused by scholars such as G. Vermes.

7. It appears to me that Paul understood Genesis 17 as an example of the ✓ renewal of the covenant already in principle made in Genesis 15.

8. Forensic rhetoric is the rhetoric of attack and defense, used in the courtroom.

9. Cf. R. B. Hays, "Have We Found Abraham to Be Our Forefather According to the Flesh? A Reconsideration of Rom. 4:1," *Novum Testamentum* 27 (1985): 76–98.

10. Ibid., 78.

11. For the construction "to find someone to be something" in Paul, cf. 1 Cor. 4:2; 15:15; 2 Cor. 5:3; 9:4; 12:20; Gal. 2:17.

12. One wonders if Paul's reading of the order of the Abraham story in Genesis 15 and 17 helped to lead him to the conclusion he arrives at in Romans 11 that God is first including mainly the uncircumcised in the true people of God and then will include "all Israel" (cf. Rom. 4:11–12 to 11:11–26).

13. This would support Hays' argument that Paul sees parallels not just between Abraham and believers, but also between Abraham and Christ. As Rom. 3:22 says, the righteousness of God was manifested through the faith of Jesus Christ for all who believe, just as it was earlier manifested through the faith of Abraham. Jesus and Abraham are the paramount examples of faith for believers to follow. To read Rom. 3:22 to refer to the believer's faith in Jesus rather than Jesus' faith in God makes the following clause ("for those who believe") redundant.

14. S. Fowl, *The Story of Christ in the Ethics of Paul* (Sheffield, Eng.: JSOT Press, 1990), 94.

15. J. A. Zeisler, *Paul's Letter to the Romans* (Philadelphia: Trinity Press International, 1989), 124.

16. It may also be worth pointing out that the recent detailed study by M. J. Harris, *Jesus as God* (Grand Rapids: Baker Book House, 1992), 45–50, shows that when Paul uses the term *theos* he always means the one Christians call the first person of the Trinity, not Christ, except in a very few places, such as Rom. 9:5, where a doxological mode of speaking leads Paul to call Christ "God."

17. Hays, *Echoes of Scripture*, 34–35.

18. See my *Jesus, Paul, and the End of the World* (Downers Grove, Ill.: I-V Press, 1992), 111–25.

19. See Wright, *The Climax*, 236: "The main subject-matter of Romans 9—11 . . . is the covenant faithfulness of God, seen in its outworking in the history of the people of God. . . . He is arguing, basically, that the events of Israel's rejection of the gospel of Jesus Christ *are* the paradoxical outworking of God's covenant faithfulness. Only by such a process—Israel's unbelief, the turning to the Gentiles, and the continual offering of salvation to Jews also—can God be true to his promises to Abraham, promises which declared *both* that he would give him a worldwide family *and* that his own seed would share in the blessing."

20. See my *Jesus, Paul, and the End*, 115.

21. The NRSV translation "not all of Abraham's children are his true descendants" is completely misleading, because the text in fact reads literally, "nor

because they are Abraham's seed, [are] all children, but . . . "; cf. C.E.B. Cranfield, *Romans II* (Edinburgh: T. & T. Clark, 1979), 470.

22. Noticing again the corporate sense of election, being "in Isaac" is rather like being "in Christ."

23. Another viable possibility is suggested by Wright in *The Climax* , 157–74. He suggests that the term "Christ" in Gal. 3:16 refers to Christ in his role as inclusive personality, as "the one in whom the people of God is summed up precisely *as* the people of God" (p. 165). Wright, however, doesn't pick up the echo of Genesis 17 in Galatians 3 in the way he should.

24. Ibid., 170ff.

25. The Holy Spirit, which christens the believer, like circumcision before it sets the person in question apart from an unholy and fallen world. However, one does it outwardly, the other inwardly. The Holy Spirit brings about the circumcision of the heart.

26. I take Galatians to have been written prior to Romans as a piece of forensic rhetoric meant to defend Paul's gospel and his converts' freedom in Christ from the influences of certain Jewish Christians zealous for imposing the Mosaic law on Gentile converts to Christianity.

27. C. K. Barrett, "The Allegory of Abraham, Sarah, and Hagar in the Argument of Galatians," in *Essays on Paul* (Philadelphia: Westminster Press, 1982), 154–170, suggests that the various texts Paul actually cites in Galatians 3 were the very ones being used by his opponents to argue their own case for Judaizing the Gentile Christians. He may well be right, but in forensic rhetoric it is also always possible that Paul is forestalling possible, not actual, arguments or mere rumors. Paul's question in 3:1 may suggest that he knows little about who is troubling the Galatians.

28. See H. D. Betz, *Galatians* (Philadelphia: Fortress Press, 1979), 245.

29. See my discussion in *Jesus, Paul, and the End*, 107–8.

30. Ibid. p. 106.

31. W. D. Davies, *Jewish and Pauline Studies* (Philadelphia:Fortress Press, 1984), 136.

32. This also involves reading the story from back to front as well as vice versa.

33. The word *pascha* could allude to the whole passover feast, the passover meal, or the passover lamb, but the reference to sacrifice in 1 Cor. 5:7 suggests that the latter is the reference here. On the idea that Christ's death averts the wrath of God from falling upon believers, see 1 Thess. 1:10.

34. See the detailed exegesis in my commentary *Conflict and Community in Corinth: A Socio-Rhetorical Commentary on 1 and 2 Corinthians* (Grand Rapids: Wm. B. Eerdmans, 1994), ad loc.

35. See Barrett, *From First Adam*, 46ff.

36. The more detailed discussion in my Corinthians commentary should be consulted for detailed reference to the scholarly debate over this material.

37. In J.D.G. Dunn, *Christology in the Making* (Philadelphia: Westminster Press, 1980), 183–84.

38. Here is apparently the first reference to an "old" covenant, with the term "old" seemingly having a rather pejorative ring to it. The phrase "old covenant"

does not appear again until the second century A.D., where it is used by Melito of Sardis. The clear reference to Moses and the allusion to the stone tablets make abundantly clear what covenant Paul has in mind.

39. Despite the suggestions of Hays, *Echoes of Scripture*, 122ff.

40. See my *Jesus, Paul, and the End*, 109.

41. Cf. V. P. Furnish, *II Corinthians* (Garden City, N.Y.: Doubleday & Co., 1984), 203; W. Bauer, W. F. Arndt, F. W. Gingrich, *A Greek English Lexicon of the New Testament and Other Early Christian Literature* (Chicago: Univ. of Chicago Press, 1957); hereafter *BAG*, 418.

42. F. F. Bruce, *Commentary on Galatians* (Grand Rapids: Wm. B. Eerdmans, 1982), 182–83.

43. However, note the parallel between Gal. 3:22 and v. 23, and cf. Rom. 7:4, 7.

44. "Do this and live," and unless one fulfills it all, one is under a curse. See Gal. 3:10–12.

45. Some of this language is accounted for because Paul is doing polemics here to dissuade his audience from listening to the Judaizers. The more positive portrayal of the Law in Rom. 9—11 and 2 Cor. 3 needs to be compared to nuance what we find here.

46. See Barrett, *From First Adam*, 51: "Paul is not developing his own doctrine out of the Exodus narrative; he knows what he has to say and uses figures and imagery drawn from the Old Testament to give it vividness and force, though it is also true he sees in the Old Testament story positive truth, of which he learns the full meaning, not in the Old Testament itself but in Christ." Although this much is certainly true, I would put things more strongly. The Old Testament does not serve for Paul just as a repository of images and examples. It provides much of the stuff of Paul's symbolic universe. Paul adds some new elements from his Christian experience and tradition; but more than anything else, what he adds is a christological and ecclesiological hermeneutic, a new way of looking at the "old, old story."

47. Ibid., 66–67, emphasis added.

48. Hays, *Echoes of Scripture*, 57.

49. Ibid., 66.

50. See my *Jesus, Paul, and the End*, 107–8.

51. See I. H. Marshall, *1 and 2 Thessalonians* (Grand Rapids: Wm. B. Eerdmans, 1978), 80ff., on this view.

52. See, e.g., B. Pearson, "1 Thessalonians 2:13–16: A Deutero-Pauline Interpolation," *Harvard Theological Review* 64 (1971): 79–94.

53. J. Munck, *Christ and Israel: An Interpretation of Romans 9—11* (Philadelphia: Fortress Press, 1967), 63–65.

54. For Paul's use of more inclusive phrasing elsewhere when he modifies the patriarchal language of the Old Testament, see 2 Cor. 6:18.

55. On the text problems here, cf. B. M. Metzger, *A Textual Commentary on the Greek New Testament*, 519, for the reading "covenants," not "covenant."

56. C. K. Barrett, *The Epistle to the Romans* (New York: Harper & Brothers, 1957), 178.

57. That God's choice is pure grace means that it is not based on merit; it does

not mean that it was made without foreknowledge and forethought. Grace is unmerited, not blind, love.

58. Barrett, *Romans*, 183.

59. Nor does Paul say this even in Rom. 8:28–30; see cf. pp. 230–31 below.

60. Barrett, *Romans*, 186.

61. It may also be that Paul viewed the hardening of Israel in the same way that Exodus presents Pharaoh's hardening; namely, that it started with Pharaoh's own desire or inclination. Pharaoh hardened his own heart, and God merely confirmed him in that desire or made him resolute in it. See Ex. 1:8ff.; 7:3, 13–14; 8:15, 32; 9:7, 12, 34–35; 10:20, 27; 11:10; 14:4, 17. Paul nonetheless does not answer why God hardens whom he does.

62. Cranfield, *Romans II*, 495–96.

63. Cf. Rom. 10:3, Gal. 3:10.

64. Barrett, *Romans*, 194.

65. Barrett, *Romans*, 140ff.; *From First Adam*, 46–67.

66. See below pp. 215ff. on Paul's conversion, and the evaluation of S. Kim, J.D.G. Dunn, and others on its effect on Paul's thought world.

67. Although Paul phrases it the other way around in this verse, he would not be saying this at all if his faith in Christ had not caused a Copernican revolution in his thinking about almost everything Jewish, including the Law.

68. See Wright, *The Climax*, 241–42.

69. The translation of *telos* as goal is possible, but 10:3 and the reference to Israel trying to establish its own righteousness by means of the Law surely favor the translation "end." Christ put an end to the meaningfulness of the sort of efforts referred to in 10:3.

70. Cf. E. P. Sanders, *Paul and Palestinian Judaism* (London: SCM Press, 1977), 84ff.

71. Paul does not stress here Christ's fulfillment of the Mosaic covenant, which is what the translation "goal or fulfillment of the Law" suggests.

72. Barrett, *Romans*, 210.

73. Nonetheless, God has not forgotten about his old people outside Christ. God still has a plan for them at the end of history.

74. Barrett, *Romans*, 213.

75. This is possibly a reference to Abraham or faithful Israel before the time of Christ.

76. This would be an exceedingly incautious and inappropriate metaphor if Paul had held to the idea of "once saved, always saved."

77. See my *The Christology of Jesus* (Minneapolis: Fortress Press, 1990), 118ff., on Jesus' relationship to the Twelve.

78. Barrett, *Romans*, 219.

79. Cranfield, *Romans II*, 575.

80. The example from M. San. 10:1 is especially interesting here, because after stating that all Israel will be saved, a list of clear exceptions are enumerated, including all Sadducees, heretics, magicians, the licentious, and more. See Barrett, *Romans*, 223.

81. J.D.G. Dunn, *Romans 9–16* (Waco: Word, 1988), 681; cf. 1 Thess. 4:17.

82. C.E.B. Cranfield, *Romans I* (Edinburgh: T. & T. Clark, 1975), 272 n. 5.

83. The temporal flow being conveyed by the earlier phrase *achri ou*, as Dunn avers.

84. Cf. Luke 24:24; Phil. 3:17; *BAG*, 602 (see n. 41).

85. The redeemer who comes out of Zion may of course be Christ rather than God. In view of 1 Thess. 1:10, this seems likely; cf. Zeisler, *Paul's Letter to the Romans*, 286.

86. The notion that v. 27 refers to the mission to the Gentiles going forth from Jerusalem, advanced by Wright, *The Climax*, 250–51, is untenable. Jew and Gentile united in Christ, much less Gentiles alone, are never called Jacob elsewhere in Paul!

87. Barrett, *Romans*, 225.

88. See the schematic in my *Jesus, Paul, and the End*, 124.

89. See Gal. 4:26.

90. I suspect that one reason there has been so much debate over Paul's view of the Law and of Israel is that these two things have been endlessly studied outside of the narrative framework in which Paul's thought moved. To give but one example, one cannot understand what Paul says about the Law in Gal. 3—4 unless one has a clear sense of his vision of the flow of salvation history, the relationship of Abraham and Christ, and also the relationship of the first and last Adam. To denude the story of its flow and drama and assume that one could understand *nomos* in Paul just by detailed morphological or lexicographic inquiries are major mistakes.

91. From *John Donne, the Complete English Poems* (Harmondsworth: Penguin Books, 1973), 330.

Fr.
p 81 – 118

PART 3

The Surprising Story
of the Crucified Conqueror

Wilt thou love God, as he thee? then digest
My soul this wholesome meditation, . . .
The Father, having begot a Son most blessed . . .
Hath deigned to choose thee by adoption,
Coheir to his glory, and Sabbath's endless rest;
And as a robbed man, which by search doth find
His stol'n stuff sold, must lose or buy it again:
The Son of glory came down, and was slain,
Us whom he had made, and Satan stol'n, to unbind.
'Twas much that man was made like God before,
But, that God should be made like man, much more.

—*John Donne*
"Divine Meditations" 15[1]

PAUL'S thought world had a dominant sun—the Son of God, Jesus Christ.[2] Paul's thoughts about Christ inform and transform the entire rest of his thought, sometimes even absorbing aspects of his thought that one might have expected would have gone relatively untouched by christological reflections. Who would have expected Paul to tell his Corinthian listeners that the rock that gave forth water to the Israelites during their period of wilderness wanderings *was* Christ (1 Cor. 10:4)? Here he is drawing on sapiential ideas about the role of personified Wisdom in Israel (cf. Wisd. Sol. 11:2–4: "They journeyed through the uninhabited wilderness. . . . When they were thirsty, they called upon [Wisdom], and water was given them out of flinty rock"). Yet Paul's view of Christ was so broad that he could conceive of Christ's being involved in God's dealings with his people long before he was born and began his earthly ministry. This is apparently because he sees Christ as Wisdom come in the flesh (cf. 1 Cor. 1:24), and therefore whatever had been said of Wisdom in early Jewish thought, including its existence in heaven before creation (cf. Proverbs 8, Sirach 24, Wisdom of Solomon 7), is now predicated of Christ.[3]

There are two opposite dangers that need to be avoided in the study of Paul's thoughts about Christ. The first is to underestimate the significance and weight of the reflection on the story of Christ for Paul's thought world. Paul's thinking about Christ may be seen as a subspecies of his thinking about God. For Paul, "Jesus is Lord" is not merely a functional description of Jesus' tasks since the resurrection. Many though not all of the names, titles, roles, and functions of God are predicated of Christ precisely because Paul believes that he is dealing with God in Christ, and in some sense God as Christ. Christ is one way God is manifested to the world. Christ can be an object of confession and worship for Paul. He does not believe he is advocating a violation of Jewish monotheism by worshiping Christ, precisely because he believes Christ is divine, or part of the Godhead.

L. W. Hurtado has ably demonstrated that early Jewish monotheism could include the idea of divine agency, which on occasion involved seeing a human being such as an Enoch or a patriarch as a divine agent of God.[4] In such a context, seeing the Christ as a divine agent of God, or as Wisdom in person, is not such a radical departure as has sometimes been thought.

This is not to say that one can find in Paul's letters any sort of developed Trinitarian doctrine or any lengthy explanation of the interrelationships in the Godhead, but the raw data for such a doctrine that predicates divinity of Father, Son, and Spirit is in evidence in Paul's letters. Christology is a form, though by no means the only form, of theology for Paul. It is thus not proper to talk about Christology being dissolved into theology in a text like 1 Corinthians 15, as if the two things were originally separate categories in Paul's Christian thought world.[5]

The other major error that must be avoided is Christomonism, in which Christology is seen as almost the sole form of theology in Paul's thought. It is one thing to say that Paul reenvisioned the world and even God through Christocentric glasses. It is quite another to suggest that Paul had no significant place in his theological thought for persons other than Christ. It is only the Father that sent the Son, and it is only the Son that died on the cross, and it is only the Spirit by whom believers are baptized into the one body of Christ, according to Paul. These three then are distinguished by Paul by some of their functions and even, at least in regard to Christ's human nature, by nature (i.e., the Father and the Spirit did not have a human nature). A Christomonistic approach to Paul's theology does not give adequate attention to the distinctive roles, functions, and characteristics of Father, Son, and Spirit that the apostle presents.

The discussion of Paul's understanding of the story of Christ has too often dealt with the subject as though it could be adequately treated by simply gathering up the various references to one title or another and analyzing them. This unfortunately often amounts to ripping ideas out of the fabric of Paul's thought. When this is done the balance between Paul's thought and the context or contingent situation in which it is expressed is lost. Beker is right that one must attend to both the coherency of Paul's thought through time, but also its contingency as it addresses particular situations and concerns.[6] Although the titles approach can be helpful, it can also be reductionistic, resulting in the treatment of Paul's thought world in a history-of-theological-ideas fashion. But Paul's theological thought is woven together with his ethical and social concerns. Furthermore, the whole of Paul's christological thought is much greater than the sum of its parts, especially in view of the fact that it is grounded in the sacred story of the Christ, which in turned is grounded in the story of Israel and, by way of the Last Adam Christology, in the story of the whole human race.[7]

Much more adequate is the recognition that Paul's thought about Christ had a narrative shape. His vision of the story of Christ is in large measure what dictates how he views the various aspects of his Christology. That narrative framework, which we will explore in detail shortly, tells a tale of a being who was in the very form of God (Phil. 2:6) but who set aside his divine prerogatives and status in order to take up the status of a slave and die a slave's death, because of which God exalted him. Paul seems to have derived this much of the story from reflecting on the pre-Pauline christological hymns (cf. Philippians 2, Colossians 1, Hebrews 1, and also John 1), which in turn were largely adaptations of what early Judaism had said about personified Wisdom. He also comments not only on Christ's ongoing roles in heaven, but also his future return to earth to act as divine judge of human beings. Thus, Paul goes beyond the idea that Christ's exalted state recapitulates his preexistent state. The story of Wisdom informs the telling of the story of Christ.

But even beyond this, because the Son is a part of the ongoing life of God, looking at the story of the interrelationship of Father, Son, and Spirit in the end tells us a lot about Christology. For example, Christology normally and properly looks at the Christ, which is to say, Jesus as a redeemer figure. To judge, however, from the christological hymn in Col. 1:15–20 (cf. 2 Cor. 4:4), Christology must deal with the fact that it is creatures that the Son came to redeem, creatures that he had a role in creating in the first place. He accomplished this task not merely by coming among us but by being one of us. Besides involvement in the acts of creation, the Son also has a role in the cosmos, subduing powers and principalities. This story of the cosmic Christ intertwines at various junctures with the earthly redeemer Christ, but unless one sees the larger narrative context one will miss the nuances of the story (cf. 1 Cor. 15:24). Although the contingent circumstances being addressed in Colossians seem to have provided the occasion for the further expression and development of a cosmic Christology, this sort of Christology can already be seen to be alluded to in texts like 1 Cor. 8:6 or 15:24–26.

There is, however, also another story, the story of Israel, that informs Paul's Christology as well. Jesus was one who was born of woman and born under the Law (Gal. 4:4). But there is a sense in which he was sent as God's Son to be that Jesus. This Son was sent to redeem those under the Law, namely, Israel. This clearly presupposes the story of the lostness of Israel, but more important, that larger story affects how Paul views both the name and the roles of the Christ. Jesus is God's royal and even preexistent Son, sent to redeem God's people. It was Israel who expected and who was promised the coming messiah (cf. Rom. 9:5). From and for Israel, the messiah was to come. The Sonship of Jesus is in part another way of talking about Jesus as a Jewish royal or messianic figure who came to set his people free. It is thus hardly surprising that Paul says the gospel is for the Jew first (Rom. 1:16).

Yet a third story that Christ and Israel are a part of is the story of the world. Paul is quite convinced that the world is a fallen place (Romans 1). Indeed, it is a place living on borrowed time; the form of this fallen world is in the process of passing away (1 Cor. 7:31). This on the one hand relativizes relationships and other social realities that may have seemed of paramount importance in the past. On the other hand, the fact of the world's gradual demise makes decisions about the critical issues in life all the more crucial. The world is bent on self-destruction yet longs for liberation; this is true not just of the human world but also of the very material creation itself (Rom. 8:20–22). One must add to this the Pauline concepts of the existence of malevolent supernatural beings, including both Satan and demons (cf. 2 Cor. 2:11; 1 Cor. 10:20–21).[8] It is against the dark backdrop and in fact in the very midst of this sort of world that the drama of Israel and her Messiah and the Christian community is played out.[9]

The various narratives about Christ alluded to or mentioned in Paul's letters provide a setting for understanding his Christology. The identity of Christ is revealed by his words and deeds, the parts he plays in the human and divine drama. This story is an eschatological story, for it is about the final things God does for creatures and creation. The story has both an eschatological framework and eschatological substance. In this portion of this study we intend to examine how various of the stories and factors mentioned have affected Paul's telling of the story of Christ. First we must consider two primary factors that generated much of Paul's Christian thought—his initial encounter with and his worship of the living Christ.

8

The Origins of a Symbolic Universe

DOWN AND OUT ON DAMASCUS ROAD

My life closed twice before its close;
It yet remains to see
If Immortality unveil
A third event to me.

—*Emily Dickinson*[10]

IT would be wrong to say that Paul's thought world was solely shaped by stories other than his own story. We will have occasion to say a good deal more about Paul's own story as a Jew and as a Christian in Part Four of this study, but here we must reflect upon the interface between Paul's own experience and his reflections on the story of Christ.

What can we deduce, from examining Gal. 1:11–23 and other key texts, that Paul may have learned about Christ from his Damascus road experience? First, the apostle believed he learned on Damascus road that Jesus was still alive. This likely would have implied to Saul, for he was a Pharisee who believed in resurrection, that the claims about Jesus having risen must be true. That Paul did draw such a conclusion is evident from 1 Cor. 9:1 and 15:8: "He appeared also to me." Certain things necessarily followed from this conclusion in Paul's mind. If Jesus was exalted in heaven by God after his death, then this surely meant a vindication of Jesus' claims or at least the claims made about Jesus. Thus Paul in Rom. 1:4 says that Jesus was vindicated to be or even designated to be the Son of God in power by his resurrection from the dead.

86

Inasmuch as Jesus did not reject the claim to be messiah, Paul could have concluded that if Jesus was alive in heaven then he must be God's anointed one. Why else would God vindicate someone who had died a death by crucifixion, a death that, in light of Paul's understanding of Deut. 21:22, meant that person was accursed? As Gal. 3:13 makes clear, Paul came to believe that Christ became a curse for believers in order to redeem them from the curse of the law (1 Cor. 12:3). In short, Paul's experience of a risen and exalted Jesus occasioned a completely different estimate of Jesus and his crucifixion.

Paul once looked at Jesus from a fallen human point of view (cf. 2 Cor. 5:16),[11] but after Damascus road he did so no longer. This means he viewed Jesus as the Son of God as was revealed to him on Damascus road. It does not mean that he had no use for apostolic traditions about or actual sayings of Jesus. Previously he had viewed Jesus in the light of the cross as a failure, perhaps a fool, and certainly not the Jewish messiah. Damascus road changed all that.

The second major thing Paul may have deduced from his Damascus road encounter was that Jesus closely identified with persecuted Christians. This would suggest that the Christians must be God's people. If God's special Son was labeling Christians as his own by so identifying with them that he could say "Why are you persecuting me?" then Paul had to reevaluate the character of the people of God. This meant that Paul, far from doing God's will by persecuting Christians, found himself to be opposing God's Christ and thus God (so Gal. 1:23, 1 Cor. 15:9–10). It is also not impossible that Paul's theology of the body of Christ in part arose out of his Damascus road experience, for that experience suggested that what happened to Christians also happened to Christ.[12]

Third, Paul could have learned that he had been saved or converted on Damascus road quite *apart* from his own deserts and actions (1 Cor. 15:10), indeed in spite of those actions. This could only lead to the conclusion that salvation was a grace gift. J.D.G. Dunn puts it this way:

> It was the experience of seeing Jesus risen and exalted on the road to Damascus which stopped him dead in his tracks and turned his whole life into a new channel . . .; for Paul this was not merely a flash of insight or intellectual conviction, but a personal encounter, the beginning of a personal relationship which became the dominating passion of his life (Phil. 3:7–10 . . .). To put it another way, it was his own *experience of grace* which made 'grace' a central and distinctive feature of his gospel— grace as not merely a way of understanding God as generous and forgiving, but grace as the experience of that unmerited and free acceptance embracing him, transforming him, enriching him, commissioning him.[13]

This in turn meant that Paul had to assume a new attitude toward the Law. Christ was now the center around which all turned, whereas the Law had been central previously. The story of Christ and the experience of Christ were the integrating factors in his life. All had to be seen through the eyes of Christ, not through the lens of the Law. For Paul, Christ was the terminus of the Law, insofar as the Law might be seen as a means of salvation. Salvation by works, or even salvation by responding to the initial work and grace of God by obedience to the Mosaic law (covenantal nomism), was no longer, if it ever had been, possible. It could no longer be a matter of "do this and you shall live." Rather, it became a matter of a righteous status received by grace through faith that enabled one to obey the Law of Christ (which was a different matter than Moses' law) out of gratitude.

Nevertheless, none of this meant that Paul saw no value in the Mosaic law. Indeed, he saw it as holy, just, and good, and some of its instruction was seen as a valuable moral guide for Christian living, particularly the narrative portions that could be used in a typological manner (cf. 1 Corinthians 10). But its splendor was eclipsed by Christ's—the fuller and final revelation of God's good and perfect will and character (cf. 2 Cor. 3:4–18).

It is not surprising that Paul concentrates so heavily in his preaching on Christ crucified and risen, for these are, in his mind, the decisive events that changed the human situation so that one who formerly stood under the Law and its condemnation could now stand under grace and its justification. If salvation is by grace through faith in the Lord Jesus crucified and risen, then there is nothing standing in the way of anyone, including Gentiles, from being saved apart from the Mosaic law. For Paul, the removal of the Mosaic law as a means of right-standing with God as a way of being saved *or* working out one's salvation broke down the barrier between Jew and Gentile (Eph. 2:14–15). If faith in the risen Lord was the way of salvation, then it could be offered without prior religious commitment to early Judaism, with its requirements of circumcision and food laws—indeed, the keeping of the whole of Torah.

Paul, according to Gal. 1:16, saw as the purpose of his conversion that he might become the missionary to the Gentiles. This is not surprising, for if all is of grace, then there is no reason why grace cannot be offered to all without Mosaic preconditions. It is very possible that Paul deduced the heart of his gospel from reflecting on his conversion experience. In Paul's mind, the revelation of Jesus in glory on Damascus road signaled the arrival of the eschatological age in which old things were passing and would pass away and new things were coming to pass.[14] The arrival of the new age meant a new Christocentric view of the Law and ethics in general. This was but a part of the larger enterprise of reevaluating the story of Israel in light of the story of Christ. Thus a reasonable case can be made that Paul's experience of Christ significantly affected how he told not only his own story but the story of Christ.

STIRRING SONGS IN A MESSIANIC KEY

There were a variety of stories through which Paul reflected on the meaning of the Christ. There was first the community-generating narrative called the Good News, which is partially summed up in 1 Cor. 15:1–10. Paul is quite clear that he is passing on in this text something he had received from those who were before him in the faith. What was of first importance was that "Christ died for our sins in accordance with the scriptures, and that he was buried and that he was raised on the third day in accordance with the scriptures," and that he appeared to a variety of witnesses including two who were not among his followers during his ministry—James, Jesus' brother, and Paul himself. There may have been more to this narrative, including a statement about God having sent his Son, about Jesus' birth as a Jew under the Law (Gal. 4:4), and about Jesus' pedigree—"descended from David according to the flesh" (Rom. 1:3). This summary is similar to various of those summaries of speeches found in Acts (cf. 2:22–36; 3:13–16; 4:10–12; 5:30–32).

It will be noted that the focus in this story of the Good News, both in Paul and in Acts, is on the death and resurrection of Jesus and to a lesser degree on Jesus' birth and pedigree. It was apparently early on concluded that one must concentrate on the portions of the story that had salvific weight, hence on the remarkable conclusion of Jesus' earthly career. Furthermore, it was seen as critical early on to show how this story was grounded, indeed foretold, in the Hebrew scriptures, including its surprising conclusion.

But this foundational community-generating story was not merely proclaimed. It was also sung about, and especially in its hymnic form it was subject to expansion by means of appropriating a variety of scriptural stories, including the story of Wisdom and the story of the Suffering Servant. Perhaps the earliest summaries of the close of Jesus' life encouraged such creative exploration of the scriptures. After all, if Jesus died and was raised according to the scriptures, it would be natural to assume there were some intimations in scripture about his origins, both divine and human, and about his destiny of exaltation to God's side after the close of his human sojourn. I would suggest that very early on, the outline of the whole career of the Son of God, not merely from womb to tomb but from and back to the side of God, was being reflected on and sung about in the light of scripture in the early Christian community.

Though it is an exaggeration to say that early Christology was born in song, one may certainly say that early Christology grew out of the worship

of Christ and was accordingly expressed in various liturgical forms—
hymns, prayers, creedal statements, testimonia, and doxologies.[15] Some of
these forms likely came initially from a spontaneous response in worship to
what was felt to be the leading of the Holy Spirit, but some also seem to
reflect a careful and calculated composition prepared in advance for
liturgical use. Various sources suggest that psalms, hymns, and spiritual
songs were perhaps the most crucial forms not only in the earliest period (c.
A.D. 35–55) but at least well into the second century. It is not only Pliny the
Younger (Ep. 10.96.7) who bears witness to the fact that what distinguished early Christians was that on the first day of the week they arose at
dawn to sing "hymns to Christ as to a god."[16] Indeed, there is telltale
evidence of such practices well before the time of Pliny.[17]

For instance, note the reference in 1 Cor. 14:26 to each one having a
psalmos (psalm) to share in worship. Paul wrote this in the early 50s.
Somewhat later we hear of a threefold characterization of the singing as
involving psalms, hymns, and spiritual songs (Col. 3:16), a passage that
seems to be further expanded upon in Eph. 5:19. Perhaps one can make a
distinction between these three types of songs. The first may reflect the
deliberate early Christian use of the psalms in a messianic way; the second
would refer to newly composed Christian hymns; and the third would refer
to spontaneous songs offered in worship at the prompting of the Holy
Spirit. There probably was some overlap, especially between the psalms
and the composed hymns, and it is not possible to make hard and fast form
critical distinctions on the basis of the slender evidence available. It is also
probable that these songs included hymns to God as well as to the Lord
Jesus, but it would be the latter that made Christians stand out and be
recognizable to even an outside observer such as Pliny.

In the pagan and Jewish world there was already a close connection
between hymn writing and singing coupled with significant theological
content. For example, Menander of Laodicea in a somewhat later period
instructs pagan hymn writers to dwell on "the naming of the god, or a
valedictory, or on the god's nature or story or birth or form" (*De Hymn.*
1ff.)[18] Christianity needed hymns to match or outstrip its competitors in
the Greek-speaking world.

W. Wink points to several pieces of revealing extracanonical evidence
coming from the fringes of early Christianity. For example, the Nag
Hammadi Tripartite tractate makes quite clear that the material found in a
somewhat different form in Col. 1:15–20 was viewed and used as a hymn.
Wink also refers to evidence from the Odes of Solomon (cf., e.g., 16:1–2)
as well as the Acts of John (94:1–96:51) that both groups on the fringe of
Christianity as well as orthodox groups were regularly in the practice of
composing and singing hymns to and about Christ.[19] Also important for

our purposes are the words of Philo (*Vit. Cont.* 28–29, 68–80) about the Jewish group called the Therapeutae in the first century A.D. They were "yearning for Wisdom" (68), so they studied scripture:

> Then the President rises and sings a hymn composed as an address to God, either a new one of his own composition or an old one by poets of an earlier day who have left behind them hymns in many measures and melodies. . . . They all lift up their voices, men and women alike (80) . . . [in] two choirs one of men and one of women (83). . . . After choric dancing they form a single choir and sing until dawn (89).[20]

Strikingly, Eusebius interprets this discussion in Philo as referring to early Christian worship (cf. *Historia Ecclesiae* 2, 17, 21ff.).

If one considers the possible analogies with Qumran (the Dead Sea community), one will not be surprised that Christians were in the business of composing hymns. Certainly this was a regular practice in the Qumran community (cf. esp. the 1QH material), and there is evidence that the psalms and perhaps also such hymns were the result of being filled with God's wisdom and Spirit, which resulted in a prophetic utterance. This is what is claimed for David in 11QPs.,[21] which reads in part: "And Yahweh gave him a wise and enlightened spirit. . . . [T]he sum (of his songs) was 4050. These he uttered through prophecy (*bnbw'h*) which had been given him by the most high." This should be compared with what is said about Solomon in Wisd. Sol. 7:7: "Therefore I prayed, and understanding was given me; I called on God and the spirit of wisdom came to me."[22] This is followed by the Wisdom hymn in 7:22ff., which near its conclusion says, "In every generation she passes into holy souls and makes them friends of God and prophets; for God loves nothing so much as the person who lives with Wisdom." The point of the previous discussion is to show that there is a precedent and there are also parallels both in early Judaism and elsewhere for the earliest Christians composing hymns and, in particular, hymns influenced by sapiential material.

To a significant degree, the earliest Christian worship practices seem to have reflected and grown out of early Jewish practices. The connection between Wisdom and the singing of hymns in the Philo quotation, and also in the quotation from the Qumran material should not be missed, for there is also such a connection in the christological hymn fragments in the New Testament, as will be shown shortly.[23] It was the focus on Christ, not the composition of hymns, even sapiential ones, that made early Christian worship and hymns stand out.[24] In order to appreciate the two Pauline hymn fragments found in Philippians 2 and Colossians 1 that we will be considering, it is necessary to give a summary statement of what was said about Wisdom, the personification of an attribute of God, in early Judaism, realizing that this material must be handled with caution because it is a composite picture.

THE PROFILE AND PILGRIMAGE OF WISDOM[25]

1. Wisdom has her origin in God (Prov. 8:22; Sir. 24:3, 9; Wisd. Sol. 7:25–26).

2. Wisdom preexisted and likely has a role in the work of creation (cf. Prov. 3:19; 8:22–29; 24:3; Sir. 1:4, 9–10; Sir. 16:24–17:7; Wisd. Sol. 7:22; 8:4–6; 9:2, 9).

3. Wisdom is infused in creation, accounting for its coherence and endurance (cf. Wisd. Sol. 1:7; 7:24; 27; 8:1; 11:25).

4. Wisdom is identified with the divine spirit (Wisd. Sol. 1:7; 9:17; 12:1) and in some sense is immanent in the world (Wisd. Sol. 7:24; 8:1).

5. Wisdom comes to the human world with a distinctive mission (Prov. 8:4, 31–36; Sir. 24:7, 12, 19–22; Wisd. Sol. 7:27–28; 8:2–3).
   a. The mission entails personally addressing the world (Proverbs 1, 8, 9; Sir. 24:19–22; Wisd. Sol. 6:12–16; 7:22a; 8:7–9; 9:10–16).
   b. To her devotees Wisdom offers life, sometimes prosperity, and a panoply of other blessings (Prov. 1:32, 3:13–18; 8:1–5, 35; 9:1–6; Sir. 1:14–20; 6:18–31; 15:1–8; 24:19–33; Wisd. Sol. 7:7–14).

6. Wisdom is especially associated with Israel.
   a. By divine order she dwells in Israel (Sir. 24:8–12).
   b. Wisdom can be identified with Torah (Sir. 24:23; cf. 1:25–27; 6:37; 15:1; 19:20; 33:2–3; Bar. 4:1).
   c. Wisdom was at work in Israel's history (Wisd. Sol. 10:1–21).

7. Wisdom, although a gift from God (Prov. 2:6; Sir. 1:9–10, 26; 6:37; Wisd. Sol. 7:7; 9:4), is associated with disciplined effort to obtain her (Prov. 4:10–27; 6:6; Sir. 4:17; 6:18–36; Wisd. Sol. 1:5; 7:14).

The further development of this personification or hypostasis can be found in other early Jewish literature. In 1 En. 42:1–3, which can be dated at least as early as the first century A.D.,[26] one finds one further step in the pilgrimage of Wisdom—she returns to heaven because she found no dwelling place on earth and resumed her rightful place, sitting down among the angels. The relevant portion, which appears to be part of an early hymn to Wisdom, reads:

> Wisdom could not find a place in which she could dwell; but a place was found (for her) in the heavens. Then Wisdom went out to dwell with the children of the people, but she found no dwelling place. (So) Wisdom returned to her place and she became settled among the angels.[27]

Once one has examined all the relevant data on the personification of Wisdom in early Judaism, one can only agree with R. E. Murphy about the malleability of this personification—"defined anew in successive generations."[28] It is clear from the flexibility of what is predicated of Wisdom in all this material that the sages are not dealing with a person and certainly not with a goddess, but with the personification of an idea, concept, attribute, or quality that was seen as desirable for humans to obtain and already something that characterized God and God's orderly creation. Nevertheless, a certain particularization of the tradition has been detected as the personification develops, so that Wisdom obtained names. She could be identified with or as Torah in Sirach or Baruch, or as God's Spirit in the Wisdom of Solomon. It may be that in the Wisdom of Solomon there is a hypostasis of Wisdom. It is striking that what happens to personified Wisdom is what happens in general in Ben Sira's book and the Wisdom of Solomon, for in both these books one sees a drawing on the particularistic traditions of Israel's history and a focus on God's elect people and their future direction. This trend of particularization takes a further and dramatic step in the New Testament wisdom material, and in particular in the New Testament hymns where a historical person, Christ, is clothed in the garb and attributes previously attributed to Wisdom.

We have suggested in this section that the origins of Paul's thoughts about the christological drama lie to a great degree in his experiences both on Damascus road and also in Christian worship. They are also indebted to and expressed in terms of the Christian traditions that were passed down to him, the scriptures, and other early Jewish traditions.

We will investigate first how the story of Wisdom and the Suffering Servant informs Paul's telling of the story in Philippians 2 and Colossians 1. This in turn will be followed by an examination of how messianic thinking about the story of Israel and of messiah affected Paul's christological thought. This will be followed by reflecting on how Paul appropriates the story of Adam to reflect on Christ. Finally, we will investigate how Paul is informed by and reflects upon the Christian narrative about the close of Jesus' life; we will also investigate how he is informed by the sayings of Jesus. Many stories are drawn upon to tell fully the story of the crucified conqueror, God's Wisdom, the suffering sage.

9

The Redeemer Stoops to Conquer

Hail the heav'n-born Prince of Peace!
Hail the sun of righteousness!
Light and life to all he brings,
Ris'n with healing in his wings.
Mild he lays his glory by,
Born that [we] no more may die,
Born to raise the [ones] of earth,
Born to give them second birth.
Hark! The herald angels sing,
"Glory to the new-born king!"

—*Charles Wesley (1707–88)*
"Hark the Herald Angels Sing"
alt. by G. Whitefield (1714–1770)

THE earliest use of christological hymn fragments is found in the Pauline corpus, and it is appropriate at this juncture to ask where Paul may have heard such hymns.[29] Perhaps the most likely answer is in contexts where Greek was the primary language of worship among Christians; such hymns would have been composed in Greek so that everyone might participate in the singing.[30] Some of the hymns—such as the one in Philippians 2, but especially the ones in Hebrews 1 and Colossians 1, which so clearly draw

94

on the *Greek* text of the Wisdom of Solomon—were surely first composed in Greek.[31] This may mean that Paul could have first heard such hymns in Syrian Antioch or possibly even in Damascus in the early years of his Christian life. Paul was not likely the originator of the christological hymns, nor of the use of wisdom traditions to construct them. These hymns suggest a widely held common form of wisdom Christology in early Christianity.

There seem to have been three primary sources that are drawn on to compose the christological hymns: (1) earlier Jewish discussions about personified or even hypostasized Wisdom; (2) the earliest Christian preaching about the life of Jesus—in particular, about his death and vindication beyond death; and (3) the christological use of the psalms, especially Psalm 110, but also Psalm 8, among others.[32] It appears that in general the preexistence and incarnational language draws on the sapiential material; the language about Jesus' death or sacrifice draws on the passion material and the early preaching; and the references to Jesus' exaltation and vindication draw on material from the psalms.

The V narrative pattern of these hymns—discussing in turn the pretemporal, temporal, and post-temporal nature, life, and activity of the Son—favors the suggestion that the dominant influence on these hymns is the earlier Jewish reflection on the career of personified Wisdom. Even the return of Wisdom to a place in glory once she was rejected is found in the material from 1 Enoch. All of the hymn fragments include preexistence material at least by implication, which is hardly surprising if the wisdom material is the dominant influence here. Wisdom thinking, to the extent that it is theology, is a form of creation theology. Thus one should not be surprised that a considerable amount of space could be devoted in a Christian wisdom hymn to what was true of the Son before and during the event of creation. Indeed, in some of the christological hymns at least as much time (and in some instances more time) is spent on these matters than on anything else (cf. Colossians 1 and John 1). Christ's career is envisioned as having both heavenly and earthly scope. The attempt adequately to express the theological significance of this career led early Jewish Christians to draw on the most exalted language they could find—Jewish wisdom speculation, coupled to some degree with messianic interpretation of the psalms and soteriological reflections on Christ's death. Because wisdom thought is a form of creation theology, it is also not surprising that it is in these sorts of Christian hymns (rather than in hymns that were simply a form of messianic exegesis of a psalm) that we find the first reflections about what it might mean to say that the preexistent redeemer took on human flesh or became a human being.

I would thus differ with M. Hengel about the sapiential influence reflecting a later stage of development of these hymns.[33] In view of the degree of development of the personification of Wisdom in early Judaism well before these christological hymns were composed, there is no good reason in principle why this material could not have been used by the earliest Jewish Christians when these hymns were first composed. Indeed, the use of the sapiential material and the christological use of the psalms to compose these hymns point to early Jewish Christians, still closely connected with Judaism and its living holy traditions and ways of contemporizing scripture, as the composers of these hymns.

If any elements seem to be added later by Paul and others, it is the making explicit that the rejection of Wisdom in the person of Christ entailed death on a cross, the making of peace thereby, the offering of purification for sins, and the like. In short, particulars are added later about the historical death of Jesus and its significance. It does not necessarily follow from this that atonement theology is a later invention of Paul, Mark, or others, but it does mean that the passion and resurrection narrative material or the early preaching about the same is not *the* primary source for these hymns.[34] Indeed, in the later hymns or hymn fragments found in 1 Tim. 3:16 and John 1, references to Christ's death and its implications are notably absent, and in the hymns in general not resurrection per se but exaltation to heaven (in particular to the right hand of God) or vindication is spoken of (cf. Phil. 2:9; 1 Tim. 3:16; Heb. 1:3b).[35]

R. P. Martin argues that the descent/ascent plot of these christological hymns replaced an earlier "Judaic" contrast involving rejection/vindication seen in the Acts kerygma. This, however, is too simplistic; both descent/ascent and vindication are seen in Philippians 2, the earliest of these hymns; vindication is seen in one of the latest, 1 Tim. 3:16. One must keep in mind that the V pattern *and* the theme of rejection are already found in the earlier Jewish material about personified Wisdom.[36]

The point of these remarks is just this—these hymns do not appear to be hymnic adaptations of the early Christian kerygma or basic teaching about Jesus' death and resurrection. One should look for their provenance elsewhere. Even where soteriology is suggested in these hymn fragments, one must not forget that in the Wisdom of Solomon, written probably only a few decades before the christological hymns, not only does one find various hymns praising Wisdom, but also the words "Who has learned your counsel, unless you have given Wisdom and sent your Holy Spirit from on high? And thus the paths of those on earth were set right, and people were taught what pleases you, and were saved by Wisdom" (9:17–18). E. Schüssler Fiorenza is right to stress how astonishing the exalted language of the christological hymns is, for "they do not belong to a later stage of christological development but are among the earliest christological statements found in the New Testament."[37]

THE SERVANT'S SONG (PHIL. 2:6–11)

Part I
> Who being in the form of God,
> did not consider the having of equality to God
> something to take advantage of,
> but stripped/emptied himself,
> taking the form of a servant,
> being born in the likeness of human beings.
> And being found in appearance like a human being,
> humbled himself,
> being obedient to the point of death,
> even death on a cross.

Part II
> That is why God has highly exalted him
> and gave him the name
> the one above all names,
> in order that at the name of Jesus
> all knees will bend—
> heavenly, on earth, and under the earth,
> and all tongues confess publicly
> that Jesus Christ is Lord,
> unto the glory of God the Father.

The literature on this hymn, as on the Logos hymn in John 1, is so voluminous that it is impossible to survey or summarize it all.[38] There have always been those who have been skeptical about the view that the fragments under scrutiny in this chapter were originally parts of christological hymns.[39] Almost all such skeptics share one notable trait in common—they have failed adequately to evaluate these hymns in light of late Jewish sapiential material and especially in light of the personified Wisdom material, which itself in some cases appears to be hymnic material.[40] But the degree of similarity in grammatical form, key terms, overall pattern, and substance in these hymns surely points to more than a remarkably similar appropriation by various New Testament authors of some common early Christian ideas that were "in the air." The correspondences are too notable not to suggest the use of earlier Christian material.

I am not suggesting that Paul is simply "quoting" hymn fragments. Rather, he takes them over, sometimes modifying them slightly to suit the purposes for which and the contexts in which he intends to use them. Furthermore, the use of this material in the context of Paul's letters undoubtedly means he *agrees* with the sources he is using, so naturally the hymn material can also be used to deduce something about the views of Paul.

Christological hymns or hymn fragments are normally introduced with –*hos* ("who"), in particular when they are quoted in mid-sentence. J. C. O'Neill has pointed out that this sort of usage is characteristic of the style of the late sages such as Ben Sira (cf. Sir. 46:1; 48:1ff., 12).[41] This does not mean that they are not frequently well integrated into their present context. For example, Philippians 2 consists of an exhortation to humility and unity by means of humble mutual service, and the example of Christ is appealed to as an exemplar.[42] As G. Strecker points out, there is a terminological and possibly compositional connection between the hymn and its context by means of the themes of humility and obedience (cf. vv. 3–8, 12).[43] The parenetic function of this Christ hymn should be clear from its introduction. The chapter is rounded out by Paul speaking of two emissaries he is sending to Philippi, Timothy and Epaphroditus, both of whom serve as further examples of humble service that leads to unity and the building up of the body of Christ. Paul is calling Christians to be self-forgetful, as the following example of Christ suggests.

The word *tapeinophrosune* ("humility") is an important one. Humility was not generally seen as a virtue in Greco-Roman antiquity, though in the Hebrew scriptures the Suffering Servant is set forward as an example of one who acts humbly.[44] This word in secular sources means something like base-minded, shabby, of no account, and in its adjectival form it was no compliment at all; it meant having the mentality of a slave. But in the Old Testament one already finds humility and lowliness exalted, for instance, in the Psalms. Paul's contribution to this development is that he connects this idea with the founder of his faith; indeed, he sees Christ as Exhibit A of what humility ought to mean. Jesus was one who took the form of a slave, or perhaps better said, a servant.

This hymn is not an attempt to contrast Christ with Adam,[45] a view largely based on a very doubtful interpretation of *harpagmos*.[46] The language of the last Adam is missing entirely from this hymn.[47] There is nothing here about Christ beginning a new race of people, or being the firstfruits of the resurrection, or being a life-giving Spirit. When one comes to the climax of the hymn where Christ is given the name *Kurios* ("Lord"), it is appropriate to ask whether a monotheistic Jewish Christian like Paul could ever have thought that a mere human being such as Adam, even an obedient and resurrected one, had the right to be called, treated, and worshiped as the God of the Old Testament was worshiped.[48] Nor is there anything here about Jesus making a choice while on earth that is parallel to Adam's choice while in the garden.[49] C. A. Wanamaker is quite right that J.D.G. Dunn fails to give an account of what glory or status Christ could have had and given up that was not available to other human beings. "In effect Dunn mythologizes the humanity of Christ by making him qualitatively different from the rest of humanity without any explanation of the origin of the supposed difference."[50] As T. F. Glasson points out, the Genesis story says nothing about Adam or Eve desiring absolute equality with God, but rather desiring to be *like* God in the knowledge of good and evil. "In the form of God" is not simply equivalent here to "according to the image of God," for Christ is said to set aside the former *morphe* (form) for the form of a servant.[51] The servant language here comes to Paul, or whoever composed this hymn, through the later reflection on such language in Sirach and especially the Wisdom of Solomon.[52] That it is not merely a recapitulation of earlier ideas, however, is shown by Phil. 2:5–7.

Verses 5–7 are talking about a being who has a particular mindset and makes particular choices—a mindset and choices that Paul wants his audience to emulate. Furthermore, as I. H. Marshall points out, the recapitulatory phrase "and being found in form as a human being" is all but inexplicable if it refers to a person who has never been anything else but a human being. "[A]gain the *contrast* clearly expressed between 'being in the form of God' and 'becoming in the form of [human beings]' is extremely odd if the contrast is between two stages in the career of a man."[53]

Furthermore, all such language is very odd indeed if Paul is simply applying the Suffering Servant language to Jesus here. In the Isaianic material, the Suffering Servant gave up no divine prerogatives or heavenly existence to become a servant. It is much more convincing to suggest that various sorts of wisdom ideas are here being predicated of Christ, including the concept of servanthood, but the wisdom material in Sirach and Wisdom of Solomon draws on the Isaianic material.[54] Both Wanamaker's and G. Howard's[55] criticisms are rightly directed against J. Murphy-O'Connor's attempt to apply only a wisdom anthropology to this hymn.

After talking about the Wisdom who has formed humankind, Solomon in Wisd. Sol. 9:4 prays, "Give me the Wisdom that sits by your throne, and do not reject me from among your servants, for I am your *doulos*, the son of your serving girl" (i.e., Wisdom). Because there is interplay in Q between Jesus as Wisdom and Jesus as Solomon figure,[56] it should not surprise us to find the same sort of thing here. D. Georgi was in part on the right track in pointing to the Wisdom of Solomon as the background of this material.[57]

The material in Wisd. Sol. 5—7 can illuminate the second half of this hymn as well as the first half. For example, in Wisd. Sol. 5:16 one hears of the righteous ones (called servants of God's kingdom in 6:4) who will receive a glorious crown; or again in 6:3ff. "for your dominion was given you from the Lord" for being obedient servants while on earth. Earlier in 5:1 the righteous are promised that they will at the final judgment stand in the presence of their oppressors, who will be amazed and forced to confess the truth about them (cf. 5:4). All of this is interspersed with the discussion of hypostasized Wisdom (cf., e.g., 7:22f.). Seen in this light, Philippians 2 becomes a hymn on the one hand about a royal figure who, like Solomon, humbles himself by becoming God's servant, obeys God, and is rewarded in royal fashion in the end. On the other hand, it is a story about a king who *is* the very embodiment of Wisdom, both before, during, and after his earthly career, as is shown by his behavior during all three stages of his career.

One may also consider the words of Ben Sira: "The wisdom of the humble lifts their heads high, and seats them among the great. Do not praise individuals for their good looks, or loathe anyone because of their appearance alone [cf., e.g., Isa. 53]. . . . Many kings have had to sit on the ground, but one who was never thought of has worn a crown" (Sir. 11:1ff.). One may also consider Sir. 3:17ff.: "My child perform your tasks with humility. . . . [T]he greater you are the more you must humble yourself; so you will find favor in the sight of the Lord. For great is the might of the Lord; and by the humble he is glorified."

Philippians 2:6–11 is a story about the exaltation of the obedient and humble one, one who had humbled himself willingly. The juxtaposition of (1) preexistence language; (2) servant language; (3) humility and exaltation language; and (4) the bestowal of kingship and kingdom is found in both the Christ hymn in Philippians 2 and also in the sapiential material in Sirach and the Wisdom of Solomon. The whole of this hymn, except the Pauline additions (e.g., even death on the cross), probably derived from early Jewish Christian attempts to paint an adequately laudatory portrait of Christ, a portrait reflecting on and using sapiential material. A few comments on some exegetical particulars and implications of such an interpretation must now be made.

G. Hawthorne is right that v. 5 really does parallel the frame of mind Christians ought to have and the frame of mind Christ both as preexistent one and as incarnate one did have. He deliberately took a lower place. He deliberately did not take advantage of the divine perogatives that he had and were rightfully his. He deliberately submitted to death on a cross—a punishment reserved for the most notable and notorious criminals, slaves, and rebels. The analogy drawn here between Christ's behavior and the proposed behavior of Christians is just that—an analogy, which presupposes that both similarities and differences exist.[58]

There are obviously some aspects of the model of Christ that the believer cannot follow, but Paul is concentrating on one main point— acting in a self-sacrificial fashion to the benefit of both others and self. It may be added that even in the second half of the hymn there is some analogy hinted at, for in Paul's thought world believers *will* be made *like* Christ. Beyond death there is resurrection, the final stage of being conformed to the image of the Son (Rom. 8:29). Just as Christ was exalted by God beyond death, so too God will perform a similar miracle for those in Christ. Thus the first half of the hymn provides an example for parenetic purposes, and the second half reveals the way God responds to such obedient and self-sacrificial living.

There is furthermore a good reason here to stress obedience even unto death. Paul says in Phil. 1:29 that the Philippians have been granted the privilege of suffering for Christ; indeed, 2 Cor. 8:2 says the suffering was severe. Paul exhorts them to persevere and make good Christlike decisions "so that in the day of Christ you may be pure and blameless" (Phil. 1:10). He reminds them that "the one who began a good work among you will bring it to completion by the day of Jesus Christ." In such a context it is hard *not* to see the story of the crucified conqueror as being set up as an exemplar for Paul's audience. Again I must stress, the first half of the hymn provides them with a model of Christlike behavior to emulate on a lesser scale. The second half suggests to them the rewards or results of doing so that God will produce. Paul is looking forward to that day when he will be able to boast before God about the faithful and obedient converts in Philippi (2:16). The apostle himself longs for Christlikeness even to the degree of death and resurrection: "I want to know Christ and the power of his resurrection and the sharing of *his* sufferings by becoming like him in his death, if somehow I may attain the resurrection from the dead" (3:10–11).

This imitation of Christ in Paul's life is also meant to provide a further model for his converts in Philippi to follow. They are to have the same mind as Paul about such things, just as they were exhorted to have the same mind as Christ about such things. Paul says, "I press on toward the goal for the prize of the heavenly call of God in Christ Jesus. Let those of us then who are mature be of the same mind. . . . Brothers and sisters, join in imitating me" (3:14–17).[59] What we see here is the connection in Paul's mind between the story of Christ and the story of Christians (in particular Paul's own story), also between what is sometimes called the indicative and what is sometimes called the imperative. The career of Christ is the model for the life of the believer, though on a lesser scale. Although the Christian did not come from heaven as a divine being, nor will he or she be proclaimed to be such at the resurrection, nonetheless on a lesser scale

Christlikeness must be exhibited and striven after in the believer's life now, so that the completion of the process of being conformed to Christ's image at the parousia will be a reality.

That the believer has obtained from God a "righteousness" through faith in Christ and apart from works (3:9) negates none of the parenetic thrust of this material.[60] Indeed, Paul assumes that the gift of right-standing with God is the basis for exhorting his charges to Christlikeness and promising them the completion of the process if they remain faithful to the end. In view of the larger context, to "gain Christ" (3:8) can surely be only another way of speaking of gaining full Christlikeness at the resurrection (3:10–11). Then indeed, Paul will be found in Christ, because Christ's likeness will be found not only spiritually but even bodily in the apostle. Herein we see the degree to which the stories of Christ, Paul, and believers are interrelated, but several more aspects of the telling of the Christ story itself in 2:6–11 call for comment.

Three words are used to describe Christ's "form," likeness, or appearance: *morphe, homoioma, schema*. Of these three the one that most obviously connotes outward recognizable appearance is *schema*, not the other two. *Morphe* suggests the way in which a thing or person appears to one's senses. However, *morphe* always signifies an outward form that truly, accurately, and fully expresses the real being that underlies it.[61] Thus, when applied to Christ it must mean that he manifested a form that truly represented the nature and very being of God.

This is why there is the further phrase "the having equality to God." The hymn makes clear that Christ really had this. Grammatically, *isa* could be an adverb that if translated as such would lead to an elliptical rendering such as "the being *equally* (something) to God." Presumably the something is the phrase *en morphe theou* from v. 6a. Thus the expanded phrase would mean "the being equally in the form of God as God [is]." Wright points out that the use of the articular infinitive (*to einai*) normally refers to something previously mentioned, and this usage is known elsewhere in Paul (cf. Rom. 7:18; 2 Cor. 7:11).[62] It has been argued that this adverb has a neuter plural ending and is being used adjectivally.[63] If so, then one must ask why a masculine adjectival form was not chosen and why it is in the plural. This would lead to a rendering something like "the having equal (attributes) to God."[64] In either case the meaning is that Christ by right and by nature had what God had.[65] As for the third term, *homoioma*, it does mean likeness, but again the sense is not an illusory outer appearance that belies the real nature, but rather that Christ really took on human likeness. He was truly human.

Dunn's interpretation of the combination *morphe doulou* as becoming a slave (like Adam as a result of the Fall) makes no sense of the text or its context. The function of this hymn as Paul uses it is to inculcate humble self-sacrificial service, not slavery to sin. Furthermore, it is hardly likely that Paul is trying to argue here that Jesus, like Adam, became a slave to sin.[66] Although admitting in general that wisdom material affected early christological thinking, Dunn fails to apply this insight to the hymn in Philippians 2. When Wisdom's attributes are transferred and predicated of Christ, it is only natural to assume that because it is said of Wisdom that she was present at the creation of the world, and in the later wisdom hymns apparently a helper in the act of creation, this is also assumed or stated to be the case about the person Jesus Christ. This becomes especially clear in the christological hymns at least as early as the one in Colossians 1, but the idea is not likely absent here in Philippians 2. The choice being described in Philippians 2 is the choice *to* take on human flesh, a choice only a preexistent one could make.[67] Furthermore, as the parallel passage in 2 Cor. 8:9 suggests, not only was a conscious choice made by the preexistent one, but also an *exchange* of something was involved—some sort of riches for some sort of poverty. Note also both the contrastive *alla* in Philippians 2 and the verb *ekenosen* ("empty"), which must have some significant content to it.

The word *harmagmos* has caused endless debate and dispute. It has been assumed to mean either robbery (as the Western Church came by and large to interpret it), in which case the verse reads that Christ did not consider it robbery being equal in attributes to God (i.e., he was no usurper or interloper grabbing for more than what was rightfully his),[68] or it may mean, as J. B. Lightfoot suggested, that Christ did not consider being equal to God consisted in clutching to something,[69] perhaps his rightful divine prerogatives. Most likely, as R. W. Hoover has argued, it means not taking advantage of something one rightfully has.[70] This latter sense makes the best sense of the text.

It is important that one give full weight to the contrast between vv. 6b and 7a. Christ did not see being equal with God something he had to take advantage of; rather, he stripped himself, or emptied himself. G. F. Hawthorne is frankly too eager to deny that Christ stripped himself of anything when he became incarnate.[71] However, the verb stripped, or emptied, must have some content to it, and it is not adequate to say that Christ did not subtract anything because he actually added a human nature. The latter is true enough, but the text says he *did* empty himself, or strip himself. It does not tell us explicitly what he emptied himself of. However, the contrast between vv. 6b and 7a suggests that Christ set aside his rightful divine prerogatives, or perhaps his glory.[72] This does not likely mean he set aside his divine nature, but it does surely indicate some sort of self-limitation, some sort of setting aside of divine rights or privileges or glory.[73] He lived among humans as one of them, drawing on the power of the Spirit and prayer through which God revealed much to him. He lived as a servant king among humankind, even outshining Solomon in this regard. We now begin to see why Paul is able to draw analogies between the story of Christ and the story of Christians. It is the *human career*—beginning with the taking on of servant form, continuing on through death and resurrection—that is seen as some sort of pattern for behavior and belief. Even Jesus' suffering and resurrection can be seen as a repeatable pattern precisely because they are things that can happen only to the Son of God *in his human nature*. Paul is not offering some sort of apotheosis ethic here, as if believers now or later could become divine, but he does believe that in their human natures they can be made Christlike.

Christ not only stripped himself but also shunned any rightful human accolades or dignity; he took on the very form of a servant or slave. He identified himself with the lowest of the low, and he died a slave's death. This hymn places a special stress on the fact that the preexistent Christ had a choice about these matters, and he *chose* to act in the way he did. Christ was *obedient* even to the point of dying on the cross. He could have done otherwise.

The reason for this stress is that Paul is engaging in an argument about what the *imitatio Christi* (imitation of Christ) means. Paul does not think it is ridiculous idealism to appeal to the example of Christ as a moral pattern for believers; rather, he believes by God's Spirit and grace Christians can be obedient even unto death. Paul seems to stress the gospel principle in this hymn that those who humble themselves (an action, not an inferiority complex) will be exalted. If this is so, then Paul is suggesting to his converts that there will be a crown of glory for them as there was for Christ, whom God exalted to the highest place.

The name that is above all names is surely the name of God, and in this hymn the name that Jesus is given when he is raised and exalted beyond death is not Jesus—he had that name since human birth—but the name of God in the Old Testament—that is, LORD, which is the LXX equivalent to Yahweh. This is especially clear because Paul is alluding here to Isa. 45:21ff., where it says that only God is God and Savior of God's people, and only to God should anyone bow. At the name of Jesus all will bow and recognize his new and rightful title of Lord when history ends.

This is an example of what Wright calls "christological monotheism," which asserts the divinity of Christ, but at the same time "never intends to assert that Christ is divine in a sense apart from or over against the one true God."[74] Here is surely a new formulation of Jewish monotheism that draws strongly on what was previously said of Wisdom, but transforms it and goes beyond it, not only applying Wisdom ideas to Christ, but transforming them so that the author could speak about a divine person, not simply a personification of a divine attribute.

The hymn then is divided into two parts between what Christ chooses to do (he is the actor in vv. 6–8) and, in vv. 9–11, what God has done for Christ. Notice that confessing that Jesus is Lord (likely the earliest Christian confession) does not detract from but in fact adds to the Father's glory, for God has made this all possible by raising and exalting Jesus. Verses 10–11 suggest that all sentient beings will make this confession, including angels, persons, and demons. This does not necessarily mean all will in the end be converted. More likely, as in Wisdom of Solomon 5, it means all will be forced to recognize the truth. Already as early as the formulation of the hymn in Philippians 2 or at the very least as early as the Pauline use and modification of the hymn, one finds a new view of monotheism emerging that involves Christ as God's Wisdom in person— someone who had and has equal attributes with God, and in the end is given the same throne name.[75]

CHORUS TO THE COSMIC CHRIST (COL. 1:15–20)

Part I   Who is the image of the invisible God,
           firstborn of all creation;
           because in him were created all things
           in the heavens and upon the earth,
           the seen and the unseen,
           whether thrones or dominions
           or sovereignties or powers.
           Everything [created] through him was also created for him.
           And he is before everything, and everything coheres in him.
           And he is the head of the body, the church.

Part II   Who is the beginning (source),
           the firstborn from the dead,
           in order that he may take precedence in all things.
           Because in him is pleased to dwell all the "pleroma,"
           and through him is reconciled everything for him,
           making peace through the blood of his cross,
           whether things on earth or in the heavens.[76]

The parallels between this hymn and material in the Wisdom of Solomon are so numerous that they must be listed at the outset of the discussion.[77] W. Wink rightly argues that most of those who have tried to parcel out the hymn to source and redaction have failed to take into account "the heavy dependence of the entire passage on the Wisdom of Solomon,"[78] with a few possible minor Pauline additions.

1. *Wisd. Sol. 7:26*—"For she is . . . a spotless mirror of the working of God, and an image of his goodness" (cf. Col. 1:15a).
2. *Wisd. Sol. 6:22*—"I will tell you what Wisdom is and how she came to be. . . . I will trace her course *from the beginning of creation*" (cf. Col. 1:15b).
3. *Wisd. Sol. 1:14*—"For he created all things so that they might exist" (cf. Col. 1:16a).
4. *Wisd. Sol. 5:23d; 6:21; 7:8*—on thrones, scepters (Col. 1:16d).
5. *Wisd. Sol. 7:24b*—"For Wisdom . . . because of her pureness pervades and penetrates all things" (cf. Col. 1:16–17, 19).
6. *Wisd. Sol. 1:7*—"That which holds all things together knows what is said," (and) *8:1b*—"She reaches mightily from one end of the earth to the other, and she orders all things well" (cf. Col. 1:17b).
7. *Wisd. Sol. 7:29c*—on priority and superiority (cf. Col. 1:17a, 18d). One may also want to compare the wisdom hymns in Sirach, particularly 1:4: "Wisdom was created before all other things"; and in the first person in 24:9: "Before the ages, in the beginning, he created me, and for all ages I shall not cease to be."[79]

It might be possible to conclude from the listing of these parallels that the Christ hymn likely stopped at Col. 1:18 or v. 19 originally, but it is more likely that what this shows is that Wink's judgment must be somewhat tempered. Some of the material in this hymn is drawn from reflection on some other source, in this case probably the story of Jesus' death.[80] One cannot say of Sophia (personified Wisdom) that she is the head of the body.[81] Even if Col. 1:20b proves to be a Pauline addition, it is possible that the original phrase is found in Col. 1:22, which speaks of reconciliation in his body through death. E. Schweizer argues that whereas the first stanza can be explained from the sapiential material in Sirach and Wisdom of Solomon, stanza two is originally Christian.[82] But only parts of the second stanza, in particular the so-called Pauline additions plus the body = church language, seem to be specifically Christian; the wisdom influence is not absent even there.

Upon closer scrutiny, it becomes evident that the composer of this hymn is not simply transferring what was once said of Wisdom to Christ, for there are various small emendations or additions along the way. Thus, for example, although it appears in the wisdom hymns in both Sirach and Wisdom of Solomon that the authors are speaking of something created by God, this is not so certain in the Colossian hymn. Furthermore, the composer is not simply interested in form for form's sake.[83]

E. Norden long ago pointed out that the absence of articles, the piling up of participles, and the frequent use of relative clauses are formal clues that one is dealing with a hymn as a closing doxology of some sort (cf. Phil. 2:9ff.).[84] To this can be added the absence of the name of the one praised and the frequent use of third person singular aorist verbs.[85] This suggests that the praise and the greatness of the theme to some extent engendered and explains the form. The composer cannot offer enough superlatives.

The similarities between the hymn in Philippians 2 and that in Colossians 1 have often been noted, yet there is no servant language in Colossians 1, a fact that in itself suggests that Philippians 2 cannot be explained by means of Isaiah alone.[86] Philippians 2 and Colossians 1 being the most similar of the hymns may suggest that they are the earliest and least revised of the lot. This should not cause one to overlook the differences: Colossians 1 is about a cosmic victory, whereas Philippians 2 is primarily about a personal vindication.[87]

The majority of scholars are likely right that this is a pre-Pauline hymn for at least two important reasons. First, there is the distinctive non-Pauline vocabulary and content (e.g., in 1 Corinthians 15 Paul calls Christ the firstfruits from the dead, not the firstborn). Second, this hymn manifests the basic V pattern so characteristic of early sapiential christological hymns, chronicling the drama of creation, salvation, and glorification in its three christological stages. In Col. 1:15ff. Christ is seen as Creator, Sustainer, and Redeemer all wrapped up into one.

These hymns reveal that early Christians were not at all bashful about not only giving Christ divine names but also ascribing to him the deeds that only the deity can do. Here we are told that in him the "pleroma" (i.e., the fullness of God), not just a part, was pleased to dwell—a point Paul amplifies in 2:9.[88]

Probably Paul has added several elements to this hymn. The phrase "the church" may be a Pauline explanatory addition in v. 18. What is unique about this particular hymn is that the nadir of the V is not the incarnation, but rather the body. Though this might originally have referred to the cosmos, in Paul's use it refers to the *ekklesia* (Christian congregation), the locus where Christ is even now present on earth. Paul does go on to refer to making peace through the blood of Christ's cross, which was perhaps the original nadir of the song that the apostle then transposed to a spot later in the hymn.

Those scholars who see only two strophes in this hymn—vv. 15–18a and vv. 18b–20—are likely right. Verse 18a serves as a sort of transitional part of the hymn. That there are only two strophes is shown by the following parallels in the two parts: (1) *hos* begins each strophe, in v. 15a and v. 18b; (2) "he is the image" corresponds to "he is the beginning or source"; (3)

prototokos (literally, "firstborn") in v. 15 and v. 18; (4) each of the relative clauses is in turn followed by a causal clause *hoti* in v. 16, ("because in him all things were created") and v. 19, ("because in him the fullness"); (5) the cosmic dimension rounds out each strophe: first the cosmic dimension of his creation role, v. 16 ("whether thrones") and then the cosmic dimension of his redemption role ("whether things on earth"). The term *pas* (all) recurs frequently, and we have the emphatic use of *autos* (himself) in vv. 17–18. The hymn keeps ringing the changes on "in him," "through him," "for him," "he himself," stressing the christological focus.

In regard to the meaning of the hymn, Christ is said to be the image of the invisible God. This does not mean he is merely a likeness of God, but rather that he is the exact representation of God, in character and otherwise. When it says he is the firstborn of all creation, this probably does not refer to his being created, for it is about to go on to say he is the author of all creation.[89] Clearly, he is depicted here as on the side of the creator in the creator-creature distinction. *Prototokos* then emphasizes Christ's relationship to that creation, just as *eikon* ("image") emphasizes the relationship to the creator.[90] Schweizer points out that in Philo "image" and "beginning" are two interchangeable predications of heavenly Wisdom.[91]

Possibly the term *prototokos* reflects the Old Testament idea found in Ps. 89:27 where God promises to make the king his "firstborn," meaning preeminent, supreme in rank, not first created. In this usage there is also some sense of temporal priority. Thus the point is that he is prior to and supreme over all creation. When the term is used again in v. 18, the meaning is also of temporal priority, but again the idea of being created is not present. Christ was not literally born or created by the resurrection; he was transformed by it. Thus, in both cases the term connotes temporal priority and supremacy, not createdness.[92]

Verse 16 stresses that Christ even created the supernatural powers—thrones, dominions, sovereignties—powers being rather common terms for such beings.[93] Apparently, Paul envisions all these as good angels/supernatural forces, at least at the point of their creation. What this hymn seems to presuppose but does not speak of is the fall of some of the angelic host, as well as humans, for otherwise they would not need reconciling, and clearly, v. 20 speaks of reconciling things in heaven.

The language of Col. 1:15–20 surely refers to the personal activity of One who is the image of God and participates in the acts of creation. This is the most logical conclusion when one sees that the author is applying the language about the role of Wisdom in creation to a person whom the author worships. The first stanza of this hymn is not merely about the *power* that God exercised in creation being fully revealed or embodied in

Christic.[94] The concept of incarnation is present, however inchoate or
unexplained, in *all* the christological hymns, probably even including 1
Tim. 3:16.

This is hardly unthinkable for early Jewish Christians. It is simply a
further development of the idea found in Sirach 24 that suggests that
Wisdom expressed herself in concrete historical form in the Torah. To be
sure, Ben Sira does not offer a discussion of a *personal* incarnation, but once
early Christians began to transfer what had previously been said about
Wisdom and, in particular, Wisdom as manifested in Torah to Jesus, such
a development is not totally surprising. C. R. Holladay is right to criticize
Dunn for giving too little attention to the partial antecedents for the idea of
the incarnation.[95] Although there is an element of uniqueness involved in
talking about the preexistence and incarnation of a personal being who
took on flesh and became Jesus the Messiah, the sapiential story with its
exalted praise of Wisdom helped prepare the way for such an idea.

Verse 17 indicates not only the priority of Christ to all things, but also
that he is the glue, the one in whom all things cohere or are established. He
is the sustainer of all things, which is a present ongoing role. These same
sorts of things in regard to a role in creation and sustaining the universe are
said about Wisdom in Wisd. Sol. 1:7ff. (cf. Sir. 43:26).

The term *ekklesia* surely refers to the universal church, which is Christ's
body, for the emphasis in this hymn is on "all"—on the universal, both in
the human and in the natural realm.[96] The point is, the term *ekklesia* refers
to the people of God and does not always carry the sense of the assembled
people of God. The body metaphor in a cosmic context like this has
universal implications and does not just refer to the body of believers in
one place. Here one finds the first development of the idea of Christ as
head of the body, Christ being identified with a particular part of the body.
Whereas in 1 Corinthians and Romans "body" is primarily a metaphor
about the interrelationships between believers in the church, it is used here
to speak of the relationship of Christ to the church.

The second strophe begins by saying that Christ is the beginning or
source (probably the former) of the resurrection from the dead (i.e., from
the realm of dead persons). Verse 18c makes clear the sense of *prototokos* in
both cases; it is a matter of Christ taking precedence both in the realm of
creation and in the realm of redemption.[97]

The term *pleroma* in later Gnostic thought came to mean all the
intermediaries, the aeons, and things that existed between God and the
material realm as a sort of buffer zone so God would not be tainted by the
material that was thought to be inherently evil. Colossians 2:9 is the proper
commentary on what "pleroma" means here. In Christ the fullness of deity
was pleased to dwell. This is likely a polemical statement against the idea

that there were other divine beings that had some divinity in them. This seems to have been part of the theology of the false teachers in Colossae (Col. 2:18).[98]

It is often asked whether "all" really means all in v. 20, in which case there is universalism here—Christ will in the end save all persons and creatures and the universe. No one will finally be lost. O'Brien, however, rightly suggests that we read this in the light of the way Paul tells the story in Philippians 2, where some will bend the knee to Christ by being forced to do so in the end, not because of faith in and trust in Christ. The universe will be at peace in the end; but some will have that peace in them, and some will simply be pacified—laid to rest.[99] Wisdom of Solomon 5:1ff. supports such an interpretation, and in view of the other parallels between Wisdom of Solomon and the Colossian hymn, such an interpretation is likely correct. This verse does make clear the idea that redemption is not just for those on earth.[100]

Though it is less obvious than in the case with the hymn in Philippians, there is here too a latent connection between the story of Christ and the appropriate way Christians should live. It is precisely because Paul and his audience share this story of Christ in common that he can draw out its implications, such as is clearly being done in Col. 2:9, as a basis for his exhortations to focus on Christ alone and abstain from any practices that might suggest there was some salvific value to viewing or participating in angel worship or being involved with any lesser, created supernatural being. Paul is writing to a community "founded on the stories of the life, death, and resurrection of Christ,"[101] and those stories are not merely historical curiosities. In Paul's mind they have clear implications for how a believer should live out his or her own story. Even when the subject matter does not suggest emulation is being called for, the implications of the fullness of deity dwelling in Christ, of Christ being God's Wisdom, are that one should look nowhere else for life or enlightenment. There is a clear and firm link in Paul's mind between theology and ethics, or more particularly between Christology and ethics, and that link is made possible especially because of the human story or career of Christ, but also because even Christ as divine does things that should affect how believers live and worship. The believer's relationship to angelic beings should be guided by the knowledge of what the angels' relationship is to the Christ in whom all God's fullness dwells.

We have seen in our somewhat detailed study of two of Paul's retellings of the story of Christ in hymnic form that for Paul Christ has a divine face, like Wisdom, but also a human face, like Solomon or the Suffering Servant. Furthermore, at different points in his heavenly and earthly career Christ undertakes activities, or things happen to him, that are appropriate to either his divine or human condition or both. The rest of our discussion in this chapter must always keep the outline in these hymns in mind, for they reveal the narrative framework that affects how Paul thinks about Jesus. We must now consider the divine face and the divine activities of Jesus more fully.

THE INSIDE STORY OF THE GODHEAD: SON, FATHER, SPIRIT

Father, part of his double interest
Unto thy kingdom, thy Son gives to me,
His jointure in the knotty Trinity
He keeps and gives me his death's conquest.
This Lamb, whose death with life the world hath blessed,
Was from the world's beginning slain, and he
Hath made two wills, which with the legacy
Of his and thy kingdom, do thy sons invest.

—*John Donne*
excerpts, "Divine Meditations" 14, 16[102]

If we are right that Paul's theological reflections originate out of his narrative thought world, as is suggested by his use of the christological hymns, among other things, then it is worth pondering further how Paul conceived of Christ's role in the story of God, which is to say Christ's place and role in the divine economy vis-à-vis the Father and the Holy Spirit. We have already seen rather clear evidence in Philippians 2 and Colossians 1 that Paul does place the story of Jesus within the context of the story of God and God's creating, sustaining, and saving activity. There is, however, evidence of this elsewhere in the Pauline corpus, and we must now consider several possible samples: (1) 2 Cor. 5:19; (2) Rom. 9:5; and (3) 1 Cor. 8:6.[103] This will be followed by a discussion of the interrelationships of Father, Son, and Spirit.

Paul's use of the christological hymns indicates that Paul saw the Son as existing before he took on human flesh. Paul also saw the Son both as the Wisdom of God, God's agent in creation (1 Cor. 1:24, 30; 8:6; Col. 1:15–17) and also one who accompanied Israel in the wilderness (1 Cor. 10:4).[104] In view of the role Christ plays in Philippians 2, Colossians 1, and 1 Cor. 10:4, Paul is basically *not* founding the story of Christ on the archetypal story of Israel, but rather on the story of Wisdom, who helped Israel in the wilderness. Furthermore, it seems likely that the sapiential ideas we find in 1 Cor. 1:24, 30 and 8:6 reflect Paul's growing concept of the cosmic Christ—not just over land and universe but also involved in its creation. The full flower of this sort of wisdom thinking comes to expression in the hymn in Col. 1:15–20. Paul, of course, adopts and adapts this sort of wisdom material to his own ends, but the implications of its use are important—the apostle is predicating divine attributes of Jesus Christ as they were previously predicated of Wisdom. Are there other telltale signs of Paul's thinking along these lines?

One could ask, What is to be made of the phrase "God was in Christ (*en Christo*) reconciling the world to himself" (2 Cor. 5:19)? Perhaps the most obvious answer would be that this verse should be interpreted by the one that immediately precedes it, where it is said that God reconciled us *through* Christ (*dia Christou*). If this is a proper interpretation, then these verses are likely suggesting that Christ is the agent or mediator through whom God reconciled the world. This interpretation would also make sense of the verbal form in v. 19 indicating God *was* in Christ. Presumably, if Paul had meant to be discussing ontology here he would have been careful to say God *is* in Christ, but instead, because the actual subject here is the historical activity of God through Christ at a particular point in the past, he uses the word "was." It is necessary to look elsewhere to find evidence of Paul's view of Christ as someone who was more than human.

Two difficult texts come immediately to mind—Rom. 9:5 and Phil. 2:6–7. The latter we have already explored and have seen that that material does convey the idea that the preexistent Christ had divine attributes and prerogatives and the right to use them. Romans 9:5 is a more difficult text and comes at the outset of Paul's discussion of the advantages of the nation Israel. The problem in Rom. 9:5 is a matter of punctuation.

F. C. Burkitt once said with some exaggeration that the punctuation of Rom. 9:5 has probably been more discussed than that of any other sentence in literature. Because there is little or no punctuation in the earliest Greek manuscripts, this text can be read in various ways.[105] The argument turns on whether we read Rom. 9:5b with the NRSV, "Messiah, who is over all, God blessed forever"; or with the NRSV margin, "Messiah, who is God over all, blessed forever"; or with the NEB, "Messiah. May God supreme over all be blessed for ever," so that v. 5b is a separate sentence from v. 5a, or at least a separate clause. The JB, NIV, and NKJV support the reading "who is over all, God blessed for ever" as qualifying Christ. It appears that both the context and the grammar favor the reading of the NRSV or the NRSV margin. As Metzger points out, at Rom 1:3–4 and elsewhere it is normal to expect a contrast when we get the phrase *kata sarka*—"according to the flesh." This phrase is unnatural in its present form if the speaker is not going to go on and say what Christ is according to something else besides the flesh. Second, the phrase "who is" should and is normally taken as introducing a relative clause, and we have a perfectly good parallel to Rom. 9:5 at 2 Cor. 11:31.[106]

Metzger also notes that Pauline doxologies elsewhere are always attached to some previous antecedent; they are not asyndetic. Further, the almost universal pattern for doxologies in the Hebrew and LXX is "blessed be God," not "God blessed," as we have here if one sort of translation is followed.[107] The early versions also favor the reading of the NRSV or the reading listed as NRSV margin above. If it is asked why Paul nowhere else so explicitly calls Christ God, I would suggest that Paul does in other terms elsewhere call Christ God, for example, in Phil. 2:6–7 or Col. 2:9. M. J. Harris rightly points out:

> [I]n Pauline usage *Theos* was a sufficiently broad term to allow for its application to figures other than Yahweh. If he could apply the term to any being thought worthy of worship (1 Cor. 8:4; 2 Thess. 2:4c; cf. Acts 17:23) or to the so-called gods of polytheistic religion (1 Cor. 8:5 . . . ; Gal. 4:8b; 2 Thess. 2:4a) . . . and if he could describe Satan as "the god of this age" (2 Cor. 4:4), there is no *a priori* reason why he should not use the term of a being whom he considered to have identity of nature and parity of status with the one true God, particularly because *Theos* could be used qualitatively and as a generic title as well as the personal name of God the Father. . . . It cannot be deemed incongruous for Paul, who taught that one of the signs of the *Antichrist* would be his laying claim to the title *Theos* (2 Thess. 2:4), on one or two occasions himself to speak of the true Christ as *Theos*.[108]

We thus conclude that Paul calls Christ "God" here, which shows how far indeed Paul's experience of the risen Lord had caused him to qualify his Jewish monotheism or transform it.[109]

One final text is of particular interest at this point—1 Cor. 8:6.[110] This verse comes in the midst of an argument about food offered to idols and is part of Paul's polemic against polytheism in general and participating in feasts in the presence of idols in particular. The discussion begins in 8:1 with Paul quoting the Corinthians' claim to possess all knowledge. The connections between wisdom and knowledge are plentiful in Hellenistic Jewish sapiential material, as R. Horsley has shown.[111] For example, in Wisd. Sol. 10:10 the claim is made that Wisdom gave the righteous man knowledge of holy things, which is paralleled with a phrase about being shown the kingdom of God (see Wisd. Sol. 15:3).

It is relevant to point out that if in fact "there are no idols in the world" is a *Corinthian* slogan that Paul quotes, the use of the term *eidola* ("idols") points to the Jewish critique of polytheism and encourages one to think that Jewish polemic versus idols such as that found in Wisd. Sol. 13:10–14; Isa. 44:9–20; Jer. 10:1–16; or in 1 Enoch 19; 99:6–10 was being drawn on.[112]

The close association of God with *Sophia* ("Wisdom"), even to the point of Sophia being said to sit by or even on God's throne is significant (Wisd.

Sol. 9:4, 10). In this source Sophia is also said to reach mightily from one end of the earth to the other and to order all things well (8:1). "For she is an initiate in the knowledge of God, and an associate in his works. . . . [W]ho more than she is fashioner of all that exists?" (8:4, 7). Philo in *Quod Det.* 54 urges faithful Jews: "Accord a father's honor to Him who created the world, and a mother's honor to Sophia, through whom (*di' hes*) the universe was brought to completion." The use of the term *Father* for God is rare in early Judaism before the turn of the era, but when it is used it almost always appears in sapiential literature (cf., e.g., Wisd. Sol. 2:17; Sir. 23:1—in prayer coupled with Lord).[113]

Some Corinthians seem to have drawn some wrong conclusions from the slogans about only one God and no idols. They had assumed, because idols were nothing, that there could be no harm in participating in feasts in pagan temples. Paul must correct this mistaken assumption, and he does so drawing on some of the same Hellenistic-Jewish sapiential material from which the Corinthians themselves had drawn their conclusions.[114]

Paul, in order to counter this, goes back to first principles, drawing on the Jewish Shema (see Deut. 6:4–5) and putting Jesus right in the midst of the most fundamental assertion in early Judaism of its monotheistic faith.[115] Here Paul is reading the Shema through the later sapiential reflections on monotheism, Wisdom, and idolatry. The quotation from Philo *Quod Det.* 54 is especially relevant at this point. Paul is taking what was formerly said of God the Father and Sophia, and is now saying the same of the Father and Jesus Christ. But there is even more to this, because Paul is also willing to use the term "Lord" of Christ, which in the Shema refers to Yahweh.[116] Whatever the Corinthians may have been looking for in terms of divine knowledge or wisdom, Paul's assertion is that they will find it in Christ.

> If—as Paul clearly believes—Jesus is the one through whom his people are reconciled to the creator, through whom therefore is being brought about the dawn of the new creation, then it must follow that he is indeed the *sophia theou*, the one through whom the creator himself is operating to remake that which, already made, had been spoilt through sin and corruption.[117]

This formula has to do not just with redemption but even more with creation, as would be expected in light of the immediate context that discusses matters of creation (are idols anything?) and also in light of the sapiential background and the roles predicated of Wisdom in texts like Wisdom of Solomon 9. Dunn's and Murphy-O'Connor's views will not stand up to close scrutiny in view of these contexts.[118] Christ is the one through whom God made the universe, just as the same was said in

Wisdom of Solomon of Wisdom. Once one believes this, then a statement like 1 Cor. 10:4 ("the rock was Christ") hardly comes as a surprise. Furthermore, Paul shows that because the initiative for both these things stands with God, then religious knowledge must be conceived as primarily theocentric rather than anthropocentric. What really matters is loving God and *being known* by God (8:3).

This new Christian Shema is exactly what Paul needed at this juncture of his argument to reassert a proper Christian monotheism and also the primacy of love as well, and perhaps also to counter any underestimation of Jesus Christ that might have existed in Corinth at the time.[119] When a crucified Christ who took on the form of a slave for the world's redemption becomes part of the definition of deity, there is no more room for self-indulgent practices such as eating in pagan temples in religious feasts that violate the conscience of fellow believers. No knowledge but the knowledge of one God the Father and one Lord Jesus Christ will do as the heart of the Christian faith.

Once one admits, however, that Paul sees Christ as a legitimate part of the story of God in God's creating, sustaining, and redeeming activities, the question then becomes *how* Christ fits into this story vis-à-vis the other *divine actors* in the drama. That Christ is seen as *functionally subordinate* to the Father is clear from several texts. First, it is the Father who sent forth the Son from heaven (Gal. 4:4), and, in texts like 2 Cor. 5:18–19 Christ is definitely presented as God's agent through whom God the Father works. This comports with the fact that no fewer than thirty-three times in the Pauline corpus *Theos* (God) is linked with *pater* ("father") to form a single compound expression.[120] In the vast majority of occasions when Paul simply uses *Theos*, it is quite clear he means the one Jews call Yahweh (cf. 2 Cor. 13:13).

Second, God acts in behalf of Christ when he is killed; it is God who raised him from the dead (cf. 1 Cor. 15:4, 15). A further extension of this is what is said in Phil. 2:9, namely, that God has highly exalted him to the preeminent position in heaven and over earth.

Third, when Christ has fulfilled his role in the drama of redemption, he will be called upon to hand the kingdom back over to the Father and assume a subordinate position again (1 Cor. 15:24–28). This last text suggests that in God's story, Christ is seen as playing the leading part, assuming most of the roles of God in heaven between the time of the resurrection and the final handing over of the kingdom. However, he assumes not all such roles, for Christians are still expected to pray to the Father using Abba (Rom. 8:15). It is the Christ who makes the eschatological age possible, and that age focuses on him. In that age Jesus functions as Lord, and functions of God are often identified as Christ's.

Furthermore, the preexistent Son is seen as at least a colaborer in the work of creation. It follows from this that it is chiefly during his earthly career that Christ is subordinate to God and needing his aid, which is hardly surprising, for we are told that Christ did not make use of his divine prerogatives while in the form of a servant on earth (Phil. 2:6–7). The Son acts for, and as the agent of, the Father while on earth, and agents are by definition subordinate to the dictates of the one who sends them.

What about Christ's relationship to the Holy Spirit? It would appear that Paul sees the Spirit's role in the drama as subordinate to Christ and acting for Christ on earth, after Christ's exaltation.[121] Christ is the life-giving one, the one who sends the Holy Spirit (1 Cor. 15:45). As Christ was God's manifestation while Christ was on earth, so the Spirit is Christ's surrogate during the eschatological age. Although certainly Paul can distinguish Christ from the Spirit or the Father (e.g., only Christ died on the cross), by and large Paul is willing to say that what Christ does or conveys, the Spirit does or conveys in "this age."

For example, the believer (1) is righteous through Christ (Phil. 3:8, 9) but also in the Holy Spirit (Rom. 14:17); (2) has life in Christ (Col. 3:4) but also in the Spirit (Rom. 8:11); (3) has hope in Christ for the life to come (1 Cor. 15:19) and in the power of the Spirit to give eternal life (Gal. 6:8); (4) has joy in Christ (Phil. 4:4) but also in the Spirit (Rom. 14:17); (5) has *koinonia* in Christ (1 Cor. 1:9) but also the *koinonia* of the Spirit (2 Cor. 13:14); (6) is sanctified in Christ (1 Cor. 1:2) but also in the Spirit (Rom. 15:16).

It does not follow from this, however, that Paul is a binitarian. Even in 2 Cor. 3:17 Paul is not completely identifying the Spirit with Christ. The text seems to mean "Now the word 'Lord' here (in this text) means the Spirit, and where the Spirit rules."[122] In Second Corinthians 3 Christ is indeed identified with his agent, the Spirit, but only in activity.[123]

Thus far we have seen how Christ is placed in the story of divine redemption, especially in the christological hymns where he appears as God's Wisdom; and we have seen how it can even be said that Christ is part of the story of the Godhead itself, acting for the Father, being acted for by the Spirit, interacting with both Father and Spirit. For the most part we have been considering pretemporal or posttemporal matters in this section.

There are two ways that Paul binds the whole story of Christ together—by his use of the Son of God language and by his use of the Christ language—to describe who Jesus is in every act of the salvation drama. It was needful for him to do this in order to indicate to his audience that it was the same person he was referring to in the various ways he reflects on the drama of salvation. The former seems to reflect a bit more of Christ's divine face and roles, the latter his human face and roles. So we will deal only with his being called Son of God in this section.

I. H. Marshall summarizes Paul's use of Son of God as follows:

> M. Hengel has demonstrated that Paul kept it for use at the climax of theological statements and that he used it to demonstrate the close bond between Jesus and God in virtue of which Jesus is the mediator of salvation. Thus it is the Son who is the theme of the gospel (Rom. 1:3, 9), and it is by means of this title that Paul emphasizes the supreme value of the death of the One who stood closest to God as the means of reconciling men with God (Rom. 5:10; 8:32; Gal. 2:20; Col. 1:13f.). The same idea is used to express the closeness of Jesus to God and appears when Jesus is described as being in the form or image of God and as his Firstborn. It should be noted that for Paul Jesus was God's Son during his earthly life, and that it was as God's Son that he died. Consequently, he did not cease to be divine in his earthly existence, and his self-emptying cannot mean that he gave up his divine nature to assume human nature.[124]

This is essentially correct but requires some expansion. Paul can speak of "the son of God" or "the Son" or "God's Son." Jesus' special relationship to the Father is expressed in the Gospels by the use of the term "Abba" (Mark 14:26). This same term seems to have characterized Paul's thinking about believers' role as sons, which is implicitly derived from Jesus' role as Son at Gal. 4:6. Believers say Abba by the same power of the Spirit that Jesus did. However, Rom. 8:15 makes clear that Paul sees believers as "adopted" sons. What about Jesus?

Romans 1:3–4 is the paramount text for those who insist that Paul has an adoptionist Christology—that is, that Jesus became or was adopted as "son of God" at his resurrection. Several things need to be made clear at this point: (1) there are two parallel phrases being applied to Jesus—born of the family of David according to the flesh, and appointed Son of God in power according to the Spirit of holiness; (2) the phrase "in power" is a crucial one and likely qualifies "son of God," not "appointed";[125] (3) the word *horisthentos* must surely mean "appointed" or "installed" here;[126] (4) the phrase "*ek* the resurrection of the dead" likely means "since," not "by" his resurrection. If these judgments are correct, then it follows that what is being described in v. 4a is what Jesus has been appointed as since the resurrection. The word *horisthentos* seems to favor the adoptionist view except for the phrase "in power," and it is in fact the key phrase. Jesus did not become Son of God in power till after the resurrection. The phrase then does not tell us when he became Son of God, but it seems to imply that before the resurrection he was Son of God in weakness. This comports with what Paul says elsewhere in Phil 2:6–7; Rom. 8:5; and 2 Cor. 8:9. Further, it is probable that the two initial phrases mean "in the sphere of the flesh" and "in the sphere of the Spirit." Jesus' birth and Davidic sonship happened in the sphere of the flesh, but his divine Sonship in power happened in the sphere of the Holy Spirit. Here then we do not likely have the idea of Christ's two natures, but rather two conditions before and after resurrection. In other words, Paul is commenting on what is true about Christ during two stages of the drama of salvation. Here again we find more evidence that it is Paul's narrative framework that explains why he expresses himself as he does here. Dunn rightly stresses: "Jesus did not first become God's Son at the resurrection; but he entered upon a still higher rank of sonship at resurrection. Certainly this has to be designated a two-stage Christology . . . though . . . [t]o describe the Christology as 'adoptionist' . . . is anachronistic since there is no indication that this 'two-stage Christology' was being put forward in opposition to some already formulated 'three-stage Christology.' "[127]

There are numerous other uses of the term "Son of God" by Paul (cf. 1 Cor. 1:9, 15, 28; 2 Cor. 1:19; Gal. 1:16; 4:6; Rom. 1:9; 5:10; 8:3, 29, 32). In 1 Cor. 1:9 we read of the *koinonia*, the sharing in common of God's Son (i.e., the sharing Jesus made possible that allows us to become adopted children of God). Second Corinthians 1:19 makes clear there is only one divine Son of God in Paul's vision of the story of the world. At Gal. 1:16 Paul sees his Damascus road experience as a "revealing by God of His Son in me." Romans 1:9 speaks of the gospel of God's Son, which means the gospel about Jesus as Son that Paul preached. It is telling that Paul is able to summarize the content of the gospel in this way and supports the thesis that the term *Son* is one way Paul binds his telling of the salvation drama together. Romans 5:10 is important because it indicates that Paul thought Jesus died as Son (so Rom. 8:32). This confirms our interpretation of Rom. 1:3–4. Romans 8:3 pushes it even further back in that Paul talks about the Son being sent in "likeness of sinful flesh." In view of all we have discovered in investigating the christological hymns, this surely implies Jesus' preexistence even as Son.[128] Galatians 4:4: "But when the fullness of the time had come, God sent forth the Son" further confirms what we have just suggested. By contrast, Rom. 8:24 insists that believers are destined to be conformed to the Son's image. Thus as Son, Christ is the one who is sent, who is born, who dies, and who at his resurrection enters a new and higher stage of his Sonship. It is to this last image of Christ as the risen and powerful Son that believers will finally be made to conform, becoming sons and daughters of God in a fuller sense, just as Christ entered a higher stage of Sonship at his resurrection. Wherever one ranges across the narrative of Christ, the term *Son* is applicable.

We need to consider how Christ fits into the story of Israel and of the world as a human being and yet more than merely human. In that context we will have things to say about his roles and his names, such as Christ or last Adam. Then we will consider what is said about Christ as Lord, which is especially predicated of Jesus as a result of his death, resurrection, and exaltation. This will lead us to a reflection on how Paul handles the Christian narrative about Jesus' life, teachings, death, and resurrection.

NOTES TO PART 3

The Surprising Story of the Crucified Conqueror

1. John Donne, *The Complete English Poems*, 315.
2. Some of the material in Part 3 appears in a rather different form in an article on Pauline christology to appear in the forthcoming *Dictionary of Paul and His Letters* (Downers Grove, Ill.: I-V Press) and some portions of the discussion on the hymns in Philippians 2 and Colossians 1 are found in a rather different and more detailed form in Chapter 7 of my *Jesus the Sage and the Pilgrimage of Wisdom* (Minneapolis: Fortress Press, 1994)
3. See my *Jesus the Sage*, chaps. 7–8.
4. L. W. Hurtado, *One God, One Lord* (Philadelphia: Fortress Press, 1988), 17–92.
5. Contra J. C. Beker, *Paul the Apostle: The Triumph of God in Life and Thought* (Philadelphia: Fortress Press, 1980), 152ff.
6. Beker, *Paul the Apostle*, 23–36.
7. See N. T. Wright, *The New Testament and the People of God* (Minneapolis: Fortress Press, 1992), 407: "The story of Jesus, interpreted precisely within the wider Jewish narrative world, was the hinge upon which Paul's rereading of that larger story turned."
8. See the discussion above pp. 17ff.
9. See N. T. Wright, *The Climax of the Covenant* (Edinburgh: T. & T. Clark, 1991), 18–40.
10. From *Judge Tenderly of Me: The Poems of Emily Dickinson*, ed. W. T. Scott (Kansas City, Mo.: Hallmark, 1968), 49.
11. On the interpretation of this important text, see my *Conflict and Community in Corinth: A Socio-Rhetorical Commentary on 1 and 2 Corinthians* (Grand Rapids: Wm. B. Eerdmans, 1994), ad loc. Here Wright, *The New Testament*, 408, fails to convince by suggesting that *kata sarka* means according to Jewish nationalistic ways of thinking about messiah. This is not what Paul means elsewhere by *kata sarka*.
12. See J.A.T. Robinson, *The Body: A Study of Pauline Theology* (Philadelphia: Westminster Press, 1977), 58.
13. J.D.G. Dunn, *Unity and Diversity in the New Testament* (Philadelphia: Westminster Press, 1977), 190.
14. Cf. S. Kim, *The Origins of Paul's Gospel* (Grand Rapids: Wm. B. Eerdmans, 1984), 71ff.; and E. deW. Burton, *A Critical and Exegetical Commentary on the Epistle to the Galatians* (Edinburgh: T. & T. Clark, 1921), 42–43.
15. Some of what follows in this section may be found in a somewhat modified and more detailed form in Chapter 7 of my *Jesus the Sage*.

16. That Pliny is referring to hymn singing seems clear in light of the way Tertullian interprets the text in *Apol. 2.6.*

17. In what follows I am indebted to M. Hengel's seminal essay "Hymns and Christology," in *Between Jesus and Paul* (Philadelphia: Fortress Press, 1983), 78–96.

18. Cited in R. MacMullen, *Paganism in the Roman Empire* (New Haven: Yale, 1981), p. 17 from a source unavailable to me.

19. W. Wink, "The Hymn of the Cosmic Christ," in *The Conversation Continues: Studies in Paul and John in Honor of J. L. Martyn* (Nashville: Abingdon Press, 1990), 235–44, here pp. 235–39.

20. Compare above what Pliny says about Christians singing at dawn.

21. J. A. Sanders, "The Psalms Scroll of Qumran Cave 11," *Discoveries in the Judean Desert Journal* 4 (1965): 91–92.

22. This document seems to have already been extant in Jesus' day and probably even earlier, for it seems to have influenced the Qumran community.

23. I agree with E. Schweizer, "Paul's Christology and Gnosticism," in *Paul and Paulinism: Essays in Honour of C. K. Barrett*, ed. M. D. Hooker and S. G. Wilson (London: SPCK, 1982), 115–123, that the parallels between the Gnostic use of hymns and Wisdom and Paul's use diverge in important ways. The hymns in Paul and elsewhere in the New Testament do not devalue creation, nor do they stress the idea of a redeemer figure who in essence passes through the intervening layers of creation separating God and humanity, yet escapes the taint of the material universe. Indeed, in the christological hymn fragments in the New Testament not only is creation seen as good but the Redeemer has a hand in making it. "While Gnosticism took up and radicalized a notion which had, perhaps, been at the root of Jewish Wisdom literature, the idea of a divine order inherent in all things and particularly in man's mind, Christianity, on the contrary, did so with the typically Jewish idea of Wisdom as a gift of God to his elect people, manifest . . . definitively, 'eschatologically' (Heb. 1:2) in Jesus Christ" (p. 120).

24. Another text pointing to early evidence of christological hymn singing is Ignatius, *Eph.* 4:1–2, which speaks not only of singing through Christ to God but also of Jesus Christ being sung.

25. Cf. Proverbs 1, 8, 9; Job 28; Sir. 1:9–10; 4:11–19; 6:18–31; 14:20–15:8; 51:13–21; Bar. 3:9–4:4; Wisd. Sol. 6:12–11:1.

26. Cf. my *The Christology of Jesus*, (Minneapolis: Fortress Press, 1990), 234–35, on dating the material in the parables of Enoch.

27. I am following the translation in J. H. Charlesworth, *OT Pseudepigrapha I* (New York: Doubleday & Co., 1983), 33, with minor modifications.

28. R. E. Murphy, *The Tree of Life* (New York: Doubleday & Co., 1990), 146. The chart on Wisdom is adapted with some changes from this study.

29. One must distinguish between where Paul likely first heard such hymns and where they originated. I would not rule out a Palestinian origin, at least for the primitive V pattern that stands behind all these hymns. In view of what was said about personified Wisdom in earlier wisdom literature, it is neither necessary nor plausible to insist on a Gnostic redeemer myth as the basis of the christological hymns. Cf. Schweizer, "Paul's Christology and Gnosticism," in *Paul and Paulinism*, 115ff., but also this from L. W. Hurtado, "Jesus as Lordly Example in Philippians

2:5–11," in *From Jesus to Paul: Studies in Honour of F. W. Beare*, ed. P. Richardson and J. C. Hurd (Toronto: Wilfred Laurier Press, 1984), 113–26: "In general, and for reasons sufficiently well known to require no explanation here, the appeal to a pre-Christian Gnostic redeemer-myth has fallen on hard times in recent years." Cf. E. Yamauchi, *Pre-Christian Gnosticism: A Survey of Proposed Evidences* (Grand Rapids: Wm. B. Eerdmans, 1973).

30. It is possible that some of the hymns were originally composed in Aramaic – or even Hebrew (though this seems less likely than Aramaic); for example, see H. Gese, *Essays on Biblical Theology* (Minneapolis: Augsburg Publishing House, 1981), 174–175.

31. Even in regard to the earliest of these hymn fragments in Philippians 2, Wright, *The Climax*, 98, is quite right to point out that Phil. 2:6, with its "nuanced idiom [used] in a characteristically Hellenistic way . . . does not *prove* that the passage was originally composed in Greek, but it makes it very easy to imagine it was" (p. 98). I would say it makes it quite likely.

32. See the important article by M. Hengel, "Psalm 110 und die Erhöhung des Auferstandenen zur Rechten Gottes," in *Anfänge der Christologie*, ed. C. Breytenbach and H. Paulsen (Göttingen: Vandenhoeck & Ruprecht, 1991), 43–73. The attempt to argue that the hymns were originally thanksgiving hymns on the basis of what comes before Col. 1:15–20 seems strained at best. As E. Schüssler Fiorenza points out in "Wisdom Mythology and the Christological Hymns of the New Testament," in *Aspects of Wisdom in Judaism and Early Christianity*, ed. R. L. Wilken (South Bend: University of Notre Dame Press, 1975), 17–41, a standard psalmic thanksgiving formula is not used in connection with these hymns. Furthermore, the psalms of thanksgiving do not seem to have been the main quarry used to construct these hymns (p. 25).

33. M. Hengel, *Between Jesus and Paul: Studies in the Earliest History of Christianity* (Philadelphia: Fortress Press, 1983), 94.

34. The general lack of much developed atonement theology in Acts, except possibly on the lips of Paul in Acts (cf., e.g., Acts 20:28), makes one wonder if it did not take a while for the early Christians to fathom the full weight and significance of Jesus' death and draw out its positive implications. The early summaries in Acts suggest that the earliest Christians continued to go to the Temple (cf. Acts 2:5ff.; 2:46; 5:20), and one wonders if this did not include, among other activities, offering sacrifices. Even the speech of Stephen in Acts 7 does not critique the offering of sacrifices per se, but only Jewish corruption and sin in various forms, and the supposition that God dwells in houses made by human hands (7:47ff.). Surely the Pauline letters, especially Galatians, bear clear witness to the fact that many early Jewish Christians continued to be observant Jews. Paul is castigated by some for living like a Gentile and breaking down the barriers of customs that separate Jew and Gentile (e.g., circumcision, table fellowship). Paul's letters are all written to people who lived in the Diaspora, and thus it is not surprising that Temple sacrifices are not a topic of any significant discussion in the apostle's writings. Perhaps Paul was the first to articulate clearly a theology of the atoning death of Christ.

35. It is possible that the reference in John 1:14 about having seen his glory

may allude to the resurrection, but Jesus in the Fourth Gospel is presented as full of grace and truth throughout his career, so even here it seems doubtful. The difficult phrase "vindicated in spirit" or "by the Spirit" in 1 Tim. 3:16 could possibly allude to resurrection. In any case, this is not the language of the early kerygma about Jesus' death and resurrection.

36. R. P. Martin, "Some Reflections on New Testament Hymns," in *Christ the Lord: Studies Presented to Donald Guthrie*, ed. H. H. Rowden (Leicester, Eng.: IV Press, 1982), 37–49.

37. Schüssler Fiorenza, "Wisdom Mythology," in *Aspects of Wisdom*, 19. Cf. also the new preface to the revised edition of R. P. Martin, *Carmen Christi: Philippians 2:5–11* (Grand Rapids: Wm. B. Eerdmans, 1983), xiff.

38. For a helpful summary of the literature on Phil. 2:6–11, cf. Martin, *Carmen Christi*, xi–xxxix, 63–95.

39. S. Fowl, *The Story of Christ in the Ethics of Paul* (Sheffield, Eng.: JSOT Press, 1990), 31–45; Gordon Fee, unpublished IBR lecture on Phil. 2.5ff. given the 1990 SBL meeting; J. F. Balchin, "Colossians 1:15–20: An Early Christological Hymn? The Arguments from Style," *Vox Evangelica* 15 (1985): 65–94; J. Frankowski, "Early Christian Hymns Recorded in the New Testament: A Reconsideration of the Question in Light of Heb. 1:3," *Biblische Zeitschrift* 27 (1983): 183–94.

40. For the suggestion that in Wisdom of Solomon we have parallel and polemical use of a hymnic form used elsewhere to praise Isis, see my *Jesus the Sage*, chap. 1.

41. J. C. O'Neill, "The Source of Christology in Colossians," *NTS* 26 (1979): 87–100, here pp. 90ff.

42. This was despite the protests of some. Contrast Martin, *Carmen Christi*, xii, with Hurtado, "Jesus as Lordly Example," in *From Jesus to Paul*, 113–26; Fowl, *The Story of Christ*, 49ff.

43. G. Strecker, "Redaktion und Tradition im Christushymnus Phil. 2:6–11," *Zeitschrift für die neutestamentliche Wissenschaft* 55 (1964): 63–78, here 63–64. In its present form, of course, this hymn is Pauline, for he has adopted it and adapted it for his purposes. It is not really possible to decide whether the hymn originally had a parenetic function apart from the Pauline context, but cf. Hurtado, "Jesus as Lordly Example," in *From Jesus to Paul*, 113–26.

44. Fowl, *The Story of Christ*, 61ff.

45. The best attempt to make a case for such a view is Wright's in *The Climax*, 56ff., but he is trying to have it both ways—both an Adamic Christology and a Christology of preexistence and incarnation in this hymn. Here C.F.D. Moule's critique of Dunn applies also to Wright: "Phil. ii . . . speaks not of man's glorious destiny as something to be achieved. It speaks of one for whom it was a humiliation to take man's likeness, and who only thereafter was exalted—and exalted not to the status of man but of *Kurios*. Can this be squeezed into a purely Adamic pattern?" (from his review of Dunn's *Christology in the Making* in *Journal of Theological Studies* n.s. 33 [1982]: 259–63, here p. 260). Not only is Paul not engaging in speculation about some Ur-Adam who preexisted in heaven; he is also not identifying Christ as an Adam figure by saying he took on the form of a *doulos*.

46. Very helpful is the philological study of R. W. Hoover, "The Harpagmos

Enigma: A Philological Solution," *Harvard Theological Review* 64 (1971): 95–119. He is right in stressing that the word *harpagmos* here must be evaluated as part of an idiomatic phrase, not as an isolated term. His suggested translation "as something to take advantage of" or "as something to use for his own advantage" is on the right track. His suggestion of a parallel with Rom. 15:3 is helpful, and one must stress his final conclusion: "In *every instance* which I have examined, this idiomatic expression refers to something already present and at one's disposal. The question in such instances is not whether one possesses something, but whether one chooses to exploit something" (p. 118, emphasis mine).

47. See now Fowl, *The Story of Christ*, 71–72. As Fowl stresses, Dunn's view is flawed in many ways, including the fact that it is based on an assumed equivalence of *morphe* and *eikon*, a supposition for which there is no linguistic evidence whatsoever. It is also worth remembering that elsewhere, when Paul wants to draw an analogy between Christ and Adam, he mentions the latter by name, unlike here.

48. As the allusion to Isaiah 45 surely indicates; cf. Wright, *The Climax*, 75, 93ff.

49. Pace J.D.G. Dunn, *Christology in the Making* (Philadelphia: Westminster Press, 1980), 119.

50. C. A. Wanamaker, "Phil. 2:6–11: Son of God or Adamic Christology?" *New Testament Studies* 33 (1987): 179–93, here p. 183. The alternative to Dunn's view—that is, a sonship Christology that totally neglects the wisdom overtones of this material—is not much more convincing. Jesus is never called Son in the hymn or in its immediate context. Nor is the relevance of the observation that children bear a likeness to their parents immediately apparent. This hymn is not about parent-child relationships, even divine ones.

51. T. F. Glasson, "Two Notes on the Philippians Hymn (II:6–11)," *New Testament Studies* 27 (1974): 133–38.

52. See J. T. Sanders, *The New Testament Christological Hymns* (Cambridge: Cambridge University Press, 1971), 73–74. I agree with him that it is unnecessary, as Georgi tried to do, to posit a specific Jewish hymn behind Philippians 2. The background is more general than that.

53. I. H. Marshall, "Incarnational Christology in the New Testament," in *Christ the Lord: Studies in Christology Presented to Donald Guthrie*, ed. H. H. Rowdon (Downers Grove, Ill.: I-V Press, 1982), 1–16, here p. 6.

54. J. T. Sanders, *NT Christological Hymns*, 66ff.

55. G. Howard, "Phil. 2:6–11 and the Human Christ," *Catholic Biblical Quarterly* 40 (1978): 368–87, here pp. 369–72.

56. I have demonstrated this at some length in *Jesus the Sage*, chap. 6.

57. D. Georgi argues in particular for Wisdom of Solomon 5 and 8 (!) being alluded to here, the latter of which is problematic. D. Georgi, "Der vorPaulinische Hymnus Phil. 2:6–11," in *Zeit und Geschichte. Dankesgabe an R. Bultmann zum 80. Geburtstag*, ed. E. Dinkler (Tübingen: J. C. B. Mohr, 1964), 263–93.

58. See now Fowl, *The Story of Christ*, 95ff.

59. Cf. esp. 2:5–3:15a.

60. I do not rule out the translation "through the faithfulness of Christ" in 3:9,

which would provide yet a further link between the story of Christ and that of believers. On the whole, however, in light of our previous discussion of the reckoning of righteousness in the story of Abraham, this seems less likely. See pp. 38ff. above. There it is clear that faith is counted instead of righteousness. One would have expected Paul to say the righteousness comes *from* (*ek*) the faithfulness of Christ, not merely through Christ and from God, if Paul were attempting to formulate some sort of notion of imputing to the believer Christ's righteousness as a result of his obedience even unto death.

61. See Fowl, *The Story of Christ*, 50–54.

62. Wright, *The Climax*, 83.

63. F. Blass, A. Debrunner, and R. W. Funk, *A Greek Grammar of the NT*, 434.1.

64. J. B. Lightfoot, *St. Paul's Epistle to the Philippians* (London: Macmillan & Co., 1898), 110, is right to say that if the reference was to the person, one would have expected *ison*, not *isa*.

65. It makes no sense, if this is a *plural* predicate adjective, to render it "having equal office, equal status, equal position." Here Fowl, *The Story of Christ*, 49ff., goes astray. It must refer to something Christ could have had that amounted to more than just an abstract singular concept like status. Nor does the rendering "equality," as in "the having equality to God," much improve things. It would be better either to render it as an adverb modifying *einai* or as a plural neuter adjective.

66. Pace Dunn, *Christology in the Making*, 115ff. Cf. the telling critique by C.E.B. Cranfield, "Some Comments on Professor J.D.G. Dunn's *Christology in the Making* with Special Reference to the Evidence of the Epistle to the Romans," in *The Glory of Christ in the New Testament*, ed. L. D. Hurst and N. T. Wright (Oxford: Clarendon Press, 1987), 267–80, here p. 271.

67. The arguments of J. Murphy O'Connor, "Christological Anthropology in Phil. 2:6–11," *Revue biblique* 83 (1976): 25–50, are no more convincing than Dunn's. The preexistence issue is raised immediately by the use of the wisdom material in the hymns to say things about the career of Christ even before his earthly existence. Only by ignoring this background can one claim that one has to bring the preexistence idea to the text to find it here.

68. C.F.D. Moule, "Further Reflexions on Phil. 2:5–11," in *Apostolic History and the Gospel*, ed. W. W. Gasque and R. P. Martin (Exeter, Eng.: Pater Noster, 1970), 264–76. On p. 266 he argues for the translation "as consisting in snatching."

69. Lightfoot, *Philippians*, 111, argued in the last century that *harpagmon hegesato* was an idiomatic phrase meaning "to prize highly," "to set store by," or "to clutch greedily." The idea of robbery for *harpagmos* had largely dropped out of sight by New Testament times, and the Greek Fathers almost universally understood the phrase as Lightfoot suggests. Cf. Glasson, "Two Notes on the Philippians Hymn," 133–36. Clearly, the weakest of the translations in terms of the philological evidence is the robbery/seizure translation.

70. Hoover, "Harpagmos," 118–19, points out against a common view that the idiomatic expression with *harpagmos* does not mean "to retain something" or "to hold something fast." The linguistic evidence is against such a translation; cf. also rightly Moule, "Further Reflexions," 267.

71. G. F. Hawthorne, *Philippians* (Waco, Tex.: Word, 1983), 78ff. So too Wright, *The Climax*, 83ff., who seems at first to assume that *ekenosen* means no more than that Christ took a different *attitude* toward the attributes or rights he had and kept all along. But surely "emptying" in v. 6 refers to an action that parallels the action in v. 7 of "taking on." Later Wright (p. 92) says Christ renounced the rank and privileges that he had. This is right, but what does this entail? If he renounced certain rights and privileges, this means at the very least that during his human existence Christ did not draw on these things. In short, he accepted certain limitations.

72. Wanamaker, "Phil. 2:6–11," 184–86.

73. Perhaps it means that Christ did not act on or draw on his ability to be omnipotent, omnipresent, and omniscient; that is, he accepted human limitations of time, space, and knowledge.

74. Wright, *The Climax*, 116.

75. First Corinthians 8:6 also shows that Paul had already made this sort of mental leap at least by the early 50s.

76. For another view similar to the one taken here of the structure, cf. Wright, *The Climax*, 102–4. Wright argues for an ABBA pattern, with vv. 15a and 18c being parallel and vv. 17 and 18a being parallel.

77. E. Schweizer, "The Church as the Missionary Body of Christ," *New Testament Studies* 8, no. 1 (1961): 1–11, here 7: "One could quote the parallels to the first stanza word by word in Wisdom literature."

78. Wink, "Hymn of the Cosmic Christ," 235–46, here 235. The hymn in Colossians 1, however, is as far as it could be from a Gnostic hymn, in view of the very positive view it takes of both creation and redemption in Christ. Cf. Wright, *The Climax*, 107.

79. J. Jervell, *Imago Dei. Gen. 1.26f im Spätjudentum, in der Gnosis und in den paulinischen Briefen* (Göttingen: Vandenhoeck & Ruprecht, 1960), 200–213.

80. It is a puzzle why Wink, having cited all these parallels, then proceeds to focus on parallels with a Gnostic source, the *Tripartite Tractate* (Trimorphic Protennoia), which is clearly later than the New Testament data. As J. Ashton notes in "The Transformation of Wisdom: A Study of the Prologue of John's Gospel," *New Testament Studies* 32, no. 2 (1986): 161–86, here 182 n. 4, this material is much too late to have been of direct influence on New Testament hymns, even the one in John 1.

81. J. T. Sanders, *NT Christological Hymns*, 82. In both Hebrew with the word *Hokmah* and in Greek with the word *Sophia* we are dealing with nouns with feminine endings, which may in part explain the feminine imagery used to describe personified Wisdom.

82. E. Schweizer, "Die Kirche als Leib Christi im dem paulinischen Antilegomena," *THLZ* 86 (1961): 241–56, here 243–44.

83. O'Neill, "Source of Christology in Colossians," 87–100. He does not think there is a hymn here, but apparently some sort of hymnic prose.

84. E. Norden, *Agnostos Theos* (Darmstadt: Wissenschaftliche Buchgesellschaft, 1956), 168ff., 201ff.

85. Martin, *Carmen Christi*, xxxiv.

86. Rightly, J. T. Sanders, *NT Christological Hymns*, 75.

87. J. T. Sanders, *NT Christological Hymns*, 86 n. 1. The theme of cosmic ‐ victory seems also to be found in the so-called "Song of the Star" in Ignatius *Eph.* 19:2–3.

88. Fowl, *The Story of Christ*, 103ff., badly underestimates the force of this material. Nice distinctions between being and status are far from Paul's mind. Paul believes that what Christ does and is acclaimed is an expression of who he is.

89. Philo calls Wisdom the *arche* in *Leg. All.* 1.43.

90. T. F. Glasson, "Col. 1:18, 15 and Sirach 24," *Novum Testamentum* 11 (1969): 154–56 notes that the Old Latin of Sir. 24:3 reads, "I went forth out of the mouth of the Most High, first born before every creature . . . and in every people and in every nation I had the preeminence." Cf. Ps. Cyprian *Testimonies* 2.1. Philo, *Quest. in Gen.* 4.97, calls Wisdom "first born mother of all things." Cf. *De Fuga* 109; *De Virtu.* 62. It is as important to note how the biblical writers alter their wisdom source as it is to note how they reuse it.

91. Schweizer, "Church as the Missionary Body of Christ," 1–11; cf. Philo *Leg. All.* 1.43.

92. In view of the parallels with the wisdom material, it is possible that this hymn originally did speak of some sort of pretemporal creation of the Redeemer, but Paul does not understand the hymn in that sense, and it is impossible to reconstruct in any full sense the hymn's earlier form.

93. Cf. *Test. Levi* 3.7–8—"in heaven below them are . . . thrones and dominions"; 1 En. 61:10—"all the angels of power"; 2 En. 20:1—"I saw there [i.e., in the seventh heaven] dominions, . . . and the authorities, cherubim . . . thrones."

94. Contrast Marshall, "Incarnational Christology," 9, with Dunn, *Christology in the Making*, 187–94. Marshall is also right that the mention of the body of his flesh in 1:22 would be quite gratuitous if the redeemer was here envisioned as simply a human being. "[T]he phrase is meaningful only as a way of emphasizing the fact that the One described in the preceding 'hymn' became incarnate in order to die on the cross" (p. 8).

95. C. R. Holladay, "New Testament Christology: Some Considerations of Method," *Novum Testamentum* 25 (1983): 257–78, here p. 264.

96. P. T. O'Brien, *Colossians, Philemon* (Waco, Tex.: Word, 1982), 48–50, 57–61.

97. See Fowl, *The Story of Christ*, 113–14.

98. It is possible that Paul is referring in Col. 2:18 to a mystical vision of the worship of angels obtained through ascetical practices. See Fowl, *The Story of Christ*, 140ff.

99. O'Brien, *Colossians, Philemon*, 53ff.

100. Some have seen a christological hymn fragment in Eph. 2:13 or 2:14–18, but for formal and content reasons this appears to be a soteriological reflection on the implications of the death of Jesus, perhaps in particular as it is expressed in the hymn in Col. 1:20. The Ephesians passage then seeks to make clear the implications of Jesus' death for the reconciliation of Jews and Gentiles. Now, through Christ's death even Gentiles have been brought near to God. This has happened because Christ himself (noting the emphatic *autos*) is the believer's peace. It is

interesting that the author of this material seems to be attempting to answer or rebut the arguments of a Ben Sira, who maintains that Torah is the locus of wisdom on earth and that which brings God's people together. In Ephesians the abolition of Torah is necessary in order that one new person could be created out of the two peoples, Jew and Gentile. In this way both groups could be reconciled to God in one body, rather than having separate plans of reconciliation for Jews and Gentiles. Ephesians 2:13–18 is not likely a hymn, but rather a theological reflection on the Colossians hymn.

101. Fowl, *The Story of Christ*, 130.

102. Donne, *Complete English Poems*, 313–14.

103. Some of the following material appears in a different form in my article on Pauline Christology in *The Dictionary of Paul and His Letters*.

104. F. F. Bruce, *Commentary on Galatians* (Grand Rapids: Wm. B. Eerdmans, 1982), 195.

105. Two key discussions of this text are B. M. Metzger, "The Punctuation of Rom. 9:5," in *Christ and the Spirit in the New Testament*, ed. B. Lindars and S. S. Smalley (Cambridge: Cambridge University Press, 1973), 95–110; and M. J. Harris, *Jesus as God* (Grand Rapids: Baker Book House, 1992), 143–72.

106. N. Turner, *Grammatical Insights into the New Testament* (Edinburgh: T. & T. Clark, 1965), 15, stresses this: "The text of the N.E.B. simply closes the sentence at 'Messiah' and begins anew with an exclamation. 'May God, supreme above all, be blessed for ever!' So it avoids assigning the quality of godhead to Jesus Christ, but it introduces asyndeton, and there is no grammatical reason why a participle agreeing with 'Messiah' should first be divorced from it and then be given the force of a wish, receiving a different person as its subject. It would in fact be unnatural to divorce it from its antecedent. It is better to follow the margin and read, 'sprang the Messiah, supreme above all, God blessed for ever.' "

107. Metzger, "The Punctuation of Rom. 9:5," in *Christ and the Spirit*, 111–12.

108. Harris, *Jesus as God*, 168.

109. See Wright, *The Climax*, 237.

110. A different version of the next few paragraphs appears in my *Jesus the Sage*, chap. 8.

111. R. Horsley, "Gnosis in Corinth: 1 Corinthians 8:1–6," *New Testament Studies* 27 (1980): 32–51.

112. So Horsley, "Gnosis in Corinth," 37.

113. Cf. my *Jesus the Sage*, ad loc.

114. I agree with Wright, *The Climax*, 124, in his critique of Horsley that Horsley distinguishes too sharply between different sorts of polemic against idols, on the basis of a false dichotomy between Palestinian and Hellenistic Jewish thinking about such matters. This does not negate the fact that he seems to have put his finger on the proper background for understanding the discussion here.

115. Wright, *The Climax*, 129.

116. On Paul not flinching in calling Christ "God," see Wright, *The Climax*, 237–38.

117. Wright, *The Climax*, 131.

118. Contrast Dunn, *Christology in the Making*, 181–82; and J. Murphy-

O'Connor, "I Cor. VIII.6: Cosmology or Soteriology?" *Revue biblique* 85 (1978): 253–67; with Wright, *The Climax*, 131ff.

119. Wright, *The Climax*, 132.

120. See Harris, *Jesus as God*, 45.

121. Yet Paul may also say that it is by the power of the Spirit that Jesus is enabled to be Son of God in power in heaven (Rom. 1:3–4).

122. See my discussion in *Conflict and Community in Corinth*, ad loc.

123. C. K. Barrett, *The Second Epistle to the Corinthians* (New York: Harper & Row, 1973), 123.

124. In *Dictionary of New Testament Theology*, III, ed. C. Brown (Exeter: Pater Noster, 1978), 644–45.

125. C. K. Barrett, *From First Adam to Last* (New York: Charles Scribner's Sons, 1962), 71, is likely right that "the naive adoptionism of 'who was appointed Son of God, according to the Holy Spirit after the resurrection from the dead' was incompatible with Paul's own belief in the incarnation of a pre-existent Son of God; hence Paul's addition of 'in power.' . . . At the resurrection Christ came to be Son of God *in power*, whereas previously (during the ministry) he had been the Son of God in weakness."

126. Cf. C.E.B. Cranfield, *Romans I* (Edinburgh: T. & T. Clark, 1975), 61ff.; C. K. Barrett, *The Epistle to the Romans* (New York: Harper & Brothers, 1957), 18–20; J.D.G. Dunn, *Romans 1–8* (Waco, Tex.: Word, 1988), 13–14.

127. Dunn, *Romans 1–8*, 14.

128. See Cranfield, *Romans I*, 381.

PART 4

The Omega Man

His Identity, Ministry, and Majesty

Five! the finding and sake
And cipher of suffering Christ.
Mark, the mark is of man's make
And the word of it Sacrificed.

But he scores it in scarlet himself on his own bespoken,
before-time-taken, dearest prized and priced—
Stigma, signal, cinquefoil token
For lettering of the lamb's fleece, ruddying of to rose flake.

—*Gerard Manley Hopkins*
"The Wreck of the Deutschland," Part 2.22[1]

ONE of the most remarkable discoveries one makes when studying Paul's narrative thought in light of the Hebrew scriptures is that for Paul the controlling stories and analogies are those of Adam and Abraham, not the later stories of Moses and David, which were in some ways the most crucial for ethnic Israel. Paul has precious little to say about David at all, unless one counts his use of the term "Christ," and even then the echoes of the David story are very faint and infrequent. Likewise, if we did not have 2 Cor. 3—4, there would be very little to say about Moses, unless one wanted to push the Law of Christ concept further than the evidence probably warrants. If we ask why Adam and Abraham are writ large on Paul's thought but Moses comes in for lesser mention and David almost none at all, I suspect the answer lies in the fact that the Apostle to the Gentiles, whether consciously or unconsciously, is trying to ground his own telling of the drama of salvation in the more universal stories, stories that would be more congenial for Gentiles to appropriate, identify with, and in some respects model themselves on. If the faith of Abraham is the model of Christian faith, and one is told that Abraham was given promises about both Gentiles and Jews, the relevance of this to a mixed audience is immediately apparent. Or again, if one is told that Christ is the eschatological Adam, the beginner of a whole new humanity encompassing both Jew and Gentile, none in the audience would be made to feel an outsider, or a second-class citizen, of this Adam's domain. It is in the context of these broader and more inclusive stories that Paul reads the story of Moses, David, and other Jews. What Paul will say about Moses must fit into the framework linking Abraham and Christ, faith and Christians. This must be kept steadily in view when we consider Paul's use of the term "Christ."

10

The Christ

God's Anointed
and Appointed One

IN order to begin to examine what Paul meant when he called Jesus Messiah, Son of David, eschatological Adam, a human being, we must remind ourselves that Rom. 1:3–4 says, "In the sphere of the flesh," Jesus is "born of the seed of David."[2] The phrase in itself indicates not only Jesus' Jewishness and humanness, but also in fact his proper ancestry and thus his fulfilling one prerequisite for being Messiah/Christ. There may be here a secondary stress on his royalness. Only at Rom. 15:12 do we get any other stress on this fact by Paul, and it is likely that in both places he is quoting sources. Mentioning this here at Rom. 1:3 is probably the natural sequel to Rom. 1:2—Jesus is the fulfillment of Old Testament prophecy. He is the promised and prophesied Messiah. Thus his story is immediately grounded at the beginning of Romans in the story of Israel and in the Hebrew scriptures, a singularly important point in view of what follows in Rom. 9—11.[3] Paul is in the extraordinary position of having to stress Jesus' Jewishness and the general blessing and benefits of being a Jew to a largely Gentile audience (11:13) without compromising the more universal stories in the light of which he is convinced one needs to understand Christ. Not even in Rom. 11:25–26 does he revert to a more ethnic or nationalistic approach to Israel; all must relate to God and God's promises on the basis of unmerited justifying grace and faith.

It is well to bear in mind that for the Jews, Messiah was a term generally referring to a human being, not a God, even if he had certain "divine" gifts or endorsements.[4] It is thus appropriate to stress Jesus' humanity born of David's seed, in a context where messiahship is mentioned. One of the great difficulties, however, in dealing with Paul's idea of Jesus as Christ or Messiah is that so often Paul simply uses the term "Christ" as a part of the name of Jesus without any particular messianic significance. In such cases it is just a way of distinguishing this particular Jesus from others. On the other hand, Paul is well aware of the larger significance of the term *Christos/Mashiach.* In 2 Cor. 1:21 we find this play on words: "God establishes us in Christ (*eis Christon*) and anoints us (*chrisas*)." Yet, strikingly, Paul rarely speaks of *the* Christ, but rather simply Jesus Christ, or sometimes Christ Jesus, or even the Lord Jesus Christ.[5] This strongly suggests that already before Paul wrote his letters the term "Christ" was used widely in early Christianity as part of the name of Jesus. Were this not the case, we would expect Paul to explain to his audience(s) what the term meant.

Careful study of the Jewish and Greek background[6] does not explain the extraordinary frequency and way[7] in which Paul uses the term *Christos.*[8] The term *Christos* is used by Paul 270 out of a total of 531 uses in the New Testament, mainly as a name for Jesus rather than as a title or descriptive term. This is especially remarkable, because Paul was mainly writing to Gentiles who may or may not have been familiar with the Jewish background for this term.

I would suggest that Paul's usage is best explained by the fact that Paul received a tradition associating the term "Christ" with the core of the early Christian message, that is, the narrative about the death and resurrection of Jesus (1 Cor. 15:3).[9] This received tradition coupled with the singular experience Paul had of Christ on Damascus road go far in explaining the distinctive ideas the apostle associates with being the Christ.

There is, however, no clear explanation or rationale for the particular permutations and combinations that we find in Paul's letters where he juxtaposes "Christ" with various other names and titles. *Christos* most often seems to appear where Christ's death, resurrection, and return are under discussion. The *en Christo* formula in many ways best encapsulates Paul's view of the condition and position of Christians—they are "in Christ." It is thus one key to a proper reading of Paul's telling of the salvation story, and so we must examine it in some detail.

Though Jesus is called *Christos* as a virtual second name by Paul, he has not lost sight of the fact that *Christos* was likely originally a title.[10] This is shown by the creative wordplay in 2 Cor. 1:21; also, Paul never juxtaposes "Lord" with *Christos* alone, for this would amount to awkwardly combining two titles.[11] Moreover, Paul never adds a genitive to the term *Christos* (as one does find in early Judaism, e.g., the Anointed of the Lord). In fact, he does not use the term in any sort of possessive expression (e.g., God's Christ). *Christos* is also never used as a simple predicate in the Pauline letters. Furthermore, Paul never feels it necessary to state the formula "Jesus is the Christ," nor does he argue for the idea. On the other hand, he among others was a conveyor of that earliest of Christian confessions "Jesus (or Jesus Christ) is Lord." This strongly suggests that the messiahship of Jesus was not under debate in the Pauline communities, and Paul himself takes it as a presupposition for all other confessions. He does not, for example, try to demonstrate by proof texts the messiahship of Jesus in his letters. "[Paul] makes no attempt to prove that Jesus really is 'the Christ' despite his suffering and death. 'Christ' is no longer a title whose fitness in its application to Jesus has to be demonstrated. The belief in Jesus as the Christ has become so firmly established in his mind and message that he simply takes it for granted, and 'Christ' functions simply as a way of speaking of Jesus, as a *proper name* for Jesus (so even in 1 Cor. 15:3)."[12]

One of the most important ways Paul uses the term *Christos* is in a daring phrase meant to characterize his preaching—"Christ crucified" (1 Cor. 1:23). The phrase must have had some shock value for Jewish listeners, for there is no real evidence that early Jews expected a crucified Messiah. Crucifixion was a punishment reserved for the worst criminals and revolutionaries, and seems to have been understood by early Jews as a sign that the crucified person was cursed by God, on the basis of a certain understanding of Deut. 21:23 (cf. Gal. 3:13). There is no evidence that Isaiah 53 was ever applied to the Messiah before Jesus' day.[13]

Careful scrutiny of the way and places in which Paul uses the term "Christ" suggests that in the main what Paul means by "Christ" he has *not* derived from early Jewish ideas about God's anointed, but rather from traditions about the conclusion of Jesus' life and its sequel, coupled with Paul's own Damascus road experience.[14] These events have forced Paul to rethink what it meant for someone to be the Davidic Messiah.[15] Because the term *Christos* is used by Paul to refer to someone who died on the cross and rose from the dead, this has greatly transformed what is meant by the term. *Christos* brings redemption to his people by dying, rising, and assuming, at the right hand of God, authority and power over all the principalities. He does *not* bring redemption by throwing off the yoke of Roman rule during his earthly ministry. In short, Paul has something rather different in mind than what we find in such texts as *Pss. Sol.* 17—18, where Messiah is seen as a conquering hero throwing off the yoke of a foreign rule. Yet it is not completely true to say, as W. Grundmann does, that "the understanding of the Messiah loses its national, political, and religious significance and the significance of the Messiah in human history is attested and expounded. This is the distinctive theological achievement of Paul."[16] Very clearly, in Rom. 15:8 Paul recounts the fact that Christ became a servant to the circumcision, and Paul holds out the hope of the salvation of many Jews at the eschaton (Rom. 11:25–26). Christ is now a savior to the Gentiles through his ministers and apostles like Paul (cf. Rom. 15:16–18), but this does not nullify the significance in Paul's mind of Christ's prior mission and service to Jews. Indeed, Paul insists to his largely Gentile audience that salvation is from and for the Jew first and also the Gentile (Rom. 1:16).

Paul is well aware of early Jewish ideas about Messiah being a Jew born under the law (cf. Gal. 4:4) with Davidic ancestry (cf. Rom. 1:3), and he is happy to affirm these characteristics of Jesus. There are also various places where Paul refers to the fully human character of the *Christos* he believes in (Rom. 5:17–19; Phil. 2:7; Rom. 8:3). He is doubtless also aware that early Jews by and large did not think of Messiah as some sort of superhuman figure, but rather as an exemplary human being especially anointed with God's Spirit.[17] Yet here too Paul goes beyond the views of the majority of his Jewish contemporaries about the Davidic Messiah, for the most natural way to read the grammatically difficult phrase in Rom. 9:5 is "comes the Christ who is over all God blessed forever."[18] This suggests that Paul saw the Christ as not only assuming divine functions in heaven but in some sense properly being called God. Here we have a very clear example of Paul speaking of *the* Christ, which once more indicates he clearly understands the larger significance of the term.

The use Paul makes of the term *Christos* in his salutations also points to an exalted view of Jesus. Thus, for instance in Phil. 1:2, grace and peace are said to come not just from God the Father but also from the Lord Jesus Christ. "The position here occupied by Jesus in relation to God, as well as in many other opening formulae of the New Testament letters, is nothing short of astounding—especially when one considers that they are written by monotheistic Jews with reference to a figure of recently past history."[19] Here Jesus Christ is seen as one who dispenses what only God can truly give—shalom.

A possible clue to why Paul so persistently uses the term *Christos*—and occasionally gives hints that it was originally a title—rather than, for instance, using *Soter* (savior) to refer to Jesus is found in Rom. 1:16. Though Paul is the apostle to the Gentiles, he wants to continue to affirm to his audience, and even stress, that salvation is from the Jews and for the Jews before it is for others. One way of doing this is to continue to juxtapose the two terms *Iesous Christos*. Paul, as a Jew, wants it never forgotten that Jesus, who is savior of the world, is such only as the Jewish *Mashiach*—the *Christos*. Thus it may be that for Paul the use of the term *Christos* as a virtual name for Jesus and also the way he refrains from using the term are not merely matters of habit but attempts by Paul to provide a reminder to an increasingly Gentile church of the Jewish source and character of salvation and of the savior. Yet it is also clear enough that Paul was willing to modify the earlier Jewish stories about Messiah, sometimes radically.

It cannot be stressed strongly enough that early Christians, including Paul, saw no contradiction in affirming Jesus as crucified *and* Jesus as the anointed one or Messiah/Christ in the same breath. Indeed, when Paul characterizes his preaching he sees its essence as the preaching of "Christ crucified" (1 Cor. 1:23), and he categorizes Jesus' "cross" as "the cross of Christ" (1:17). It is striking that he does not feel he has to defend the use of such paradoxical phrases as this.

The story of Jesus (i.e., his death) is one factor causing a rethinking of what it meant to be the Davidic Messiah. To judge from Paul's lack of polemics on the subject, all this appears to have happened at least before he began to write letters, perhaps even before his conversion. It is clear that Paul intends to indicate Jesus' uniqueness by the term "Christ"—he is the anointed one, the Messiah of the Jews and the world. Paul still sees "Christ" as a term of honor and dignity. Paul frequently refers to the gospel (or preaching) of Christ, by which is meant the Good News about Christ as God's anointed and appointed one. Galatians 3:13 reveals that Paul did not shy away from the idea that dying on the cross was seen as a sign of God's curse. He simply asserted that Christ as Messiah bore that curse for us and in our place (Phil. 3:18). Furthermore, because Jesus is seen as a suffering Messiah, he could also be seen as an atoning Messiah or ransoming Messiah (cf. 1 Cor. 6:20; 7:23; Gal. 3:13; 4:5). He is even the Paschal Lamb (1 Cor. 5:7). In a sense then, 2 Cor. 5:19 is a summary of how Paul viewed Jesus as the Christ, especially when he says, "God was in Christ reconciling the world to himself, not imputing their trespasses to them." Being Christ, then, is being Mediator, Reconciler, and Savior from sins.

This is a different vision of Messiah than what one finds in various other early Jewish sources such as the Talmuds and Targums. The Messiah was indeed regarded as God's anointed one in these sources, the one who was to usher in the messianic kingdom, but this was to be a penultimate state of affairs prior to the end of history, the resurrection, and the final judgment. As one viewed the kingdom, so one viewed the king, and there was a variety of expectations about the nature of that kingdom. Obviously, for Paul the resurrection of Jesus begins, not ends, the kingdom's coming in power. Paul may also enunciate a millennial view (1 Corinthians 15), but we cannot be sure of this. Some early Jewish teachers believed that the Messiah's coming would be prepared for by conversion and obedience to the Law; it would not precipitate such conditions. The messianic kingdom is often viewed as a political and material one involving a reestablishing of

Israel's Solomonic borders, a time of fruitfulness in the land and peace. Jerusalem would be rebuilt more beautifully; human life would grow longer.[20]

Paul and early Christianity transformed the concept of Messiah when they saw it in light of the historical Jesus' death. It was never just a matter of retelling any of the Jewish stories about the Messiah and claiming that Jesus should be seen as the Anointed One in those stories. A transformation of the Jewish narratives was necessary, and was undertaken in light of Christian traditions about the end of Jesus' career and about Wisdom, to mention but two catalysts for generating a whole new narrative.

The term *Christos*, if studied in the context of its varied uses in the Pauline corpus, reveals how the apostle draws on, amplifies, transforms, and transcends some early Jewish ideas about the Messiah. For Paul, the content of the term *Christos* is mainly derived from the Christ event and his experience of that event. This leads to three elements in his preaching about Christ that are without clear precedent in early Judaism: (1) Messiah is called God; (2) Messiah is said to have been crucified, and his death is seen as redemptive; (3) Messiah is expected to come to earth again. Non-Christian Jews apparently did not speak of a crucified Messiah,[21] much less of a *Second* Coming of Messiah. Nor do I know of any evidence that early Jews were willing to call the Messiah one in whom the fullness of deity dwells.

It is probably due to careful reflection on some of the three elements listed above that Paul comes to use the phrase *en Christo* ("in Christ") as he does. *En Christo* is without question one of Paul's favorite phrases, appearing 164 times in the earlier Paulines and another half-dozen in the form "in Jesus Christ" in the Pastorals. This total is especially remarkable in view of the fact that other New Testament writers hardly ever use the phrase (but cf., e.g., 1 Peter 3:16, 5:10, 14). Paul never uses the term "Christian," that is, *Christianos*, rather, *en Christo* seems to be his substitute for this noun (cf. 1 Cor. 3:1).

At other points the phrase *en Christo* seems to have a more pregnant sense, indicating the environment, or atmosphere, in which Christians live; that is, they are "in Christ." A good example of this usage is found in 2 Cor. 5:17: "If anyone is in Christ, she or he (or there) is a new creation" (cf. Phil. 3:8–9). In fact, whole congregations can be said to be "in Christ" in the same way they are said to be "in God" (cf. Gal. 1:22; Phil. 1:1; with 1 Thess. 1:1). There are a variety of other passages that seem to have a locative sense (1 Thess. 4:16; Gal. 2:17; 1 Cor. 1:2; 15:18). Paul does speak of Christ being in the believer (Gal. 2:20; Rom. 8:10), but this is not nearly so characteristic of the apostle as the phrase *en Christo*. It does not seem possible either to argue that Paul is simply using the language of exchange or to eliminate completely the locative sense of *en Christo* in various instances. Nor can these texts simply be explained as another way of saying one belongs to Christ or that things are accomplished for the believer through Christ. Rather, for Paul both logically and theologically the concept of being *en Christo* is central. One cannot do something *for* or *with* Christ unless one is first *en Christo.* One cannot approach the Father through the Son unless one is *en Christo.* The effects of being in Christ involve nothing less than human spiritual transformation by means of death to sin, possession of the Spirit, being made a new creation or creature, having one's inner person and mind renewed, being given both hope and assurance of one's own bodily resurrection like unto Christ's, and being united spiritually with a great host of other believers in a living entity Paul likens to a body and calls "the Christian community" (*ekklesia*).

The christological implications of this sort of use of *en Christo* have been ably summed up by C.F.D. Moule: "If it is really true that Paul thought of himself and other Christians as 'included' or 'located' in Christ; . . . it indicates a more than individualistic conception of the person of Christ. . . . [A] plurality of persons can find themselves 'in Christ,' as limbs are in the body."[22] This means that Paul conceives of the exalted Christ in heaven as a divine being who has some sort of omnipresence and in whom one can dwell. Thus in the end, for Paul the story of Christ must be exegeted not merely in the context of the story of Israel or Israel's Davidic anointed one, but in the context of the story of God.

11

A Human Being and the Eschatological Adam

TRULY HUMAN

IF Paul had no difficulties associating Jesus with the term "Christ," and Jesus was a human being who died, how did Paul look at Jesus' humanity in general? What Paul has to say on this subject is in fact very little, and it can be summed up in a few short phrases. There is enough to suggest that Paul saw Jesus as fully human, but there is not enough to tell us much of what Paul thought about that humanity. This may be because Paul is writing to those who have already accepted the earthly Jesus and his ministry, and did not need to hear it all over again. It probably also reflects where Paul places the emphasis in his own writing—on matters that begin with Jesus' death and resurrection and go forward from there in time to life in the Spirit and in the church. Paul is a preacher of salvation, and it appears he believed that believers would still have been saved if Jesus had never raised Lazarus, or told the parable of the sower, or walked on water. It is his living in flesh, dying, and rising that is of pure theological weight for Paul. Even when Paul uses Jesus as a pattern or example of Christian behavior, Paul usually talks about believers dying to sin and rising to new life, or reckoning themselves dead to sin, or acting self-sacrificially as Christ did when he came to earth and when he died. Paul seldom holds up the life of Christ *after* his coming to earth and *prior* to his passion as an ethical example, though he does draw on Jesus' ethical teaching for this purpose. Even when there is a certain amount of exhortation to be humble or loving like Christ, Christ's death is always the prime example of being humble. All the above explains the paucity of what follows.

138

✓ Humanly speaking, Jesus was born of woman (Gal. 4:4), a phrase that does not distinguish Jesus from other human beings. As Bruce points out, ✓ Paul's wording is applicable to anyone born of a woman.[23] The text implies nothing special about Jesus' manner of birth. Nor, for that matter, do the Gospels. Matthew 1 and Luke 2 imply and state something miraculous about the means of Mary's conceiving Jesus, and so we ought to talk about the virginal conception, *not* the virgin birth. Paul does not mention the virginal conception here or elsewhere, and many scholars have taken this to mean Paul did not know of such an idea. Thus they conclude that such an idea arose later.[24] It must be said that this is probably reading too much into Paul's silence.

There may even be a hint of Paul's knowledge of such an idea in his use of the phrase "sending his own Son in the *likeness* of sinful flesh" (Rom. 8:3). This verse is carefully worded. It says that Jesus condemned sin in the flesh; that is, he took on flesh to do so. Any sort of docetism must be ruled out. Jesus was real flesh and blood. But v. 3a is probably worded as it is to indicate that Jesus did not participate in the sinfulness of human flesh. Barrett cautiously puts it this way:

> Paul certainly does not mean that Christ was sinful like the rest of [hu]mankind (2 Cor. 5:21), or that he was a man only in appearance—his insistence upon the Cross as a real event makes it impossible to think that he believed in a docetic Christ. One possible suggestion is that Paul distinguished between flesh as it was created by God, and "flesh of sin," that is, flesh which had fallen under the dominion of sin. Christ (on this view) had perfect, unfallen flesh, which nevertheless was indistinguishable in appearance from "flesh of sin"; he came in flesh, so that the incarnation was perfectly real, but only *in the likeness* of "flesh of sin," so that he remained sinless.[25]

But Barrett thinks it doubtful that this is what Paul means; he goes on to suggest that Christ took on precisely the same fallen nature as all humans have had since Adam and Eve.[26] There are several problems with this reading of Paul's thought. First, Dunn is right that the language here seems to allude to Christ as a figure like Adam—but in what regard?[27] I would suggest that the very reason the word "likeness" (*homoioma*) is used here is intentionally to avoid simply saying he came in sinful flesh.

It must appear strange that he would go on in this same epistle and elsewhere to suggest that Jesus is a new Adam, starting a new creation, if in fact he was merely participating in the fallen nature of the old Adam. There is little doubt from Romans that Paul believed in the concept of a sinful nature inherent in all fallen humans that places all such people in bondage to sin (Rom. 5:12ff.; Romans 7). But Paul surely does not want to portray Christ as being like Adam or the Adamic descendants described in Romans 7.[28] Indeed, in the very next verse after Rom. 8:3 he goes on to stress that this Jesus, who came in the likeness of sinful flesh, was presented as a "sin offering." One must remember that a sin offering, to be an atoning sacrifice, must have unblemished and spotless flesh.[29] The juxtaposition of Rom. 8:3 with 8:4 makes it very likely that Paul is implying that like Adam, Jesus was born with an unfallen nature, though one that had the capacity to sin; but *unlike* Adam, Jesus remained sinless and so could be an unblemished sacrifice for sin. Thus Paul uses the term "likeness of sinful flesh" not to deny Jesus' sinlessness in regard to his behavior (cf. 2 Cor. 5:21), nor to deny his sinless human nature, but to affirm that he was in the flesh and was in this respect like all other human beings, "save without sin" (cf. Heb. 4:15, 2:17). The eschatological Adam starts humanity over again without blemish.[30] A further confirmation of this interpretation can be found in Phil. 2:7–8, where we are told Christ is born in the likeness of human beings. This is intended to tell us that Jesus took on human flesh, being a man who was subject to human frailty and weakness, even death. Romans 8:3 is not suggesting anything significantly different from Phil. 2:7–8.

A second fact about Jesus as a human being that Paul mentions in passing is that he was born under the Law (Gal. 4:4). This means his mother was a Jew and so was he. Galatians 4:5a may suggest that Paul saw Jesus' earthly ministry as essentially one to Israel; he came to redeem those who were under the Law. Because Paul is apostle to the Gentiles, this could explain in part why he says so little about Jesus' earthly ministry; that is, it was directed to the lost sheep that made up Israel, and when they did not respond a new door was opened to go to the Gentiles (cf. Rom. 9—11). Paul then, as an apostle writing to these Gentiles, might not have a lot of reason—in view of the new situation for God's people since Jesus' death and the expansion of the ministry of Jesus beyond a Jewish context—to refer back to that earlier stage in redemption history. What applied to the Jews then does not fully apply since the death and resurrection of Jesus. If Paul believed Christ's death and resurrection really did change things for the Gentiles, then it is not surprising that he only deals with those Christ events that affected and involved the Gentiles.

This is not to say that Paul does not draw on Jesus' sayings in various ways and apply them in new situations, but he is notably silent about Jesus' deeds and ministry prior to his death. I suspect this is because Paul's ministry is largely directed to a different audience, and Paul believes he must do what is appropriate in view of the point in the eschatological timetable in which he is now ministering.

There is little else we can say from Paul's letters about the earthly Jesus except on aspects of the passion narrative. The Last Supper is referred to

(1 Cor. 11:23) and indicates that Jesus was a person who broke bread, who poured wine, who gave thanks, and thus was human like us, needing to thank the heavenly Father for such earthly gifts. Paul does not say Jesus ate at the Last Supper, but that is certainly implied. Apart from the references to Jesus' death and burial, indicating he was truly dead and resurrected (1 Cor. 15:4), there is little else to say.

ADAM WITH A DIFFERENCE

Another line of inquiry may be to pursue the whole question of what is meant by calling Jesus the last Adam. Paul does not call Jesus the Son of Man; indeed, no one does in any of the New Testament epistles. This is likely because this title had such a Jewish background and could so easily be assumed to mean simply that Jesus was a real human being, that as a title it was seen as too obscure or too simple for the Gentile mission and the expanding church.[31] Whatever the reason for this phenomenon, Paul certainly does use the Adam typology of Jesus and at 1 Cor. 15:45 calls Jesus the last or eschatological Adam. J. Jeremias also stressed that Paul avoids using the term "son of man" because he addresses a largely Gentile audience. However, he goes on to show how Paul appears to know of the "son of man" tradition, because at 1 Cor. 15:27 we have a messianic application of Psalm 8 to Jesus, and this psalm is well known for the line that precedes the part Paul is quoting: "or the son of man that thou shouldst care" (v. 4).[32] In preparation for examining Paul's typological comparison between the first Adam and the eschatological one, there are certain references, which speak of Jesus as the man, that need to be examined.

At Rom. 5:15, in the midst of the Adam-Christ typology Paul says that just as death came by one human (Adam), so God's grace and the gift that went along with it (righteousness, v. 17) came by one human (Jesus). Again, at 1 Cor. 15:21 death comes through a man (Adam), and the resurrection of the dead comes through a man (Jesus).[33] What is the point of saying that salvation comes to humankind, as does resurrection and reconciliation, by a human being? Sin was a human problem that was resolved only by a human being. Perhaps our tendency may be to think of salvation coming to humankind because of Jesus as a divine one, but Paul wants to assert just the opposite. If Jesus had not been a human being, humans would not have had redemption, resurrection, reconciliation. This is especially so because only human beings can die and rise again. Paul seems to think that Jesus as divine, or God, was not subject to, nor could he be subject to, death.[34] He had to stand on both sides of the fence in order to experience and fully know both the God who grieves over sin and the sinner who causes God grief. In short, for salvation to reach and to redeem humankind, it had to take the form of a human being. This is an extremely important point for Paul. It meant for him that Christ must be situated not merely in the story of God, but also in the story of the human race, in particular in the story of Adam and, as we have already stressed in the story of the father of all who have faith, Abraham.[35]

Let us examine first the 1 Corinthians 15 material, in particular vv. 21–23, 44–49. This passage is quite unlike the Adam reference we find in the later Paulines (e.g., 1 Tim. 2:13–14). There Adam is first in creation but not first in sin, and the point there is an appeal to the creation order to prevent the Christian community from reflecting disorder or some kind of order antithetical to God's creation plan. Here by contrast we have the blame for sin and its consequences placed squarely on Adam's shoulders, and Eve is not mentioned.

There are both similarities and differences between Adam, the type, and Christ, the antitype. Both are truly human; both are representative heads of humankind, and both have a dramatic effect on those who come forth from them. However, in some ways the differences outweigh the similarities. The powerful effect of Adam's action on all humanity was death (v. 21), but the powerful effect of Christ's action was life (in the specific form of the resurrection of the dead).

The question may be raised, Is the parallelism in 1 Cor. 15:22 a perfect one? "In Adam all die." Does then the "all" in v. 22b mean that all humans will one day be made alive in Christ? First Thessalonians 4:16 shows that elsewhere when Paul talks about resurrection he means resurrection of the dead in Christ. This is likely also meant in 1 Cor. 15:22. In fact, v. 23 makes this interpretation all but certain, because it speaks of the resurrection of those "who belong to Christ." Thus the parallelism of vv. 22a and 22b is not perfect.

In order to understand the Adam-Christ typology, one must bear in mind several things. First is the idea of collective personality, or at least federal headship. It appears that Paul thinks that in a sense all persons were "in Adam"; he was humankind and sinned for us, and we died in him. Unless you understand the idea of collective personality, this will make little sense. Second, salvation comes only in Christ. One must be in Christ to benefit. Believers died and were raised in Christ. If one thinks the idea of federal headship is more to the fore here, this would mean Christ as head of a new humanity did deeds that shaped his own thereafter. He died in the believers' place as their representative, just as Adam sinned in their place and for them.[36]

Jeremias provides us with the following chart in regard to vv. 44–49.[37]

| v. 45 | The first Adam, a living being. | The last Adam, a life-giving spirit. |
| vv. 47–48 | The first person from the earth, earthly. | The second person from heaven, heavenly. |

Jesus here is called the last, or eschatological, Adam. All of what Paul says here has an eschatological flavor. In a sense, Jesus is starting a new creation, being firstfruits of the dead. But in another sense he is the end and goal of the whole human race. There will be no more founders of humanity after him. He is bringing in the last age, the new creation, the end of God's plan. Further, Jesus is the *second human being*. Obviously, this is only in the representative sense.[38] He is the second start and starter of the human race.

We must also note the differences here. Adam was strictly an earth creature. He came from the earth, he returned to the earth, and his body and life were natural and physical. Insofar as humans are his descendants, they are earthly, physical, contingent, and have a natural life principle in their bodies. Jesus, on the other hand, was heavenly and of heaven.[39] There was something unearthly about him; he was also a life-giving spirit.

Several implications come out of this discussion: (1) Jesus is not merely living, like Adam; he is life-giving, whereas Adam gave humanity death. (2) When Paul calls Jesus a life-giving spirit, he does not mean to imply Jesus had or has no body, but that he lived in a form of life characterized by the Spirit. (3) Obviously, v. 45 is a quotation from Gen. 2:7, except that Paul has added the word "first" and the word "Adam." The Hebrew does not mean Adam gained a "soul," but that God animated his body with a natural life principle; thus he became a living body, a living being. *Psuche* here and elsewhere in Paul, like *nephesh* in the Hebrew, means "being" (Adam was a living being), not the Greek idea of a soul. (4) When Paul uses the term "spiritual body," he does not mean a body made out of nonmaterial substance, but a body empowered by the Spirit.[40] Jesus did not become a life-giving Spirit until after he rose, and the life he gave was eternal life, unlike the life Adam gave. Further, it was given to the believer by the Spirit—in part now, in full later.

It is not impossible that Paul got some of these ideas from Jewish speculation about Adam and the coming Messiah. Philo saw Genesis 1 as discussing an ideal being, a Platonic type, whereas in Genesis 2 Philo talks about Adam in the same way Paul does (*Leg. All.* 1:31; *Conf.* 41, 62–63, 146–147). Yet in Paul's thought, it is not the first man, but the last one who is the ideal or true model, or at least the true representative of the race.[41] Further, we never find the redeemer described in rabbinic literature as the last Adam.[42] Thus Paul has reflected on the Christian gospel and has modified any previous ideas he may have had in light of the story of the historical Christ and his death and resurrection and their effects.

Rom. 5:12ff. can now be considered. At v. 12 we are told that not only sin, but death, entered the world through Adam. Death came through or because of sin. Paul likely accepted Gen. 1—3 as a straightforward account of historical events, but that is not the focus here. His concern is with the story's theological significance. Whatever humans may inherit from Adam and whatever effect his sin may have on them, there is a real sense in which human beings dig their own grave. It is implied that if humans lived without sin, they would not die, or at least the converse is true—death came to all humanity because all sinned. Thus God did not unjustly punish any with death. Nonetheless, it is true that none would be dying if Adam had not sinned in the first place. So Paul can also add in v. 15: "Many died by the trespasses of the one man."

It is also important that in v. 14 Paul says that Adam is a "type" of *ho mellon*. Should this be translated straightforwardly as a virtual equivalent of *ho erchomenos*—"the Coming One"?[43] Or is he looking at things from the time frame of the first Adam, and so in fact "from his own time" means "the one who *was* to Come" (so NRSV)? Barrett believes that Paul is thinking of the whole career of Christ, including his future coming at the Parousia.[44]

Yet surely, when Paul draws an analogy between Adam and Christ he is *mainly* thinking not of the preexistent Son, nor even of the Son born of a woman, nor of the Christ yet to come. Rather, he is thinking of the events that allowed Christ to become a life-giving spirit or, as Paul says in Romans 5, allowed Christ to offer the free gift of right-standing with God. Romans 5:19 pinpoints the matter rather precisely; Adam's disobedience at the tree in Eden is countered by Christ's act of obedience on the tree at Calvary.[45] In 1 Corinthians 15 the focus is on the event that made it possible for Christ to become a life-giving spirit, namely, the resurrection.

It is thus primarily, perhaps almost exclusively, because of the death and resurrection that Paul came to draw an analogy between the first Adam and the eschatological one. As Dunn stresses, Paul is not interested in some sort of urMensch mythology or Platonic prototype like Philo, nor is the focus in the Adamic analogy on the Christ yet to come at the Parousia. Christ is the eschatological Adam because of what happened in the death and resurrection.[46] Only so could he become the founder of a new humanity, the conveyor of resurrection to all those in Christ.[47]

Through Adam's sin death reigned (Rom. 5:17), but Paul stresses that God's antidote is not merely an equal and opposite reaction. It goes above and beyond in a positive direction what Adam's mistake did in a negative one. Thus Paul can say that the gift is not like the trespass (v. 15); and what is implied is that salvation is not just paradise regained. If one trespass could affect so much and so many, how much more of an effect did the overflowing grace and gift of righteousness have for believers (v. 15)? Again, the death penalty followed just one sin, but God's grace came after many sins; and quite apart from what anyone deserved, it brought right-standing with God. Verse 17 implies that the life believers have in Christ is not merely more powerful than the death Adam bequested to all; it is of a wholly different order. As 1 Corinthians 15 makes clear, it comes from the spirit and heaven, and as such it goes beyond natural life and triumphs over natural death. Romans 5:19 goes on to point out that Christ's obedience even unto death (his righteous conduct and sinlessness) made possible the undoing of all that was caused by the first Adam's disobedience.

> The important thing here is to remember that vv. 15–17 have specially stressed the vast superiority of Christ to Adam, and made it abundantly clear that Adam's sin and Christ's obedience are not on an equal footing and that there is no equilibrium between their respective consequences. [Judgment] does indeed result for all . . . from Adam's sin, but this is no absolutely irreversible, eternal fact: on the contrary, Christ has in fact already begun the process of its reversal.[48]

imputed dress

Romans 5:19b has often been understood to mean "put into a right relationship with God," and in this sense "make righteous."[49] This argument is not entirely satisfactory in view of what follows in Rom. 7:14–25, where Paul does indeed say that a person "in Adam" does involuntarily sin. This leads one to wonder if "made righteous" does not also mean more than just "given right relationship with God," for only something imparted to a fallen person could change his or her nature so that he or she might do what God requires of him or her. We will have opportunity to say more on this in the last part of this study.

A few final thoughts about the so-called Adam Christology are in order. Paul sees Christ as Adam's antitype even before he became the eschatological Adam at his resurrection from the dead, at which point he became the firstfruits and firstborn of the many included in the new humanity. Adam's death was punishment for sin, but Christ's death was in obedience to God. Christ willingly accepted the consequences of Adam's sin (i.e., death), which is probably what "obedience" means in Rom. 5:19b, as in Phil. 2:8. Jesus was what Adam was not—an obedient, hence righteous, child of God. As a human being there is a certain sense in which one can say Jesus followed in the footsteps of Adam, yet refused to fall and fail, and so began a new humanity. He even died like Adam, enduring the punishment due all humanity for sin; yet his death, rather than inaugurating a curse, absorbed and reversed it. Because of the obedient path that Jesus followed even unto death as "the one man Jesus Christ" (Rom. 5:17c), God highly exalted him (Phil. 2:8–9), not merely raising him, but in effect placing him in a position so that as Lord he could do what only God can do, give life to the dead, be a life-giving spirit. For Paul, then, there is a sphere in which the story of Adam no longer has the first and last word on humanity, that sphere is "in Christ," who in Paul's thought is the Omega man, the eschatological Adam, God's final Word to and about humanity.

12

The *Koinonia* of Jesus and Paul

IT is precisely because, as Paul himself claims, his gospel is one that in its essentials came to him not from human beings but from a revelation of Jesus himself, that we have difficulties assessing Paul's relationship to and knowledge of the words and deeds of Jesus during his earthly ministry. In all honesty, we must recognize that Paul's letters are not loaded with quotations from or allusions to the Jesus tradition, though they are not so scarce as many might lead one to believe. This has led some scholars, such as R. Bultmann, to conclude that Paul was not really interested in the historical Jesus and his claims, but rather only in the risen Christ. In now famous words, he argues: "Paul's theology proper . . . is not at all a recapitulation of Jesus' own preaching, nor a further development of it, and it is especially significant that he never addresses any of the sayings of Jesus on the Torah in favor of his own teaching about Torah. . . . [I]n relation to the preaching of Jesus, the theology of Paul is a new structure."[50] Elsewhere Bultmann argues: "The historical Jesus plays no role or practically none in Paul."[51] It is precisely this sort of assessment that has led so many to see Paul as the first great corrupter or distorter of Christianity. This in turn has led to a movement in the church that might be called "back to Jesus," with the clear implication "away from and away with Paul"! But there is an alternative and more satisfactory way of explaining the relative paucity of Jesus material found in Paul's letters. Bultmann's influential criticism is mitigated, if not vitiated, in five ways: (1) by considering where in the story of salvation history Paul locates himself and Jesus; (2) by recognizing that they shared a common eschatological outlook; (3) by noting that Paul's letters are addressed to those who are already Christians, and thus they likely do not contain much of the material that Paul would have preached to these people if they were not yet Christians; (4) by recognizing that in fact Paul *does* at various points rely on the Jesus material, both quoting from and alluding to it; (5) by recognizing that there is a profound agreement between the essence of Paul's theology, even the theology that he received by revelation, and various parts of the Jesus material especially the parables.

"TIMING IS EVERYTHING"

One of the most important observations a student of history can ever make is that when and why and to whom something is said makes all the difference in the world in how one ought to assess that pronouncement. It needs to be said, therefore, that all of Jesus' teaching and all the deeds of his earthly ministry preceded the watershed events in salvation history, Jesus' death and resurrection, whereas everything that Paul said and did as a Christian took place after Jesus' death and resurrection. Paul looked back on those events as the turning point in the battle against sin and evil. It is thus not all that surprising that Paul's perspective on Jesus and his ministry includes and benefits from the fact that Paul knew how things turned out. Paul also knew about the ensuing developments, including the beginnings of the church and its spread over all the Mediterranean; whereas Jesus, if he alluded to such things at all, could only look forward to such happenings. The time element necessitates a difference in perspective. For Jesus, the kingdom is just coming, just at hand in his person and ministry. For Paul, the kingdom is not merely near or at hand, but here, especially because Jesus' death and resurrection were past facts for him. There is a difference between Jesus' "repent, for the kingdom of God is at hand" (Mark 1:15) and Paul's "now is the favorable time" (2 Cor. 6:2). The difference is not one of kind, but of time. In Jesus and his ministry, the kingdom, the eschatological age, was dawning; by Paul's day it would be looked back on as something that had already in part happened—the kingdom had dawned. No fair estimate of the relation of Paul's and Jesus' thought should leave this out of account.

A SHARED ESCHATOLOGICAL OUTLOOK

Second, there is the matter that Paul and Jesus shared a common eschatological outlook in general. I have argued this case at great length elsewhere, and here I only summarize the results. In regard to the character of the dominion of God both in the present and the future, Jesus and Paul seem to stand together. It is present partially and in individual lives now; it

will be present as something that can be entered or inherited later. Both
Jesus and Paul affirm the death and vindication beyond death of the Christ.
Both affirm the future gathering and resurrection of "the righteous," or
the believers. Both affirm the future final judgment and the dispatching of
evil. Both envision some sort of final messianic banquet, or *koinonia*, of all
believers with their Redeemer when the dominion of God finally comes in
fullness.[52]

A. Schweitzer, despite misreading Paul and Jesus in many regards, is
right when he says, "Paul shares with Jesus the eschatological worldview
and the eschatological expectation which all these imply. The only
difference is the hour in the world clock in the two cases. To use another
figure, both are looking toward the same mountain range, but whereas
Jesus sees it as lying before him, Paul already stands upon it, and its first
slopes are already behind him."[53]

By eschatological outlook, I mean that both Jesus and Paul see human
history as the place where divine activity has and will happen. Jesus and
Paul are primarily concerned with God's saving acts in history, not just any
kind of history. We may call this salvation history or eschatological history,
for what it entails is that the salvation of God, so often expected only at the
end of history, at the eschaton, was breaking into space and time now.
Some scholars, such as Schweitzer, have thought that because Jesus and
Paul saw the eschatological events breaking into history during their
lifetime, they must also have believed that these events and all of history
would conclude in their lifetime. This is a questionable assumption. There
is a difference between the beginning of the end of salvation history, and
the end of the end of salvation history.

Both Jesus and Paul believed that God's decisive and climactic work of
salvation was happening in their day or era. Jesus speaks of the time being
at hand (Mark 1:15) or the acceptable Day of the Lord being "now" (Luke
4:22). And Paul also says in one of his earliest letters, "But when the time
had fully come, God sent forth his Son" (Gal. 4:4). Though Jesus and Paul
spoke at somewhat different points in the eschatological timetable, it is true
to say that so far as their *future* expectations are concerned, they speak in
similar fashion.

Jesus speaks of the coming of the Son of Man at an unknown hour, at an
hour not even the Son knows of (Mark 13:32). This event will conclude
human history and bring in the final judgment. Elsewhere, in an important
Q parable (Luke 12:39f., cf. Matt. 24:43f.) Jesus says: "If the householder
had known at what hour the thief was coming, he would have been awake
and would not have let his house be broken into. You must be ready, for the
Son of Man is coming at an hour you do not expect." Paul says the same
thing in effect in 1 Thessalonians, another of his earliest letters. At 5:2–5 he

says the Day of the Lord will come like a thief in the night, and because one does not know that day or hour, one must be vigilant, always alert and ready.

This belief that they were living during the climactic days of history, during the beginning of the end, and thus looking anxiously toward the conclusion of that end colors much of what Jesus and Paul say and do. Both look toward the final coming of a person *other than* Yahweh on the Day of the Lord. That is one future event they both relate to and speak of frequently. No comparison of Jesus and Paul will be satisfactory if it does not take this into consideration.

"TO THE JEW FIRST AND ALSO . . ."

Third, there is the matter of audience. Jesus primarily if not almost exclusively addressed Jews. There is little reason to think he ever wandered far beyond the boundaries of Israel. This Jewish audience in some cases included his disciples, his opponents, and those who were simply interested bystanders. The Gospels also record some private discussions with his disciples alone. But even in the latter case, we must realize that it would be anachronistic to think of Jesus' disciples during his ministry as full-fledged Christians. The Gospels freely admit that when Jesus addressed them they did not yet understand or believe in the coming death and resurrection of their Master. Their faith was at most pre-Christian or on the way to becoming Christian simply because Jesus' death and resurrection and the coming of the Spirit still lay ahead. What Jesus said to his disciples was conditioned by these factors.

On the other hand, with Paul we have in his letters not treatises written to the non-Christian world, not proclamations of what Paul taught in the synagogues, but rather words to those who were already Christians (or at least were supposed to be). Everywhere Paul presupposes in his letters that his listeners know about Jesus' death and resurrection, about the coming of the Spirit, about the Christ being Jesus of Nazareth. He seldom stops to rehearse the basic story of Jesus because doubtless he or others went over such basics when he first preached to them. These letters may in some cases be addressed to those who are immature in Christ, but everywhere Paul presupposes they are in Christ. He calls them brothers and sisters, and he attempts to supplement and in some cases to interpret properly the information they had received previously from others and from himself about Jesus and the Jesus tradition.

Only in the case of Paul's letter to the Romans, and perhaps in Colossians, do we have Paul writing to those whom he has not personally been involved in converting and evangelizing, but even in Romans, Paul presupposes they have long since heard the basic Christian message and are ready to hear his extrapolation or interpretation of its significance to all Christians. No comparisons of Jesus and Paul will be adequate that do not carefully take into consideration whom Jesus, on the one hand, and whom Paul, on the other hand, were addressing.

PAUL AND THE JESUS TRADITION

Despite not writing to non-Christians, Paul does have occasion to quote or allude to the Jesus tradition, sometimes by way of reminding his listeners of what he already taught them, sometimes to reinforce his own teaching. This material is not to be found in every verse of Paul's letters, but also by no means can this material be dismissed as inconsequential in quantity or quality. Even in Paul's great pronouncement that he received his gospel by revelation, he goes on to admit that after three years in Arabia and Damascus he did go up to Jerusalem to see Peter and James (and he spent fifteen days with Peter). We may be sure that they didn't discuss the weather or Peter's fishing trips! In point of fact, the Greek verb in Gal. 1:18 (*historesai*) means "to inquire of" or possibly "to make the acquaintance of" (if it is used in its classical sense). It is highly probable that on this occasion Paul gathered information about Jesus, the Jesus tradition, Jesus' appearances to others besides himself, and perhaps other matters, supplementing whatever other information Paul may have already known as one who had sought out and persecuted the followers of Jesus.[54]

As we have already considered, in 1 Cor. 15:3 Paul says to the Corinthians that he had delivered to them the traditions he had received about Christ's death, burial, resurrection, and appearances. It is thus a reasonable hypothesis that Paul received this sort of summary tradition about the conclusion of Jesus' life from Peter on that first trip to Jerusalem. We also have in 1 Cor. 11:23 a reference to the fact that Paul received a tradition about the Last Supper. Though Paul says he received this information from the Lord, he probably means that the Lord is the ultimate originator of the Supper and its tradition, but that he received the information from those who were there, that is, Peter and others.

In that same letter, Paul refers specifically to what Jesus taught about divorce: "The Lord says that the wife should not separate from her husband" (1 Cor 7:10). Paul, however, feels free, under the guidance of the Spirit, to add instructions of his own to the teaching of Jesus, even though he knew no word of the Lord to deal with such cases.[55]

It is significant that Paul often refers to Jesus or church traditions in 1 Corinthians. Probably the reason is that he had so many free spirits in Corinth that he had to try to bring them more into line with beliefs and practices elsewhere in the Christian church. Thus, in 1 Cor. 11:2 he asks them "to maintain the traditions even as I have delivered them to you." He wants there to be some sort of order, structure, and traditions as there is in all the churches (cf. 1 Cor. 14:32). Elsewhere, when he is writing to another group of Christians he does not stress the Jesus and church traditions so strongly, probably because he did not need to.

Not only did Paul receive traditions about the passion narrative, the Last Supper, the resurrection, Jesus' teaching on divorce, but we also have other sorts of materials and traditions that Paul received. Thus we know from 2 Thess. 3:10 (cf. v. 14) that there were various ethical traditions he learned, such as "If anyone will not work, let him not eat!" We cannot be sure whether this is just a tradition of the church in general or whether it goes back to something Jesus said, but the point is that Paul certainly felt free to rely on and use such traditions. More explicitly, we have in 1 Cor. 9:14 the saying: "The Lord commanded that those who proclaim the gospel should get their living by the gospel." This appears to go back to Jesus' words in Matt. 10:10: "The laborer deserves his food," or possibly to Luke 10:7: "The laborer deserves his wages."

In Rom. 13:7, when speaking about the Roman government Paul says, "Render to all their dues," which could be a generalization of Matt. 12:11: "Render to Caesar what is Caesar's and to God what is God's." There is in fact much material that we cannot go over here, especially in Rom. 12—14, that is strongly reminiscent of various teachings of Jesus encapsulated in the compilation known as the Sermon on the Mount (cf. Rom. 12:19–21 to Matt. 5:38–48 and par.).[56] In both collections we find teachings about love, forgiveness, bearing one another's burdens, preparation for the Day of the Lord. This is sufficient to show that Paul had and used various traditions that went back to the Palestinian church and even to Jesus himself.

Our list of teachings shared by Paul and Jesus even on a conservative reckoning includes sayings about the Last Supper, Jesus' death, resurrection, postresurrection appearances, and a variety of ethical matters (marriage, divorce, support of missionaries, relationships to worldly authorities). But it would be wrong to say that these are the only points of contact between Paul and the historical Jesus' teaching, because there is a profound similarity between Paul's doctrine of justification by grace through faith and Jesus' teaching in some of his parables.

J. Jeremias rightly says, "Nowhere is the connection between Paul and Jesus so evident as here."[57] Thus, for instance, in the parable of the Pharisee and the tax collector (Luke 18:14a), there is clear reference to the ungodly tax collector being justified by God, not because of something he did or deserved, but because of God's grace. This is very close to the concept of justification by grace through faith that Paul advocates in

Romans, Galatians, and elsewhere. Romans 3:23 says, "Since all have sinned and fallen short of the glory of God, they are justified by grace as a gift."

Again in Matt. 20:1–16, we have the parable about the workers hired for labor in the vineyard, the last one hired receiving the same pay as the first because, as it turns out, the payment is not based on what the workers deserved but on the owner's generosity. Again, in the parable of the two debtors (Luke 7:42) the creditor forgives them both their whole debt because of his own generosity. In the parable of the prodigal son (Luke 15:11–32), we see the father who forgives and readopts the son despite what the son really deserves. Further, when Paul speaks of the redemption that is wrought by the death of Christ, he is not saying anything very much different from the Jesus tradition, where it talks about Jesus giving his life as a ransom for many (Mark 10:45).

Both Jesus and Paul apparently felt free to relate to the Father as Abba (cf. Mark 14:36; Rom. 8:15; Gal. 4:6). Both also talk in terms of the kingdom of God, the reign of God now breaking into history (Mark 1:15; Rom. 14:17; 1 Cor. 4:20; 15:24, 50). There are so many profound theological correspondences that without minimizing the differences of emphasis and perspective, we may say that for Jesus, as for Paul, religion is indeed grace and ethics is gratitude. Their fundamental orientation is the same. Without discounting the differences, I would urge that it is not at all appropriate or correct to say there is a great chasm between the thought of Jesus and that of Paul. They stand together and in contrast to a goodly number of their Jewish contemporaries.

Nor can we conclude from 2 Cor. 5:16, as Bultmann did, that Paul had no interest in the historical Jesus but only in the risen Christ. In order to understand the flow of the argument leading up to 2 Cor. 5:16, one must take into account that Paul has been showing his concern for the wayward Corinthians. He indicates that what he has been doing and saying to them was on the basis of Christian motives: "The love of Christ constrains us" (5:14). He points out that Christ has died for all, and therefore all have died. Verse 15 stresses that Christians (i.e., those who live) should no longer live for themselves but for Christ. Verse 16 then follows and leads immediately into his discussion of Christians being, or being part of, a new creation. It seems clear that Paul is contrasting the perspective one has (or ought to have) since one's conversion, and the perspective one had before that new creation happened. Barrett is right to stress that 5:16b must be seen as a special case of 5:16a (i.e., of not viewing anyone from a fallen human perspective anymore).[58]

Thus this text really says nothing about Paul's view of the importance of the Jesus of history. Rather, it contrasts his pre-Christian false estimation of him with his postconversion view. On both sides of the Damascus road experience, the historical Jesus is the object of this knowledge—the one whom Paul now knows died for all so they might live. Second Corinthians 5:14–15 could hardly make clearer Paul's interest in and emphasis on a Jesus who died in space and time. Second Corinthians 5:16 means that after his conversion Paul no longer viewed Jesus from a fallen worldly perspective. This meant he could no longer tell the story of Jesus as he had done before he became a follower of Christ. What he thought of Jesus had to be reenvisioned in light of Christian tradition and the Hebrew scriptures. The narrative of faith had to change. Paul believed it was this same Jesus whose followers he had once persecuted who was now Lord in heaven. He was adamant that salvation had been and had to be wrought by Jesus of Nazareth in space and time in Israel—on a cross outside Jerusalem, not in heaven. Thus he dared not denigrate or ignore the importance of the earthly Jesus.

That he does not focus primarily on the earthly Jesus prior to his death and resurrection in his letters is probably because he had moved on from the elementary teachings and traditions, like those one now finds in the Gospels, to deal with their implications for specific situations in the Christian churches. Paul received much of what was distinctive about his gospel through reflecting on the implications of his encounter on Damascus road, it is true. But he supplemented it not only by material from the Hebrew scriptures but also with the traditions about Jesus that he believed also ultimately came from the Lord himself and thus were also a permanent source of revelation, instruction, and inspiration.

NOTES TO PART 4

The Omega Man: His Identity, Ministry, and Majesty

1. From *The Harper Book of Christian Poetry*, ed. A. Mercatante (New York: Harper & Row, 1972), 223.

2. This is a phrase we find again at the end of the Pauline corpus in 2 Tim. 2:8.

3. See pp. 57ff. above.

4. God's royal Messiah is also called God's Son in a variety of places; see 2 Sam. 7:14; Ps. 2:7; 1QSa 2:11–12; 4QpsDanAa. Paul, however, uses the term "Son" to allude to more than just this fact.

5. N. A. Dahl, "The Messiahship of Jesus in Paul," in *The Crucified Messiah and Other Essays* (Minneapolis: Augsburg Publishing House, 1974), 30–47, here 37.

6. In secular Greek usage, the term *Christos* simply means "for external application" or "externally applied" in regard to ointments and cosmetics, but apparently it never referred to the one anointed (cf. Euripides *Hipp.* 516).

7. In early Jewish literature the term is found infrequently (cf. Ps. Sol. 18:5; 4

Q patr 3; CD 12:23–24; 14:19; 19:10–11; 1 En. 48:10; 52:4) and does not seem to have been "an *essential* designation for any future redeemer." M. De Jonge, "The Use of the Word 'Anointed' in the Time of Jesus," *Novum Testamentum* 8 (1966): 132–48, here 147; idem, "The Earliest Christian Use of *Christos:* Some Suggestions," *New Testament Studies* 32, no. 3 (1986): 321–43. There were various forms of messianic expectation in early Judaism, but it does appear that the terms translated in English as "Messiah" were not frequently used in early Judaism and probably were not *technical* terms for a future redeemer figure.

8. One should compare the more detailed discussion of Paul's use of *Christos* in *The Dictionary of Paul and His Letters.* (Downers Grove, Ill.: I-V Press, 1994) ad loc. What follows here is an adaptation of some of that article.

9. M. Hengel, "Erwägungen zum Sprachgebrauch von *Christos* bei Paulus und in der 'vorpaulinischen' Überlieferung," in *Paul and Paulinism. Essays in Honour of C. K. Barrett*, ed. M. D. Hooker and S. G. Wilson (London: SPCK, 1982), 135–59.

10. J.D.G. Dunn, *Unity and Diversity in the New Testament* (Philadelphia: Westminster Press, 1977), 43.

11. W. Grundmann, *"Christos," TDNT* 9 (1976): 540–62, here 542ff.

12. Dunn, *Unity and Diversity*, 43.

13. It has been reported that such evidence is forthcoming from the materials only recently published from Qumran, but the jury is still out on this data.

14. We should include also some wisdom traditions.

15. See S. Kim, *The Origins of Paul's Gospel* (Grand Rapids: Wm. B. Eerdmans, 1984), passim.

16. Grundmann, *"Christos,"* 555.

17. Ibid., 526; but cf. the parables of 1 Enoch, which suggest a more than merely human figure, and possibly Dan. 7.

18. See above pp. 112ff.

19. C.F.D. Moule, *The Origin of Christology* (Cambridge: Cambridge University Press, 1977), 150.

20. Grundmann, *"Christos,"* 526ff., on this paragraph.

21. This is so unless Qumran provides an exception to this rule.

22. Moule, *Origin of Christology*, 62, 65.

23. F. F. Bruce, *Commentary on Galatians* (Grand Rapids: Wm. B. Eerdmans, 1982), 195.

24. Against this idea, cf. my detailed article "Birth of Jesus," in *The Dictionary of Jesus and the Gospels* (Downers Grove, Ill.: I-V Press, 1992), 60–74; cf. also R. E. Brown, *The Virginal Conception and Bodily Resurrection of Jesus* (New York: Paulist Press, 1973); J. G. Machen, *The Virgin Birth of Christ* (Grand Rapids: Baker Book House, 1930).

25. C. K. Barrett, *The Epistle to the Romans* (New York: Harper & Brothers, 1957), 156.

26. Cf. C.E.B. Cranfield, *Romans I* (Edinburgh: T. & T. Clark, 1975), 381–382.

27. J.D.G. Dunn, *Romans 1–8* (Waco, Tex.: Word, 1988), 421–22.

28. Cf. pp. 14ff. above on Romans 7.

29. Cf. esp. Lev. 4:32 in the English, and in the LXX the use of the phrase *peri hamartias* (Lev. 5:6–7, 11; 16:3, 5, 9; Num. 6:16; 7:16; 2 Chron. 29:23–24).

30. It will not do to argue that Christ became the eschatological Adam only at the resurrection. What Paul says in 1 Cor. 15:45 is that the last Adam became a life-giving spirit at the resurrection, which surely implies that he was already this Adam before then. See 15:22.

31. See Moule's discussion in *Origin of Christology*, 10ff.

32. J. Jeremias, "*Adam*," *TDNT 1* (1964): 141ff.

33. At 1 Tim. 2:5 Christ as mediator between God and man is said to be the man Christ, Jesus.

34. First Timothy 2:5 goes a bit beyond this in stressing Christ's mediatorial role. Jesus, it may be implied, had to be fully God and fully human in order properly to represent God to humans and vice versa.

35. Cf. pp. 40ff. above.

36. A contemporary example of federal headship would be if our president declares war, U.S. citizens are all at war, even if we did not personally choose to be.

37. Jeremias, "*Adam*," 142.

38. See a somewhat different discussion of this in my *Jesus, Paul, and the End of the World* (Downers Grove, Ill.: I-V Press, 1992), 192ff., where I deal with more of the eschatological overtones.

39. Though the focus here is on what Christ is since the resurrection—namely, a life-giving spirit—it is not impossible that Paul is talking about the first Adam's origins (from the earth) as well as his character. The same is true of the second Adam as well; namely, that he came from heaven, thus implying his preexistence.

40. See my discussion in *Jesus, Paul, and the End*, 198ff.

41. See G. D. Fee, *The First Epistle to the Corinthians* (Grand Rapids: Wm. B. Eerdmans, 1987), 789 n. 11.

42. See C. K. Barrett, *From First Adam to Last* (New York: Charles Scribner's Sons, 1962), 68–77.

43. Ibid., 92.

44. Ibid., 92ff.

45. In poetic form I have put it this way:

> A tree, always a tree,
> That shadows forth his shade to me.
>
> God's ways are not human
> Our eyes cannot see
> The logic of love,
> Nailed to a tree.

46. See J.D.G. Dunn, "1 Cor. 15:45: Last Adam, Life-Giving Spirit," in *Christ and Spirit in the New Testament*, 127–41.

47. See Dunn, *Romans 1–8*, 278.

48. See Cranfield, *Romans I*, 290.

49. Barrett, *Romans*, 117.

50. R. Bultmann, *Theology of the New Testament*, 2 vols. in one (New York: Charles Scribner's Sons, 1951, 1955), 189.

51. Bultmann, *Theology*, 35.

52. See the chart and the conclusions in my *Jesus, Paul, and the End*, 225–231.

53. A. Schweitzer, *The Mysticism of Paul the Apostle* (New York: Holt, Rinehart & Winston, 1931), 113.

54. On the pre-Christian Paul, see now M. Hengel, *The Pre-Christian Paul* (Philadelphia: Trinity Press International, 1991).

55. This is so, for example, in the case of religiously mixed marriages.

56. Cf. also Luke 21:28; Rom. 13:11; and the discussion below of the eschatological traditions in 1 Thess. 4—5 and 2 Thessalonians 2, pp. 190ff. below.

57. J. Jeremias, "Paul and James," *ET* 66 (1954–55): 369.

58. This may be so from a purely human point of view, or perhaps even more strongly from a fallen human point of view, as Paul judged Christ before Paul's own conversion. See pp. 215ff.

PART 5

The Power and the Glory

The End and Beyond

STRANGE as it may seem, just when one might have thought the Pauline story of Jesus was over, once he died on the cross, the story takes a sudden upturn as it discusses Jesus' resurrection, exaltation, and glorification, including his ongoing role as Lord in heaven—as a risen, exalted one. Paul's encounter with Jesus changed his whole perspective on Jesus and on "the faith."

It is right to say that Paul saw Jesus' life and death retrospectively through the eyes of Easter faith. Jesus' death has the significance it has only because Jesus rose; God vindicated him, even in his decision to go to the cross (cf. Gal. 3:13). Thus Paul did expect his audience to look at the cross in light of the resurrection. It is the risen Christ, now in heaven, who is the focus of the church. Christology and eschatology intersect in Jesus' resurrection precisely because many early Jews saw resurrection as a phenomena of the eschaton, the end things, not as something that would happen before then. Let us follow Paul down the way of the cross and see where it leads.

13

All Roads Lead to the Cross

PERHAPS the question that takes us back to the beginning of this matter more than any other is, Why did Jesus have to die on the cross? If Jesus was merely showing God's love for human beings, there were many other ways God could have done it, and in fact did do it. What was it then, in Paul's view, about the human situation that necessitated the scandal of a crucified messiah? If Jesus' death was optional, not absolutely necessary for the salvation of the world, it is hard to see how anyone could view God as a truly loving God. No parent who loved an only child would send him to die such a hideous death unless it was absolutely necessary and the situation demanded it. Yet Paul tells us that God did this as an act of love and mercy. This means that of necessity we must ask this question: In Paul's view, what sort of God is the Father of Jesus? What in God's character, as well as in our situation, necessitated this gruesome event? What we must do is ask about Paul's understanding of God's holy and just character and will, as reflected in Paul's thoughts about God's wrath and Christ's death.

Paul speaks about the wrath of God more in Romans than elsewhere in his epistles. To begin with, Paul sees God's wrath not as an inevitable force or an impersonal principle of retribution structured into a moral universe, but rather as an expression of a trait of God as a person. To be sure, Paul would not want to predicate of God any *irrational* passion nor any vindictiveness in any normal sense of the term. Paul sees God's wrath as falling into the category of "righteous indignation."[1]

Thus, when in Rom. 1:18 we are told of the "wrath of God" revealed against all ungodliness and unrighteousness, we may ask, Where is this revealed? We should likely see vv. 17 and 18 as parallel here, in which case

160

the "righteousness of God" is intimately connected to the "wrath of God" (the latter being a manifestation of his righteous character), and both are revealed in the gospel Paul preached (v. 16). God's offer of salvation and God's judgment of sin are two sides of the same coin and go together.

> The preaching of Christ crucified, risen, ascended and coming again, is at the same time both the offer to [humankind] of a status of righteousness before God and the revelation of God's wrath against their sin. In the gospel the divine mercy and the divine judgment are inseparable from each other: the forgiveness offered to us is forgiveness without condoning. . . . [W]e do not see the full meaning of the wrath of God in the disasters befalling sinful [humans] in the course of history: the reality of the wrath of God is only truly known when it is seen in its revelation in Gethsemane and on Golgotha.[2]

This wrath is poured out on Christ in the place of sinners. Though for Paul this wrath comes ultimately from God, as 2 Thess. 1:7 intimates, the angels will have a role to play in the process at the day of judgment, but apparently not now.

Just as salvation in Paul has an already–not yet aspect to it, so does judgment. It has already happened to Jesus on the cross, yet it will happen to unbelievers on the last day. There are certain factors that act as a stimulus to sin and thus "incur wrath" in the interim, such as is indicated in Rom. 5:20: "Law entered that the offense might abound." Then there is an aspect of wrath being exerted now by magistrates. Romans 13:4–5 says, "He is . . . an avenger to execute wrath on him who practices evil." Romans 9:22–23 suggests that God is a God who wants to show both righteous wrath but also mercy and power to save. It is not a case of one or the other as alternatives. Indeed, it may be said that the whole of Rom. 1:18–3:20 (or v. 26) describes the eschatological manifestation of God's wrath, which is expressed both on the cross and through the current temporal authorities, and later on the "day of wrath."

Even in Rom. 1:18–3:20, Paul is not depicting God as a tyrant or a capricious being who indulges angry impulses. It is, rather, a matter of God's righteous wrath against sin—precisely because God loves people and sin separates the Almighty from them. A key word at this juncture is found in Rom. 2:8—*thumos* ("indignation"). It may be that wrath and indignation are simply two ways of saying the same thing. Cranfield suggests that *thumos* refers to the outward expression of wrath, *orge* to the inner feeling, but it is probably going beyond Paul's intention to make such a distinction. What may be said is that God's anger is a righteous indignation against sin. God's wrath is determined and prompted by God's righteousness and holiness. Romans 2:6 indicates that God will judge fairly, not punishing more than one's deeds deserve (cf. 2:11).

From Paul's point of view, one cannot claim that God is unjust in judging the world, even the world who knows not Christ, for all have sinned and fallen short of God's glory. If God were to be merely fair, all ought to be condemned. Fortunately, God does not operate simply on the basis of fairness. Notice how Rom. 3:5 talks about inflicting wrath; here God's wrath is seen as the actual punishment of sin, not the feeling or attitude behind it.

The future aspect of wrath (the day of judgment) is expressed numerous times in Paul (Rom. 5:9; 1 Thess. 1:10); in the later Paulines we especially find the phrase "the wrath to come" (Col. 3:6; Eph. 5:6). If, however, one compares Rom. 1:18 with 2:5, one sees that the day of wrath is already revealed but not yet consummated. Romans 2:9 indicates that the day of wrath will be a time of tribulation and anguish as a result of the wrath and indignation of God. It is not a pretty picture at all.

In the later Paulines there is a stress that all are, because of their fallen natures, "children of wrath." This seems to mean "children destined for wrath" unless they are in Christ (Eph. 2:3). Lostness outside of Christ is not merely a possibility; it is seen as a fact. Second Thess. 1:7–9 presents a most disturbing picture of Jesus taking vengeance on disbelievers and disobeyers. Judgment is said to come in the form of flaming fire and entails "everlasting destruction." This destruction is what ensues *after* all stand before the judgment seat of Christ—both Christian and non-Christian (cf. Rom. 14:10). Second Corinthians 5:10 speaks in similar fashion, but it adds that the works or deeds of even Christians will be judged. This same idea comes out clearly at 1 Cor. 3:13–14: a Christian's works (in this case a missionary's) will be tested, but the person in question will not be condemned. Barrett questions:

> Is this consistent with his doctrine of justification by faith? . . . Paul saw no inconsistency, for his references to judgement are much too frequent, and are too closely connected with Christ, to be dismissed as an unthinking recollection of his now abandoned Jewish past. He never ceased to think that obedience to the command of God was required of all . . . , not least of Christians; such obedience is not abrogated but made possible by justification. This is the foundation; on it [humans] may build, and what they build is exposed to judgement (1 Cor. iii. 10–15). Worthless building is destroyed, but the builder is not destroyed with it.[3]

This leads us back to 2 Thess. 1:7–9 and the fate of those who in person as well as in works must face the judgment and the wrath. What does "everlasting destruction" mean? In all probability it means unending punishment—not annihilation. This is also a view predicated of Jesus in the Synoptics (cf. Matt. 5:29f.; 12:32; 18:8f.; 21:41, 46; Luke 16:23–25) and was a common Jewish view.

Quite clearly, Paul does not believe in annihilation in the sense of the person losing consciousness at death and never recovering it. Rather, he says all must rise and appear before the judgment seat, where Christ, on God's behalf, will judge. Verse 9 also implies that those who are damned are separated from God's presence forever, which is the very essence of eternal punishment, whatever else may be experienced.[4] Nor is there any support for the annihilationist view in 1 Cor. 5:5 or even 1 Tim. 6:9, which deals with physical deterioration at death, or the wages of sin causing such deterioration.

God's wrath is a mixture of divine intervention on the cross and on the last day, but also in part in the present (Romans 1). It cannot be confined to the idea of the inevitable moral consequences of sin. Paul uses this stern language in order to affirm that God is just, righteous, and holy, and it is this aspect of God's character that is manifested not only on judgment day but on the cross. We are now prepared to understand the cross properly in Paul's thought. It is interesting that outside of Paul, in the epistles there is hardly any theology of the cross; indeed, there are hardly any references to Christ's death. Apart from one verse in Hebrews, Paul is the only New Testament writer to use the term "the cross." E. Käsemann wants to stress that Paul does not call Jesus' death a sacrifice and deduces from that that there is no vicarious punishment idea in Paul. This is unlikely, as we will see.[5]

Let us begin with Rom. 3:25 and deal immediately with a key Greek term—*hilasterion*. This is an adjective or noun sometimes used to mean "lid of the ark," that is, the spot where atoning blood is normally sprinkled, but it can mean any place of atonement. In its verbal form it normally means to "propitiate" or to "placate," although in the LXX there may be some cases where it means to "expiate" (to wipe clean or cover over). Propitiate means to appease the anger of *someone*, in addition to any of the concepts "expiate" usually connotes. The latter term focuses on the covering or cleansing of *something*. In Rom. 3:25 it is clear that God is the subject. God sent Jesus forth as a *hilasterion*. Some have objected, Does God propitiate God's own anger? The answer, however paradoxical, must be yes. At Rom. 3:25, *hilasterion* should be seen as an adjective, "propitiatory," with a noun "sacrifice" understood. This makes sense in light of the fact that it is by Christ's blood that the propitiation takes place, which presupposes his death as a sacrifice.

The foregoing is confirmed when we study the verb *hilaskomai*. This verb is used to mean "propitiate" in all the Hellenistic Jewish and Greek texts we have, and the early church fathers used it that way as well. Further, there are even three places in the LXX that it might mean "propitiate" (cf. Zech. 7:2; 8:22; Mal. 1:9). Also, we may note that atonement in the Old

Testament *did involve* appeasing God's wrath (see Num. 16:46ff.). This supports the view advocated above about Rom. 3:25. It is true that there are texts where Christ's death is seen as an expression of love toward us (Rom. 5:8; 8:32), but these do not negate the texts that indicate that the cross was the place where God expressed divine wrath against sin and was propitiated. There are, in addition, various texts where Jesus' death is viewed as a sacrifice, despite Käsemann's protest.

First Corinthians 5:7 reads, "Christ our passover was sacrificed for us." The context here is important because the practice of Passover is being used as an analogy here. Various Old Testament passages suggest the efficacy of blood, and the Passover had to do with appeasing God's wrath (cf. Ex. 12:13; 24:5–8). In Passover, the leaven would have to be cleaned out before the feast could be celebrated. Here the bad and old leaven is purged *after* the Passover has transpired, and here it represents pride and other sin. "Paul nowhere works out in detail a theory of Christ's sacrifice, but as in Rom. 3:25 he alludes to one great Jewish festival (the Day of Atonement), so here he alludes to another . . . Christ as the Lamb of God summed up God's action for the deliverance of [God's] people; and the context suggests . . . that he delivered them by bearing for them the burden of their guilt and thus removing their sin."[6]

When one says, "Christ bears our sins," this is shorthand for saying he bears the punishment for our sins. Also, having a clear sacrificial implication is Paul's presentation of the Lord's Supper in 1 Cor. 11:23–26. Ephesians 5:2 is more explicit yet—Christ is an offering, and a sacrifice to God. Just as significant are the texts that indicate that Christ's death was a representative substitution. First Thessalonians 5:10 is the earliest evidence for this in the Pauline corpus. Jesus is the one "who died for us." A question may be raised about the sense of the preposition *huper* (for) here and elsewhere in such phrases. Some scholars have suggested that it is significant that Paul uses *huper* instead of *anti* (instead of). They argue that if he had meant substitutionary atonement he would have used the latter, which more strongly carries the sense of "instead of." It is true that, generally speaking, *huper* means "in behalf of," but this can overlap with doing something "in the place of" a person. In the papyri, *huper* often has a substitutionary sense.[7] W. Bauer notes at least two other Pauline texts where *huper* means "instead of"—Rom. 9:3 and possibly 1 Cor. 15:29a (cf. 2 Cor. 5:14, 15ab, 21).[8] Philemon 13 can be added as well. Thus there is nothing at all unlikely about Paul using *huper* to mean "in the stead of" as well as "in behalf of."

After all, substitution was at the heart of the sacrificial system in the Old Testament and is brought into the picture when Paul draws analogies between Christ's death and Old Testament practices, especially sacrifice.

Notice how at Gal. 3:13 Christ is said to bear a curse *huper humon* ("for us"). Because believers do not bear this curse, this phrase must also imply "in our place." Second Corinthians 5:14–21 is especially important at this point. Christ died *huper panton*, literally, "for all." He says "all" here—not many; and it is very difficult to argue that "all" means "many" here.

Paul's deduction is that because Christ died for all, all died. He does not say all are potentially dead or reckoned as dead, but all are dead. He can draw this inference only if the one has been substituted in the place of all as their representative. All died in the one who died, and his death took the place of theirs. In what sense? Do not believers still go on to experience death? Yes, but Paul seems to think that Christians no longer experience it as punishment for sin, nor do they experience its eternal extension—eternal death. Paul then goes on in v. 15 to add that it is not the case that because Christ died for all, all *must* be given eternal life. The purpose of v. 15 is to show that the living, because Christ died for them, *ought* to live for him.

Second Corinthians 5:19 indicates that Christ was in the business of reconciling the world to himself. In a special sense, of course, he has effectively reconciled Christians (v. 18), but it was God's intention for Christ to die for all and to reconcile all the world. Thus Christ's death is seen as *sufficient* for all, but only *efficient* for those who respond to the offer of salvation. It follows from this that Paul did not see it as God's intention or desire that any should perish.[9] The distinction is made on the basis of who responds in faith and who does not. Thus we conclude: (1) These texts suggest that God did *not* limit the scope of the atonement. It was intended to be and was sufficient for all. (2) However, not all receive it and believe it, and for those there is the fate of facing eternal destruction. (3) It therefore follows that Paul is not a universalist, but also that it is humans who limit the atonement by the way they respond to it.

Second Corinthians 5:21 is a significant verse as well. Verse 21a indicates that Jesus did not engage in sin; he experienced ("knew") it not. It is only as the sinless one that Jesus can be the perfect sacrifice and atone for human sin, bearing humankind's punishment in its place. When Paul says, "Christ was made to be sin," he does not mean that Christ became a sinner. The contrast here is between what Christ was in himself and what he became for others—a sin offering. In addition, there is what believers have become as a result of Christ's death—"the righteousness of God." Barrett claims that we should see these as purely relational terms.[10]

There are at least three problems with this whole line of approach. We have already seen how for Paul the language of justification arises not out of the courtroom but out of, and should be exegeted in light of, the Abraham story. What is substituted in that story is Abraham's faith, which

is counted instead of his own works righteousness. It seems doubtful that
we should read another and contrary meaning into the text here. Second,
when Paul says that Jesus "was *made* to be sin," he is not merely using
relational language; he does not say Christ was reckoned or counted as sin.
Paul is not talking about "guilt" here, but sacrifice; Christ was through his
death literally made into a sin offering to God.

He then adds, "so that we might become the righteousness of God in
him." This does not mean that Christ's righteousness substitutes for the
believer's own personal obedience to God or that Christ's righteousness is
simply imputed to the believer, so that when God looks at the life of the
believer God simply sees Christ and so is deceived about or ignores the sins
of believers. In the first place, it is God's righteousness, not Christ's as
exhibited on the cross, that "we might become." In the second place there
is nothing said about an exchange of righteousness here. It is possible that
Paul means that the *locus* in which believers become the "righteousness of
God" is "in Christ," which may mean in the body of Christ. It is perhaps
more likely he means through Christ. Christ is the means through which
believers become the righteousness of God. In Rom. 5:2 Paul stresses that
it is through Christ that believers have not only peace with God, having
been justified through faith, but have obtained access to the grace that
enables them to stand.

It must be remembered that the context refers to the subjective change
that happens within believers (5:17) when they are "in Christ." In v. 17
Paul is not speaking about a change that happens to Christ, nor something
that is merely relational in character. If a person is in Christ, there is a
subjective change that involves the old person passing away and a new
creature emerging. This is made possible only through and because of the
death of Christ. It is likely, then, that 5:21 implies something about the
actual life of believers, not just their relational position, once they are "in
Christ."[11] In any event, it is clear from other Pauline texts (cf. Phil. 3:12)
that Paul does not mean that believers become perfect when they become
part of a new creation, although there is a world of change and difference in
them.

What we have been saying thus far may be summed up as follows: (1) It
was God's will that Christ died. (2) Christ's death propitiated God's wrath
caused by sin. (3) Christ died in our place and also in our behalf. (4) Christ
died for all; it was God's intent that he be sent to reconcile the world. (5)
Some do not respond to the atonement properly, and they go on to eternal
punishment, not everlasting life. (6) It is human beings, not God, who limit
the atonement.

Certain other views of the atonement are less than satisfactory. For
instance, C. H. Dodd's view that Christ's death was merely an expiation, a

√ covering or wiping out of the effects of sin, is not adequate. Certainly Paul means at least this, as his quoting Ps. 32:1, 2 in Rom. 4:7, 8 demonstrates. It is striking, however, that Paul hardly ever talks about forgiveness of sins or a wiping of the slate clean, except here where he quotes Ps. 32:1 and in some of the latter captivity epistles (cf. Eph. 4:32; Col. 2:13; Eph. 1:7; Col. 1:14). In 2 Cor. 2:7, 10, and 12:13 forgiveness has nothing to do with the cross, but rather with interpersonal relationships between believers. This is surprising, and I would suggest that we could expect more of such language if Paul simply saw the atonement as a matter of expiation, covering, cleansing, or forgiving.

We must also ask, Why does sin need to be expiated if God's wrath does not endanger a person? The reason sin needs to be expiated, in Paul's view, is that until this happens people stand in danger of dying in their sins with a hostile God standing against them on the last day. Thus it is fair to say that for Paul only propitiation gives meaning to expiation. Expiation of sin would not be necessary if there were not also a God who needed to be propitiated. As Paul understands the story of God and of God in Christ, sin cannot merely be covered over or put away—it must be dealt with. God is not viewed by Paul as an overly indulgent parent precisely because God loves humankind so greatly. Sin is something that affects humanity's relationship with God, not merely human character or human relationships.

At this point, it may prove useful to look briefly at those passages where blood is referred to by Paul: Rom. 3:25; 5:9; Col. 1:20 (cf. Eph. 1:7). It has been claimed that the use of the term "blood" by Paul points to life, for the Old Testament says that "the life of the flesh is in the blood" (Lev. 17:11).[12] Against such a view are several key texts. At Rom. 3:25 blood is the means of propitiation, and furthermore, v. 25b mentions God passing over sins previously. It was not life by itself that propitiated God in the Old Testament, but a life poured out in death, and blood here is likely a synonym for Christ's death. Romans 5:8–9 is another context where we have the connection of blood and death even more explicitly. The sequence is that Christ died for us, and we are consequently justified by his blood and saved from the wrath to come. Here and elsewhere blood in isolation from flesh means death and not life. Blood is associated with death, not life, and sometimes a penal substitutionary view of the atonement.

At Eph. 1:7 we are told that believers have redemption through Christ's blood. Surely this does not mean to imply that simply because Christ lived people have redemption. Rather, it was his lifeblood poured out in death that made redemption possible. Colossians 1:20 is very explicit: "making peace through the blood of the cross." The last phrase clearly associates death and blood, and both with an act that makes peace between God and humanity, which necessarily implies hostility beforehand.

Another inadequate view of the Pauline understanding of the atonement is one that sees it as merely a representative act and not also a substitutionary act. Sometimes this view seems to imply that Christ is simply an example of suffering love for all. This Paul certainly believed (cf. Phil. 2:6ff.), but it is an insufficient view of the atonement. Sometimes the representative view sounds as if believers chose Christ as their representative, whereas Paul is clear that God delivered and gave him over to death, though not without Christ's voluntary cooperation. Sometimes the representative view seems to see believers' dying and rising with Christ as in some sense atoning. This is to cross over the line from the imitation of Christ to acting as one's own Christ or savior, something Paul would certainly repudiate. To become like Christ, whether through physical suffering and dying for the faith or spiritual dying to sin, is not of the same order as Christ's death, in Paul's view. He believed that before there were any Christians and quite apart from them God did something in Christ to take care of sin, while the as yet future converts were still sinners and ungodly (Rom. 5:6–8).

Romans 6:10 makes it plain that in Paul's mind Christ died to sin "once for all." This last phrase translates *ephapax*, which means "a decisive and unrepeatable event."[13] Because it is once for all, believers do not need to atone for themselves or for their sins at any time. Paul believes that one decisive historical death took care of all that. Thus one must conclude that the only fully adequate view of Paul's understanding of the atonement is that it is a penal substitutionary atonement limited in its effects only by human response to it.

14

First Up from the Dead

Firstfruits of the Harvest

Lord, who createdst man in wealth and store
Though foolishly he lost the same,
Decaying more and more,
Till he became
Most poor:
With thee
O let me rise
As larks, harmoniously,
And sing this day thy victories:
Then shall the fall further the flight in me.

My tender age in sorrow did begin:
And still with sickness and shame
Thou didst so punish sin,
That I became
Most thin.
With thee
Let me combine,
And feel this day thy victory:
For if I imp my wing on thine,
Affliction shall advance the flight in me.

—*George Herbert*
"Easter-Wings"[14]

WHEN Paul reflected on the climax of the story of Jesus' earthly ministry, he did not stop with the story of Jesus' death or burial but went on to reflect on the meaning of the early Christian tradition that Jesus rose from the dead. For Paul, this is the most crucial part of the whole story, not just because it is the climax of Jesus' story, but also because this is the juncture where he believed he enters the story, by means of the Damascus road encounter. All that goes before resurrection in the story of Christ and all that comes after it hinges on Jesus' rising. If he is not raised, then his death has not effected atonement for sins and his ministry has ended in failure. Though Paul does not say so explicitly, 1 Corinthians 15 certainly implies that there is also no return of Christ and no future resurrection of Christians if Christ was not raised. The story of Christ and the story of Christians are intimately intertwined at this point, and the story of Christians cannot turn out well if Jesus' story did not also turn out well. Christology, eschatology, ecclesiology, and ethics are all combined in one potent mixture in 1 Corinthians 15, with the latter two being in various ways dependent on the successful resolution of the former two.

As we have already seen, when Paul wants to expand and expound on the meaning of Jesus' resurrection he turns to the story of Adam. For Paul, Jesus' resurrection is a story about endings that turn into new beginnings. The conclusion of the story of Jesus' earthly career inaugurates the new eschatological age, an age in which Jesus is but the firstborn from the dead, firstfruit of a harvest of raised ones. Just as the story of Adam is a story about an absolute beginning of the human race, so the story of Jesus' resurrection is the story of the new beginning of and for humanity. Paul does not reflect on the early Christian story just in the light of the climactic events in Jesus' life; he reflects on it in the light of the primal narrative of God's breathing life into Adam.

Paul's encounter with the risen Christ on Damascus road was by definition an eschatological experience not only because resurrection was not supposed to happen until the end times, but also because messiah was not to come until then. It is not clear from 1 Cor. 15:3 whether Paul received the Christian credo orally or in written form, but clearly he is relying here on some sort of church tradition that includes vv. 3–7. Only at v. 8 is he able to speak on the basis of his personal experience, and it is entirely likely that Paul's thinking on this subject is a combination of insights from (a) his Jewish background, (b) the church tradition he received, (c) his personal encounter with Christ, and (d) the story of Adam.[15]

The great merit of J. C. Beker's treatments of Paul's theology is that he clearly shows that Paul's understanding of resurrection, including the resurrection of Jesus, must not be studied apart from the eschatological framework of which it is an integral part.

Resurrection language is end-time language and unintelligible apart from the apocalyptic thought world to which resurrection language belongs. . . . Thus, the resurrection of Christ, the coming reign of God, and the future resurrection of the dead belong together. . . . When the resurrection of Christ is isolated from its linguistic apocalyptic environment and from the reality of future apocalyptic renewal, it may well retain its traditional nomenclature in expositions of Paul's thought, but it becomes something radically different. It becomes . . . an event in the midst of history rather than at the end of history for the sake of history's transformation. Attention now shifts to the resurrection as the end of the incarnation, as a closure event rather than an inaugural event.[16]

Beker's judgment is on target, though I think the term "eschatological" rather than "apocalyptic" should be used to describe what Beker is discussing.[17] He is also right that the attempts to remove the ontological and historical referents from Paul's views on resurrection do less than justice to Paul's perspective. Whether or not we are comfortable with the idea, Paul believed not only in the spiritual resurrection of the human spirit in this life and the new perspective on life which that brings, but also in the literal resurrection of Christ and of Christians at the end of history as we know it. Furthermore, this resurrection is linked to actual environmental renewal of the earth itself (see Rom. 8:18–25). The resurrection of Christ, the destiny of believers, and the destiny of the earth are inexorably linked together.

Although rightly highlighting Paul's eschatological framework, Beker has done so at the expense of Paul's Christology. What caused Paul to alter his eschatological framework, which he inherited from early Pharisaic Judaism, is precisely his experience of the risen Lord coupled with the Christian story he inherited and reflected upon about the past and future work of Christ. For Paul, not only does Christ's return trigger the resurrection of believers, but in Paul's view there will be no resurrection of believers if Christ has not been raised. In short, it is the narrative of Christ's career that causes Paul to bifurcate his doctrine of resurrection and to make the resurrection of believers dependent on both Christ's resurrection and his return. The Parousia component especially distinguishes Paul's views from those of other Jews about when and how the resurrection of believers will transpire. W. D. Davies stresses that "it is erroneous thus to make Paul conform too closely to current apocalyptic speculation. That in his eschatology, the apostle drew upon the latter for his terms will be obvious, but the character of that eschatology was determined not by any traditional scheme but by that significance which Paul had been led to give to Jesus."[18] With these general caveats in mind, we are now prepared to trace the trajectory of Paul's thought on Christ's resurrection as it is evidenced in the capital Pauline letters.

It is hardly surprising, in view of his Pharisaic background, that Paul places so much stress on resurrection, both Christ's and the believers. There was also, quite apart from Pharisaic teaching (see Gen. Rab. 14:5; Acts 23:6–8), considerable precedent for such a belief not only in the Hebrew scriptures (see Isa. 26:19; Dan. 12:1–3) but in the intertestamental period (see 2 Macc. 12:43–44; 7:10–11; 4:9; 14:46). This belief became a sort of test of true Jewishness after A.D. 70 (see Mish. San. 10:1; B.T. San. 90b; 2 Bar. 50:1–4).[19] The majority of the references to resurrection in early Judaism suggest a very materialistic view of the resurrection (but see Josephus *Wars* 2.10.11; Wisd. Sol. 3:1–4). In other words, to many if not most early Jews, and especially to Pharisaic ones, the idea of a nonmaterial resurrection would have amounted to a contradiction in terms.

G.W.E. Nickelsburg has, however, rightly cautioned us "that in the intertestamental period there was no single Jewish orthodoxy on the time, mode, and place of resurrection, immortality, and eternal life."[20] Nickelsburg has also shown that the idea of a general resurrection and judgment of all the dead (not just the believing dead) in early Jewish literature is rarely found prior to the end of the first century A.D. (see 2 En. 65:6–7; Apoc. Mos. 13:3; 41:3; Test. Ben. 10:9; Sib. Or. 4:176–190; 4 Ezra 7; Wisd. Sol. 1–6 is a possible exception, as is Dan. 12:2). When a universal resurrection is spoken of, its function is almost always to make possible the final rendering of justice for all. By contrast, in the earlier Jewish texts that speak of a resurrection of the righteous, the function of resurrection is vindication, rescue, or reward (see 2 Maccabees 7).[21] When Paul speaks of resurrection, whether of Christ or of Christians, this latter, more positive thrust and connection with vindication or reward comes to the fore (see Rom. 1:4; 1 Corinthians 15).

Very little in 1 Thessalonians will help us obtain a clear fix on Paul's view of resurrection. First Thessalonians 1:9–10 is probably a pre-Pauline fragment of the early church's preaching to Gentiles. Verse 10 speaks of God having raised Jesus from/out of *the* dead (persons). Though this implies resurrection from death, what the text actually says is that Jesus was brought back from the midst of the realm of the dead persons (Sheol). Paul normally uses the verb *egeirein*, either in the active or passive, to speak of resurrection. He does not use *anistanai* in the transitive. That is, Paul never speaks of Jesus raising himself; rather, he is always passively acted upon by God (see, e.g., Rom. 4:24–25; 6:4, 9; 7:4; 1 Cor. 6:14; 15:12–17, 20; 2 Cor. 4:14; 5:15).

In 1 Thess. 1:10 Christ's resurrection is connected with the believer's future deliverance from God's wrath. Almost always when Paul speaks of Christ's resurrection he does so in connection with the events that will transpire when Christ returns. He clearly does not see Christ's resurrection as an isolated historical anomaly but as an eschatological event that is the harbinger and in some sense the trigger or at least the prerequisite of future eschatological events. Paul is surely dealing with Christians in Thessalonica who had speculated about such eschatological matters, and it may even be that the Thessalonian Christians were reflecting the characteristics of a millenarian movement.[22] If so, then it would appear that Paul is trying to offer a certain amount of "eschatological reserve" while still affirming much of the substance of the Thessalonians' beliefs about the future. Here Paul grounds the believer's future status in the belief in the past Christ event, the story of the conclusion of Jesus' earthly life.

In 1 Thess. 4:14 the future resurrection of deceased believers is linked with the past death and resurrection of Jesus. The link here, however, is unlike that in 1 Corinthians 15. Here, belief in Christ's resurrection is seen as the proper grounds for believing that deceased Christians will likewise be raised. Verse 16 also makes clear that Paul is only referring to the future of "the dead in Christ." Christ's resurrection is not a guarantee or proof of the future general resurrection of all the dead. Finally, because in v. 17b Paul says, "and so [or "in this way"] we shall be with the Lord *forever*," this must count strongly against the idea that this text is talking about some *interim* stay with Christ in heaven during a period of earthly tribulation.

For Paul, resurrection of the believer means final conformity to the likeness or image of God's Son, even in regard to one's body. In other words, resurrection seems to have a very specific positive content that has to do with the consummation of Paul's ideas about the imitation of Christ. In such a context, it is hardly surprising that Paul never speaks of the resurrection of nonbelievers. If one has not participated in the process of being conformed to the image of the Son in this life (Rom. 8:29), it is hardly to be expected that one would get the final installment or completion of this ongoing process later. Resurrection ushers the believer into the new world and the kingdom promised to them by God. G. Vos has it right when he says this:

> If we may judge of the resurrection of believers *mutatis mutandis* after the analogy of that of Christ, we shall have to believe that the event will mark the entrance upon a new world constructed upon a new superabundantly dynamic plane. . . . The resurrection constitutes, as it were, the womb of the new aeon, out of which believers issue as, in a new, altogether unprecedented sense, sons of God.[23]

The truth of this observation will become readily apparent when we examine Romans 1 and 1 Corinthians 15 more fully below. However, this theological truth already stands behind what Paul says in texts like 1 Thess. 3:13 and 5:23, where the ongoing process of sanctification is seen as preparation for the coming of Christ. The work of the Spirit in the present in the believer is preparing that believer not only for the final judgment of Christ, but for the final work of the Spirit for the believer; that is, resurrection in the likeness of Christ's glorified body. For Paul, Christology, pneumatology, soteriology, eschatology, and ethics are so closely interwoven that any attempt to treat one or another of these aspects of Paul's thought in isolation from the others does less than justice to them all. To put it another way, any attempt to take these ideas outside of the context of the Story Paul tells of the development of salvation history from the first Adam to the last and beyond stands in grave danger of distorting Paul's meaning. This is especially true when we come to what is for Paul a *sine qua non* of Christian faith—the belief in both Christ's and the believer's resurrection. Because 2 Thessalonians adds nothing to our discussion, we will pass on to 1 and 2 Corinthians.

The first passage for consideration, 1 Cor. 6:14, comes in the middle of Paul's discussion about the proper use of the human body. Resurrection is introduced here to explain why it is important to act morally in and with the body—the body is meant for the Lord and in fact will participate in the eschatological state of salvation. Verse 14 makes the analogy between Christ's resurrection and that of believers quite explicit. Both are raised up by God's power. The context makes clear that by resurrection Paul means something involving a body. Again we see a clear connection made between the believer's present condition and conduct and his or her future condition. Ethics circumscribes bodily conduct because the body has a place in the eschatological future of the believer. "This affirmation stands in bold contrast to the Corinthian view of spirituality which looked for a 'spiritual' salvation that would finally be divested of the body."[24]

Crucial is the retelling of the Christian's credo in story form in 1 Cor. 15:1ff. What had Paul received from his Christian predecessors? Basically we find here only the heart of the creed—death, burial, resurrection on the third day, and then appearances, last of all to Paul. Verse 3 insists that Christ died for our sins according to the scriptures. We have already seen that this meant he died on account of "our" sins; it was our sins that made his death necessary if believers were to receive forgiveness and life.[25] One may ask, Where in the Old Testament is it said that Christ must die on account of sins? In all probability, Isa. 53:12 is in view here. Nonetheless, the real significance of saying it happened according to scriptures is that it "was not fortuitous, but willed and determined by God, and that it formed part of the winding up of [God's] eternal purpose, that is, that it was one of those eschatological events that stand on the frontier between the present age and the age to come, in which the divine purpose reaches its completion."[26] This also applies to what Paul says about Jesus' resurrection in v. 4; it too was "according to the scriptures." Possibly, Ps. 16:10 and Isa. 54:7 are alluded to at this point. The reference to Christ's burial is especially important on two counts: (1) it confirms that Jesus was really dead; (2) it confirms that resurrection must be from the dead and involve the body. Jesus rose not merely from the grave, but from the dead. Note the verb tenses—died and buried. Both Greek verbs are in the aorist, indicating punctiliar events in the past. "Was raised" is in the perfect, suggesting not only that it happened but that "it remains in force";[27] that is, Christ died once, he was buried once, but he rose and is alive now.

It has often been pointed out that for Paul the resurrection, ascension, and exaltation of Jesus are all lumped together and little distinction if any is made between them. For example, in Phil. 2:8–9 we go straight from Jesus' death to his exaltation, which would seem to mean his heavenly existence, perhaps including his resurrection. First Corinthians 15:45–47 deals not with where Jesus came from (from heaven) but with what his quality was—heavenly. Jesus at his resurrection became the heavenly man (1 Cor. 15:48). Romans 1:3–4 indicates that it was by the resurrection or from the (time of) the resurrection that Jesus entered the sphere of the Spirit or was Spirit-imbued to become Son of God in power. Notice how at Col. 3:1 Paul felt that the appearances of Jesus are all appearances of the heavenly, exalted Lord. Paul says nothing about the ascension. Paul sees these appearances as ending with himself, and this is also the point Luke wants to make with the doctrine of the ascension. There was a definite end to the time of the appearances, after which Jesus was strictly in heaven.

What does this tell us about Jesus' resurrection? Paul saw Jesus as experiencing a deathless, life-giving existence in a new body. Doubtless Paul thought of transformation of the old body of Jesus by resurrection, but it is notable that he nowhere discusses the empty tomb. Inasmuch as it is the one who is buried (1 Cor. 15:3–4) who is raised, it is likely implied that Paul did not think of Jesus as receiving a replacement body, but a transformed one. Paul believes there are a number of differences between the risen Christ and the risen Christian. Christ alone is a life-giving spirit (v. 45); he alone is the one who is the firstfruits; and he alone reigns over God's enemies and defeats them, even death. He alone commands and hands over the kingdom of God to the Father. Thus believers do not become like him in all respects—for example, they do not become lords by their resurrections. As we will see in the next chapter, they do, however, share in Christ's power, glory, imperishability, and spiritual life source. First Corinthians 6:3 also implies that they will share in his role as judge at the end. The language of imitation does not imply full identification.

The crucial nature of the analogy, firstfruits/latter fruits in 1 Corinthians 15, is made clear by M. J. Harris: "This essential unity between the firstfruits and the harvest is basic to the whole argument of 1 Corinthians 15. To affirm Christ's resurrection is to affirm that of his people (1 Cor. 15:12, 20, 23). To deny their resurrection is to deny his (1 Cor. 15:13, 15–16). Each implies or is involved in the other."[28]

In the Hebrew scriptures the firstfruits was the first part of the annual harvest of grain or wine or other products that was to be offered up to God (see Ex. 23:16, 19; Lev. 23:10; Num. 18:8, 12). As Harris points out, the relationship of firstfruits to the harvest is that of the part to the whole.[29] There is more to the analogy than this, however. The firstfruits both presage and also promise or prove that there will be latter fruits.[30] In short, Christ's resurrection makes possible, believable, and in Paul's mind certain that believers will one day rise. It is also likely that Paul's language of imminence in regard to the end, insofar as it involves both Parousia and resurrection, has been strongly affected by his Christology. A. L. Moore puts it this way:

> The nearness of the end is bound up with the person of Jesus Christ, in whom the events of the end, including their open, unambiguous manifestation coinhere. In him, death, resurrection, ascension, and Parousia belong together. They do not belong together as a general principle but as a matter of theological, or more exactly of Christological fact.[31]

In Paul's thought world there is a twofold proleptic realization of the end. Christ's resurrection and believers having the Spirit are both pledges and pointers that the resurrection of believers will yet happen. Thus Paul can speak not only of the firstfruits of the resurrection (1 Cor. 15:20, 22) but also of the firstfruits of the Spirit (Rom. 8:23). In both cases Paul uses the term *aparche*. It is not surprising that Paul does not speak of the Spirit as firstfruits in 1 Corinthians 15, for that would play right into the hands of the spiritualists in Corinth.

First Corinthians 15:23b makes clear that this connection between firstfruits and latter fruits is not a connection between Christ and all humanity, but rather between Christ and "those who belong to him." Christ's resurrection then does not simply trigger or guarantee the resurrection of all the dead in some sort of cause and effect relationship. The middle term between Christ's resurrection and that of others is belonging to Christ, being in him—in short, having Christian faith. The Christian's future is dependent upon and connected to Christ's past. Paul believes that Christ's history is the believer's destiny. This destiny is not something that is inevitable apart from ongoing Christian faith. Thus we must see that in the firstfruits analogy Paul is giving the Corinthians another chance to broaden their horizons and gain a salvation-historical perspective. He is also placing the discussion in the context of the larger idea of the imitation of Christ, which involves both ethics and eschatology, both the actions of believers and the action of God for them in the present and at the Parousia.

Though we have already considered Rom. 1:3–4 when we were reflecting on Paul's use of the term "Son," one other point of interest can be garnered from this text about the resurrection of Christ. The key phrase for our purposes does not mean "as from *his* resurrection from the dead" but "as from *the* resurrection of the dead." In short, the phrase associates what happened to Jesus with the general resurrection of the dead. This comports with the firstfruits analogy in 1 Corinthians 15, but it also should be compared with the unique tradition in Matt. 27:52–53, where Jesus' resurrection is seen to be accompanied by the resurrection of various saints.[32] Here the resurrection of Jesus is seen as the prerequisite to his being installed at the right hand of God as Son of God in power. Without resurrection, Jesus would not be who he has become to believers—the Son of God in power and thereby a life-giving spirit.

In Rom. 4:24–25 we begin to see Paul reflecting on the *present* benefits to believers of Christ's resurrection. We are told not only that God raised Jesus from the dead, but also at least part of the reason why—because of or for *our* justification/vindication. This makes clear again how crucial Christ's resurrection is for Paul's thought world in general. There is a sense in which everything hinges on it. Jesus would not fully be the Christ without the resurrection, nor would he be the Son of God in power, a Son who could be a present help to believers, without the resurrection. It is equally true that Christians would still be in their sins, which is another way of saying they would not be justified/acquitted without Christ's resurrection. There would be no eschatological hope of a resurrection like Christ's for believers if God had not raised him from the dead.

This makes abundantly clear how Paul's beliefs about the future have been shaped and are determined by his experience of the risen Lord and his reflection on the Christ story he inherited that interpreted the Christ event. Paul does not affirm a general resurrection of all the dead. Indeed, he does not posit any resurrection even for believers without there first being a resurrection of Jesus. Paul has reshaped his prior Pharisaic eschatological beliefs in light of his newfound christological convictions. The Christ event is both central to and determinative for Paul's eschatology. Here Beker has placed the emphasis in the wrong spot, and it has led him to make Christology something less than a form or part of theology for Paul.[33]

Romans 6:4–9 continues the trend of relating Christ's resurrection to the *present* life and behavior of Christians. Christ was raised from the dead so that (*houtos*) "we might now walk in newness of life." Lest we suspect that this stress on the present effects of Christ's resurrection has led Paul to abandon the parallel between Christ's resurrection and that of the believers at the Parousia, in the very next verse (6:5) Paul reiterates this parallel. Note how closely the theme of *imitatio Christi* is tied to the discussion of resurrection. If believers have in this present life been united with Christ in his death (experienced death to sin, the burial of the old nature), then they will also rise in a resurrection like his. The *ei* here could be translated "because" rather than "if," but in either case Paul is talking about the consequences of being united with Christ in his death. Future resurrection in the likeness of Christ depends on present faith in and union with Christ. This is stated another way in v. 8, but the point is the same. Present experience and behavior (v. 4c) determine whether one will experience a resurrection like Christ's in the future. The future tense of the verb "become" must be taken seriously in v. 5. Believers have not yet obtained the likeness of Christ's resurrection that Paul is talking about. In Rom. 8:33 there is further reference to Christ's death and resurrection with the implication that Christ has the role he does at God's right hand interceding for us as a result of the resurrection. In Rom. 10:9 belief in Christ's resurrection is seen as a *sine qua non* for being saved. Here Paul probably is citing an essential part of an early Christian creedal formula, and once again we see how the onset of the eschatological realities are seen as beginning in the climax of Jesus' life. The resurrection of Jesus is as essential for the Christian as it was for Christ. Romans 14:9 adds the thought that the reason or purpose for which Christ died and lived again was so that he might be the Lord of both the dead and the living. It has long been stressed that "the Lordship of Christ is in the theology of St. Paul always connected with His resurrection, not His life, which was a period of humiliation (Rom. viii:34; 2 Cor. iv:10, 11)."[34] We may add that assuming lordship is also in Paul dependent on Christ's death. There is for Paul a belief that Christ did not, at least in the full sense, exercise his lordship until after his resurrection. Only then did he assume the position of a Lord at God's right hand (see Rom. 8:34; Phil. 2:11). Paul always seems to look at Christ in terms of the narrative of the drama of salvation and the successive stages of the Christ event. We will consider more fully Paul's understanding of Christ as Lord in the next section of this chapter.

In Romans a new theme emerges in Paul's discussion of the resurrection. In various texts Paul closely connects the believers' present condition or behavior either to Christ's resurrection or to believers' resurrection or to both. It appears that the common denominator is the Holy Spirit, who is involved in the resurrection both of Christ and of Christians, and in the present in the ongoing conforming of the believer to the image of the Son (see Rom. 8:23–29). Paul does not isolate belief from behavior or events past and future from their present consequences or importance. Rather, these matters are all closely bound together in Paul's gospel, the story of salvation. At the heart of the matter is resurrection of both the Christ and the Christian, *and* walking in newness of life, as even Christ walked and was obedient unto death.

The resurrection of Christ is the foundation stone of Paul's gospel, providing the basis for the offer of forgiveness of sins and justification. Resurrection is also the goal for believers; it is what one strives to attain. There is a sense in which the theme of resurrection circumscribes the Pauline narrative of salvation, providing both its basis and its dramatic climax. In the end, being a Christian means being like Christ not only in character here and now, but also in body and in power then and there. Without the very concrete basis of hope in Christ's resurrection there is no object of hope, preaching is pointless, and Christian living is in vain. In short, for Paul the basis of ethics, Christian living, preaching, and even Christology (for there would be no living Lord Jesus Christ without the resurrection) is the resurrection.

The implication of affirming resurrection as the ultimate form of eternal life is that the drama of redemption must have an earthly conclusion or else salvation is not complete. Without such a conclusion there can be no renewal of the earth as well as of believers. Without such a conclusion there can be no inheriting of the kingdom of God on earth or fulfilling of the earthly promises of God to Israel. Without such a conclusion there is no point to the idea of a Parousia, a return of Christ to raise the dead and to be with his people forever in the dominion of God.

Thus, just when we might have expected the story to be over, it goes on. Although Paul could have argued that as Christ was exalted to heaven and a place of honor there after death, so likewise Christians will be, instead Paul draws his analogy between the bodily resurrection of Christ and Christians. This in turn involves an ongoing purpose for history and role for Christ in heaven during the eschatological age. Moreover, the turning point of human history, the resurrection of Jesus, requires an earthly sequel!

The drama of salvation has at least four main acts: (1) the establishing of an eternal covenant with Abraham on the basis of faith, which is reckoned as righteousness—a covenant that entails promises to bless all the nations as well as Jews, and which covenant Christ comes and brings to fulfillment; (2) the death and resurrection of Christ, which makes possible the realization of all God's promises, including the promise of salvation; (3) the new creation, firstfruits of the Spirit, newness of life, forgiveness, and justification that the believer experiences now as a result of Christ's resurrection; and (4) the ingathering of Jews and Gentiles in Christ, which culminates in the future resurrection/transformation of believers at the close of human history. This requires the return of Christ to triumph finally and completely over the powers of darkness—including the supernatural evil ones, disease, decay, and death. In the end Paul varies little from the early Jewish-Christian picture in Revelations 21 of what final salvation will and must look like. It will entail not only new believers but also a new heaven, a new earth, and a new Jerusalem on earth that has come down out of heaven (compare Gal. 4:26 to Rev. 21:9ff.). The realities that already exist in heaven will find their final purpose and resting place on earth. Then and then only will the kingdoms of this world become the kingdoms "of our God and of his Christ." But once again we jump ahead of the story; we must reflect first briefly on Christ's present status and role in heaven as risen Lord.

15

Therefore God Has Given Him the Name "Lord"

THE term *kurios* ("Lord") became in the early church the essential thing one had to confess Jesus to be if one wanted to be a Christian (cf. Rom. 10:9; 1 Cor. 12:3; Phil. 2:11). Paul was well aware and freely admits that there were many competitors who were addressed as "lords" in the world of pagan religion: "Even though there may be so-called gods in heaven or on earth, as in fact there are many gods and many lords (*kurioi*), yet for us there is one God, the Father . . . and one Lord Jesus Christ" (1 Cor. 8:5–6). He was doubtless also cognizant that in his own day the emperor was also called *kurios* in a more than human sense,[35] but it is doubtful that his use or the content of the term is derived from secular sources.

In the first place, the term *kurios* occurs in the LXX over nine thousand times, and in over six thousand of these occurrences it is used in place of the proper name of God—Yahweh. This amounted to a circumlocution to avoid saying the Tetragrammaton. We also find *kurios* used some twenty-seven times in place of Yahweh, or some transliteration thereof, in Wisdom of Solomon (cf. Wisd. Sol. 1:1–9; 2:13). In Aramaic the term *mare* or *mara* to refer to God as Lord is found as early as Dan. 2:47 and 5:23, and from Qumran 1QapGen provides an example where *mari*, meaning "my Lord," is used in an address to God.

In 1 Cor. 16:22–23 we find the terms *marana tha* being used, probably meaning "come Lord," as a prayer for Jesus' return. What is striking about this is that Paul does not even bother to translate this phrase for his largely Gentile audience, which strongly suggests he assumes they know its meaning, as a long-used Christian phrase, likely going back to the first Aramaic-speaking Jewish Christians.

181

Converging lines of evidence suggest that not only in the case of Paul, whose essential justification for his ministry was that he had seen "Jesus our Lord" (1 Cor. 9:1), but also in the case of many Jewish Christians, who were in Christ before him and originated the *marana tha* invocation, the belief that they had personally encountered the risen Christ after his death generated the confession "Jesus is Lord." L. W. Hurtado puts it this way:

> Rather than trying to account for such a development as the veneration of Jesus by resort to vague suggestions of ideational borrowing from the cafeteria of heroes and demigods of the Greco-Roman world, scholars should pay more attention to this sort of religious experience of the first Christians. It is more likely that the initial and main reason that this particular chief agent (Jesus) came to share in the religious devotion of this particular Jewish group (the earliest Christians) is that they had visions and other experiences that communicated the risen and exalted Christ and that presented him in such unprecedented and superlative divine glory that they felt compelled to respond devotionally as they did.[36]

It should then come as no surprise that Paul especially associates the term "Lord" with what is true of Jesus as a result of and since the resurrection. The christological hymn in Philippians 2 had already strongly linked the exaltation of Jesus with the term "Lord," the *marana tha* prayer implied that he was a divine Lord who was to return from heaven, and the earliest confession was "Jesus is Lord." Both because of his own Christian story and because of the Christian traditions that were passed on to him, Paul had ample reasons to think of Jesus as *kurios*.

"Lord" was a role that in Paul's mind Jesus did not, or at least did not fully, assume until after his resurrection and exaltation. The early Christian confession "Jesus is Lord" was one only the resurrection community could make. He was Lord precisely because he was risen and alive, proving his lordship even over death. He was Lord because he was believed to now reign from heaven. Neither of these factors was true of Jesus before his death.

"Lord" is a favorite Pauline term for Jesus. He uses it some 275 times (43 in Romans, 67 in 1 Corinthians alone), which certainly shows that Paul is comfortable in using this early affirmation as reflecting his own thoughts and devotion. According to Phil. 2:9, it is at the point of exaltation in the recounting of Jesus' career that he is given the name that is above all names. The commentators are right to stress at this point that the name that is above all names is the name of God, or as God was so often called in the Old Testament, "Lord."[37] This passage is a truly astonishing one, for it is saying that the name that God went by in the LXX, *kurios*, is now bestowed on someone who, whatever else can be said about him, was clearly a human being. With such a title goes an implied bestowal of the function or office that that name implies—lordship over all. One must bear in mind that we are not merely dealing with Jesus assuming a new name here, nor even just a new status, but a new role. R. P. Martin reminds us that the name above every name is a descriptive phrase patterned on Yahweh being the "all-excelling" name of God.[38] Surely the best way to interpret the gift of a new name is to regard it as the Almighty's bestowal of God's own lordship on the exalted Christ. "Lordly power is to be seen as committed to the hands of the historical person of Jesus of Nazareth, who is not some cosmic cipher or despotic ruler but a figure to whom Christians could give a face and a name."[39]

So vital was the applying of this term *kurios* to Jesus in early Christianity that the confession "Jesus is Lord" was used by the church as a criterion to determine whether or not one was a Christian (cf. Rom. 10:9; 1 Cor. 12:3) and perhaps was the confession by which one entered the church. Romans 10:9 gets to the heart of the matter. To say that Jesus is Lord is another way of saying that God raised him from the dead, or at least they are two sides of one coin. Romans 14:9 says clearly that Jesus would not have been Lord, at least in its normal sense, before he did certain things or if he had not done these things. It appears certain that Jesus was not worshiped as Lord until after Easter.

Calling Jesus "Lord" had a special meaning for Paul. When Paul recognized Jesus as the risen Lord on Damascus road, he began to see himself as the Lord's slave and servant commissioned for a special task and "bought with a price." In other words, he saw himself as owned by and ruled, or controlled, by Christ (cf. Rom. 1:1; Phil. 1:1). In this Paul is not distinguishing himself from other Christians insofar as they too are servants of their Lord (cf. Rom. 6:16; 1 Cor. 7:22b). They too are bought with a price (1 Cor. 6:20). Moreover, there is only one Lord whom they could serve—Jesus (1 Cor. 8:5–6). To say that Jesus was the one Lord was a staggering confession for Paul to make, for Jews recognized no other Lord than God the Father.

It seems possible to see a certain development in Paul's thinking. In the early and middle epistles, Jesus is mainly seen as "our Lord," the Lord of Christians (Rom. 1:3; 2 Cor. 1:3–11; 1 Thess. 3:11–13; 1 Cor 16:21–22 is especially interesting). However, by the time we get to Philippians, Colossians, or Ephesians, there is at least a new stress on Christ as Lord over all the earth and the cosmic Lord of the universe (Phil. 2:10–11; Col. 1:15–20).[40] Moreover, Christ in this expanded notion is seen as both Lord over creation and Lord over redemption. The key difference between the church and the universe is, however, that the church is Christ's "body"; the universe is not. Colossians 2:10 stresses that Christ is the Lord over hostile

and evil powers. Ephesians 1:22 says that he is Lord over all things for the
sake of the church. Thus the cosmic perspective does not replace, but
serves, the ecclesiastical one. Notice how Paul uses "all things," not *kosmos*,
to speak of Jesus' cosmic lordship. This is perhaps because *kosmos* is used by
Paul to mean corrupt human society, the world as organized by fallen
humanity against God.

When Paul thinks of this risen and exalted Lord, he thinks of unending
glory (*doxa*), Christ being the very mirror of God reflecting the bright and
shining presence of God (cf. 2 Corinthians 3 and Col. 1:15ff.). He also
thinks of Christ as the source of all the heavenly blessings, such as grace,
that only God can give (cf. 1 Cor. 16:23). In such a context one must say
that nice distinctions between Christ's name, function, and character have
broken down. For Paul, no one but a divine being can act as the risen Lord
does, no one should be worshiped or prayed to as Lord without deserving
to be called by the divine name. Indeed, there are even times, though rare,
when lordship is seen as such an intrinsic attribute of Christ that Paul
speaks of Christ being Lord even on the cross (Gal. 6:14). He even can
speak of believers doing things "in the Lord," which means more than just
in the power of the Lord (cf. Phil. 4:2, 4; Col. 2:6).[41] "Lord" is a relational
term, and the relationship Christians have with Christ, and the things they
are able to do "in the Lord" suggest that Paul sees this as an example of the
divine-human encounter.

Thus for Paul, the V-shaped pattern that is the trajectory of the career
and story of God's Son ends as it begins—in heaven, in glory, with the Son
seen as a divine figure. He is seen as one who deserves to be called by the
name above all names and is now reigning in heaven over believers, over
the earth, over the universe. He is seen as not just a lord, but the "one Lord
Jesus Christ," the confession of whom does not in Paul's mind violate
Jewish monotheism, but certainly stretches the meaning of the term.[42]
This is a story Paul likely heard in miniature in early Christian worship
when the christological hymns were sung. It was a story he heard confessed
by those who joined the *ekklesia*; it was a story the authenticity of which
Paul himself felt he could attest from his own personal experience. The
story of God and the story of humankind intertwined in the person of Jesus
so that redemption was fully and finally wrought upon the earth by means
of a birth, a death, a resurrection—the most remarkable story ever told.

Yet Paul also knew, as O. Cullmann was fond of putting it, that the
D-Day encounter of Christ with the powers of darkness on the cross only
signaled and initiated the process that would lead to V-E Day. Paul knew
that the victory on Golgotha and in the appearances of the risen Lord for a
select and mostly believing audience was at best an open secret. It was not
yet a full and public triumph that excluded all evil and righted all wrongs.

Taps could not be played; the death knell of death could not be wrung before the last trumpet sounded. Jesus' personal triumph over death and his personal exaltation had to be transferred and translated into a victory not only in heaven but on earth. It was needful that Christ's personal triumph become a triumph in which Christ's people could fully share, not only spiritually but also physically. In short, it was needful for Christ to return one final time to finish what he began—to redeem fully both the earth and his followers. It was a consummation devoutly to be wished by Paul and many other early Christians. To a very great degree they appear to us as saints standing on tiptoe eagerly scanning the horizon for Christ's return. It is fair to say that this future hope colored much of what Paul says about many subjects. It is our task, however, to conclude this portion of our study by considering Paul's reflections on the final act of the drama of Christ—the return of the King and the recovery of the sacred upon the earth.

16

The Royal Return

> At the round earth's imagined corners, blow
> Your trumpets, angels and arise
> From death, you numberless infinities
> Of souls and to your scattered bodies go. . . .
> Death be not proud, though some have called thee
> Mighty and dreadful, for thou art not so,
> For, those whom thou think'st thou dost overthrow,
> Die not poor death, nor canst thou kill me; . . .
> One short sleep past, we wake eternally,
> And death shall be no more, Death thou shalt die. ◄
>
> —*John Donne*
> *excerpts, "Divine Meditations" 7,10*[43]

IN another study I have sought to demonstrate at some length that Paul did not seek to provide his listeners with a precise chronology of the end of the End, nor did he go for the eschatological jackpot of setting a date, either more or less specific, for the return of Christ.[44] Rather, he urged constant readiness precisely because Christ would come like a thief in the night, at a time least expected, on a date no one could predict. The time might be soon; it might not. But it was the *possible* imminence of this event coupled with a strong belief that whether sooner or later it would *certainly* happen that led Paul to affirm in such strong terms the return of Christ and the events that would ensue thereafter. If the king was *definitely* coming to dinner, though traveling from afar, one had to have all in readiness for the feast, whenever it might transpire. We will examine first what Paul says

186

about the return of Christ and will then consider what he says will transpire after Christ's return.

It was not a part of early Jewish expectations about a messiah that he would *return* to earth after his death. The idea of a *second* coming does not appear in the literature prior to the time of Jesus and Paul. We might expect, then, to find something unique here about the teaching of Paul, something that stands out from its Jewish matrix. Paradoxically, these traditions about a return owe a great deal of indebtedness to Old Testament stories about theophanies, in particular, the theophanic event known as the *Yom Yahweh*, the Day of Yahweh. It is also true that Paul's story of Christ's return is indebted to early Christian traditions about the coming of the Son of Man on the clouds, but also to stories about the coming of a royal figure to a city. What his story of Christ's return is not indebted to are either the christological hymns that end with the exalted Christ or the basic credo that was passed on to Paul, as we find it in 1 Cor. 15:1ff. In short, for the sequel to Christ's exaltation, Paul drew on a variety of narratives that were not necessarily always right at the heart of early Christian preaching or worship. We will first spend some time investigating Old Testament ideas about the "Day of the Lord."

THE *YOM YAHWEH*

Most scholars agree that the concept of the *Yom Yahweh* first emerges in the Old Testament with Amos in the middle of the eighth century B.C., though it draws on previous accounts of theophanies in the Old Testament.[45] It seems probable that the Sinai theophany and other Old Testament theophanies, with some influence from the Holy War traditions, have been drawn on to portray the *Yom Yahweh*. What is more certain is that possibly as early as Amos, but more certainly in Zephaniah and the later prophetic literature, the *Yom Yahweh* had taken on eschatological overtones and was used to describe a definitive and possibly final manifestation of God's redemptive judgment. I use the term "redemptive judgment" intentionally because almost always the concept that the phrase *Yom Yahweh* represents is both an act of God's judgment on some and an act of redemption of others. This is especially the case when the *Yom Yahweh* is said to be judgment on Israel's enemies and thereby redemption of Israel. Yet even when the *Yom Yahweh* is said to be directed against Israel there is also almost always talk of a remnant that survives or is saved "though as through fire" (see Zech. 14:2). When a prophet uses the idea of the *Yom Yahweh*, most often the stress lies on judgment, though this is not always the whole picture. Amos is conveying the most characteristic idea when he says, "Woe to you who long for the *Yom Yahweh*! Why do you long for the *Yom Yahweh*? That day will be darkness, not light" (5:18). Amos is suggesting that, contrary to popular belief, when Yahweh does indeed come it will be for judgment, even on Yahweh's own people. There is something of this in Paul's portrayal in 1 Corinthians 3 and in 2 Cor. 5:10 of the final judgment by Christ of believers.

The following motifs, found in the Sinai theophany story recorded in Exodus 19 (cf. 1 Kings 19), recur in various of the *Yom Yahweh* passages: descriptions of lightning, smoke, fire, earthquake, and even cosmic upheaval. To these accompanying manifestations the *Yom Yahweh* traditions add the concept of judgment, sometimes even on Israel. This may also entail judgment on the land, sometimes taking the form of a locust plague (Joel 2) or some other form of destruction. For instance, Zeph. 1:2–3 reads: "I will sweep away everything from the face of the earth. . . . I will sweep away both men and animals; I will sweep away the birds of the air and the fish of the sea. The wicked will have only heaps of rubble." It is not surprising that this day is then sometimes called "the Day of Yahweh's vengeance/wrath" (Isa. 22:5; 34:8; Zeph. 1:18; Ezra 7:19).

The specific phrase *Yom Yahweh* is never used to describe days and events in the past. It is always applied to a coming or imminent judgment from God, and certainly as early as Zephaniah the concept has eschatological overtones. Several times the *Yom Yahweh* traditions are connected with the idea of the flow of the nations to Israel at the end of history; however, in this case the nations are not said to be converted to Judaism but are said either to be instruments of God's wrath against Jerusalem (Zechariah 14) or to be more faithful to the one true God and God's justice than are "the people of the house of Jacob" (Isaiah 2). That the *Yom Yahweh* is not something confined to a literal twenty-four-hour day but rather is an event that goes on for some time is made clear in Isa. 34:8, where *yom* parallels *sāna* (year). The day of judgment is also called a year of retribution. By the time Malachi was written, we find the idea of a prophet sent before "the great and terrible Day of the Lord" not merely to warn of that day's coming, but possibly by effecting change among Israel to avert the coming that will "smite the land with a curse" (Mal. 4:5–6).

In the intertestamental literature the stress on judgment is developed even further than in the Hebrew scriptures, though the idea of redemption is also not absent from this material. For instance, 1 En. 100:4–5 says:

> In those days, the angels shall descend into the secret places. They shall gather together into one place all those who gave aid to sin. And the most high will arise on that day of judgment in order to execute a great judgment upon all the sinners. He will set a guard of holy angels over all the righteous and holy ones, and they shall keep them as the apple of the eye until all evil and sin are brought to an end.

Here the primary character of "that day" is judgment from which the righteous get protection. In 2 En. 66:6–11 the righteous simply escape "the Lord's great judgment." It is not surprising in literature that arises out of a persecuted or oppressed group of Jews to find a stress on God's judgment on the nations, but it is telling that we also find in the Testament of the Twelve Patriarchs a stress on redemption, as well as on judgment. For instance, in Test. Jud. 22:2 we read, "My rule shall be terminated by people of an alien race until the salvation of Israel comes, until the coming of the God of righteousness, so that Jacob may enjoy tranquility and peace, *as well as all the nations*" (cf. Test. Levi 4:4). There are also clear passages like Test. Jud. 23:3, where God's judgment against faithless Israel is spelled out in graphic detail. The *Yom Yahweh* is usually called the great day of the Lord or the day of judgment. It retains and in some cases enhances the Old Testament's stress on judgment, even on God's people, but there is also a message of redemption of the righteous connected with it.

THE ROYAL PAROUSIA

Material from an entirely different storied world has bearing on our study and is found when one explores the meaning and use of the term "parousia" before and during the New Testament period. The word means "presence" or "arrival." From the Ptolemaic period to the second century A.D. there is clear evidence that the term was used for the arrival of a ruler, king, or emperor.[46] For instance, a third-century B.C. papyrus refers to a crown of gold to be presented to a king at his parousia. Or again, a parousia of King Ptolemy the Second, who called himself savior, is expected, and it is said that "the provision of 80 artabae . . . was imposed for the parousia of the king." In memory of the visit of Nero to Corinth, special *adventus*/parousia coins were cast.[47] These coins were cast during the period when Paul was writing to Corinth (1 Cor. 15:23).

Equally interesting is the evidence G. D. Kilpatrick has collected showing that "parousia" often was the Hellenistic term for a theophany.[48] For instance, in the Greek form of the Testament of the Twelve Patriarchs, at Test. Jud. 22:3(2) and Test. Levi 8:15(11) we find it used to refer to the final coming of God. Josephus uses the term "parousia" for the divine appearances in the Old Testament theophanies (*Ant.* 3.80, 202–203; 9.55; cf. 18.284). Of perhaps equal importance is another sort of "sacral" use of the term, found in an inscription from the Asclepion at Epidaurus, which reads, "and Asclepius manifested his parousia"[49] (cf. 2 Thess. 2:8). One should not make too sharp a distinction between the sacred and the profane use of "parousia," not least because by Paul's time the emperor was already being given divine status of a sort. E. Best puts it this way:

These two usages are not so far apart as may seem for court and sacral language are closely linked. It is difficult to believe that those who used the term in the Hellenistic world were unaware of this significance. . . . The word then was chosen to express the concept in Greek because it carried the nuance of movement and probably . . . because it also carried from Hellenistic culture the idea of a ceremonial visit of a ruler to his people which would be for them a joyful occasion.[50]

With this background we are prepared to examine the Pauline story of the return of Christ.

PERUSING THE PAULINE STORY OF THE PAROUSIA

Paul may have been the first person to use the term "parousia" to refer to the return of Christ. The term itself does not mean "return" or a "second" coming; it simply means "arrival" or "presence." Applying it to Christ's coming from heaven in a sense changes what the word connotes. The word occurs twenty-four times in the New Testament, fourteen of which are in the Pauline letters, sometimes in a mundane sense to refer to the arrival or presence of Paul or one of his coworkers (cf. 1 Cor. 16:17; 2 Cor. 7:6–7). This shows that the term does not have to connote the arrival/presence of a deity or king.

It may seem puzzling that Paul uses the term "parousia" of the coming of Christ from heaven in only three letters, all of them early: 1 Thess. 2:19; 3:13; 4:15; 5:23; 2 Thess. 2:1, 8–9; 1 Cor. 15:23. This is perhaps explained because the situations Paul was addressing in the Thessalonian correspondence and in 1 Corinthians required him to speak at some length on matters pertaining to the eschatological future. In 1 and 2 Thessalonians Paul must correct certain misunderstandings about future eschatology, whereas in 1 Corinthians Paul must correct an overrealized or overspiritualized eschatology by setting over against it the eschatological future.

The phrase Paul more frequently uses to speak of Christ's return is the "Day of the Lord" or the "Day of Christ." As W. Baird has so clearly demonstrated, linguistic variety in talking about things eschatological is characteristic of the way Paul approaches these matters even within one letter.[51] It is impossible to demonstrate a clear developmental schema in regard to Paul's thinking about Christ's return, not merely because in the latest generally undisputed Pauline letter Paul is still talking about the "Day of Christ Jesus" (Phil. 1:6) and "eagerly awaiting" his return from heaven (Phil. 3:20), but also because it is impossible to know how much weight to give to the contingency/coherency factor. The stress on future eschatology early on and less emphasis in later Pauline letters may as easily reflect the change in audience and problems Paul is addressing as a change or shift in the apostle's thinking.

The idea of a decisive and enduring shift in Paul's eschatological thinking from a predominantly horizontal to a predominantly vertical (otherworldly) eschatology somewhere between the time of 1 and 2 Corinthians is confounded by the fact that in the crucial 2 Corinthians 5 text Paul speaks not only about being "at home with the Lord" in heaven (v. 8) but also of "all appearing before the judgment seat of Christ" at some time subsequent to being at home with the Lord (vv. 9b, 10).[52]

Paul's eschatological language manifests a rich variety and complexity, and as time went on he put less stress on future eschatology than he did in some of his earlier letters, for reasons that are not completely clear. This did not, however, amount to abandoning one form of eschatology for another, as Romans 13 and Philippians 1 and 3 make clear. As time went on and it became clearer to Paul that his death was likely to come before the Parousia, he quite naturally reflected more on life in heaven with the Lord. This increased focus on vertical eschatology is evident in those letters where his death may have seemed rather near (such as 2 Corinthians and Philippians). In short, the contingent circumstances of Paul's audience or of Paul's own life may best explain the differences of eschatological emphasis and focus in Paul's various letters. Paul never really de-eschatologizes his thought. In fact, he does not even expunge the purely future elements of this eschatology even in his latest letter. His thought has an eschatological framework from start to finish, but unless we bear in mind the interplay of Paul's soteriology, Christology, and *theology* with that eschatological framework, we will not fully understand his thinking. The eschatological framework is shaped especially by Paul's belief that Jesus is the crucified and risen Messiah who has *already* made salvation available to all but has *not yet* completed the full work of salvation. This is why Paul can speak of salvation as both present and yet future.

Also, because of the christological story he inherited, Paul (1) speaks without precedent from his Jewish background of a *return* of Messiah from heaven; (2) bifurcates the resurrection into that of Christ and that of those who belong to him; (3) speaks of the final judgment sometimes as an act of God and sometimes as an act of Christ; and (4) speaks of the *Yom Yahweh*, sometimes focusing on Christ's role and sometimes focusing on God's. The already–not-yet tension in Paul's eschatology is caused by what he believes is already true about Jesus Christ and has been accomplished by him, *and* by what he will yet do at the Parousia. Paul never fully resolves this tension either by stressing the already at the expense of the not yet or vice versa, because he always believes that he stands between the resurrection of Christ and his return. Philippians 3:20 must be given its full weight; Paul was still eagerly awaiting the Lord from heaven even as his life approached its end.

Behind all Paul's theologizing stands the christological narrative of faith about one Jesus who came, died, rose, and would return. For Paul the performance of this narrative on the stage of history is still in the middle of things. Paul cannot conclude the drama prematurely, for the main actor must first return to the stage for one final act. I would thus suggest that partially fulfilled messianism is the essence of Paul's thought and largely explains why the eschatological framework takes the shape it does in his thought. Bearing these things in mind, we return to the discussion of Paul's use of parousia language.

It is reasonable to expect Paul to use the royal imagery and accompanying appropriate metaphors and terms when he speaks of Christ's parousia, and we might expect the description of the Day of the Lord to draw more on Old Testament theophanic and *Yom Yahweh* traditions. To a certain extent this expectation is justified; but because it is also the case that "parousia" could refer to the arrival of a deity, it is not surprising that in some Pauline texts where the term is used we also find theophanic terms and imagery. First Thessalonians 4:13–5:11 bears evidence of this sort of cross-fertilization of ideas. For Paul, the Parousia, the final judgment, and the resurrection of the dead are closely intertwined, the latter two being dependent on the former event. Thus there is some overlap of ideas from traditions about resurrection as well as from those about the *Yom Yahweh*.

Paul's first reference to the Parousia is at 1 Thess. 2:19. It is clear that the meaning of the term here is "arrival," because Paul conveys the idea of presence by another phrase, "before our Lord," and because he says "in/at his arrival/coming." A note of joy permeates this whole passage, and there is no hint that the converts will undergo judgment. Paul's converts are his crown about whom he will boast when the Lord comes. It seems probable that Paul is drawing on the idea of a joyful celebration when a parousia of a king happens. It may also be that the reference to the crown is drawn from such a complex of ideas. What Paul will present to the King when he returns is his converts who are his crown. "When Christians spoke of the parousia of their Lord, they probably thought of the pomp and circumstance attending those imperial visits as parodies of the true glory to be revealed on the day of Christ."[53]

First Thessalonians 3:13 has a similarly worded phrase, except that God the Father has been added to what was said in 2:19. Now converts will be in the presence of the Father "at the parousia of our Lord Jesus with all his holy ones." Here Paul has drawn not only on secular parousia tales but also on the *Yom Yahweh* material found in Zech. 14:5 (LXX), which speaks of the coming of the Lord God with "all his holy ones." Not surprisingly, overtones of judgment are found in 1 Thess. 3:13. The converts are being presented to God and Christ for their final review. The hope is that they will be seen to be blameless and holy on that day. In view of the Zechariah 14 echo here, it seems likely that *hagioi* in 1 Thess. 3:13 refers to angels, not believers. Thus Paul affirms that Jesus will not come alone at the Parousia.

The next reference to the Parousia is in the midst of a complex paranetic section in which Paul is trying to reassure the audience about Thessalonian Christians who have already died. The function of 1 Thess. 4:13–18 is to encourage (v. 18) the Thessalonians by assuring them that the Christian dead are at no disadvantage because they have died prior to the Parousia. Indeed, Paul makes clear that the dead will take precedence over the living in the resurrection and in going to meet Christ in the air.

Paul clearly connects the Parousia here with both the resurrection and the meeting with Christ in the air. The latter two are precipitated by and thus dependent on the Parousia. Paul sees all three of these eschatological events as made possible only by Jesus' own death and resurrection. This comports with 1 Corinthians 15 where, for Paul, Jesus' resurrection is presented as the first portion of the general resurrection. The apostle believes that Christ's resurrection makes certain that believers will likewise be resurrected. This is implied in 1 Thess. 4:14–16 and stated explicitly in 1 Corinthians 15. Second, there are no connotations of judgment here. Paul here is sailing in waters that are basically uncharted in early Jewish apocalyptic and eschatological literature.

Third, v. 14 says that God will bring with Jesus the dead. This might suggest that the Christian saints are returning with Christ from heaven. If v. 16 is an explanation of what Paul means by "bring with him" in v. 14, then when Christ comes, the dead in Christ will be raised. Paul does not pause to explain how the dead in Christ are reunited with their bodies, or whether at this stage in his thinking he believes that the Christian dead are "asleep" with their bodies rather than being in heaven until Christ returns. In view of what Paul says elsewhere in 2 Cor. 4—5 and in view of precedents in early Jewish literature for a belief in life in heaven, it is probable that Paul already believed when he wrote 1 Thessalonians that to be away from the body means to be present with the Lord.[54] Paul's purpose here, however, is not to offer speculation on the relationship of the resurrection to life in heaven. Here, as in 1 Corinthians 15, Paul says nothing about the resurrection of the non-Christian dead. What vv. 14–15 *suggest* is that Paul sees the dead Christians as persons who still can be addressed and commanded at the Parousia.

From Paul's description of what accompanies the Parousia—namely, the loud command, the voice of the archangel and the trumpet call of

God—it seems certain he sees the Parousia as a public event. Here only audible rather than visible factors make this apparent. The reference to clouds in v. 17 perhaps also reflects the use of the Old Testament theophanic imagery; but this is uncertain, for Paul is talking about a meeting in the air, which naturally suggests the reference to clouds. It is possible that the three audible components that announce the Parousia are three different ways to describe one phenomenon. Paul is likely drawing on *Yom Yahweh* traditions for the idea of the trumpet blast (see Isa. 27:13; Joel 2:1; Zech. 9:14; 1 Cor. 15:52), though the other two audible phenomena are apparently unprecedented in the literature. The reference to the archangel confirms our earlier interpretation of the holy ones in 1 Thess. 3:13.

It is probable that Paul is drawing on the secular parousia imagery, for when a king went to visit a city his herald would go before him to the city walls to announce with trumpet blast and audible words the coming of the king. It might even include the "cry of command" to open up the city gates so as to let the visiting monarch in (cf. the entrance liturgy in Ps. 24:7–10). This suggestion becomes more than a conjecture when we compare 1 Thess. 4:17, where Paul refers to meeting and greeting the Lord in the air. Cicero, in his description of Julius Caesar's tour through Italy in 49 B.C., says, "Just imagine what *apanteseis* (greetings) he is receiving from the towns, what honors are paid to him" (*Ad. Att.* 8:16.2). This word refers to the action of the greeting committee that goes out to meet a visiting king or dignitary at his parousia and escort him back into the town on the final part of his journey. "These analogies (especially in association with the term *parousia*) suggest the possibility that the Lord is pictured here as escorted on the remainder of his journey to earth by his people—both those newly raised from the dead and those who have remained alive."[55] The recipients of 1 Thessalonians would surely have been familiar with what Paul was implying by the use of the secular Hellenistic language of a parousia.

Although Paul does not tell us where the Lord and the Christians go after meeting in the air, the probable inference that he intended, and that his audience would have taken, was that they all would return to earth together. This means that although Paul does speak of a "rapture" into the clouds to meet the Lord, he is not to be taken as an early advocate of the Dispensationalist view of a pretribulation rapture of the saints so that they will avoid the messianic woes that precede the end of history.[56] Indeed, Paul seems to affirm that he and other Christians have already been experiencing such woes since Christ's death and resurrection. Thus he speaks of "the sufferings of this present time" (Rom. 8:18) or "the present distress" (1 Cor. 7:26). First Thessalonians 3:4 would seem to point in the same direction: "We told you beforehand that we were to suffer affliction." Romans 1:18 says, "The wrath of God is *presently* being revealed from heaven." Finally, if Colossians is Pauline, it points in the same direction: "I complete what is lacking in Christ's afflictions" (1:24).[57]

That Paul might have affirmed that Christians would suffer in the great tribulation before the end is not surprising, for in early Judaism a belief in the saints going through the tribulation was not uncommon. We find the idea in Dan. 7:21–22; Jub. 23:23; Assump. Mos. 9:1–7; Apoc. Elij. 4:21; and 1QH III, 13—IV, 26. Evidence also exists that some early Jews, such as some of those at Qumran, believed that the great tribulation had already begun or was beginning (see 4 Ezra 5—6; 9:3; M. Sota 9:15; Assump. Mos. 8—9; 1QH III—IV). If this was indeed Paul's belief, as seems to be the case, it may in part explain why he could so readily speak of the possible imminence of the Parousia. Yet when we consider 2 Thessalonians 2, even if Paul does believe he and other Christians are already suffering the messianic woes, it does not follow that Paul could not also conceive of certain important events still being yet to come prior to the Parousia.

It is appropriate, however, to ask whether Paul is drawing on oral or written sources in 1 Thess. 4:13–5:11, for he tells us in 1 Thess. 4:15 that he is drawing on sources. Most scholars have of late tended to favor the view that Paul is quoting an utterance of a Christian prophet or sharing his own personal revelation (but cf. Matt. 24:31).[58] Yet we should not lightly dismiss Paul's drawing on the Jesus tradition not only in 1 Thess. 4:15 but throughout 4:13–5:11. For one thing, there are many echoes in this material and in 2 Thess. 1—2 of the eschatological discourse recorded in Mark 13/Matthew 24/Luke 21.[59]

The two most solid parallels in 1 Thess. 4:13–5:11 to the synoptic eschatological discourse are the thief-in-the-night motif and the coming of the Lord from heaven. It appears that Paul has drawn on and added to one or two Jesus logia in his eschatological discussions in 1 Thess. 4—5, and that he seems to be most heavily dependent on such traditional material in 2 Thess. 1—2. Because 1 and 2 Thessalonians were written at such an early date (circa A.D. 50), we may have evidence here that Paul was familiar with important parts of the Jesus tradition even before he began his missionary work. If so, it should not surprise us that Paul's essential views on eschatological matters are consonant with what we can reconstruct of Jesus' views on these matters.[60]

First Thessalonians 5:23 is in essence the reformulation of what we have seen at 3:11–13. In both cases we are dealing with a wish prayer. Here again, Paul stresses the prerequisite of a certain sort of moral character as necessary if one is to be prepared to meet the Lord at his Parousia. Here the emphasis is on God's sanctifying work in the believer, which Paul expects to be complete at the Parousia or at least to be complet*ed* at the

Parousia, more likely the former. Verse 24 reassures the audience that God will finish the good work God has begun in them. The paranetic thrust and function of this material is evident.

When we turn to 2 Thess. 2:1, 8–9, we find a tale of two parousias, one of Christ (vv. 1, 8) and one of the "man of lawlessness" (v. 9). The former is a royal and divine one, whereas the latter is a pseudo-divine one. The man of lawlessness, as in the story of a pagan god's parousia into his temple (see above on Asclepius) will come into God's temple, proclaiming himself to be God (or a god). In 2 Thess. 2:8, Jesus, by contrast, is said to take on the role of the Prince of the House of David mentioned in Isa. 11:4 (LXX), who comes to "smite the earth with the word of his mouth and destroy the wicked one with breath through his lips." In this same verse we have the only New Testament occurrence outside of the Pastoral Epistles of the term *epiphaneia*. Like "parousia," this term is another cultic word meaning "appearing" that was also used of divinized emperors or the visible appearing of a god. The point of the seemingly redundant phrase "with the appearing of his coming" is to make Christ's Parousia seem more grand and significant than that of the man of lawlessness. Christ's coming involves the appearing of one who is truly royal *and* divine, whereas the coming of the man of lawlessness is simply the coming of a false god. The use of *epiphaneia* may also be because Paul sees this man of lawlessness as a political figure in the mold of an Antiochus Epiphanes, who desecrated the Temple in Jerusalem. Perhaps more fresh in Paul's mind would be Gaius Caligula, who in A.D. 40 attempted to have his statue set up in the Jerusalem Temple in order to assert his claims of divinity (Philo *Leg.* 203–346; Josephus *Ant.* 18.261–301). Jesus then is presented as a counter political force of greater power who will come as the Prince of David and will destroy the man of lawlessness.

Much in 2 Thess. 2:1–12 is obscure. What can be said with reasonable certainty can be summed up briefly. First, Paul is trying to correct the impression of some Thessalonians that the Parousia, also called the "Day of the Lord" (v. 2), is already present. Second, Paul corrects this impression by referring to certain events that must precede the Parousia, namely, the *apostasia*—which can mean political rebellion or religious apostasy and here may convey some of both ideas—and the coming of the man of lawlessness. These events, or at least the latter of them, have not yet occurred (cf. vv. 7–8), so Paul's point is that even the necessary preliminary events that immediately precede the parousia of Christ have yet to transpire. Third, 2:1 refers to the same idea we have seen in 1 Thess. 4:17, namely, the gathering of Christians to Christ when he comes. Fourth, in addition to this positive notion, parousia as applied to Christ in this passage clearly is associated with an act of judgment by Christ on the "son of perdition." The purpose of this material is to inject a note of eschatological reserve into a group of Christians with some form of over-realized eschatology, which in turn may have affected the willingness of some of them to work (see 3:6–11).

Finally, in early Jewish and Christian eschatology the theology of imminence or of a sudden end could be and often was juxtaposed with an accounting of some events usually involving a time of tribulation and distress that must transpire before the end. Sometimes the language of imminence is even accompanied by periodization or calculations. The New Testament writers are notably reticent about offering specific calculations, but they do juxtapose the language of imminence with the recounting of preliminary events that must come first. This is seen not only in the Thessalonian correspondence, the synoptic apocalypse, and the book of Revelation, but also in the Qumran literature and in some of the pseudepigraphical material (see 1QM passim, 2 Bar. 36—40, and 2 Esd. 10:60–12:35 on calculation).

One should not argue that 2 Thessalonians 2 is non-Pauline, for it entails the chronicling of events prior to the Parousia. Paul would have seen no contradiction between what is said in 1 Thess. 4—5 and what is said here. For Paul the mystery of lawlessness is already at work, but the "man of lawlessness" has not yet made his appearance, nor has Christ come back. There is an "already" and a "not yet" even to the preliminary eschatological events. The mystery of lawlessness that may perhaps be associated with the suffering of the messianic woes is already happening. The "apostasy" and the man of lawlessness are yet to come.

The final parousia text is in the middle of Paul's lengthy discussion about the resurrection in 1 Corinthians 15. At v. 23 Paul is in the midst of chronicling the climactic events of human history in some sort of order (*tagma*).[61] Here the resurrection of believers is integrally connected with and dependent on the parousia of Christ. As such, this material varies little from 1 Thessalonians 4. The Parousia is what triggers the final triumph of Christ over the forces of darkness.

We must now consider those passages where Paul uses the phrase "the Day," or "the Day of the Lord/Christ." That Paul means the same event by these phrases as the Parousia is evident from the fact that the terms are used interchangeably in some of the passages we have already discussed (see 1 Thess. 5:2, 4, which has both "the Day" and "the Day of the Lord"). It is interesting that in Paul's earlier letters we find either the phrase "the Day" (1 Thess. 5:4; 1 Cor. 3:13; Rom. 2:5; cf. 13:12) or "the Day of the Lord" (1 Thess. 5:2; 2 Thess. 2:2; 1 Cor. 5:5) or even "the Day of our Lord

Jesus Christ" (1 Cor. 1:8) or "the Day of the Lord Jesus" (2 Cor. 1:14). Philippians, however, has "the Day of Christ Jesus" (1:6) or "the day of Christ" (1:10; 2:16) without the qualifier "Lord."

Probably Paul has taken over the "Day of the Lord" phrase from the Septuagint, and instead of using it to refer to Yahweh, he now predicates it of Christ. This transfer is made clear by comparing 1 Thess. 4:14–17 to 5:2. Whether Paul is the first to make this transfer of the *Yom Yahweh* language is uncertain. However, this usage is perfectly logical in view of the early Christian confession "Jesus is Lord," which Paul takes up and uses. It is simply a matter of pursuing the logic of the confession to its end.[62] The christological importance of this transfer of the titles of Yahweh to Christ should not be minimized, for it means that, for Paul, Christ is to be confessed and worshiped as in some sense God. In the use of the *Yom Yahweh* language, however, the focus is on Christ's taking over the *functions* of Yahweh, bringing in the final judgment and redemption that is predicated of Yahweh in the Old Testament.

When Paul uses the *Yom Yahweh* language, the theme of judgment is usually found in the immediate context. Thus, for instance, in 1 Thess. 5:3, which follows our first reference to "the Day of the Lord," we read, "destruction will come on them suddenly." This comports with the use of the thief in the night metaphor that stresses the sudden unexpected intrusion aspect of the Parousia. In both 1 Thessalonians 5 and Romans 13 there is a play on the contrast between day and night in conjunction with talking about preparedness for the coming of "the Day." Though Christ will come like a thief in the night, when he does so, "the Day" will dawn. In 1 Thess. 5:5 "the Day" is associated with light, and Christians are in Semitic fashion labeled "sons of the Day."

In 1 Cor. 3:13 we read again of judgment on "the Day," involving a fire that will test the quality of a Christian's, or perhaps in particular, a Christian church planter's works. The individual Christian escapes but only like one passing through the flames even if his or her work is burned up (v. 15). First Corinthians 3:15 is an analogy (cf. Amos 4:11) that is meant to indicate a narrow escape, not literally to describe the condition of the believer on that day. Nonetheless, the theme of judgment somehow affecting the believer strikes a note we have already come across in our discussion of the Old Testament. The theme of exposure of the true character of something at the final judgment is conventional. Once again the material has a paranetic function meant to inculcate care in one's actions especially in regard to how one builds the *ekklesia*.

In Rom. 2:5 Paul speaks of "the Day of God's wrath," a day when God's righteous judgment will be revealed. The subject of this activity is God, not Christ (cf. 2:2–3). Yet 2:16 shows that for Paul both God and Christ are involved in this final judgment, for he says that God will judge people's secrets through Christ. He has already mentioned in 1 Thess. 4:14 the idea of God and Christ working together on "the Day"; it is God who brings Jesus at the Parousia. Here, as in Rom. 13:11–14, the reference to "the Day" of judgment serves a paranetic purpose—to encourage moral earnestness, good deeds, repentant hearts, preparedness, and the like. The use of the term *apokalupsis* ("revelation") makes evident that only on "that Day" will the condition of a human being become fully evident. God is not unjust, for God renders "to each according to his works," quoting the Old Testament principle from Ps. 62:12 and Prov. 24:12. It may also be that Paul is drawing on Zeph. 1:15, 18; 2:2–3; and 3:8 for the idea of the *Yom Yahweh* as a day of wrath. In the Romans passage Paul seems to be drawing on the Jewish idea of a treasury of works that provides a sort of "heavenly bank account."[63] This idea is found in the Jesus tradition (Matt. 6:19–20; Luke 12:33) and is well known in early Judaism (see Tob. 4:9–10; 4 Ezra 6:5; 7:77; 8:33, 36; Apoc. Bar. 14:12). Paul, however, has turned the treasury of merits into a treasury of wrath. What some are storing up is more and more judgment for themselves![64]

First Corinthians 1:8 stresses moral preparedness for the Day of the Lord, though it makes clear, because this is a promise, that God is the one who keeps them strong to the end. In content, 1 Cor. 1:8 is almost exactly the same as 1 Thess. 5:23, though the language has been modified a bit. First Corinthians 1:8 involves a promise; 1 Thess. 5:23 a wish prayer. First Corinthians 1:8 speaks of "the Day of the Lord Jesus Christ," the most expansive of Paul's phrases for the return of Christ; 1 Thess. 5:23 speaks of the Parousia. First Corinthians 1:8 speaks of being "irreproachable"; 1 Thess. 5:23 of "being kept blameless." Both verses use "in" to introduce the phrase about the Parousia/Day. The nearly identical phrasing in these two verses must be taken as strong evidence that for Paul the Parousia equals the Day of the Lord Jesus.

In 1 Cor. 5:5 Paul speaks of a redemptive judgment that happens on "the Day of the Lord." On the one hand, this verse could mean that the body will be destroyed but the human spirit saved on the Day of the Lord. On the other hand, the contrast could be between *sarx* as sinful inclination/nature, the "flesh" in a moral sense, and the human spirit. In view of 1 Corinthians 15, where Paul indicates that the body will have a part in final salvation, it seems unlikely that Paul might be suggesting some sort of spiritual salvation apart from the body. Although some Corinthians might have believed that the body was doomed to destruction but the spirit was immortal or savable, Paul did not. In addition, if in fact the phrase "destruction of the flesh" means physical death, here it is difficult to see how that could be remedial. Perhaps Paul means that the man should be put outside the Christian community for the destruction of what was carnal in him, his sinful inclinations, so that he might ultimately experience eschatological salvation. If this is the correct interpretation, then Paul is talking about temporal judgment now, but salvation at the Day of the Lord.

In 2 Cor. 1:14 Paul boasts of his converts (presumably to the Lord) "in the Day of the Lord Jesus." This seems to suggest that Paul expects to be a witness at the final review of Christians. One of the distinctive features of the Pauline letters is the way Paul uses *kauchema*, "boasting." Of the fifty times this word and its cognates appear in the New Testament, forty-six of them occur in Paul's letters. Ordinarily this term refers to an arrogance or vanity that deserves condemnation. Paul, however, uses it most often in a positive sense to refer to justified pride in something or someone. G. B. Caird suggests that the use of this language is a carryover from Paul's Pharisaic days when he believed that a person's destiny depends on his or her record.[65] For a Pharisee like Paul, it was not enough just to pass God's scrutiny; one must excel in life so that one could be justly proud.

It is crucial to remember that when Paul speaks of the events that ensue at the Parousia and he associates them with the end (*telos;* see 1 Cor. 1:8; 15:24), he is referring to the end of the present world order; he also believes, however, that at "the end" another world order will begin. He calls this eschatological world order "the dominion of God." In short, when Paul speaks of "the end" he is not referring to the "end of the world" in the sense of the complete destruction and termination of the earth and universe or the end of all human life or relationships. In 2 Cor. 1:14 Paul suggests a time of celebration when he may converse with his Lord and brag about the faith and perhaps also the lives and deeds of his converts. On the whole, Paul is noticeably reticent to describe or discuss the life to come on earth when Christ returns. He simply uses phrases like "we shall be with the Lord forever" or "we shall inherit the dominion." There can be little doubt, especially in view of 1 Corinthians 15, that he does envision such a future life happening on earth. Resurrection of the body and renewal of the earth (see Romans 8) are integral to Paul's view of the completion of the process of redemption.

Philippians 1:6 is very much of a piece with 1 Thess. 5:23 and 1 Cor. 1:8 in being a word of encouragement. Paul assures his converts that God will carry to completion his work in them "until the Day of Christ Jesus." The advice and encouragement Paul gives on such matters he gives with a real sense of urgency. This is because "the advent was imminent . . . in the sense that it might happen at any time, not because it must happen within a given period of time."[66] Philippians 3:20 shows that Paul loses neither his belief in imminence nor the urgency that comes from that belief in his later letters. Sometimes this sense of urgency involves real anxiety for Paul when some of his converts seem in danger of apostasy and of missing out on the dominion of God (cf. 1 Cor. 9:27; Rom. 11:21–22; Gal. 5:21).

Philippians stands out from the earlier letters in its use of the phrase "the Day of Christ" or "Day of Christ Jesus," but the content differs little from what we have heard before. Philippians 1:10 in fact is an even closer parallel to 1 Thess. 5:23 and especially 1 Cor. 1:8 than is Phil. 1:6. Once again Paul offers a wish prayer that his converts may be morally discerning in their choices and conduct and so be blameless/faultless "in the Day of Christ." Philippians 2:15 echoes this same theme, and v. 16 reiterates Paul's desire to boast of his converts when Christ returns. The ideas Paul associates with the Parousia/Day of the Lord vary little from the earliest to the latest of Paul's undisputed letters.

Paul is not limited to using either the word "parousia" or the phrase "Day of" when he wants to talk about the return of Christ. For instance, at 2 Thess. 1:7 he speaks of "the revelation of our Lord Jesus Christ from heaven" (cf. Phil. 3:20), and we read virtually the same words in 1 Cor. 1:7. In both cases Paul uses apocalyptic language to describe the Parousia.

Finally, note how Paul can speak of Christians appearing before the *bema* (judgment seat) of Christ for review of their deeds and receiving their just due accordingly (2 Cor. 5:10): "The life of faith does not free the Christian from the life of obedience."[67] Rather, one may insist that grace or justification by faith equips the believer for such a life. There is little doubt that the middle aorist subjunctive "receive" has a retributive force here (cf. Eph. 6:8; Col. 3:25). Paul also makes clear that this judgment is distributive; each will receive according to what she or he has done. Believers are not judged as a group, but the whole life of each believer is seen as a unity that can be looked back on. Although it is possible that the "we all" refers to all persons, in light of whom Paul is addressing in vv. 9–10, the object of this judgment is probably the sum total of all Christians. Paul can equally well speak in Rom. 14:10–12 of Christians appearing before the *bema* of God and giving an account to God. Paul's basic view of what will happen at the Parousia does not seem to change much throughout his letters, but he uses a variety of ways to express the same set of ideas.

These ideas may be summarized as follows: (1) Christ will return with his angels. (2) The elect will be gathered to him in the air, and whether they are dead or alive, they will also receive resurrection bodies. (3) The deeds/words/intentions of Christians will be reviewed and judged, and they will be rewarded or punished accordingly. Thus Paul repeatedly urges and prays for his believers' moral preparedness for "the Day," which is associated with both judgment and redemption by God or Christ or both. It is not clear where Paul draws the line between conduct that keeps one out of the final dominion of God and conduct that is merely punished although the believer ends up being saved. (4) Paul is also notably silent on the future resurrection or judgment on nonbelievers, though clearly he believes that various morally unprepared people will be excluded from the dominion (see Gal. 5:21). This is probably because he is too busy exhorting and preparing those who are Christians to comment on the fate of others (but cf. Rom. 2:7–10). (5) Paul envisions being able to boast about his converts to Christ on "the Day." (6) In view of the various events Paul associates with the Day, it is clear that he does not envision the Day as a twenty-four-hour day but as a period of time that begins with the event of Christ's return from heaven to earth. Also, Paul uses the term "parousia" or the phrase "Day of the Lord" interchangeably for the same event. It is also striking that Paul's use of these terms is confined to some of his earlier letters—1 and 2 Thessalonians and 1 and 2 Corinthians. Yet this is primarily a matter of terminology, for the idea of "the Day" is also evident in Rom. 2:5–16 and 13:11–14, and is especially clear in Phil. 1:6, 10, 2:16, and 3:20, though now Paul calls it "the Day of Jesus Christ." We should not argue that Paul abandoned his theology of the return of the Lord at any point during his ministry. Nor does he exchange a purely future eschatology for a realized one. There is, however, understandably more emphasis given to vertical eschatology as time goes on and Paul sees himself as more likely than not to die before the Parousia.

Paul uses the parousia language to conjure up in his audience's mind the story of a royal and divine coming of Christ, whereas he predominantly draws on the *Yom Yahweh* story from the Hebrew scriptures when he speaks of the Day of the Lord. Yet the imagery does overlap. Judgment can be discussed even when the term "parousia" is used, and redemption can be in focus when either the parousia or the *Yom Yahweh* language is used. The parousia language is used to express the idea of a rapture of living and dead believers when Christ returns, but the use of this terminology leads one to think that Paul believes that the sequel entails a return to earth with Christ. Paul is also capable of holding in tension a belief in events that must precede the Day, but also a belief in the possible imminence of the Day. In most of these matters Paul does draw on Jewish eschatological and apocalyptic ideas. However, because Paul now views such matters in the light of Christ, and in particular in the light of the early Christian story about the returning Lord, or the coming Son of Man he reinterprets the tradition he has inherited from the Old Testament so that he may convey the unique idea of a *return* of Messiah from heaven, and of Messiah sitting on the *bema* to judge the life of Christian believers. We must now consider the way Paul portrays Christ's completion of the unfinished business of disposing of the effects of the Fall.

IN GOOD TIME AND GOOD ORDER

In 1 Cor. 15:23 Paul begins to explain the order of events, and it seems most likely that he intends a chronological sequence here, though doubtless he is not trying to give an exhaustive account of what will happen. The word *tagma*—translated "rank," "band," "order," or "turn"—is a key one here. It is normally a word used in military contexts. Here it implies each in its proper order or sequence. The question then becomes, Are we talking primarily about a chronological ordering or some sort of hierarchical ordering in terms of authority? It would seem we have some of both here. Verse 23 suggests that believers will rise before the end of things, but not until Christ returns. Here then we see yet another way that believers' resurrection is linked to Christ; unless and until he comes, believers will not experience resurrection. It does not happen to them automatically simply because Christ has risen and they are Christians.

At v. 24 matters get complicated. This can hardly be an exhaustive description of the end, not only because it fails to mention what happens to nonbelievers, but also because it gives no mention of the final judgment, which Paul clearly believes will occur (cf. 1 Cor. 6:2–3; 2 Cor. 5:10). Verses 24–28 have been taken to mean either (a) that Paul sees Christ reigning in a millennial realm between his Parousia and the end or (b) that the end comes only shortly after his Parousia, in which case Christ is now reigning over the principalities and powers, and slowly is destroying his foe so that at the resurrection of believers the last enemy, death, is destroyed. In view (a), it would appear that Christ does not destroy death until after the millennial reign, which would create the anomalous situation of Christians in resurrection bodies still being subject to death. Barrett argues for view (b), saying that the *eita* in v. 24a could be translated "there upon" rather than "then."[68] This is plausible, but it must be admitted that view (b) has its own special problems. The destruction of the principalities and powers would then be going on in the present.[69]

In this section of 1 Corinthians 15 there is a strong subordinationist strain: Jesus hands the kingdom over to God the Father: moreover, Jesus will subject himself (or be made subject) to the Father. This implies several interesting things about the Son. First, between exaltation and parousia, Christ is the ruler of God's realm and has the job of subduing or destroying God's and humankind's enemies, the principalities and powers, and also death. Second, the situation reverts to a different expression of monotheism, after a Christocentric interval since Christ's resurrection. Christ hands the kingdom back over to the Father and becomes once again functionally subordinate to the Father. Barrett puts it this way:

The Son has been entrusted with a mission on behalf of his Father, whose sovereignty has been challenged, and at least to some extent usurped by rebellious powers. It is for him to reclaim this sovereignty by overcoming the powers, overthrowing his enemies, and recovering the submission of creation as a whole. This mission he will in due course execute, death being the last adversary to hold out, and when it is completed he will hand the government of the universe back to his Father.[70]

What this would seem to imply is that during the eschatological age, Christ is even functionally equal to God, and this remains true until God's salvation plan is completed. Philippians 2:9–11 does not conflict with this picture but refers to the situation at present until the end. Paul believes that eventually Christ's victory over evil will be total, and when that happens believers also will be totally conformed to his image by means of resurrection, after which "we shall always be with the Lord" (1 Thess. 4:17). Romans 8:20–21 suggests that creation itself will participate in this final liberating act by Christ, which in turn suggests that the eternal dwelling place of believers will be on earth with God in Christ.

It is plausible that Paul envisioned the same sort of scenario as did other early Jews, including Jesus, where there is a gathering of all the believers and sharing by them in the messianic banquet (cf. Mark 14:25; Luke 14:15–24 and par.). In one sense this is a neverending story, for it is a story about everlasting life with Christ, but we must move on to discuss the story of believers, after a synopsis of the discussion thus far.

17

Flashback

A Twofold Trip
from Heaven to Earth

IT is true that "Paul is interested in nothing less than the whole story of
[hu]mankind from beginning to end, for the whole story stands under the
righteous and merciful design of God."[71] This latter is particularly the case
with the story of Jesus Christ. It is important to note, however, where the
emphasis lies in the telling of the tale. If the Gospels have been called
passion narratives with a long introduction, Paul's telling of the story of
Christ may be called a passion narrative with a short introduction. The
focus in both cases is clearly on the climax of Jesus' earthly ministry, his
death and resurrection, and what followed from these remarkable events.
Paul, like the evangelists, is especially interested in those aspects of Christ's
career that are of soteriological, christological, and ecclesiological weight.

It is wrong, however, to overlook the cosmic scope of the story as well.
Humankind's dilemma could not fully be dealt with unless the powers and
principalities were also dealt with. Thus, although Abraham could be a
paradigm of faith for all, "Abraham . . . had no power to retrieve the cosmic
situation; and the deliverance under Moses had been local, partial, and
fundamentally social and political; it had led, moreover, to a worsening of
the anthropological situation, because the cosmic powers had taken the
opportunity of perverting law."[72] What was needed was a redeemer, not
merely an example or an informer. This meant a Story about heaven and
earth, a divine and a human Story, for the problems in the cosmos were
larger than human life.

Accordingly, Paul reflects upon and articulates a narrative that involves
both God's story and the story of humankind. It is a story that begins and

ends with God's action, first in creation, then in redemption, then in the completion of redemption. Redemption requires a twofold trip from heaven to earth by the savior, because Paul believes in a messiah who came in the middle of things, not at the very end of things, and who was resurrected in isolation.

There are many stories that Paul draws on to tell Christ's story: (1) the story of Wisdom's role in the Godhead and in Israel's history; (2) the story of Adam; (3) the Christian story about the life of Jesus Christ, particularly its close; (4) the story of Abraham; (5) the story of the Suffering Servant of Isaiah; (6) the story of royalty who comes for a visit; (7) the story of the *Yom Yahweh*, the Day of the Lord.

There are a variety of ways Paul binds the divine and human elements of this story together. First, especially in the christological hymns the Son is given a role both in heaven and on earth, as both creator and redeemer. He is said to be divine; yet God sent him, and he became a human being as well. Paul is not really an early advocate of kenotic Christology, for he continues to call Jesus the Son throughout the trajectory of his career, maintaining some continuity of identity throughout. The name "Christ" also binds the story as a whole together and is used in all of the acts of the drama. This is also made clear in the way that Paul transfers stories about God to Christ and even on occasion calls Christ "God" in a moment of worship or doxological praise. No one can fully understand the tale Paul tells unless he or she recognize that for Paul the Christ has both a divine and a human face.

Paul talks in various ways about the Christ when he wants to emphasize the human dimension of the story. He will call him "the man"; he will label him the eschatological Adam; he will allude to his being the Son of David or the seed of Abraham. This echoes and conjures up all those marvelous stories in the Hebrew scriptures that Christ has come to fulfill or in some cases to correct. He is the truer, more obedient, Adam. Like Abraham, he is a paradigm of faith as well as faithfulness. Like David, he is a royal personage who at the end of "the Day" will by means of his Parousia pay a final royal visit to God's people. What is missing in all this is any attempt to stress Jesus is a latter-day Moses figure; this is because Paul believed in a Christ in whom there was in some sense "no Jew or Greek" (Gal. 3:28).

Though Jesus is the Jewish messiah, the salvation he offers is available, not on the basis of ethnic or cultural affiliation, but purely on the basis of faith; thus salvation is offered to Gentile and Jew on the same terms. Paul does not believe in two people of God at any point in human history. Thus not only does he affirm that it was always God's plan, as is shown in Abraham's case, to relate to people on the basis of a covenant originally grounded in faith, not in circumcision and the law (see Rom. 9—11), but he also tells a tale of a Christ and a community that, though they come out of Israel, are nonetheless different from ethnic Israel as it now stands. The true Israel grows out of the old Israel, but there are certain senses in which it outgrows the Mosaic expression of that Israel. For Paul, the Mosaic covenant was temporary, until the messiah came, until the people of God came of age.

For Paul, Christ is not simply seen as or identified with Israel "according to the flesh" in his telling of this story for two good reasons: (1) the non-Christian portion of Israel he believed has been temporarily broken off from the people of God so that the full number of Gentiles may come in; (2) true Israel is Jew and Gentile united in Christ on the basis of faith, not Mosaic requirements. Paul knows that this was not true during Jesus' ministry, only after Easter, and so he does not portray the death and resurrection of Jesus as the death and resurrection of all Israel or even as the representative head for just Israel.

Jesus is the seed of Abraham; Jesus is the singular one who keeps the line of God's faithful people alive. But the Israel of God Paul believes in (Gal. 6:16) only arises as a result of Christ's resurrection. Only after that can others be "in Christ"; only after that can he be a divine inclusive personality. Furthermore, the proper response to this Christ is not covenantal nomism on the Mosaic model, but faith, and then faithful living according to the new "Law of Christ."

There was, of course, a cost to telling a Story of Christ and Israel in this fashion. There would be not only Jews but also fervent Jewish Christians who would see justification by grace through faith, a faith like unto Abraham's but a faith that leaves much of Moses behind, as a betrayal of the stories told in the Hebrew scriptures about Israel and messiah. Paul knew this, and the evidence suggests he did battle with both Jews and Judaizers over these very matters both early and late in his career. He felt he could not deny either his experience of the risen Christ, or the scriptures, and so he believed that a reenvisioning and retelling of the stories in the Old Testament was required, in light of his own experience and in light of the actual course of Jesus' earthly career, especially the close of it. Some may fault him for the way he tells the tale, but none can deny he was perhaps the greatest early Christian storyteller, and his telling of the tale has shaped the community who has listened to it ever since.

It should not be ignored that this is not just a story about properly understanding who Christ was, is, and will be. It is a story about the actions of the Christ, particularly in his death, and about how God vindicated him beyond death. In Paul's view, when one reaches the bottom of the V-shaped pattern that traces the arc of Christ's career, one has plumbed the very depths of the meaning of this story. Without the death and resurrection there would be no retelling of the story of Christ and God's people, for without the death and resurrection there would be no redemption for creatures or creation. The story is not just about Jesus, from womb to tomb, but about God's Son from heaven to earth, even unto death on a cross, and back to heaven again. Then, to finish all unfinished business, he comes back to earth once more.

At the heart of all this is an atoning sacrifice of a sinless person—a sacrifice that satisfies God's righteous requirements, averts God's wrath for those who have faith in Christ, and expresses God's great love for humankind, for this is a substitutionary sacrifice. All the stories in the Pentateuch about sin offerings come to fruition in this story, just as all the stories of the revival of God's people from bondage come to fruition in Christ's resurrection; and all the theophanies of God and the tellings of the future theophanic *Yom Yahweh* come to fulfillment in Christ's return. All of the great stories of the Hebrew scriptures are summed up in Christ's story or are given fulfillment or new life in Paul's telling of the tale. This is even true of the story of Adam, for in Paul's mind, by means of resurrection Christ was made the founder and firstborn of a whole new humanity. We are perhaps also entitled to add, in light of 1 Corinthians 15, that "Paul asserts that Christ will exercise kingship for a limited time, during which his enemies will be forced one by one to submit to him, so that in him [humankind] will regain the lordship (even over death) that was originally entrusted to [them]."[73]

Yet the telling of this story was not meant to be a mere recital of facts. It was meant as a summons to believe and obey, to trust and to emulate. Loving the story of Christ meant committing oneself to striving for and looking forward to Christlikeness. It is then necessary in the final major section of this study that we examine in detail Paul's telling of the story of Christians, including his own story. Like Christ's story, it has many surprises, many twists and turns involving both tragedies and triumphs. As we turn to that narrative, we remember the words of John Donne: "We think that paradise and Calvary, Christ's Cross and Adam's tree, stood in one place; Look, Lord, and find both Adams in me; As the first Adam's sweat surrounds my face, May the last Adam's blood my soul embrace."[74]

NOTES TO PART 5

The Power and the Glory: The End and Beyond

1. C.E.B. Cranfield, *Romans I* (Edinburgh: T. & T. Clark, 1975), 109.
2. Ibid., 110.
3. C. K. Barrett, *The Second Epistle to the Corinthians* (New York: Harper & Row, 1973), 161.

4. Eternal pain is not clearly stated.

5. See E. Käsemann, *Commentary on Romans* (Grand Rapids: Wm. B. Eerdmans, 1980), 33ff.

6. C. K. Barrett, *The First Epistle to the Corinthians*, (New York: Harper & Row, 1968), 128.

7. J. H. Moulton and G. Milligan, *The Vocabulary of the Greek New Testament* (Grand Rapids: Eerdmans, 1930), 151.

8. *BAG* 846.

9. This is also the view one finds in 1 Tim. 5:6, where it is stated that God is the Savior of all persons, but especially of those who believe.

10. Barrett, *Second Corinthians*, 180.

11. I would suggest that Paul is talking both about the position and the condition of the believer here.

12. Among the scholars holding such a view at one time or another are W. Sanday and A. C. Headlam in their *Romans* (Edinburgh: T. & T. Clark, 1902), V. Taylor, and D.E.H. Whiteley in his Pauline theology.

13. See Cranfield, *Romans I*, 314.

14. In J. Hollander and F. Kermode, eds., *The Literature of Renaissance England* (Oxford: Oxford University Press, 1973), 668.

15. What follows here may be found in a different and fuller form in my *Jesus, Paul, and the End of the World* (Downers Grove, Ill.: I-V Press, 1992), 184ff.

16. J. C. Beker, *Paul the Apostle: The Triumph of God in Life and Thought* (Philadelphia: Fortress Press, 1980), 152, 155–56.

17. See my discussion in *Jesus, Paul, and the End*, 16ff.

18. W. D. Davies, *Paul and Rabbinic Judaism* (New York: Harper & Row, 1970), 290.

19. Ibid., 300–301.

20. G.W.E. Nickelsburg, *Resurrection, Immortality, and Eternal Life in Intertestamental Judaism* (Cambridge: Harvard University Press, 1972), 180.

21. Ibid., 93–143.

22. C. A. Wanamaker, "Apocalypticism at Thessalonica," *Neotestamentica* 21 (1987): 1–10.

23. G. Vos, *The Pauline Eschatology*, rpr. (Grand Rapids: Wm. B. Eerdmans, 1972), 156, 155 n. 10.

24. G. D. Fee, *The First Epistle to the Corinthians* (Grand Rapids: Wm. B. Eerdmans, 1987), 257.

25. See pp. 164–65 above.

26. Barrett, *First Corinthians*, 338–39.

27. Ibid., 339.

28. M. J. Harris, *Raised Immortal: Resurrection and Immortality in the New Testament* (Grand Rapids: Wm. B. Eerdmans, 1985), 111.

29. Ibid., 110.

30. Barrett, *First Corinthians*, 350.

31. A. L. Moore, *The Parousia in the New Testament* (Leiden, Neth.: E. J. Brill, 1966), 172.

32. See J.D.G. Dunn, *Romans 1–8* (Waco, Tex.: Word, 1988), 16–17.

33. J. C. Beker, *Paul's Apocalyptic Gospel* (Philadelphia: Fortress Press, 1982), 90ff.

34. Sanday and Headlam, *Romans*, 388.

35. See my article on "Lord" in *The Dictionary of Jesus and the Gospels* (Downers Grove, Ill.: I-V Press, 1992), 484–92.

36. L. W. Hurtado, *One God, One Lord* (Philadelphia: Fortress Press, 1988), 121.

37. See the discussion of this hymn above pp. 100f.

38. R. P. Martin, *Philippians* (Greenwood, S.C.: Attic Press, 1976), 101.

39. Ibid.

40. This idea is probably already suggested by texts like 1 Cor. 8:6, but Paul further develops the "cosmic" lordship idea in his later letters.

41. See J. A. Zeisler, *Pauline Christianity*, rev. ed. (Oxford: Oxford University Press, 1990), 40.

42. See pp. 113f. above.

43. John Donne, *The Complete English Poems*, 311, 313.

44. See my *Jesus, Paul, and the End*, esp. 15ff.

45. For a more detailed version of what follows here, in a somewhat different form, see ibid., 147ff.

46. The Latin equivalent was *adventus*.

47. For the details on these inscriptions, see my *Jesus, Paul, and the End*, 150–51 and the notes.

48. G. D. Kilpatrick, "Acts 7:52 ELEUSIS," *Journal of Theological Studies* 46 (1945): 136–45.

49. See my *Jesus, Paul, and the End*, 278.

50. E. Best, *A Commentary on the First and Second Epistles to the Thessalonians* (London: A. & C. Black, 1972), 353.

51. W. Baird, "Pauline Eschatology in Hermeneutic Perspective," *New Testament Studies* 17 (1970–71): 314–27.

52. Ibid., 323.

53. F. F. Bruce, *1 and 2 Thessalonians* (Waco, Tex.: Word, 1982), 57.

54. See my *Jesus, Paul, and the End*, 157ff.

55. Bruce, *Thessalonians*, 103.

56. See my discussion of the problems of Dispensationalist handling of prophecy in general in *Jesus, Paul, and the End*, 243ff.

57. E. Lohse, *Colossians and Philemon* (Philadelphia: Fortress Press, 1971), 71.

58. See my *Jesus, Paul, and the End*, 280.

59. G. R. Beasley-Murray, *Jesus and the Future* (London: Macmillan & Co., 1954), 226–30.

60. I have sought to demonstrate this at length in *Jesus, Paul, and the End*, 15ff.

61. See the discussion below pp. 203ff.

62. On this confession, see above pp. 181ff.

63. Dunn, *Romans 1–8*, 84.

64. See L. J. Kreitzer, *Jesus and God in Paul's Eschatology* (Sheffield, Eng.: JSOT Press, 1987), 99–112.

65. G. B. Caird, *Paul's Letters from Prison* (Oxford: Clarendon Press, 1976), 126–27.

66. Ibid., 107.

67. R. P. Martin, *2 Corinthians* (Waco, Tex.: Word, 1986), 114.

68. Barrett, *First Corinthians*, 354ff.

69. See Davies, *Paul and Rabbinic Judaism*, 291–96.

70. Barrett, *First Corinthians*, 360.

71. C. K. Barrett, *From First Adam to Last* (New York: Charles Scribner's Sons, 1962), 92.

72. Ibid., 93.

73. Ibid., 101.

74. From John Donne's "Hymn to God My God in My Sickness," lines 21–25, in *The Complete English Poems*, 348.

PART 6

"A Good Likeness"

The Story of Christians

The cruciform life to which we are called,
In the crucible of life we give you our all,
    shaped and sharpened
    enlightened and led
In the footsteps of he
    who rose from the dead
By dying to sin and living anew
We boldly embody Immanuel who:
    —through his grave has brought us,
    —with his hand has taught us,
    —by his blood has bought us
      Lord Jesus Christ.

          —*Ben Witherington, III*
            "*Imitatio Christi*"

SOMEWHERE between experience and behavior lies the provenance of
ethics. When Paul was dealing with his converts, at times it was his task to
remind them of their own story, what they left behind in order to become
Christians (cf. 1 Thess. 1:9). Sometimes he had to draw out the implications of their Christian experience to explain how they ought to behave.
And sometimes he had to correct the behavior of Christians because they
were living in a fashion inconsistent with their own story and the stories the
Christian story was grounded in—chiefly the story of Christ, but also the
story of other exemplars such as Abraham, Paul, or even some of Paul's
coworkers and other churches. We have already discussed the story of

Christ and the story of Abraham; we must now consider in some depth the story of Paul, as well as the stories of other Christians.

The relationship between these stories is partly a matter of similarity in difference (between Christ and Christians) or shared experience (in the case of Abraham, Paul, and Christians) that provides a basis for Paul's repeated call for imitation. Abraham, Christ, Paul, Paul's coworkers, and even other whole assemblies (see 1 Thess. 2:14) are to be seen as models that both are imitatable and ought to be imitated. This theme of imitation comes up chiefly in the very places where one would expect it to—in those letters or subsections of letters[1] of Paul where he is using deliberative rhetoric in order to advise his converts about the future course of their lifestyle and behavior: (1) 1 Thessalonians (see 1 Thess. 1:6, 14); (2) 1 Corinthians (see 1 Cor. 11:1); and (3) Philippians (see Phil. 2:2ff.).

I would argue that what binds the story of Christ and Christians together is not only that God does similar things in the life of Christ and in the life of Christians but also that God requires similar things of Christ and Christians—faith, faithfulness, and obedience, even unto death. *Imitatio Christi* both in experience and behavior is meant to point and advance the believer toward the ultimate goal—conformity to the image of the Son, even in bodily form through the resurrection. We thus must reflect carefully on the story of Paul first, as a particular instance of the story of Christians, and then turn to what Paul says about the experience and behavior of various of his converts.

18

Saul Searching

Only now that you have taught me (but how late) my lack.
I see the chasm. And everything You are was making
My heart into a bridge by which I might get back
From exile, and grow man. And now the bridge is breaking.

For this I bless you as the ruin falls. The pains
You give me are more precious than all other gains.

—*C. S. Lewis*
"As the Ruin Falls"[2]

HARDLY any figure in Christian history has been so beloved or alternatively so belittled as St. Paul.[3] The great English cleric and poet John Donne once said, "Wheresoever I open St. Paul's Epistles, I meet not words but thunder, and universal thunder, thunder that passes through all the world." St. Ambrose called Paul "Jesus' second eye," and the modern psychologist Carl Jung remarked, "It is frankly disappointing to see how Paul hardly ever allows the real Jesus of Nazareth to get a word in." The church historian A. von Harnack once said, "No one understood Paul until Marcion, a century after Paul, and he misunderstood him." What we hope to accomplish in this section of our study is to allow Paul to tell his own story. We will also consider the reports of a friend of Paul's, Luke, who reflected on the conversion of Paul in some depth.

SAUL OF TARSUS

Paul was the product of the confluence of three cultural orientations—Jewish, Hellenistic Greek, and Roman. It is easy to see why he would have

215

been so influenced by all three of these cultural factors, for he was a Roman citizen, as his parents before him were. Paul was born in one of the centers of Hellenistic culture in the ancient world (Tarsus in Asia Minor). He was a child of orthodox Jews, who apparently took him while just a child to Jerusalem with the eventual goal of having him study at the feet of the notable teacher Gamaliel in order to become a good Pharisaic teacher. To all these influences Paul owed a considerable intellectual and personal debt.

Jews were not granted Roman citizenship very regularly, so we may surmise that Paul's family must have provided some service to the empire to be granted this status. Perhaps they had made leather tents for the Roman army, but we cannot know for sure. What we do know is that Paul's Roman citizenship provided him with free access to the whole Mediterranean and beyond, and his citizenship by and large protected him from local injustices and prejudices. For instance, when he was in jail in Philippi, his citizenship provided release for him (see Acts 16:37). This citizenship likely extricated Paul from many a tight spot. Paul was no doubt proud of his citizenship, and it is fair to say that he had a generally positive view of the Roman Empire and its system of justice (cf. Romans 13; 2 Thess. 2:7). Paul took advantage of Roman roads, Roman justice, and Roman order once he became a missionary for Christ. Moreover, if Paul died a Roman citizen, he would have been exempt from crucifixion, unlike his Lord. This last event likely happened during the outburst against Christians in Rome in the late 60s.[4]

The evidence suggests that Paul was in the upper 1–2 percent of well-educated people in his day. This may partly be reflected in the few quotations Paul makes from the Greek poets and philosophers (cf. 1 Cor. 15:33; Acts 17:28), but it is difficult to know how deep Paul's knowledge was of Greek writings. Paul was influenced, however, by Greek rhetorical style in the way he formed and developed his letters, not just in the use of occasional conventional rhetorical devices, and so one must assume some considerable Greek education.

This was all good preparation for Paul to be an apostle to Gentiles. No doubt it also provided him with a broader view of Jews and Greeks, women and men, and slaves and free persons (cf. 1 Cor. 9:19ff.) than would have been the case if he had been raised in a cultural backwater somewhere in the rural parts of the Holy Land, as some of the early Jewish Christians apparently were. Paul knew something of how to be the Jew to the Jew and the Greek to the Greek, and this served him well once he found his Christian calling in life.

Without question, however, Paul was most shaped in his early and middle years by his Jewish origins and faith. Under some provocation he says in 2 Cor. 11:21–22: "What anyone else dares to boast about, I am speaking as a fool, I also dare to boast about. Are they Hebrews? So am I. Are they Israelites? So am I. Are they Abraham's descendants? So am I." In Phil. 3:4–6 he says:"If anyone else thinks he has reasons to put confidence in the flesh, I have more—circumcised on the eight day, of the people of Israel, of the tribe of Benjamin, a Hebrew of Hebrews, in regard to the law, a Pharisee, as for zeal persecuting the church, as for legalistic righteousness, faultless." Paul considered himself a Jew among Jews, without many peers in his pedigree. It appears likely too, as Hengel has argued, that when Paul says he is a Hebrew of Hebrews he is claiming to know and speak the language of the scriptures—Hebrew and Aramaic.[5]

As a Pharisee, Paul is said by Luke to have trained under Gamaliel, one of the more broadminded of early Jewish teachers, but Paul in his zeal against the fledgling church showed no such temperate character.[6] Rather, he saw himself as a zealot for God's law and its enforcement, and anyone who compromised or disputed that Jews should follow such a course he would adamantly oppose. The Pharisees in general were attempting to extend some of the Levitical standards of holiness to all God's people, which in the Old Testament were applied particularly to the priesthood. They wanted to organize all of life, every human activity, in accord with God's Word. They were especially concerned about purity of diet, clothing, and religious observances such as worship, prayer, fasting, and tithing. The Pharisees believed they represented Israel at its best. Though they were the largest of early Jewish sects, they numbered perhaps as few as 6,000 in a population somewhere around 600,000 in Israel.

The Pharisees believed in the sacredness of oral traditions about the various parts of the Old Testament, and they accepted such ideas as resurrection of the righteous, eternal life and eternal death, whereas the Sadducees apparently did not. The Pharisees also believed in angels and spirits, unlike the Sadducees (cf. Acts 23:8), and that everything happens through the providence of God, though human beings also have moral responsibility. Various of these beliefs continued on in Paul's Christian life.

Even once Paul had converted to Christianity, he still saw many advantages to being a Jew (cf. Rom. 11:1ff.; Rom. 3:1). Yet Paul, whose Jewish name was Saul, also had reason to look back with regret on some of the things he did as an ardent Pharisaic Jew, in particular his involvement in persecuting the church. This is one reason why later he felt unworthy to be called an apostle (cf. 1 Cor. 15:9; 1 Tim. 1:15). In one of his earliest extant Christian letters (Gal. 1:13) he says that he persecuted the church violently. His was not merely a war of words. He even went to foreign cities to try to persecute Christians because he felt they were undermining the validity of Judaism and in particular of the Law (see Acts 26:11). A person does not make a trek of over one hundred miles from Jerusalem to Damascus unless one is in deadly earnest about his work as a persecutor. Paul was likely in his early twenties or even younger when he began such campaigns against Christians, though it is difficult to tell whether he had interrupted his studies with Gamaliel to undertake such tasks.[7]

From texts like 2 Cor. 11:23–24 and Acts 26:10–11 we get a reasonably clear idea of what Paul was likely willing to do to stop Christianity. It appears rather certain that Paul was responsible not only for the beating and incarceration but even for the death of some early Christians (see Gal. 1:13; 1 Cor. 15:9). Paul has no reason to exaggerate in his remarks in Galatians 1, for he is already at a disadvantage with the Galatians due to the presence of the Judaizers. Paul reminds them that he had told them or at least they had heard the story of his previous life (Gal. 1:13). In Galatians, Paul is doing damage control in part caused by someone else trying to retell Paul's own story in an unfavorable manner.

Paul, by his own admission, had set his face like a flint against Christianity, and there is not a shred of evidence that he was in any other frame of mind than this when he met Christ on Damascus road. We must now consider that pivotal event in Paul's life, first told by a friend of Paul, then told by Paul himself.

THE CONVERSION OF SAUL OF TARSUS ACCORDING TO LUKE

Acts 9:1–19 *Third person*	Acts 22:1–16 *First person*	Acts 26:1–18 *First person*
Luke's summary based on talks with Paul	*In Hebrew/Aramaic (Paul's Greek summary given to Luke?)*	*Spoken by Paul to Festus—Luke is present*
Saul asked the high priest for letters to synagogues authorizing him to bring Christians back to Jerusalem (v. 2).	Saul refers to letters from high priest and council authorizing him to bring back Christians to Jerusalem for punishment (v. 5).	Saul received authorization from chief priests to imprison Christians and condemn them to death (v. 10).
A light from heaven flashed about him (v. 3).	At noon, a great light from heaven shone about me (v. 6).	At midday, a light from heaven shone around me and those with me (v. 13).

He fell to the ground and heard a voice (v. 4).	I fell to the ground and heard a voice (v. 7).	We all fell to the ground. I heard a voice speaking *in Hebrew* (v. 14).
"Saul, Saul, why do you persecute me?"	Same as Acts 9	Same as Acts 9 except, "It hurts you to kick against the goads."
"Who are you, sir?"	Same as Acts 9	Same as Acts 9
"I am Jesus, whom you are persecuting" (vv. 4–5).	"I am Jesus of Nazareth, whom you are persecuting" (vv. 7–8).	The Lord said: "I am Jesus whom you are persecuting" (v. 15).
"Rise, enter the city. You will be told what to do" (v. 6).	"What shall I do, sir?" "Rise, go into Damascus. You will be told all that is appointed for you to do" (v. 10).	"Rise, stand on your feet. I have appeared to you for this purpose, to appoint you to serve and bear witness to the things in which you have seen me and to those in which I will appear to you. I will deliver you from your people and from the Gentiles, to whom I send you, to open their eyes, so that they might turn from darkness to light" (vv. 16–18).
Men stood speechless, hearing a voice but seeing no one (v. 7).	Men saw the light, but did not hear the voice of the one speaking to me (v. 9).	
Saul arose. He could see nothing. For three days he was without sight; he had no food or drink. He was led by hand into Damascus (vv. 8–9).	Paul cannot see due to the brightness of the light. He is led by the hand of companions into Damascus (v. 11).	
Vision of Ananias (vv. 10–16).	Ananias says, "Brother Saul, receive your sight!" (v. 13) (no vision mentioned).	(no mention of Ananias)

Ananias laid hands on Saul and said, "Jesus sent me that you may regain sight and be filled with the Holy Spirit" (v. 17).	Ananias said, "God of our fathers appointed you to know his will, and see the just one, and hear a voice from his mouth. You will be a witness to all people of what you have seen and heard" (v. 14).
Something like scales fell from Saul's eyes; he regained his sight and was baptized (v. 18).	"Rise and be baptized, and have your sins washed away, calling on his name" (v. 16).
Saul took food and was strengthened (v. 19).	(The above was a heavenly vision; see v. 19.)

Anyone who has ever been a student of Paul and his letters will have questioned at some point whether the Paul of the letters and the Paul of Acts are reconcilable. Many scholars think that Luke reflects scant knowledge of Paul and even less understanding of Paul's message. This contradiction between the Paul of the letters and the Paul of Acts is argued to be most evident in the story of Saul/Paul's conversion and call to Christianity as told in the three places listed above in Acts and as referred to in Gal. 1—2 in particular. Much nearer the mark is the advice of Hengel to take "seriously both the main sources, Paul *and* Luke, and weigh them up critically, in broad outline to arrive at something like an overall picture of the 'pre-Christian Paul.'" The apostle's own testimonies must have priority over Luke, "but despite his contrary tendency Luke's accounts, some of which correspond with Paul in an amazing way, may not be swept away as being fictitious and utterly incredible."[8]

It is important to bear in mind at the outset that Paul in his letters does not seek to present anything like a third-person account of his conversion or life. The only evidence we have from the apostle is in passing while he is discussing other matters or in some of the autobiographical sections of Paul's letters where he is defending his pedigree or correcting a misunderstanding of his own story. This means that in Acts and in Paul's letters we have two different sorts of presentations of Paul, not to mention two different types of literature. These factors must be taken into account in evaluating the references to Saul's conversion and call in Acts and in the Pauline letters.

We will start by noting the differences in the accounts in Acts of Saul's conversion. In the first place, some of the differences are likely because these three accounts serve different purposes and may have originally been meant for different audiences, though now they are all part of Luke's account written for Theophilus. If Luke was indeed present at one of these recountings of the story (Acts 26) and was at least for a time the traveling companion of Paul, there is good reason to expect accurate summaries here of this dramatic turning point in Saul's life.

It is true enough that these accounts are *summaries*, and Luke has described them in his own way. The accounts, especially in Acts 22 and 26, appear to be condensations from speeches made by Paul himself. Paul would be presenting his story to two very different audiences here and wanting to convey some different aspects of the account to these two groups, but Luke is only summarizing these presentations at most.

A further complicating factor is that Luke tells us that Paul spoke the speech we have in Acts 22 *not* in Greek but "in the Hebrew tongue," which likely means in Aramaic. We have this speech, however, in Luke's Greek translation and condensation. Furthermore, we are told in Acts 26:14 that Jesus spoke to Saul from heaven in Aramaic or Hebrew in the first place, but in all three accounts we have only a Greek version of his words.

One may suspect that Acts 22 is Luke's own composition and account of that encounter based on Paul's summary report to him. One must bear in mind that we have no clear evidence that Luke could even understand Aramaic, for he always seems to use the LXX or some Greek version of the Old Testament in his two-volume work. Luke, of course, was not present on Damascus road either, and so the account in Acts 9 is likewise secondhand, perhaps based on Paul's relating of the account to Luke. Taken at face value, the "we" in Acts 21:17ff. and Acts 27:1 suggests that Luke was present with Paul at the occasion of the relating of the conversion to Festus.

When one compares Acts 22 and 26, one will notice that in Acts 26 Paul presents himself as a prophet called of God, and he speaks in a way that will make this clear to Festus and Agrippa. In Acts 22, however, he is trying to present himself as a good Jew, a former Pharisee, to his fellow Jews and accordingly as one who is faithful to the God of Abraham. All three of these accounts go immediately back to Luke, who wrote them. However, in the case of Acts 9 and 22, they ultimately may go back to Paul, whereas Acts 26 is probably Luke's own firsthand account.

One of the factors that must count in favor of seeing these as narratives of real events and real speeches is their obvious differences. If Luke were to set out to compose on his own multiple accounts of Saul's conversion, we would have expected the narratives to be more similar than they are. The account in Acts 9 or Acts 22 cannot be based on the account in Acts 26, where Luke was present, because Acts 26 totally omits Ananias and his role altogether.

The three accounts in Acts 9, 22, and 26 agree in essentials but differ in some details, some of which are inconsequential, some of which are quite important. The essentials on which all three accounts agree are these: (1) Saul was authorized by one or more priestly authorities in Jerusalem to do something against Christians. As the story goes on, it is implied that the authorization applied to Christians in Damascus. (2) While Saul was traveling to Damascus he saw a light and heard a voice. (3) The voice said, "Saul, Saul, why do you persecute me?" (4) Saul answered, "Who are you, sir?" (5) The voice said, "I am Jesus, whom you are persecuting." In other words, all three accounts confirm that Saul had an encounter, including a real communication from Jesus in the context of a bright light, that turned Saul from an anti- to a pro-Christian person. At the very least, one may say that this distilled summary comports with what one finds in Paul's letters when the apostle speaks of or alludes to his conversion.

Luke also stresses that this encounter was not merely subjective, for it also affected those who were with Saul to some degree. In Luke's portrayal of these events, Saul's name does not change at the point of his conversion. Rather, when he first begins to be the missionary to the Gentiles he adopts a Greek name—Paulos (see Acts 13:9).[9] It would appear, especially in view of the way Acts ends, that Luke's interest in Paul is not purely personal but is chiefly because Paul is part of and a vital player in the growing early Christian movement. Luke is not trying to present an encomium or even simply an apologia for Paul in Acts, and thus there is no good reason to think he has significantly recast the telling of the story of Paul's conversion.

When we turn to consider the differences in the three Acts accounts, they must be examined very carefully. We must realize that ancient historians were not nearly so concerned as we are today about minute details.[10] Often they were satisfied with general rather than punctiliar accuracy so long as the details presented the right gist, thrust, and significance of a speech or event. It is thus wrong to press Luke to be precise at points where he intended only to give a summarized and generalized account. Luke, like Paul, exercised a certain literary freedom with his material, arranging it so as to get across a particular point. This is only what one would expect from people who grew up in an environment saturated with and enamoured of rhetoric.

An example of Luke's literary freedom may be found in the Acts 26 account where we have the interesting sentence not found in the other two accounts: "It hurts you to kick against the goads." A goad was a wooden stick with metal spikes against which it was fruitless to kick because one would only hurt oneself. This expression was a *Greek*, not a Jewish, idiom, and it meant "It is fruitless to struggle against God or against one's destiny." This proverbial saying was one that Agrippa or Festus would likely have understood and perhaps even have heard before, but it is hardly something one would expect to originate on the lips of Jesus in Aramaic. Paul or Luke inserts this line into the discourse to make clear that Jesus had indicated to Paul that he was struggling against God by persecuting Christians, and indeed against his own destiny. This phrase, which Jesus did not likely use when he spoke to Saul originally, indicated to the audience that Paul was pursuing his present mission because God had mandated for him to do so, and "woe unto me if I don't preach the Gospel"—to borrow a phrase from a Pauline context.

Another piece of evidence of literary license is that when one compares Acts 22 and Acts 26 one notices that the commission that comes to Saul from Ananias's lips in Acts 22 comes directly from Jesus in Acts 26, where there is no mention of the intermediary, Ananias. Thus we must conclude that in Acts 26 either Luke or Paul has telescoped the account. This should not trouble us, for the commission that came to Saul was ultimately from Jesus even if it did actually come *through* Ananias. Ananias could be left out of the account in Acts 26 because the crucial point was that Paul was authorized by God to do what he was doing. The differences between the three accounts on this matter can be accounted for in terms of Paul's or Luke's editing of the account to suit the purpose and audience currently being addressed.

Another point of difference in the accounts is that we are told in Acts 26:14, "We fell to the ground," whereas in Acts 9 and 22 it is only Saul who falls to the ground while the others stand (cf. Acts 9:7). Here again Paul or Luke is simply generalizing, because Saul was not alone in this encounter. The others also saw and heard something. It is in any case unlikely that Saul knew the position of his companions at this juncture, for we are told he was blinded by the light! The point then of saying "we" was to indicate that this experience involved more than one person and was not simply the product of Saul's overheated imagination.

The most difficult difference to account for in these three narratives is what seems to be a flat contradiction between Acts 9:7 and Acts 22:9. The former says, "The men stood speechless hearing the voice but seeing no one," whereas the latter says, "The men saw the light but did not hear the voice of the one speaking to me." Scholars have argued that here is clear evidence that Luke was not a careful editor of his material. There is, however, another possible explanation.

The verb *akouo* ("hear") with the genitive normally means that someone has heard the sound of something or someone, whereas this same verb with the accusative refers to both hearing and understanding something. This sort of distinction is clearly in evidence in classical Greek, and the only question is whether Luke might have used it here. If so, then the meaning of Acts 9:7 would be that Saul's companions, like Saul, heard the sound of the voice communicating to Saul; whereas in Acts 22:9, the point would be that unlike Saul, the companions did not hear intelligible words so as to understand what the voice was actually saying to Saul. In Acts 9:7 the text says that the companions saw *no one*, whereas in Acts 22:9 there is a stress that these men saw the light that accompanied Saul's personal encounter with Jesus.

Thus we can explain the differences in the two accounts as follows: (1) only Saul had a personal encounter with Jesus that involved seeing someone and hearing distinct words; (2) his companions saw and heard the phenomena that accompanied this encounter but had no such encounter themselves. Notice that Acts 22:9 does not say they did not hear the sound of the voice at all, but only that they did not hear the voice of the one speaking "to me."

One more difference is of note. Acts 9 says nothing about Saul as a missionary to the Gentiles, whereas Acts 22 and 26 stress this point. This is likely because Luke did not need to mention this matter in Acts 9, for it would be evident in what followed; whereas in Acts 22 and 26 Paul did have to mention this to his audiences to justify what he had been doing. Each of the narratives and speeches is shaped to serve a different purpose, and this is the major reason for the variables in the accounts.

Because of the enormous influence of this story, especially on Protestantism since Martin Luther, we should digress for a moment and make some pertinent observations that bear on the use of this story in the church today.

Saul's experience on Damascus road is portrayed as *a way* but not the only way recorded in Acts that a person can be brought into a personal relationship with Jesus. Too often some have tried, with disastrous results, to make Saul's Damascus road encounter the normative pattern for all conversions since Saul's day. Those who do not have this sort of dramatic experience or clear turning point in their lives are made to feel as if they are less than fully Christian or less than fully converted. This is most unfortunate, for there are many ways to come to Christ. Sometimes it involves a long arduous struggle with no euphoric climax[11]; sometimes it happens rather quickly.

Note, however, that even in Luke's telling of Saul's story the conversion experience was not instantaneous. He was blinded for three days and did not regain sight, receive the Holy Spirit, or receive baptism washing away his sins until the third day after the Damascus road experience. Conversion, even in the case of Saul, is seen as an event that precipitates a process, but the process of conversion is not completed until Saul receives sight, Spirit, and baptism.

Another aspect of Saul's conversion also requires close scrutiny. It appears that in the case of Saul God really did overwhelm the man and in a sense redeem him before he had time to give a considered response. Certain other stories in Acts do not support that sort of "irresistible grace" in action (cf. the story of Philip and the Ethiopian eunuch). Even in Saul's case, one must also note that after Damascus road, Saul must still willingly respond positively to the encounter by obeying the exhortation of Ananias to receive the Spirit and baptism. Saul surely did not act as a pure automaton in the latter stage of this conversion process. Thus, although it is clear in all these cases that the initiative is, and the transforming work always is, ascribed to God, there is still need for free human response.[12]

Luke, then, in his varying stories of conversion to Christianity in Acts would be suggesting that God can use a variety of means and amount of time to achieve this result. This is not to say that Luke is suggesting that conversion is an inevitable evolutionary process. The New Testament witness suggests that it involves a crisis experience of some sort, which may be preceded and followed by a process of greater or lesser length. What I am suggesting is that Luke probably would not have us take Saul's conversion as *the* blueprint of what all subsequent conversions must look like. Luke presents us with a variety of conversion experiences in Acts; we should take that variety seriously.

Likewise, when we look at how Paul handles this event in his own life there are points of analogy between his experience and those of other Christians, but points of difference as well. Paul, for instance, was not one who turned from idols to faith in a living, true God (1 Thess. 1:9).

PAUL'S OWN REFLECTIONS ON HIS CONVERSION AND CHRISTIAN LIFE

The clearest and earliest statement we have from Paul about his own conversion and its immediate consequences is found in Gal. 1:11–23. Paul is quite adamant in saying that he did not receive his gospel through human beings, nor is it human in origin or the result of some human instruction he received. To the contrary, Paul claims he received his gospel by revelation directly. It must be stressed that in this passage Paul is defending the source and content of his gospel, *not* his conversion to Christ, and this goes a long way toward explaining the differences in this narrative from the three Acts accounts. Various scholars have seen a notable contradiction between what Paul says here and what is said in Acts 9 and 22. But is it so?

In the first place, both in Paul and certainly in Acts 26 it is crystal clear that Paul does not see commission, mission, and message as deriving from a human source. There is no Christian instruction of Saul prior to Damascus road; furthermore, Ananias is not the ultimate source of Saul's commission and mission, as Acts 26 makes abundantly clear. This is equally clear in Acts 9:15 and to a lesser but real degree in Acts 22:14.

However, the real issue in Galatians is not Paul's Christianity or his commission to be some sort of missionary or just the source of the Pauline gospel, but the content of that gospel. Much hinges on what we make of the key phrase in Gal. 1:7: "the gospel of Christ." Does this phrase mean the gospel that comes from Christ as a source or the gospel of which Christ is the content? In this same context in Gal. 1:16 we likely have a clue to Paul's main meaning—namely, that he is talking about a revelation *about* the Son of God. This is likely the meaning in Gal. 1:7 as well. If so, then we should note that in Acts 9 and 22 Ananias does not teach Saul at all *about* Jesus Christ. Rather, in Acts 9 he tells Saul to arise, receive his sight, and be baptized, and in Acts 22 he tells Saul something about his commission. In any event, in Acts 22 we are probably to think of Ananias as speaking a prophetic word, not offering mere human instruction or opinion.

One must then conclude that what Paul means by "the gospel of Christ" is the distinctive and essential insights he received directly from Christ either during or as a result of reflecting on the Damascus road experience. We have already discussed what these distinctive elements likely were,[13] and so our focus here must be on the implications of what Paul says for his own conversion.

First, it is not surprising that Paul concentrates so heavily in his preaching on Christ crucified and risen, for these are, in his mind, the decisive events that changed the human situation so that one who formerly stood under the Law and its condemnation could now stand under grace and its justification. If salvation is by grace through faith in the Lord Jesus crucified and risen, then there is nothing preventing anyone, including Gentiles, from being saved apart from the Mosaic law. For Paul, the removal of the Mosaic law as a means of right-standing with God, as a way of being saved, or even as a way of working out one's salvation broke down the barrier between Jew and Gentile (cf. Eph. 2:14–15). If faith in the risen Lord was the way of salvation, then it could be offered without prior religious commitment to early Judaism, with its requirements of circumcision, food laws, and indeed keeping of the whole of Torah.

Second, Paul, according to Gal. 1:16, saw as the purpose of his conversion that he might become the missionary to the Gentiles. This is not surprising, because if all is of grace, then there is no reason why grace cannot be offered to all without Mosaic preconditions. It is very plausible that Paul deduced much of the heart of his gospel from his conversion experience.[14]

Recent treatment of the story of Paul's conversion by the Jewish scholar A. Segal has rightly stressed that we must look at what happened to Paul on Damascus road as a conversion, involving a major transvaluation of values, and not merely a calling, though that also is entailed in Paul's conversion.[15] One must delicately balance the elements of continuity and discontinuity between the belief systems of Saul the Pharisee and Paul the Christian. As Segal notes, Paul's conversion did not lead him to repudiate Torah, only to claim that he had badly misunderstood its meaning while a Pharisee.[16] This is why he is still able to draw on the stories in the Hebrew scriptures to present his own and others' current narratives of faith.

The language Paul uses about his own and other Christian conversions suggests that more emphasis must be placed on the elements of discontinuity with the past. As G. Lyons says, the "stark contrast between Paul the persecutor and Paul the persecuted preacher, between his 'formerly' and 'now,' is well attested throughout the Pauline corpus" (cf. Phil. 3:6; 1 Cor. 15:9, and the whole of Gal. 1:10–2:21).[17] This, of course, especially includes the way Paul formerly evaluated Jesus and the way he does so since his conversion. He used to know or at least view Jesus from a fallen human point of view, but he does so no longer (2 Cor. 5:16–17). Herein lay the most drastic of the transvaluation of values, which carried in its wake a change in Paul's view of numerous other things such as the nature of the Godhead, the Law, the basis of salvation for Gentiles as well as Jews, and a host of other matters. We must explore how Paul views his conversion by reflecting on the texts mentioned above and also some others, such as 2 Cor. 4:5–6 and 5:16–20, but first we must focus on Paul's view of God's role in this whole process of conversion to Christ. In short, we must reflect further on Paul's understanding of God's foreknowledge, predestination, and the whole concept of election.

FOREKNOWN, PREDESTINED, CALLED, CONFORMED

For over four hundred years the Protestant church has heatedly debated the meaning of the word *proginosko*, which is used only six times in the entire New Testament. In reference to the divine-human encounter, the word *proginosko* (verb) or *prognosis* (noun) is used only in 1 Peter 1:2; Rom. 11:2; and Rom. 8:29. There are, however, other words closely related to these—namely, *proorao* and *proorizo* which bring in a series of related texts (Acts 1:23; 1 Peter 1:20; 2 Peter 3:17; Acts 26:5).

Pro-orao is the word in Greek that most clearly means foresee, or to know in advance. It is used only of human beings (Acts 2:25; 2:31; 21:29) and once of scripture personified (Gal. 3:8). In Acts 2:31 it refers to David's prophetic foresight; in Gal. 3:8, to the scriptures'. In the other two references it means to see something before or in front of one, or to have seen previously. In Philo it is used of God's prophetic foreseeing, and in Ps. 139:2 (LXX) it simply means that God is acquainted with all humankind's ways. If Paul, Luke, or any New Testament writer wanted to express only prophetic foresight or seeing before one, *proorao* is the most likely choice.

At the other end of the semantic spectrum from *proorao* is *proorizo*, which is used six times in the New Testament, always with God as its subject and always meaning to decree, to predestine, or to foreordain. It is a stronger form of *horizo* (ordain), indicating God's sovereignty and that God's decree is prior to some time. The goal of *proorizo* in Rom. 8:29 is conformity to the image of Christ. K. L. Schmidt argues that "the synonyms and external history show that the reference in *proginosko* is the same as in *proorizo*."[18] This statement is a bit too strong, but the evidence does indicate some areas of crossover. In any case, we can say with some assurance that *proorizo* and *proginosko* seem to be closer in meaning than *proorizo* and *proorao*, if for no other reason than the latter one almost never has God as its subject in the New Testament. Also, *proginosko* does seem to have an element of will included beyond mere knowledge (cf. below).

The real heart of the matter comes to the fore when one studies the relationship of *proginosko* and *ginosko*. The Old Testament and LXX background are crucial here because these are the bases of the argument that *proginosko* in the New Testament (particularly in Rom. 8:29: "Those whom God foreknew, God also predestined . . .") means to elect, to predestine, to forelove. R. Bultmann says that *yada* (to know) is the Old Testament background for the New Testament *ginosko*, and the element of will emerges with particular emphasis when it is used of God, whose knowledge establishes the significance of what is known. In this connection it is argued *yada* can mean to elect an object of concern and acknowledgment. This meaning seems possible in Gen. 18:19 and Jer. 1:5; however, more often the content seems to be to separate and live in a special way, to have an intimate relationship with, without necessarily implying anything about one's ultimate destiny.

Bultmann also points out that in the LXX "there are far more passages in which [humankind] is the logical subject of *ginoskein* than there are references to the knowledge, recognition, or acknowledgement of [humankind] by God."[19] The element of will, of election, of choosing is present in some cases, but still the question must be raised, Is this a choosing for eternal salvation, or for a special purpose, or both? Most of the passages cited, although stressing God's choosing, do not make clear that this choosing has ultimate salvific consequences, but they do make clear that a special purpose or at least a special loving favor expressed by God for God's people is involved.

Bultmann stresses, "The corresponding use of foreknowledge on God's part in the sense of election, which is so characteristic of the Old Testament, is occasionally found most clearly at 2 Tim. 2:19. . . . [T]his usage is the furthest from ordinary Greek and was later abandoned."[20] We would suggest, however, that although the word *yada* in the Hebrew scriptures may occasionally mean elect to salvation, even in the passages where this is a possible meaning it is uncertain that the author is really advocating such a view. This is especially so when the concept of Sheol, not a positive afterlife, seems to have been the dominant way to think of the afterlife when such texts were written. In any case, more often if God is the subject, *yada* probably implies to choose, to love in a special way without necessarily implying anything about a person's eternal state or destiny. This latter meaning seems also to be the major sense that *ginosko* (to know) has in the New Testament, and if it has a debt to the Old Testament meanings of *yada*, this is likely it.

Proginosko is an intensification of *ginosko* if God is the subject and the basic sense of the word is to "foreknow," which in God's case would seem to mean to know from all eternity and, of course, before the event transpires. Bultmann felt that "in the New Testament *proginosko* is referred to God. [God's] foreknowledge however is an election or fore-ordination of [God']s people."[21] Despite this he also affirms elsewhere:

> If such statements about God's "foreknowing" and "predestining" or [God's] "electing" and "hardening" be taken literally, an insoluble contradiction results, for a faith brought about by God outside of [our] decision would obviously not be genuine obedience. Faith is God-wrought to the extent that prevenient grace first made the human decision possible, with the result that he who has made the decision can only understand it as God's gift. . . . [P]redestination statements express the fact that the decision of faith does not, like other decisions, go back to this-worldly motives.[22]

To some this will sound like special pleading; but even if these terms are taken literally, it is not clear that Paul and other New Testament writers meant what Luther and Calvin thought they meant. For one thing, as Bultmann goes on to point out, there is little or no evidence of *proginosko*, meaning "elect," in the earliest postapostolic literature of the Shepherd of Hermas, Justin, or Clement.[23] In 1 Peter 1:2 it appears that the author is referring to the "chosen" exiles, being "chosen" on the basis of God's foreknowledge and purpose. In other words, God's foreknowledge is seen as the basis of God's choosing, but the two are not identical here. *Proginosko* does not here mean "elect," or predestined, but rather refers to the basis on which God acted. Whatever one makes of this text, our concern is with the Pauline material.

We have already had occasion to discuss various aspects about Rom. 9—11.[24] Here it is sufficient to point out that in Rom. 11:2 the object of God's foreknowledge is clearly Israel after the flesh whom Paul is so concerned about, because they are presently outside of Christ. In other words, whatever *proginosko* means here, it does not necessarily imply the eternal salvation of particular individual Israelites. This text is especially a problem for those who insist that *proginosko* must mean or imply foreordination to eternal salvation. Paul is speaking of his people, the nation Israel in 11:1–3. Neither a remnant nor the spiritual or true Israel is in view at this point.[25]

The mention here that God "foreknows" is given as an indication that God has not cast off forever the first chosen people—the nation Israel. If *proegno* ("foreknew") means here to elect to eternal salvation, are we to infer that all the nation Israel, though apparently cast off, will ultimately be saved? We are forced to this view only if *proegno* means to elect in the salvific sense. Later, however, the argument of Paul is that the way we know that the nation Israel *writ large* has not been cast off is that a remnant (including Paul) is being saved. Yet more than this remnant is referred to in vv. 1 and 2 as "the people whom God foreknew." Even J. Murray says, "In this instance it has the more generic application as in Amos 3:2 and not the particularizing and *strictly soteric* import found in Romans 8:29."[26] Whether he is right about Rom. 8:29 we will consider in a moment. Here *proegno* may well imply more than knowing. It may imply the action of God loving Israel in advance, but this does not necessarily mean that the eternal salvation of every Israelite is a result of that action or knowledge on God's part. Election has to do with the chosen group, and individuals can be broken off from or grafted into that group.

In Romans 8:29–30, Paul in speaking to believers, showing them reasons they have for confidence. God has a glorious destiny planned for them—namely, conformity to the image of the Son, which in this case likely means gaining a resurrection body like Christ's, though progressive sanctification might also be implied. The stress on God's sovereignty is prevalent throughout all of Romans 8 and 9 and is reflected here.

The flow of Paul's thought may be summarized as follows: "We know all things work together for good for those who love him . . . for those whom he foreknew, he predestined." The *hoti* in v. 29 almost certainly means "because" or "for" introducing an explanatory and subordinate clause. Verse 29 shows how one knows that all things work together for good for believers—namely, because a loving God is working them together. It is God who is the subject of each of the verbs in vv. 29 and 30.

Paul is stressing God's sovereignty so much that even the part of salvation that is yet future, glorification, is spoken of in the aorist tense by attraction to the other verbs in this sequence. Because it is God "who is working to will and to do," glorification for the elect group is seen as a certain conclusion. That this is an election text is not to be denied, but the question is, What role does *proegno* play in this process?

Proegno is clearly first, from a human perspective, both logically and chronologically in this sequence of verbs. It is the point of departure. The *kai* here most likely means "also," rather than "and." In light of this, and also the fact that in 1 Peter 1:2 *prognosis* is to be distinguished from rather than equated with *eklektoi* ("chosen according to the foreknowledge"), probably *proegno* is not totally synonymous with *pro-orao* here. Perhaps, as in 1 Peter 1:2, the former is seen as the ground of the latter. It seems likely that mere knowledge on God's part is not referred to here, for all the other verbs here express God's actions. Perhaps the meaning is to love in advance, "to forelove."

In any case, the object of this verb, whether it means knowing or loving in advance, is *Christians*—those who love God and are called to God's purposes. We are not told *what* God knew about the ones he knew in advance, but definitely the *hous* ("those who") here cannot refer to God's knowing and choosing some unsaved individuals from out of a mass of unredeemed humanity in order that they might be Christians. The antecedent of *hous* is "those who love God."

This passage is about God's loving concern and actions for believers, to ensure that they reach their destiny of being conformed to the image of God's Son. I. H. Marshall is correct when he says:

> *Proegno*... means that God's loving regard rests upon [persons] before they are aware of it. In neither case however, is it necessary to assume as J. Calvin did, that it refers to God's selection of the elect and their separation from the reprobate. For here Paul is thinking of [people] who are actually believers, and all that he is asserting is that God's regard was fixed upon them in time past and that [God] is now carrying out the purpose which he has for those whom [God] loves. The thought of [people] who are not believers is absent from this passage, and the idea of a separation between two types of people is not there.[27]

The function of this material in Romans 8 is not to enunciate a doctrine of election, but rather to tell the story of the glorious destiny of those who are already Christians, as a means of reassuring the audience that they are in God's able hands and that God's purpose is to see that they reach the intended destiny God had in mind from all eternity. In other words, this is not about being chosen to be saved, but being destined as saved to conformity to Christ. To suggest that in Romans 8 Paul has a different concept of election from the group notion of election enunciated in Rom. 9—11, applied first to Israel after the flesh and then to those in Christ, is not convincing.

In this matter, God does not deal with Christians, including Paul, any differently than God dealt with Israel "according to the flesh." Paul's warning in 11:21 to Gentile Christians that they could be broken off from the elect group is more than an idle threat. Paul believes that one is eternally secure only when one is securely in eternity. Short of that, one has the possibility, however unlikely, of committing apostasy and being excluded from the eternal kingdom. The glorious benediction in Rom. 8:35–39 is meant to reassure believers that no outside force, not even supernatural ones, can separate the believer from Christ's love against their will. What Paul does not include in his listing in 8:35–39 is the individual himself or herself, who may indeed commit apostasy—hence all Paul's warnings and urgings about faithfulness and perseverance.

The importance of all this for Paul's own reflections on his conversion are severalfold: (1) Paul knows that being called and chosen for a great mission, being saved to serve, is the basis of his working out his salvation with fear and trembling, while God works in him to will and to do. It is not a substitute for doing so. In Gal. 1:15–16, when Paul speaks of being set apart before he was born and being called through grace, he speaks of himself in prophetic terms (Jer. 1:5; cf. Rom. 1:1) or in terms of the Suffering Servant (Isa. 49:1–6), and he speaks of being chosen for a specific mission in life, just as even Cyrus before him had been chosen. The point is that his apostleship comes from God's good pleasure, call, and endow-ment.[27] Paul does not say that this guaranteed his own personal eternal salvation regardless of what he did subsequent to conversion. (2) Paul knows that what he does with God's gift of salvation and service is all-important. For Paul, there are three tenses to salvation: I have been saved, I am being saved, and I shall be saved. In the latter two at least he has a necessary and important part to play. He must work out what God works in. (3) For Paul, God's gifts do not work automatically; rather, they are given to human beings to use responsibly. Indeed, they can be misused (like the Corinthians with their spiritual gifts) or even rejected in an act of apostasy. (4) It is as true for Paul (see Phil. 3:16) as it is for his converts that "it is by your holding fast to the word of life that I can boast on the day of Christ that I did not run in vain or labor in vain" (Phil. 2:16). There is a complexity in Paul's understanding of being a chosen one: "Not that I have already obtained this or have already reached the goal; but I press on to make it my own, because Christ Jesus has made me his own" (Phil. 3:12).

Paul belongs to Christ and does not want to be disowned by him; thus he presses on with all strenuous effort to obtain the goal of the resurrection of the dead (3:11). The reason Paul speaks in this fashion is that he believes not only in his own case but also in the case of others that God treats believers as persons, not as things to be manipulated. Therefore chosenness is but the stage upon which one may stand firmly and act out one's part in the drama of salvation, drawing on the resources of the Spirit, the Word, and the grace of God. Being foreknown and destined in advance is not the whole drama in itself. One must play one's part, even if there is a script set forth in advance in scripture. If one refuses to play one's part, one's part and role can be taken by another in the drama of salvation. God can raise up believers or even apostles from stones if necessary. Choices must be made, the Spirit's guidance must be followed, and hard work is required if the planned destiny is to become a reality. Paul, as much as the author of James, believed firmly that for those who are already justified, faith without works is dead. This leads us to consider further texts that refer or allude to Paul's conversion.

PAUL THE NEW CREATURE

M. Hengel, referring to a much neglected text, suggests that 2 Corinthians 4, and in particular 4:6, tells us more about Paul's conversion than is often realized.[28] Here we have a partial citation from Genesis 1 that refers to God making light to shine out of darkness. Paul, however, connects this text with the fact that "Christ has shone in our hearts to give the light of the knowledge of the glory of God in the face of Christ." In view of what we have seen can be distilled from the three Acts accounts about Paul's conversion, this may well be Paul's theological reflection upon that event. In other words, in Paul's mind conversion is the beginning of a whole new world of illumination that Paul found when he saw the risen Lord, when he saw the glory of God in the face of Christ. Like the great act of God's first creation, the new creation is a matter of God, who "calls into being the things that do not exist" (Rom. 4:17b). This implies a radical new start, a stress on discontinuity with the past in various crucial regards.[29] It may also be that Paul is thinking of himself in terms of the story of Adam, but more likely he thinks of his story primarily in light of the story of the last Adam—the one who gave up much and took on the form of a servant.

The above comports with what Paul says elsewhere. For instance, Paul, in distinguishing the sort of things that used to matter to him and the things that now count, contrasts circumcision with a *kaine ktisis*, which may mean a new creation or a new creature (Gal. 6:15). As R. N. Longenecker stresses, Paul is not talking just about re-creation, but a new creation, with emphasis on the word *new*.[30] A fresh start by means of God's saving activity is implied for the person in question. Likewise, in 2 Cor. 5:17 Paul says that when a person is in Christ she or he is a new creature.[31] Paul says of himself that even he had formerly evaluated Christ from a fallen and worldly point of view,[32] but that he does so no longer. There are two things being discussed here: (1) God's dynamic work on and in the person in question, which changes their spiritual makeup; (2) the believer's reevaluation of everything in the light of this encounter with God in Christ.

Again, the degree of Paul's about-face is shown by what he says he counts as rubbish, now that he has obtained Christ. Although admitting that being a Jew, a Hebrew-speaking one, a Law-obedient Pharisee could be seen from a certain viewpoint as great gain, Paul nonetheless does not place that sort of stock in such things anymore. The only thing of surpassing value is knowing Christ (Phil. 3:7–8). In this passage the telling of Paul's own story sounds remarkably like the story he has told in the previous chapter of the Christ who gave up his great divine prerogatives and took on the form of a servant. It is not an accident that one of Paul's favorite self-descriptions is "servant" in Philippians and elsewhere (cf. Phil. 1:1; Rom. 1:1). He sees his story as analogous in various ways to the story of Christ, and he models his behavior on the Christ story. He even believes that God is working things out in his life so that he has Christlike experiences—in particular, that he suffers "the sufferings of Christ" (2 Cor. 1:5). We will have more to say on this shortly, but it is sufficient to say now that Paul sees the trajectory of his own life as analogous to that of Christ's. Paul has given up great gains that were rightfully his and has taken on the form of a servant. He is being conformed to the image of Christ even in regard to sufferings, but also in his own chosen behavior. His hope is to be completely conformed to Christ's image possibly in his death, but definitely in death's sequel in the resurrection, at which point he will be more fully made like Christ.

Some of this is the sole and direct work of God in and on Paul, but some of it is a matter of imitation. Thus experience and behavior work together to produce a Christlikeness in Paul and in his converts. Of course, it is true that Paul does not see himself as a divine being giving up divine prerogatives at his conversion, nor does he expect to be exalted to the position of Lord of the universe beyond death. Furthermore, he does not view Christ's experience as a matter of conversion to a different faith orientation. Nevertheless, Christ is Paul's exemplar beckoning him to emulation, insofar as such a thing is humanly possible, by the combination of grace working in and the believer working out such a thing.

A clear indicator of the degree of discontinuity between Paul's past and present is that Paul can speak of Jews in a detached manner (cf., e.g., 1 Thess. 2:14) and can speak of being a Jew to the Jew from a point of view of one who is now something else. He can reassume that sort of identity or act in a Jewish fashion (1 Cor. 9:20ff.), but the point is, he now basically sees himself as some third sort of person—neither simply Jew nor Gentile.[33] He is part of a whole new humanity that is neither Jew nor Gentile and yet composed of both (Gal. 3:28). When Paul is required to trot out his own Jewish pedigree, it is often in a context where he must set the record straight about his own story and counter claims by his opponents (2 Cor. 11:21ff.), but he makes clear that such boasting is foolish and quite beside the point. What matters now is the new creation in Christ.

It seems very likely, in view of 1 Cor. 15:8–9, that one of the things that was being said about Paul is that his transformation from persecutor of the church to apostle of Christ was something that happened with unnatural haste. The implication of *ektroma* would seem to be that Paul was rushed into this new role and life, just as an abortion brings a human life into the world out of season, with undue haste.[34] Paul freely admits he is unfit, judging on the basis of human criteria, to be called an apostle in view of his past track record of violently persecuting, perhaps even being involved in the killing of, Christians. Paul's own answer to such plausible criticisms is twofold: (1) God's grace and (2) his hard work by means of grace, outworking the other apostles. This is a significant response, because it tells us something about how Paul views not only the life of the apostle, but also the life of the believer in general: God is working grace in, but the believer must work strenuously to work out God's will for his or her life.

Being born a new creature in midlife was no easy thing, for it meant a giving up of much. It meant in one sense a dying to the past in order to be reborn. Paul is not just speaking of others, but also of himself ("we") in Rom. 6:2–4 when he speaks of what being put into Christ means. It means being buried with Christ in baptism; it means being baptized into *his* death. Now this certainly means that the old has passed away and the new has come (2 Cor. 5:17),[35] but it also means something more.

Being converted means being in some sense put into the story of Christ. We have already discussed what for Paul was the heart of the creed—namely, that Christ died for sins according to the scriptures, was buried, and was raised on the third day in accord with the scriptures (1 Cor. 15:3–5).[36] Here in Rom. 6:2–4 he uses the very same language to describe the experience and then the behavior of Christians. Just as Christ died for sins, so the believer has died to sin (6:2). Just as Christ has been buried, so the believer has been buried with Christ into death (6:4), so that just as Christ has been raised, the believer in like manner *too* might walk in newness of life.[37] The major subject of this passage is not what water baptism accomplishes[38] but what conversion accomplishes, as is symbolized by water baptism, which depicts a sort of burial and rising to new life.[39] The point here is not merely imitation of Christ's story, though that is partially in view, but being grafted into Christ and so in a sense being grafted into his story—having his story played out again in the life of the believer.

A similar sort of discussion can be found in Col. 2:6ff. where Paul keeps bringing up the phrase "in Him." Thus, when Paul begins to talk about "the circumcision of Christ" in 2:9, one must raise the issue of whether he is talking about what happened to Christ, or what happens to the believer in Christ, or perhaps both. The phrase "in the divesting of the body of flesh" would seem to suggest that at least the primary subject here is Christ's literal death on the cross, as the clear reference to the cross in 2:14 also suggests. Yet equally clearly the writer speaks about the believer being buried together with Christ in baptism and even being raised together with him "through faith in the effective working of God who raised him from the dead." Christ's story is efficacious precisely at the point when by analogy it is recapitulated in the life of the believer who goes from being dead in trespasses to being made alive "with Him." This is not simply the language of exchange or interchange, for 2:14, among other verses, makes clear that what Christ does for the believer is the basis for what he does in the believer. Christians only experience Christlikeness in the Spirit because Jesus first experienced death and resurrection. Yet the two stories are similar enough, with the later story depending on the earlier for its efficacy, so that the same sort of language can be used about both. This leads us to some reflections on Paul's telling of his own story since his conversion.

PAUL THE SUFFERING SAGE AND SERVANT

There are a variety of ways Paul images his own Christian story: (1) as a prisoner of Christ being led around the world, like a prisoner in a Roman triumph, heading ultimately for his execution; (2) as a suffering servant or sage who endures much for his beliefs; (3) as a moral athlete enduring hard discipline, constantly in training, striving for the prize and the goal that is final conformity to Christ's image by means of resurrection; (4) as a spiritual father or even a nurse who has assisted in bringing many new creatures into the new creation God has made in Christ; (5) as the ambassador or agent (shaliach, apostolos) of Christ whose task it is to convey the message of reconciliation, using the usual tools of an ambassador— rhetoric, the art of persuasion. In all of this Paul takes it as axiomatic that he is called upon to imitate Christ to the extent that he can do so. Furthermore, for Paul his calling and his Christian living are so interwoven that it is difficult if not impossible to separate what is said of Paul the apostle and of Paul the Christian. The Christian life, every Christian life, involves being called by God to various tasks through which one works out one's calling to the imitation of Christ.

One of the most striking of all Paul's images is his use of the Roman triumph to describe his own career. This is seen quite clearly in 2 Cor. 2:14–17. I have discussed this passage in considerable detail elsewhere and agree with the treatment of S. Hafemann.[40] Here Paul envisions himself as a person formerly hostile to the will of the ruler he now serves, and hence he has been taken captive by Christ and is being led around the world by God in Christ in the triumph. While he is being led to eventual execution, an aroma of Christ, the knowledge of him, is being disseminated throughout the empire as he heads ultimately for Rome. Not all the onlookers catch this scent, however; some smell the dying of Jesus in him and take offense, for it smells like death. This same idea can be found in 1 Cor. 4:9, where Paul says he is exhibited last of all Christ's agents (*apostoloi*) being sentenced to death, and being made something of a spectacle to gawk at and be amazed by. In both these passages God is the author of the death sentence, and it is very difficult not to hear echoes of the story of Christ such as is found in 2 Cor. 5:21 or in Rom. 3:25, where God offers Christ as a sacrifice, with the result that many are saved. This is not to say that Paul sees his own story as salvific as Christ's is, but he does see it as modeled on and pointing to that salvific story, with the result that many come to Christ.

Paul is not merely using the Roman triumph as an image here. Paul is literally going around the empire exhibiting the dying of Christ (*nekrosis*, 2 Cor. 4:10) through his own bodily sufferings. J. T. Fitzgerald aptly puts it this way:

> Since death is at work in him, his own body is slowly deteriorating and decomposing. His "outer man" is being devastated . . . by the affliction to which it is subjected (4:16). As death takes its toll on him and *nekrosis* sets in, he loses even the bodily vitality that he once had. This is important for him, for it points to his own utter weakness and shows again why the power in his ministry must be seen as deriving from God and not from himself (4:7). . . . [T]he *nekrosis* of Jesus that Paul carries in his deteriorating body is what leads unbelievers to find in him the putrid smell (2:16) that is the product of putrefaction. Those who are being saved, however, find in Paul the "sweet aroma of Christ" (2:15), "a fragrance of life" (2:16), and they do so because "the life of Jesus"[41] is manifested in his body (4:10), indeed, in the very mortal flesh (4:11) that is being mortified. That "the life of Jesus" appears precisely where "the *nekrosis* of Jesus" does, is, of course, but another of the paradoxes with which Paul's theology is replete.[42]

Paul's presentation of himself as a suffering sage can be seen in a number of the tribulation catalogs found in his letters at 1 Cor. 4:9–13, 2 Cor.

6:4–10, and in an imitation of and to some degree in mockery of the *res gestae* of Caesar, of Caesar's public declaration of his mighty deeds (2 Cor. 11:23–29).[43] What is striking about Paul's presentation of himself, and stands in contrast to the bragging of Caesar, is that he boasts in weaknesses, humiliations, sufferings, and the like. This is because Paul is telling of his career in a fashion that comports with what he knows and relates about the story of Christ who is his exemplar. Christ is one who did not please himself but took on insults and afflictions on behalf of others (Rom. 15:3). Christ was one who became a servant to the Jews (Rom. 15:8) not only to confirm the promises to them but also so the Gentiles might glorify God. Christ was one who when reviled did not return the vilification, and this was likewise true of his agent, Paul (cf. 1 Cor. 4:12; 1 Peter 2:23).

As Fitzgerald points out, one of the major functions of the tribulation catalogs is to show that the sage is a person of exemplary strength and merit, one who is able to persevere in spite of great hardships.[44] Paul is a suffering sage—but also one like Christ, who is Wisdom incarnate (1 Cor. 1:30)—who triumphs over and through such suffering.[45]

Included in the tribulation catalogs are a number of interesting entries, including that Paul worked with his hands, that he had endured the thirty-nine lashes, that he had been punished by Romans with rods and by flogging, that he had been imprisoned, that he had been a hunted man—in danger from both Gentiles and Jews. As a result of all this, plus the sort of physical deprivation one undergoes when one is homeless, hungry, subject to the elements, or involved in a shipwreck, Paul had been at death's door on various occasions because of the cruelty of the natural world and human nature. On all these occasions Paul saw such misadventures as a matter of being a fool for the sake of Christ (1 Cor. 4:10) or a matter of carrying about in one's body the dying of Jesus (2 Cor. 4:10), and yet making the unconquerable life of Christ visible in Paul's all too mortal flesh (4:11). Paul has been crucified to the world and vice versa (Gal. 6:14) through Christ's cross. The close connection between what is true of Paul in his Christian life and what happened to Christ at the end of his life is quite clear in such texts.

Enduring suffering and sorrows and moral striving is in Paul's mind in part what it means to "put on Christ," or to put it another way, "put on the story of Christ." Paul claims, "I have been crucified with Christ; and it is no longer I who live, but it is Christ who lives in me" (Gal. 2:19–20). He is a walking billboard displaying the life and death of Christ in his own story: "It was before your eyes that Jesus was clearly portrayed as crucified" (Gal. 3:1). This latter text surely means more than just that Paul told the Galatians the story of Christ crucified.[46] Preaching is a matter for the ears (see Rom. 10:14–15), but Paul is speaking of something for the eyes, something that is publicly exhibited or portrayed. Paul freely admits that his public appearance was offensive by normal human standards (cf. Gal. 4:13–14).

Surely in light of Gal. 2:19–20 Paul is referring to the portrayal of Christ in Paul's own life and body—he was a suffering servant too. He appeared as a beaten man, indeed, like one who had been put up on a cross but had gotten a reprieve and was taken back down, now bearing about the scars of Christ in his body (cf. 2 Cor. 1:5; Gal. 6:17).[47] What "Paul had in mind by his use of *ta stigmata* here were the scars and disfigurements left on his body as the effects of his suffering as an apostle."[48]

The image of Paul as a moral athlete is found in a variety of places. This is not simply a matter of Paul's adopting athletic metaphors or the *agon* motif,[49] but rather he is following the example of previous sages who used such language to speak of their moral strivings.[50] What is most important about texts like 1 Cor. 9:24–27 or Phil. 3:13–14 is that they show that in Paul's view the Christian life, including his own, requires moral discipline and strenuous effort, and that this effort affects whether or not one will obtain the prize or, in a worst case scenario, be disqualified (1 Cor. 9:27). The Christian life is seen as teleological, straining forward toward a goal—conformity to Christ, even in one's body. This means that obedience to the example of Christ the obedient and faithful one and indeed to the "law of Christ" is required even unto death (cf. Phil. 2:8, 12, 30; 1 Cor. 9:21). The prize for the moral athlete is that God will grant one final conformity to Christlikeness in the body by means of resurrection (Phil. 3:11–12). Short of this, the Christian is not *teleios*—complete, fully mature, as perfect as a mere mortal can be. There is then for the Christian moral athlete an already and not yet quality to his or her life. In regard to the matter of perfection, what Paul always says, even about himself, is that short of the resurrection even he has not attained full Christlikeness, full maturity, the goal of perfection (Phil. 3:12).

Paul knows that there is a sense in which more is required of him as a special agent of Christ. He is called to model Christlikeness in such a way that he can call his converts to imitate him. These converts include his fellow leaders, whom he calls coworkers (cf. 1 Cor. 11:1; Phil. 3:17; 1 Thess. 1:6–7). This sometimes amounts to Paul setting an example of how to endure with courage the suffering that comes from being a bold witness for Christ. For example, just as Paul is a prisoner and sufferer because of the gospel (Phil. 1:13), so also the converts may have the privilege of suffering for Christ's sake (1:29) or have the opportunity to provide an example of receiving the word with joy, though in much persecution (1 Thess. 1:6–7). Imitation of Paul or of Christ is almost always linked by Paul to some kind of suffering (1 Thess. 2:14), or at least sacrificial behavior that puts the well-being of others first (cf. 1 Cor. 10:33–11:1; Phil. 2:3ff.).

It is at this juncture that the phrase "the law of Christ" comes into play. In Gal. 6:2 we are told that by bearing one another's burdens Christians fulfill (or will fulfill) the law of Christ. In 1 Cor. 9:21, Paul says that he himself is in-lawed to Christ. It seems clear enough from the context and content of both of these passages that Paul is talking about some set of principles or guidelines that the Christian lives by or in, principles like "bear one another's burdens." The discussions in both texts are about behavior, not experience. Thus it is likely correct to conclude, as Longenecker does, that Paul is referring to those "prescriptive principles stemming from the heart of the gospel (usually embodied in the example and teachings of Jesus), which are meant to be applied to specific situations by the direction and enablement of the Holy Spirit, being always motivated and conditioned by love."[51] I would suggest that the example and pattern of Christ's life, as, for instance, it was extolled in the christological hymns, is more likely than the sayings of Jesus to be primarily in mind here.

Paul frequently uses the language of family to express his relationship to his converts, but it is particularly when Paul calls himself a father to his converts, or a mother, or a nurse that we see something of how he views his Christian life and life tasks. For instance, in 1 Cor. 4:15 Paul says that he became the father of the Corinthians by means of his preaching of the gospel. He constantly feels he has the ongoing responsibilities of a father to provide for the spiritual well-being of his "children" (see 2 Cor. 12:14–15). This fatherly concern can produce parental anxieties of all sorts (2 Cor. 11:28). Paul can be the father of a whole *ekklesia*, but he can also be the father of an individual Christian and write a letter in his behalf (Philemon, see v. 10). This entire language is based on Paul's knowledge that in the Old Testament, when God calls a people, summoning them out of their moral darkness, it is at this point that God becomes a father to them (2 Cor. 6:18) and they become sons and daughters of the Almighty. In other words, Paul assumes a role that God, and more particularly God in Christ, ultimately has. This is not surprising, for Paul sees himself as Christ's agent or surrogate, empowered with the authority and power of the one who sent him. Fatherhood is also clearly related to conversion in Paul's telling of the story of Abraham in Rom. 4:11—Abraham is the father of those who become Christians through faith in Christ. One gets the feeling sometimes that the story of Abraham and the story of Christ have become superimposed on the story of Paul, or at least that Paul chiefly envisions his own story in light of these two narratives of faith.

Paul on more than one occasion uses the imagery of the nurse to describe his life and life work. This is part of a general pattern in which

Paul makes a point of not being introspective or speaking about himself, except in the roles he undertakes for others. One gets the feeling that once Paul was converted he seldom looked back with longing on his past, though at times he did experience angst over the fact that he had been a persecutor of Christians (1 Cor. 15:9). In a case of radical role reversal, Paul had since his conversion taken up the task of playing nurse midwife, bringing Christians into a new creation and nurturing them once born.

As A. Malherbe has shown, Paul is drawing on the earlier Stoic-Cynic sage traditions in speaking in 1 Thess. 2:7–8 of his role as that of a nurse.[52] Paul uses the imagery to indicate that Paul treated his converts gently and in a giving manner, not demanding the sort of support to which apostles had a right. In 1 Cor. 3:1–2 Paul says that he nurtured the Corinthians, feeding them milk because they were still infants in Christ. Paul's Christian life is wrapped up with taking care of others, helping them to grow in Christ, and providing them with a godly example to imitate. Insofar as he fulfills his function in life, that to which Paul believes he is called, Paul is at ease with himself. He does not waste time worrying about his own spiritual welfare. His actions are self-forgetful and sacrificial. Paul's choice of the image of the nurse is perhaps based most on what he believes was true of Christ during his earthly ministry—he acted with meekness and gentleness (2 Cor. 10:1).

Paul, in explaining his ministry to his wavering converts in Corinth, calls himself, and perhaps also his converts, ambassadors for Christ (2 Cor. 5:20). He chiefly is thinking of the role of an ambassador to make appeals, perhaps to a hostile audience, and in this case the appeal has to do with being reconciled to the one who sent Paul—God in Christ. I have demonstrated at some length elsewhere that this whole passage indicates Paul's commitment to use rhetoric, the art of persuasion, rather than force to get his converts to act as they ought.[53] This is also one reason Paul from time to time uses the appeal to imitation. Voluntary compliance to God's requirements is expected, for God treats human beings in a personal manner and gives them the freedom, by means of grace, to respond without compulsion. This is not to say that Paul sees his own compliance with God's demands or any Christian's as optional. Rather, it is obligatory, but is to be a response of a grateful and loving heart, and therefore it must be a free and chosen response.

Certainly, by far the main way Paul envisions his own life is as an *apostolos* of Christ. For Paul, his calling and his conversion came together and are often so interwoven as to be indistinguishable. Paul was able to claim that the normal signs and wonders and mighty works that some had come to expect of agents of Christ were things he had performed and could perform by the grace of God (2 Cor. 12:12). One might not have guessed this simply by reading Paul's letters, so self-forgetful is Paul and so concerned about building up others, not exalting himself. Nevertheless, Paul under provocation admits to performing miracles and having revelations, and this is one thing he assumes is natural for an agent of Christ. This may well be because Paul knows some of the traditions about Christ's miracles and revelations.

Apostolos is a term that likely draws in part on the Jewish concept of the *shaliach*. T. W. Manson long ago aptly summed up things in this fashion:

> What emerges from the consideration of the Jewish evidence regarding the *shaliach*? First, that he performs on behalf of someone else, whether an individual or a corporate body, functions which his principal is himself entitled to perform. Second, that the nature of his activities, and in some cases their duration, is defined; so that his authority does not go beyond the terms of his commission. Third, that his commission is not transferable. When he ceases to exercise it, the authority reverts to the principal. Fourth, that *shaliach* is not a term of status but of function. Fifth, that in so far as the *shaliach* has a religious commission it is always exercised within the borders of Jewry, and does not involve what we should call missionary activity.[54]

What this summary reveals is that Paul's concept of *apostolos* cannot be derived just from the Jewish idea of *shaliach*, because for Paul it means someone who is a missionary and is acting beyond the borders of Jewry.[55] Yet the extreme frequency of the term *apostolos* both in Paul and elsewhere in the New Testament, a term that is by no means common outside of Christian literature, requires some explanation. Barrett has argued plausibly that the early Christians, and perhaps especially Paul, adopted and adapted the *shaliach* concept to their own ends.[56] It seems apparent that when Paul uses the term to refer not merely to an agent of some local congregation given some limited task (cf. Phil. 2:25; 2 Cor. 8:23) but to an *apostolos* of Jesus Christ, such as himself, he is referring to a person under authority with an ongoing commission to do various kinds of missionary tasks, especially proclaiming the gospel and planting churches (cf. 1 Cor. 3:10–15). As such, he is a servant of Christ sent on this mission and a steward of the mysteries of God (1 Cor. 4:1).

It is characteristic of such a servant that he or she must act within the limits of his or her commission. Such persons know they are not autonomous authorities, but rather are dependent upon the one who sent them both for the manner and the matter of their mission. "It is required of stewards that they be found trustworthy" (1 Cor. 4:2). When one is authorized to speak or act for another, one becomes an extension of the one who has sent them. This is one reason why for Paul imitation of Christ is so important. His words and deeds must be the very sort of thing that Christ would have said or done in the same circumstance. Paul is perhaps aided in this task from time to time by fresh revelation from Christ, but one cannot help but get the feeling that apart from the revelation that came in his conversion Paul normally relies on traditions of and from Jesus, and the imitating of what he knows of the historical Jesus. Whatever else one may say, the fact that Paul can speak in the same breath of his converts imitating him and then immediately refer to the fact that he imitates Christ (1 Cor. 11:1; cf. 1 Cor. 4:16) may be put down to the fact that Paul, being Christ's *apostolos*, models Christ for his converts.

For Paul, being Christ's *apostolos* means a life that entails not only the necessity of living in a fashion that comports with the life pattern of Christ but also preaching as Christ requires: "For necessity is laid upon me. Woe to me if I do not preach the gospel!" (1 Cor. 9:16). In such a situation, Paul does not envision that he has a private life any more than a slave would have, nor a choice of jobs any more than a *shaliach* had. For Paul, his life work was his life, and it was all consuming. He would pursue it until he himself was finally conformed to the pattern of the close of Christ's life—being obedient unto death and being raised in fashion like unto Christ.

Yet Paul is not satisfied just to fulfill his life work, what Christ has commisioned him to do. He seeks to do even more—for instance, by not accepting support—so he will have something to boast of on the Day of the Lord (1 Cor. 9:15–18). Paul doesn't just work to rule, he works for a reward. He wants his converts to act in such a manner, going above and beyond the call of duty, both in love and in anticipation of the greater approbation of Christ in the life to come.

I have argued elsewhere that the first person in 1 Corinthians 13 must be taken very seriously.[57] Here Paul describes himself as a tongue speaker (cf. 1 Cor. 14:18), a prophet (14:37–38), one who understands revelations and mysteries (cf. 2 Cor. 12:1ff.), one who has a miracle-working faith (2 Cor. 12:12), one who has given up much (cf. Phil. 3:7), and one who had given his body up to death for the sake of the gospel on numerous occasions (2 Cor. 11:23–29). Yet without love, the love of Christ and love like Christ, all such activities are for nought. These activities are temporal and temporary, but love is the one quality in the believers' life that will transcend the boundary of death in recognizably the same form. Faith will become sight, hope will be fulfilled, but love endures forever. It has often been said that 1 Cor. 13:4–7 especially depicts Christ's character. This is true enough, but Paul is using it to depict what Christlikeness, both in his own case and that of others, should look like. Paul may have had many teachers, but in his mind he had one exemplar who eclipsed them all—hence his attempt to imitate Christ, above all else, in his thoughts, deeds, and words, his general pattern of life.

The call for imitation was a normal one for one seeking to be a sage or rhetorician, striving to teach his charges.[58] It implies a relationship of a hierarchical sort. To call someone to imitate another implies that the other's authority and example is recognized by those who would be imitators. This says something to us about not only how Paul viewed his relationship with Christ but also how he viewed his relationship with Christians. Yet Paul, modeling himself on Christ, takes on the roles and form of a servant and thus presents himself as an enslaved leader, a sage in whom God's power is manifest mainly through Paul's weakness.[59] In other words, Paul lives a life of paradox. He is a powerful-yet-weak-leader-yet-servant figure, and the call to imitation is given in the context of this sort of vision of servant leadership and resource stewardship.

Paul followed as best he could the V-shaped pattern of the life of Christ in his own life, longing for his own resurrection beyond a life of obedience unto death. There was to be no completion, no perfection short of final conformity to Christ, being like him in a resurrection body. Paul called his converts to set their sights equally high—focusing on the upward call of God in Christ. We must now consider in detail how Paul describes the various aspects of life in Christ for believers in general.

Mar
*p 245-
351*

19

The Christening of the Believer

*The Story of Life in Christ
and Life in the Spirit*

"In the coming world they will not ask me, 'Why were you not Moses?'
They will ask me, 'Why were you not Zusya?' " Even with some
adaptation, the Christian would not say this with reference to Christ. For
Christ does not simply bid me be myself, he calls me to live in him. His
Spirit is to be the source of our life, as well as director of our path.

—*G. M. Styler, quoting a saying of R. Zusya*[60]

THE story of the Christian life is a story that moves from new life to new
body, just as Paul's story did. It is, of course, a story that has antecedents,
but Paul is not much concerned with these, except occasionally to remind
his converts of what they once were and are no longer meant to be. The
Christian story proper is a story that rests on the various stories we have
already examined. For all, the story of Adam lurks in the background; for
all, the story of Abraham is umbilically linked to the story of Christians
through Christ, for some, the story of Moses and the Mosaic covenant is a
part of their sacred history; and finally, for all, the story of Christ is the
basis, ground, and generating influence that both makes possible the
Christian story and continues to make it a viable and ongoing drama. C. K.
Barrett has put it this way:

> The basic terms in which Christian existence must be understood are
> eschatological. It rests upon Christ's own resurrection and victory over
> the powers brought forward from the time of the End, and upon the
> verdict of acquittal brought forward from the last judgement. It is thus a

245

unique eschatology, since it asserts that, notwithstanding appearances, the End has already come, and further that, notwithstanding this confident assertion, the End is not yet. Out of this formula "Already-Not Yet," which is the fundamental pattern of the Christian life, we see evolving in Paul the more developed maxim of "As if not" (*hos me*).[61]

This means that the Christian lives in the shadow not of Eden but of the new creation, and that in some ways she or he gets to taste the promised fruit, which is not forbidden, of this new creation in advance of its full-fledged arrival. Life in Christ, life in the Spirit, is already eschatological life, yet it is life lived in an old world and in an old body subject to disease, decay, and death. In such a situation, Christlikeness is only possible in part before the return of Christ and the resurrection. Believers always live between new birth and new body, but their existence is in motion and is teleological. The former pole of Christian existence gradually recedes into the past, whereas the latter one comes closer and closer, at least in the form of its normal necessary precursor—death.

We must explore this story in some depth now, tracing the trajectory of Christian existence. This will entail considering at the start matters such as God's plan, God's righteousness, the believer's pardon, grace, faith, and the new creation. Then we must reflect on what life in the Spirit is like and ought to be like in terms of experience, belief, and behavior. Finally, we must look at the goal to which the believer presses—full conformity to the image of Christ in a resurrection body.

THE RIGHTEOUSNESS OF GOD AND THE RIGHTING OF THE HUMAN STORY

The story of human salvation in general, like the story of Paul in particular, begins in the mind and heart of God. This means that we must say a few more things about Paul's understanding of election, especially because it affects how one views the atonement, among other things. Certain key texts need to be discussed, such as Rom. 8:29–30; Rom. 9—11; and Eph. 1:5, 11 (if the latter is Pauline).

ELECTION RETURNS

As we have already seen in our discussion of Paul's story, it is clear in Rom. 8:28ff. that Paul is talking about Christians. Verse 28 is very explicitly talking about those who love God and are called unto God's purpose. It follows from this that it is very difficult to derive any election unto salvation here. What Paul is saying is that the Christians whom God foreknew, God also predestined to be conformed to Christ's image. I. H.

~ Marshall is right to stress the end of the passage here. The purpose of this passage is to make clear that nothing external can prevent Christians from reaching the goal of glorification. God is involved at every stage of the process, ensuring its completion. Marshall stresses:

> Paul's concern is with believers who are looking forward to the "redemption of the body" but are tempted to despair of ever reaching the goal because of their present sufferings. . . . The verb thus refers to the loving knowledge which God already has of [God's] people. It does not refer to the separation of the elect and consequent rejection of the reprobate, a thought which is not present in the context.[62]

The purpose, then, that God has already formed for those whom God knows to be believers is glorification. It is possible that Paul is saying that God has predestined those who are Christians to be conformed to the Son's image, so they need not worry about reaching that goal, so far as outside interference is concerned.

One must also ask what it means to say that God foreknows something. Some have suggested that, strictly speaking, God does not foreknow anything, but rather simply knows it. That is, Paul's language here is anthropological; from a human point of view God knows certain things in advance, but from God's point of view God simply knows it. Foreknowledge is said in Rom. 8:28ff. to be different from and the basis of predestination. We can only conclude from this that Paul believes God wills things on the basis of divine knowledge. The NIV has translated rightly, "Those whom God foreknew, God also predestined." Willing and knowing cannot be equated. It is especially incorrect to argue on the basis of this text that God knows it because God wills or determines it. This text provides no basis for the idea that God's foreknowledge is certain because it is based on God's prior divine decree.

A moment's reflection will lead to the conclusion that God can have a certain knowledge of human sin without willing it, and one would be treading on very thin ice to suggest that Paul believes that God wills sin. If God can foreknow sin, it follows that God can know things God does not decree. This being so, one must be careful how one envisions the way Paul relates God's will and knowledge in the story of Christians. Research on the Hebrew word *yada* strongly suggests that *yada* has the sense of intimate personal knowledge of something, but not necessarily the choosing of it. If *yada* is the background here, standing behind and influencing Paul's use of *proginosko*, this further supports the distinction of "foreknow" and "foreordain."[63] Thus we conclude that Rom. 8:28ff. does not provide a basis for asserting that God has limited the atonement from the divine perspective, but certainly it makes clear (a) that salvation begins and depends upon a divine initiative; (b) that salvation could not transpire unless God planned, led, enabled, and supported believers through every stage of their working out of their salvation; and (c) that no third force can separate believers from God. This text does not, however, rule out either that believers must respond in faith willingly to the divine initiative or that they may at some future date apostasize (i.e., separate themselves from God).

In Rom. 9—11 Paul wants to make clear that even with God's election of the corporate entity Israel, there are some individuals who are not "of Israel" (cf. 11:5–7; 9:6). God's promises have not been revoked. Romans 11:28 makes clear that even those Israelites currently broken off from God's people are still loved because of God's electing purpose. God's call and promises to them are irrevocable. Paul allows, however, that all throughout the drama of human salvation individual branches of Israel were broken off due to unbelief (11:20ff.), and everywhere he warns the saved Gentiles that their fate will be similar if they do not exercise faith (11:21, cf. 9:32), believe in their hearts, and confess (10:11 ff.). He also goes on to insist that people become Christians by hearing the preaching and receiving it by faith. Ultimately, salvation depends not on human desire or effort, but on God's mercy and gracious offer (9:18), so Jew and Gentile are on the same footing (10:12). It is true that at 11:26 Paul says, "All Israel will be saved," but in light of what he has said elsewhere, this cannot be apart from a faith response.[64] Thus there is nothing here that would suggest that Paul's understanding of election meant that God's grand design included the idea of salvation and atonement limited by a divine decree, before or apart from the human response of faith. Election here, as elsewhere, is a corporate phenomenon.

Finally, for the sake of completion we must consider Ephesians 1, for it may reflect Paul's thought, even if he did not personally write this document. Ephesians 1:3–4 is part of a long and somewhat clumsy sentence that does not end till v. 14. Two groups of people that in fact overlap are distinguished here: the "we" (or "us") mentioned in vv. 3–14 and the "you" mentioned in v. 13. As Marshall points out, the "we" refers to the church as a whole, and the "you" refers to the once pagan readers of the epistle who have now been added to the church.[65] This means that this passage refers to the church as a corporate entity and the audience, insofar as they are part of it. Verse 3 says that the blessings that are theirs are in heaven and in Christ. Verse 4 continues this thought saying God chose believers "in Christ." Notice that he does not say God chose believers to be in Christ, but God chose them "in Christ."

One may want to ask how God could choose believers before they existed? To be sure, God could foresee and plan to choose them, but this is not what the text says. It says that God chose them in Christ. I would suggest that this may mean that God chose Christ because the author believed that Christ was preexistent, and believers are chosen insofar as they are connected to Christ. That is, when Paul thinks of the story of Christians, he thinks of it in the context of the broader story of Christ. Just as the believer's blessing is not in herself or himself but in Christ and in heaven, so the believer's being chosen has to do with Christ, who always was and was chosen by God. Christ is God's elect one, chosen to save the world since before creation. Thus we conclude that the church is elect and chosen in Christ, who is and was in heaven. Nothing is said here about particular individuals being chosen to be in Christ. Consider the judicious conclusions of M. Barth:

> This formula describes God's relationship to the congregation of the saints rather than to individuals only. Election "in Christ" must be understood as election of God's people. Only as members of that community do individuals share in the benefits of God's gracious choice. . . . If the person of Jesus Christ is the prime object and subject, the revealed secret and instrument of God's election, and if he represents all those elected, then all notions of a fixed will, testament, plan, and program of God are not only inadequate but contrary to the sense of Eph. 1. Election does not consist of the creation of a scheme which divides [hu]mankind into two opposite groups. Much more is it that person-to-person relationship of love which exists in the relation between God and [God's] Son and is revealed only by the events that manifest this relationship. . . . God's election is not an *absolute* decree, but is relative to the Son, his mission, death, resurrection.[66]

GRACE NOTES

This leads us to consider Paul's understanding of the grace and the "righteousness of God" as it affects the story of the believer. There is no doubt that grace is a vital term for Paul. More important, grace is a term that describes an action or benefit of God that in effect changes the human story. Thus we must look at *charis* and its cognates (*charisma, charizomai*) in some detail. In Greek literature, *charis* can mean a variety of things: (1) that which causes a favorable regard (attractiveness, gracefulness of form, or graciousness of speech); (2) the favorable regard someone feels toward another (i.e., looking with favor on someone); (3) the responding feeling to favor (i.e., gratitude). The biblical idea of *charis* differs from this in that God's *charis* is not due to human charm or attractiveness, but to God's nature.

The Hebrew word *hen* has roughly the same range of meaning. In Prov. 11:16 it means "to incline to," "to favor." But it is also something someone can find—Noah found *hen* in God's eyes (Gen. 6:8). Sometimes it is pointed out that *charis* can mean something similar to the Hebrew term *hesed*, often translated "loving-kindness." However, this Hebrew word normally means covenant love and loyalty, a favor or love owed because God has promised to give it. This has little relevance for Paul's use of *charis*, which talks about a favor not owed, but that is given undeserved. The chief example of *charis* is found in the story of Christ, who "at the right time died for the ungodly" (Rom. 5:6)—in other words, for those to whom he had no obligation. Mishnah Aboth 1:2 shows, however, that *hesed* had come to mean the doing of kindnesses that go beyond the law, and this is closer to Paul's use. If, however, *hesed* is basically a covenant love or loyalty, *charis* is basically the opposite for Paul, for it is the love for those God is not obligated to love.

Charis is used in Acts and also figuratively in Paul to talk about God's including of the Gentiles law-free among his people. *Charis* then becomes almost a one-word description for Paul of the character of God and God's action toward Gentiles as manifested in Christ and through his ministry. Thus it is also not surprising that the term *charis*, like the term *dikaiosune*, for Paul is crucial precisely because it deals with the basis on which one is saved and becomes a part of Christ's community. It is about this very issue—On what basis can Gentiles be included in God's people?—that Paul had to argue so long and hard. There is an integral connection between Paul's specific mission, his message of grace, and his understanding of the basis of salvation in Christ. One also suspects that grace is so critical for Paul because of his own experience on the Damascus road.[67]

In Paul's letters, grace is often contrasted with law, works, merit. There are in fact a whole series of ideas that go together for Paul—grace, gift, righteousness of God, faith, gospel, hope, freedom—that stand over and against law, reward, sin, works, accomplishment, debt, one's own honor or righteousness or wisdom.

Let us look first at the contrast between law and grace, which is precisely a contrast between works of the law and grace. This is essentially a contrast between those who are living out of the story of Moses and his kin as opposed to those who are living out of the story Christ. At Gal. 2:21 Paul states that if righteousness came through the law, then this would mean that Christ died in vain; it would be a setting aside the grace of God. Grace for Paul, not law, is the means of obtaining that righteousness, and specifically grace as it comes to the believer in the event of Christ's death—a free and undeserved self-giving of the Son (v. 20). Obviously, Christ's death is the prime example and means on account of which believers receive grace. It is the Exhibit A of God's unmerited favor and love toward them.

A good place to see the contrast between grace and law is in Romans 6. As S. Fowl has pointed out, this section of Paul's argument is grounded in the story of Adam, as the immediately preceding section in 5:12–21 shows.[68] This is probably because the majority of Paul's audience is Gentile, or at least they are the ones Paul is primarily addressing. The old person in this discussion is defined by sin and characterized by Adam. When persons become Christian, they cease being in Adam and become in Christ, they leave the community of Adam and have joined Christ's. Adam's story is no longer their own, for they have buried that tale and have risen to new life in Christ. They have not only a new relationship with God, but a new nature and a new identity—they belong to a new community. "Having terminated activity in the oppressive domain ruled by sin, having broken all bonds and commitments to sin's power, being removed from the realm defined by sin, in short having died to sin, it would be incoherent to pursue the activities that characterized this old allegiance."[69]

For Paul, the tension in the Christian life is not between the old person, still in Adam, and the new person in Christ, but between flesh and Spirit. The tension is not between carrying over one's old preconversion identity and yet now having a new identity as well, as if the Christian were the classic example of schizophrenia. The Christian is not two persons at once, with one foot each in two different communities or with two different stories. Rather, the tension in the Christian life is between two aspects of Christian existence—having a fallen body subject to disease, decay, death, suffering, sorrow, and temptation, and having the Holy Spirit.

At Rom. 6:14ff. Paul categorizes Christians as not under law, but under grace, which does not mean that Christians are no longer required to obey God and keep divine commandments. It was Christ's death in the believer's place that obtained this grace, not Christ's obedience to the Mosaic law. Therefore the benefits of Christ's death are reckoned to the believer, but nothing is said about Christ's obedience to the Mosaic law being imputed to the believer. Paul will go on to make clear that the believer must obey God, in the form of obeying "the law of Christ" rather than the Mosaic code.[70]

Romans 6:14ff. means that the believer's relationship to God is established and fundamentally determined by grace, quite apart from the Mosaic law. To be under the law is to be under the dominion of sin, because those who sin always fall short and find themselves condemned, not saved. This grace, which establishes believers in Christ, is not only independent of human works, it is independent of human wisdom, as 2 Cor. 1:12 makes clear.

Rom. 11:5–6 shows, however, that the fundamental contrast is between grace and works. Grace is not grace if it depends on human works; the two are fundamentally incompatible as a basis of God's saving a righteous remnant. At Rom. 4:4 grace is contrasted with debt, something owed. A worker is paid what is owed him. *Charis* is that which is freely given, not because it is owed or deserved, but because it is what the giver wants to do. It is a gift in the truest sense of the word, not a payment.

When Paul wants to talk about grace not as an attitude or action but as a free gift, he uses the word *charisma*, from which our English counterpart comes. Thus, for instance, at Rom. 6:23 eternal life, which God gives believers in Christ, is called a *charisma* and is contrasted with what is owed, the payment for a person who sins—death. In Rom. 5:12ff. Paul contrasts the "free gift" of grace given by God and Christ with the offense, that is, the original sin of Adam. The former is a totally self-giving act; the latter was a self-seeking act. Because sin characterizes the story of Adam in Paul's mind, that story serves as the perfect foil for discussing the story of Christians who live by and under grace.

As Bultmann rightly stressed, grace must not be seen just as the benevolent attitude of God toward humankind. It is also the actions that result from that attitude, particularly the actions involved in the Christ event. Grace is something God gives believers as well as what he does for them (Rom. 12:3; 15:15; 1 Cor. 3:10; Gal. 2:9). It is the means by which the Christian is enabled to live out a proper Christian story—a story of emulation of the Christ.

Grace is the opposite of self-seeking. It does not look for someone worthy, it bestows worth. It does not look for love, it creates its object of love (Luther). It does not look for receptivity, it enables one to receive. It is because the law's requirements are beyond fallen human capacity that Paul contrasts *charis* and works, not because "once saved by grace" one has nothing to do thereafter. The issue is the basis of salvation, and only in part how believers should live after conversion. Nothing must compromise the truth that salvation is ultimately by grace (cf. Rom. 11:5f.). It has been noted often how Paul uses *charis* at the climax of his arguments.

But when the believer receives that grace as a gift, it brings other gifts and "graces" with it, for example, spiritual gifts. It appears at Rom. 1:5 that Paul sees apostleship as a special gift of God's grace to him. *Charisma* then can be used by Paul to refer to God's free gifts that accompany but are not identical with eternal life. In Rom. 12 and 1 Cor. 12—14, it is quite clear to Paul that such gifts are just that, gifts, not accomplishments. Thus all Christians have at least one, and many have more than one. Romans 12:6 indicates that the gifts believers have are determined by the grace given to them (cf. 1 Cor. 1:4; 7:7). Notice for instance that Paul calls his ability to remain celibate a *charisma* (1 Cor. 7:1), as well as the so-called charismatic gift of speaking in tongues (1 Cor. 14:18). What so disturbed Paul about the behavior of some Corinthians was that God's grace is fundamentally other-centered, but the Corinthians used their gifts in such self-centered ways. These gifts were given not only to build up the self but to equip the Corinthians for ministry and to build up the body of Christ. Gifts are given to serve, not sever, the body (see below).

Perhaps just as bad was the use of God's grace and grace gifts to do what violates one's relationship with God. The Corinthians, not only in the case of spiritual pride, but also in the matter of humility, were taking the gracious freedom they had as a freedom to act as they pleased, now that they were liberated from the bondage to sin. On the contrary, grace was given so they might stand before and in relationship to God in the position of those who have been justified (Rom. 5:1–2). Grace was given to equip believers for righteousness (Rom. 5:20–21), not for sin. Nor is God's grace and giving dependent on how much humans sin, as if the more one sins, the more grace God will have to bestow.

The attempt to gain right-standing with God by the Mosaic law leads to falling from grace (Gal. 5:4), and the attempt to live by that law, instead of by faith and grace, leads to guilt and condemnation. At Rom. 3:24 Paul can talk about grace as the instrument or means by which believers are justified. Paul is who he is by God's grace (1 Cor. 15:10). At 2 Cor. 6:1 Paul talks about receiving grace, but we should be wary of seeing *charis* as some material substance or object bestowed. Rather, here "receive grace" means receive the benefits or gifts that come from a gracious God. To receive grace in vain is to live or act contrary to the intention of the giver or the gift. Paul implies that it is possible to receive the grace in vain so that it becomes useless to a person and one becomes useless to God.

In Gal. 1:6, 16, Paul speaks of being called through grace or in grace. Grace, or God's undeserved favor, is the means of God's calling a person to relationship. Christians are those who are partakers of grace (Phil. 1:7; see also 2 Thess. 2:16). Colossians 1:6 talks about hearing or knowing the grace of God, which must surely be at conversion and is referring to hearing and knowing about God's free gift of and in Christ. Second Thessalonians 1:12 says that it is according to grace that God found believers. It is by grace that Christ is glorified in them and vice versa.

In 2 Corinthians 8 grace shifts around between God's giving and human giving, but it is notable that usually only God is the subject of grace and gracious giving in Paul. Nonetheless, believers too can be bestowers of *charis*—the term Paul uses to categorize the collection that the Gentiles were giving to the needy church in Jerusalem. Thus *charis* can be shared by

humans, and here surely it has the sense of benevolence, or a freely given
kindness. It may also be said to dwell in abundance in a believer (2 Cor. 9:8, 14).

It is clear that in spite of and even in the midst of suffering, personal weakness, or hardship, God's unmerited favor is sufficient to get believers through and help them triumph over it (2 Cor. 12:9). Still we are told it is God's grace, not the believer's, even when it is given to them. The whole movement and course of the Christian life is to be seen as grace and as characterized by grace (2 Cor. 6:1–9). It has often been noted how Paul uses *charis* in the opening and closing greetings of his letters. It is what he prays all his listeners will have and will continue to receive. The impression is clearly that Christians are in need of receiving grace on an ongoing basis, not just once or twice, or as an occasional booster shot.

Usually the verb *charizomai*, like the noun, is used to denote the decisive gracious gift of God in Christ (Rom. 8:32), or as in 1 Cor. 2:12, it is found where the Spirit is said to be God's free gift to the believer. The verb, however, can also mean to forgive (cf. 2 Cor. 2:7, 10; Eph. 4:32). Those who have received so great a gift of forgiveness ought likewise to forgive others. Those who have received grace should show unmerited favor on others (Eph. 4:32; Col. 2:13; 3:13). Notice that only at Col. 2:13 is reference made to God's forgiving believers, but even there it refers to the one-time forgiveness at conversion.

It has been noticed that in the later Paulines the writer tends to connect grace not so much with "justify" as with "save." This is so, for instance, in Eph. 4:5, 8f. and Titus 2:11 (but note how the three ideas are combined at Titus 3:5–7). Bultmann points out this shift because *dikaioo* is not found in Colossians and Ephesians, and thus in his view the emphasis is on effective salvation, not forensic justification. It is, however, significant that only in the latest letters in the Pauline corpus do we have the idea of a *charisma* or *charis* for a church job or task (1 Tim. 4:14; 2 Tim. 1:6; 2:1), given at the laying on of hands.

We may sum up as follows: grace is the attitude and actions of God to and for the sinner, through Jesus Christ. It amounts to an attitude of unmerited favor, an action of free self-giving, and a gift (Holy Spirit, eternal life) that brings with it many undeserved gifts (spiritual gifts). Throughout Paul's letters, grace is in God's hands, and God is the dispenser of it, though often through mediators, whether Christ or one of his ministers. Paul says nothing specific about the idea of the sacraments as means of grace, as if grace could be confined to a ritual or one particular channel. However, because Christ's self-giving is by definition grace, and because believers are participating in Christ and his body in the Eucharist, it may perhaps be seen as *a* means of grace, as is laying on of hands and various other practices. Usually, however, Paul implies that grace is the channel through which one receives gifts—eternal life and the like. It is God's instrument, and it is received directly in an encounter with Christ, not primarily through other mediators or mediating vehicles. Nonetheless, if Christians can have grace and share gifts or grace in a derivative sense, then they must take seriously that God has given it to them. Any naturalistic or quasi-substantive view of grace will not do. It is not a thing or a substance or a medicine. It is an attitude, an action, an ability, or a gift such as life or Spirit, none of which can be quantified or materialized.

Grace is the atmosphere in which Christians live, involving continual dependence on God's favor and help and gifts. Without grace they cannot become or remain Christians. Thus they must continually receive grace and learn the truth of the sufficiency of grace and their own insufficiency and weakness apart from it—"there but for the grace of God. . . ." This being so, Christians should be driven to have the same mercy and great love on others that Christ had on them while they were still sinners. Grace implies the great need of humankind—that they are lost, mired in the story of Adam. Grace implies an unmerited and undeserved benefit, and thus by definition implies an unworthy recipient.[71]

Grace is a gift and a giver. Grace is the beginner and the finisher. Grace is the saver and the guider, which is only another way of saying that God in God's free mercy is all of these, for humans know God's real character in the ultimate act of self-giving and undeserved benefit—the giving of the Son who is giving, has given, and continues to give grace to all who receive him.

Paul's gospel is assuredly *charis* from start to finish, and few had personally experienced more of the reality of how gracious God is and how much it is an undeserved favor, than this former persecutor of the church. If it is fair to say that Christology is at the heart of Paul's gospel, then grace is at the heart of his Christology. But nowhere is this more evident than when he talks about how he and others became Christians and received this grace. To the extent that the believer's story is a matter of grace, it must be grounded in the action of God in Christ, in the story of Jesus, if grace is to be received and also imparted.

REDEMPTIVE RIGHTEOUSNESS AT WORK IN THE WORLD

In many respects, when we speak of "justification" or "righteousness" we have arrived at one of the main storm centers of the Pauline discussion. Opinions about the significance of the *dikaiosune* word group for Paul have been varied. On one hand, we have A. Schweitzer, who said, "It is obvious that the doctrine of righteousness by faith is something incomplete and unfitted to stand alone."[72] In his view it was a minor crater in Paul's thought world. On the other hand, we have those in a more traditional and Lutheran vein who have seen it as the key to understanding Paul and perhaps the most central motif in his theological framework. We have already had occasion to say that when Paul thinks of these matters he is reminded of the story of Abraham, the first person for whom faith was reckoned as righteousness.[73]

Unlike those who see *dikaiosune* as central, I would argue that an idea does not have to be central to be crucial. Nor do I mean that *dikaiosune* is tangential to the warp and woof of Paul's thinking. Rather, if one is following the events of the story of the Christian in Paul's thought world, as we are attempting to do, noting the eschatological framework of his whole thought and then seeing how the elements are placed in the storied world that is driving forward toward its conclusion, then it is logical to see *dikaiosune* as having to do with the first things that are true about God and about the story of those in Christ. *Dikaiosune* comes up for discussion at the juncture where Paul is discussing the basis and beginning of the believer's relationship with God, the point of departure, not what is central to their Christian walk thereafter. It is no accident that *dikaiosune* is usually considered in a context in which grace and faith are the issues on the one hand, and where law, works, and various other judicial terms are in use on the other. It is interesting to note that this means that normally Paul discusses this matter with the story of Abraham and that of the law set in tension with one another, such as in Gal. 3—4 and Rom. 3—4, and in this case the law comes up for significant discussion. This is precisely because *dikaiosune* has to do with how one comes to have a positive relationship with God, how one came to be redeemed. Believers are saved by grace, not works; they are "righteous" because of or through faith, not through law or works of the law. In short, this word group is used (a) to describe God's character; (b) to describe God's saving activities; or (c) to describe the status, or standing, believers have through faith, as a result of those salvific activities. They are acquitted; they are reckoned as righteous. All of this has to do with the getting in (the how and the what).

When Paul does not have to defend the basis of his gospel to the Gentiles and their ability to get in by faith plus nothing, Paul naturally concentrates on what it means to be in Christ and to walk in the Spirit. Those scholars are right, then, who see Paul's participationist language as central to Paul's thought,[74] but one cannot get to the heart of the narrative structure without going through the crucial and only entrance door— Paul's view of *dikaiosune* and its cognates. Every good story needs a strong beginning, a powerful middle, and a convincing and conclusive end, and Paul's telling of the Christian story has all three.[75]

Background—Dikaiosune *Outside of the New Testament*

There is no question that the primary meaning of *dikaiosune* outside of the New Testament is forensic. In Aristotle, *Nic. Ethics* 5.1129(a), we read: "In regard to *dikaiosune* and *adikias* . . . we observe that everybody means by *dikaiosune* that moral disposition which renders people apt to do just things and which causes them to act justly." Here, as the editor in the Loeb edition of this work makes clear, "just" and "unjust" are terms applied to legal and illegal behavior, as well as to what is right and wrong in general. There is thus a forensic background and use of this term. *Dikaiosune* is doing what is due. It corresponds in some respects to the Hebrew term *sadiq* (righteous). In the Old Testament it is stressed that God must distinguish between the *dikaios* (righteous) and the wicked (see Gen. 18:25). This is how God is revealed to be a just judge.

By contrast, Paul says (1) there are none "righteous," and thus, (2) God counts as *dikaios* the ungodly. The classic questions that are asked about all this are: How can God be both just and the justifier of sinful humanity? How can God both vindicate divine righteousness and yet exonerate and pardon the sinner? These are the kinds of questions Paul strives to answer using the *dikaios/dikaiosune* word group and his understanding of substitutionary propitiatory atonement.[76] S. Westerholm stresses:

> An emphasis on divine grace as opposed to human achievement is a genuine Pauline concern, not one foisted upon him by Reformation interpreters. Judaism knows much of divine grace; its view of humanity's plight, however, is less drastic than Paul's and, as a result, it does not speak in Paul's exclusive language of the need for divine grace. Paul's convictions on both scores were formulated in the light of the cross of Christ. Held throughout his ministry, these convictions found their most memorable expression when Paul, responding to the controversy surrounding the admission of Gentiles to the Church, declared his doctrine of justification for Jews and Gentiles alike by faith in Jesus Christ, apart from works of the law.[77]

Thus, although Paul's discussion of "justification" may arise chiefly in polemical contexts, they only provide the occasion for Paul to articulate something that is fundamental to his Christian thought world.

It is axiomatic in the Old Testament that God will be fair and do what is right because God is the righteous one. Various texts use *sedek* in the context of God's doing right or pleading the divine or someone else's case. Here again the term has a juridical sense (cf. Ps. 51:4; Ex. 9:27; Jer. 11:20). Because God is *dikaios*, God will vindicate the righteous and punish the wicked (Ps. 24:5). Often righteousness and salvation are closely linked in the Old Testament (cf. Ps. 98:2; 103:6; Isa. 46:13) because God shows divine *dikaiosune* by vindicating the oppressed and saving the chosen people. We even find woe sayings against anyone who would acquit the guilty.[78]

Paul's Use of Dikaiosune

With this background in view, it ought to be clear why the Judaizers among the Jewish Christians were incensed over Paul's idea of justifying the sinner by faith. They had not seen that God, because of Christ, now relates to believers on a very different basis than God did during the period of the Mosaic law. Because of Christ, God can and does pardon the wicked and the sinner. God does justify the ungodly, for all receive salvation while they are still sinners. Paul will contrast righteousness under the law and righteousness by faith, even though he allows that he himself could be said to be blameless so far as righteousness under the law is concerned (Phil. 3:4–9). In Paul's view there is higher and prior righteousness that Paul finds in the Old Testament,[79] by which standard none are righteous ultimately, and so one may receive the status of "righteous" only by faith, as Abraham did (Romans 4). This higher righteousness is not the believer's, but God's, and one can receive the benefits of it only by believing it and receiving those benefits through faith. One must give up any sort of righteousness one may be able to have in obeying the law in order to have righteousness that comes from God, not human good or correct deeds.

In Rom. 9:30–10:4, Paul says that this is true for all people, not just Gentiles. The Jews have not obtained salvation previously because they pursued their righteousness based on law and works, not on faith. Paul seems to suggest that the problem was that God's good commandments were being used by the Jews to construct a righteousness of their own. As Sanders argues, Paul reasoned from solution to plight,[80] thinking back through the story of his own life starting from the point of conversion and working back to what came before it. "If I am righteous by grace through faith in the crucified Lord, then ipso facto, it is not by works of the law." Paul came to believe that the Mosaic law was unable to make one righteous because it could not give the kind of life and character necessary to perform it. Galatians 2:21 puts it this way: "I do not nullify the grace of God; for if righteousness were through the law, then Christ died to no purpose." Thus we see how Paul reevaluates things in light of Christ and Paul's encounter with him. "Christ died for a purpose, so that I may be righteous through faith, therefore, righteousness cannot be by works of the law. That would nullify God's grace and the significance of Christ's death." It appears that Paul's conviction about this did not change during the course of his ministry, and S. Kim and others have made a reasonable case for the view that this conviction came to Paul out of or as a result of his conversion experience.[81]

It is not accidental either that, even in personal remarks that are almost asides, Paul stresses the connection between God's grace in his being called/converted and his unworthiness (1 Cor. 15:9–10), which contrasts so dramatically with Paul's boast about his righteousness while he was a Pharisee. The argument that righteousness by faith arose out of Paul's struggles with Jewish Christians in Galatia is likely wrong. We may say that it certainly surfaced in Galatians first in its full force, however. It was the problems there that first brought it into clear light.[82] Nor is it sufficient to call this idea simply Paul's polemic against the law, which he brings forward in order to do battle with works righteousness. Paul uses this idea in polemical fashion in Galatians, but in Romans, where by and large the polemics are laid aside, we find it playing a large role. Even in Philippians it is mentioned in an important personal context, when Paul is not concerned to give a harangue about the law.

Part of the issue is whether one is going to judge oneself by God's standards or by human conscience. First Corinthians 4:4 makes quite clear that for Paul, humans cannot determine the issue or acquit themselves. Indeed, humans are not to be judges at all. When one accepts a righteousness that comes from and through faith and ultimately from God as a gift,[83] one is recognizing that only God is the proper judge and God's judgment is no condemnation. Pardon or acquittal comes, even though humans are guilty, because of what Christ has done for them.

At Rom. 1:17 we encounter a much-controverted phrase "the righteousness of God." It may refer to what is true about God's character—God has righteousness. However, the only way to see God's righteous character is through the eyes of faith. On the surface of things, God appears to be unfair—not only because God's own people suffer, but because now God is justifying the ungodly. But when that justifying is looked at through faith, by recognizing why Christ had to die, it makes good sense, and God is seen to be both righteous and loving.

On the other hand, E. Käsemann and C.E.B. Cranfield have argued well that this phrase in 1:17 means the righteousness or right-standing bestowed by God on those who have faith in Christ. In other words, Paul is talking about the eschatological redemptive activity of God when he uses this phrase. What points in this direction is that "the righteousness of God" is equated by Paul with "the righteousness of faith" (see Phil. 3:9).[84]

This may well be so; however, at Rom. 3:25–26 it seems clear that it means God's character as righteous. Christ's death showed that God was righteous and could not pass over sin forever. But it was not only to prove or demonstrate divine righteousness, but also to demonstrate that God justifies only those who have faith in Jesus. Thus Christ's death shows that God is both just/righteous and the justifier of human beings.

When righteousness is predicated of God, it refers in part to God's being a righteous judge at the last judgment. But God was manifesting that eschatological last judgment already (so far as believers are concerned), executing the sentence on Jesus. Thus for Paul, God's mercy and justice, God's love and righteousness have been shown to be operational early, prior to the end of history.

God must vindicate divine righteousness, and God does so already at the present time, not just on judgment day, by (a) Christ's death, and (b) accepting only those who have faith in Christ and his atoning work. Also, Christ's death could be seen as a demonstration of God's righteousness only to the eyes of faith. Without faith it appears that Christ was cursed by God. Paul in Gal. 3:10ff. admits this is so, but adds that Christ "became a curse for us." It was humankind who should have been cursed by God for their sins. Whatever Paul himself had achieved by way of merit under the Mosaic law, Paul counted all this as loss and renounced having a righteousness of his own so he might have that which comes by faith in Christ.

Now is the appropriate juncture to ask, In what sense then are believers righteous through faith? Is this a condition or a status? a comment on believers' duty or on their standing? It also raises another question, Is this righteousness a legal fiction? Is God deceived about believers, so that when God looks at them once they have converted, God no longer sees them but the perfectly righteous Christ? These latter questions we have already addressed earlier in our discussion of Abraham's story.[85] The first question, however, calls for further comment.

Let us begin with 2 Cor. 5:21. Obviously, it is believers who have become "the righteousness of God," though it is "in him." It is clear that one cannot become this outside of Christ, outside of being a Christian, but this still does not explain what is meant here. Barrett suggests that the terms Paul uses here are purely relational.

> Paul does not say, for by definition it would not have been true, that Christ became a sinner, transgressing God's law; neither does he say, for it would have contradicted all experience (not least in Corinth) that every believer becomes immediately and automatically morally righteous, good as God is good. He says rather that Christ became *sin;* that is, he came to stand in that relation with God which normally is the result of sin, estranged from God and the object of his wrath. . . . We correspondingly, and through God's loving act in Christ, have come to stand in that

relation with God which is described by the term *righteousness*, that is, we are acquitted in his court, justified, reconciled. We are no longer his judicial enemies, but his friends.[86]

We have already seen reasons why this approach is only partially satisfactory, for God also expects righteous behavior of believers and enables them to behave in such a fashion.[87] But even more to the point, believers like Abraham must have and exercise faith in God's promises for faith to be counted as righteousness. In short, one's objective right-standing with God must be appropriated through the subjective exercising of the gift of faith, it is not simply imputed without regard to the response or receptivity of the person in question.

We may also note in passing that the new creation of 2 Cor. 5:17 and righteousness of v. 21 are not synonymous. It is the right-standing, the new relationship with God, that is the basis of the transformation of a person and his or her moral life.[88] It must remain doubtful then that all Paul is talking about in v. 21 is Christ being righteous in the believer's stead. Paul not only says "we"; he uses the form *genometha*, "become." In Paul's thought world, Christ could hardly become righteous; he simply was righteous. Clearly, Paul is talking about what believers are as Christians.

Confirmation of some of Barrett's interpretation of 2 Cor. 5:21 comes when we examine Rom. 4:3ff., where the key term is *logizomai*—to "count" or "reckon," applied both to Abraham as prototype faith *and* to believers. Abraham's faith in God was not righteousness in itself, but it was reckoned or counted to him as righteousness. The same is true of Christians. Romans 4:3 is affirming that faith in Christ's death is reckoned or credited to believers as acquittal, leaving them in right-standing with God.

That *dikaios* and its cognates do not mean just exoneration but also have a positive connotation is clear from Rom. 5:9–10. Believers are *dikaiothentes* ("righted"/"made righteous") by Jesus' blood. Paul says in the very next breath, "We were reconciled." The two ideas clearly go together. Not merely are negative impediments to relationships removed; the positive reestablishing of the relationship is accomplished. This being reckoned righteous or acquitted or reconciled means that Christians will be saved from the wrath of God expressed by the judge on judgment day. They will be saved by Christ's life, which might imply his righteous life as opposed to his death.[89] That this is likely is seen from v. 18b, where Paul states emphatically that by one man's obedience many "were made righteous." Being made righteous must happen in a way parallel to the sense of being made sinner in Adam.

As Cranfield insists, the emphasis is on how the deed of one man has affected and determined all the others' existence, or perhaps we should say all the others' relationships with God.[90] In short, Christ makes things right between God and humankind. That is the point of all this language. The conclusion all of this leads us to is this: when Paul uses *dikaiosune* and its cognates in reference to human beings, he is referring to their status, their standing before God (i.e., being in right relationship with God). When Paul wants to talk about their moral purification or progressive sanctification, he uses a whole different set of words. Paul does not confuse the two ideas of justification, or objective righteousness, and sanctification, or subjective righteousness. As Rom. 8:33–34 says, to make righteous is the opposite of to condemn. It is a pronounced verdict of not guilty that results in right-standing with God. Second Corinthians 5:19 says that Christ became sin, but this is not in an ethical subjective sense. Because Jesus knew no sin, only in a legal sense could he become sin (i.e., take the place and the punishment of others as sinners). He was reckoned as a sinner. *Dikaiosune* deals with human guilt from the human situation. Sanctification deals with sinful tendencies, involving the human condition. The former involves a changed objective status; the latter a changed subjective nature. The former leads to or precipitates the latter, though the new creation may be virtually coincident in time with justification. The former involves the reckoning of a right-standing; the latter an imparting of a righteous condition.

Paul certainly knows all about final justification at the last day (Rom. 2:13), or final righteousness (Gal. 5:5); that is, positive vindication on judgment day. However, a preliminary judgment has already been made— "no condemnation"—which will be finalized only on that last day. Believers have the right-standing now, and they will hear the final verdict then, provided they continue to work out their salvation with fear and trembling. This means that the preliminary eschatological verdict of no condemnation that is passed when someone first trusts in Christ is provisional. Nonetheless, for Paul the present aspect of justification, being reckoned righteous, is more prominent. Notice, for example, 1 Cor. 6:11 and the aorist verb "you are already *dikaios*."

Once one realizes that one does not have to earn that verdict and right-standing but just receive it as a gift, then all one does in the Christian life can be motivated by a desire to please God, a love for living, and a gratitude for what God has already given the believer. It is the recognition of this freedom to be a new creation, no longer bound to sin or having an adversarial relationship with God, that frees one to pursue ethical Christ-likeness without looking over one's shoulder and worrying about one's past. However, this does not mean that Christians should be unconcerned about the final consequences of their actions after conversion.

IN GOOD FAITH

> The soul wherein God dwells
> What church could holier be?
> Becomes a walking-tent
> Of Heavenly majesty.
> How far from here to heaven?
> Not very far, my friend
> A single hearty step
> Will all the journey end.
> Though Christ a thousand times
> In Bethlehem be born,
> If He's not born in thee,
> Thy soul is still forlorn. . . .
> Go out, God will go in;
> Die thou—and let Him live;
> Be not—and He will be;
> Wait, and He'll all things give.
>
> —*Angelus Silesius*
> *"The Soul Wherein God Dwells"*[91]

If salvation is, as in Paul's telling of the tale, solely by grace, then it must also be solely through faith. Put another way, if grace is what may be said to characterize the divine work of salvation, faith for Paul is that which is the characteristic and proper response to such a free gift of undeserved benefit. It is fair to say that for Paul *pistis* has a variety of meanings, all basically interrelated. We will look at several of the salient meanings for Paul: (1) faith as a gift of grace; (2) faith as the means of being justified, being united to Christ, receiving salvation; (3) faith as an act of believing or trusting; (4) the faith as what is believed; (5) faith as obedience; (6) "the faith of Jesus" as a crucial and controversial phrase.

When Paul discusses faith, because he thinks of faith in terms of concrete examples from the story of salvation (in particular, Abraham), he is usually talking about what is called justifying faith. However, this is not always the case. For instance, both 1 Cor. 12:9 and 1 Cor. 13:2 suggest that to some is given a particular kind or degree of faith. We may call this a special sort of faith, or in the case of 1 Cor. 13:2 a miracle-working faith, but the point is that Paul calls this faith a gift of the Spirit (cf. 2 Cor. 4:13). At Phil. 1:29 Paul makes quite clear, however, that he is talking about saving faith, and here he says that the act of believing was granted to Christians. What this means is that not even the act of believing, the human response to grace, can be seen as something humans inherently have and can offer in exchange for salvation. Faith is not a human accomplishment, or a "work." It too is given by God's grace. This means that faith is not a quid pro quo that one offers to God in exchange for salvation. It is not a possible human response apart from God's grace. Bultmann helpfully affirms that "a faith brought about by God outside of [human] decision would obviously not be genuine [faith]. Faith is God-wrought to the extent that prevenient grace first made the human decision possible, with the result that [the one] who made the decision can only understand it as God's gift."[92]

This leads us to discuss faith as a means of receiving salvation. Fundamentally, this idea is expressed when Paul uses the word *pistis* (faith) with certain prepositions (e.g., *ek, dia, eis,* "by," "through," or "in"). One of the main concerns of Paul is to show that the salvation that he is discussing does not come by doing works of the law: "No one is justified before God by the law; for "he who through/from faith (*ek pisteos*) is righteous shall live' " (Gal. 3:11–12). Shortly thereafter, Paul again explains that the law was a *paidagogos* for (Jewish) believers until Christ came,[93] but when Christ came they were able to be justified by faith and become sons or daughters through faith (*dia pisteos;* see Gal. 3:11–12). There is thus a sense in which the coming of Christ means the coming of the age of faith as a means by which many believers might receive right-standing and salvation.

This, however, does not prevent Paul from using Abraham as Exhibit A of righteousness through faith. Indeed, he does so most prominently in the same Galatian letter (cf. 3:6ff.), because in his mind the story of Abraham is an exemplar for the story of Christians, in part because the Christian is linked to Abraham through his "seed"—the Christ. It is clear that Paul views the Abrahamic covenant as linked to the new one, which may be said to link Christians to the Old Testament people of God. Paul sees the Mosaic covenant as only an interim arrangement between two covenants that provide righteousness by grace and through faith.

Romans 3:27ff. emphasizes the same message: salvation, or justification, comes not through law but rather through the "law," or principle, of faith.[94] Other references simply confirm that Paul sees faith as the means through which such right-standing and salvation comes (cf. Rom. 5:1; Gal. 2:16; Phil. 3:9). In Rom. 10:3ff. we are told that the gospel preached by Paul is the word of faith, which must surely mean a word about receiving salvation by faith or a word about believing in Christ. In any event, the gospel is characterized here as having essentially to do with faith, and the following verses make evident that having faith in Christ means confessing with one's lips and believing in one's heart that he is the risen Lord.

Believing then involves both confessing and accepting certain things as
true. The object of this belief is properly and mainly a person; Christians
believe in Christ. However, it is also clear that for Paul believing entails
believing certain things about Jesus and God's work through him and in
him. More to the point, believing in Jesus means believing that his story,
involving words, deeds, and relationships as told by the early Christians, is
true. Faith is not faith in itself or in the believer, but faith in the story and the
person who is the central figure in the story. Paul was no advocate of
believing for its own sake. (*believism*)

As Kim stresses, this believing does not require that persons go and find
Jesus either in heaven or elsewhere,[95] but rather that they simply respond
to the preached word that tells the story about Jesus. Thus, in Rom.
10:14ff. God has made preaching the indispensable means of bringing
someone to Christ. A person cannot call upon or believe in someone she or
he has not heard about.

Usually, when Paul talks about the act of believing he always mentions
the object or subjects of that act of believing in a "that" clause. For
instance, in 1 Thess. 4:14 Paul says we believe (*hoti*) that Jesus died and rose
again. In 1 Cor. 15:2ff. he proceeds to summarize what he and his audience
had received and believed, namely, the Good News about Christ's death,
burial, resurrection, and appearances. In other words, they have believed in
the climax of the story of Jesus' earthly ministry. Whether in the phrase
pistis Christou (the faith/fulness of Christ) Paul uses a shorthand way of
alluding to this story (cf. Gal. 2:16b; Rom. 10:14; Phil. 1:29; Col. 2:5) will
be discussed in a moment. In any case, what one believes *about* Jesus is not
to be abstracted from believing *in* him, because not only does Jesus' story
reveal who he is, but in a real sense he would not have been the Christ or
Lord if his life had not had the climax it did. Faith, after all, arises in the
context of a personal relationship with Christ, which entails believing
certain things to be true about his career and accomplishments. Faith, as we
have been discussing it thus far, has related primarily to the key saving
events that happened to and through Jesus and the consequent possibility
and reality of having right-standing with God. Now we must go on to
discuss faith as the believer's ongoing trust in Christ and God.

There is some real overlap between this sort of faith and the previous
one because what one believes in, one must also necessarily trust. There is
an inherent trust element in believing. "As the verb *pisteuo* ('believe')
shows, *pistis* for Paul has the twofold sense: both of *belief that*—acceptance
of the truth/reliability of what has been said (cf. [Rom.] 4:3; 6:8; 10:9, 16;
1 Cor. 11:18; Gal. 3:6; 1 Thess. 4:14; 2 Thess. 2:11–12) but also of
consequent *trust in,* or reliance upon ([Rom.] 4:5, 24; 9:33; 10:11; Gal.
2:16; Phil. 1:29), as expressed particularly in the initial act of being

baptized, that is, identifying with Jesus in his death (6:3–4) and placing oneself under his lordship (10:9)."[96]

At 1 Cor. 2:5 Paul is really talking about placing one's trust in God's power and not human wisdom. He is not merely discussing notional assent to an abstract proposition about God's power. Especially prominent is the trust element of faith when Paul talks about the future and about walking by faith (2 Cor. 5:7). In such contexts, faith is often contrasted with sight; and though Paul did not write Hebrews, nonetheless he would have agreed that faith is at least in part an assurance or trust in and about things hoped for and a conviction about things not seen (Heb. 11:1). We must also always keep in mind that for Paul faith is not a static quality or characteristic. It can be weak or strong (cf. Rom. 14:1ff.); furthermore, it can grow (and presumably atrophy as well—see 2 Cor. 10:15). Numerous texts that do not specifically mention *pistis* nonetheless describe the trust that accompanies or flows forth from faith. One can compare 2 Cor. 1:9ff. and Phil. 3:3ff. on this score. Having this sort of faith in or trust in God means having confidence that God will complete the work God has begun in believers and will guide them throughout their earthly existence (cf. Phil. 1:6, 25; 2:24). All of this is the opposite of pride or a trusting or boasting in oneself (2 Cor. 1:9) or one's accomplishments or deeds (cf. Phil. 3:3–4).

Paul does not usually talk in terms of "the faith" as a body of things believed; however, we certainly find this usage in 1 Cor. 16:13. In the latter Paulines, this sort of usage is much more common. Thus we find it at 1 Tim. 6:12 and 2 Tim. 4:7: "I have kept the faith." We may also compare at this juncture Titus 1:1–4, where faith and knowledge are correlated, suggesting a cognitive content to the faith here and something that is held in common by believers (v. 4).

Both Bultmann and V. P. Furnish lay heavy stress on faith as obedience and the obedience of faith as the central element in Paul's view of faith. Furnish puts it this way:

> The acknowledgment of Jesus as "Lord" is not possible apart from the acknowledgment that one resides in the sphere of his sovereign power. . . . Faith, therefore, is the acknowledgment that one "belongs" to Christ, and as such it is an act of commitment to him. This is why the apostle can speak of "faith's obedience" (Rom. 1:5).[97]

There is more implied by this phrase, however. For one thing, this phrase indicates that faith and obedience, far from being at odds with one another, go together in Paul's thought. Thus Cranfield points out the parallel between Rom. 1:8 and 16:19, where in the former text the Romans' faith has been heard of and in the latter it is their obedience.[98] Notice too how at Rom. 10:16a Paul talks about becoming obedient to the gospel, and 10:16b refers to believing what was heard. When one is exhorted or even commanded to believe, believing is an act of obedience and thus becomes an action humans must perform in order to receive the benefits of Christ's story.[99]

Again, Paul, when he is discussing non-Christian Jews, speaks of their unbelief (Rom. 11:23) being persisted in, and then he speaks of their disobedience in the same terms (11:30). It is obedience to God and faith in God that Paul hopes to win from the Gentiles (Rom. 15:18), and this may be called the obedience of faith (1:5). Second Corinthians 10:5ff. speaks of taking every thought captive in order to obey Christ, and Gal. 5:7 talks about obeying the truth. In this context we might have expected Paul to say "believe the truth," but for Paul the two ideas go together. In Rom. 1:5 the phrase "the obedience of faith" closely links the two concepts: believing in Christ *is* a form of obedience, obediently accepting God's gift of right-standing on God's own terms. This also leads to further acts of obedience, modeling oneself on Christ.

Besides all of the above, there are various places where Paul talks about walking by faith, and it is well to remember that this is just another way of saying live a Christian life. The Christian is believed capable of this because not only has he or she received salvation through faith; he or she has received the Spirit through faith (cf. Gal. 3:2, 5, 14). Faith then is both the door through which one receives all the benefits of salvation and the way a Christian is expected to live after conversion.

It is for this reason that Paul, in his great hymn to love, so closely links faith to hope and love, the other two primary Christian attributes or virtues. It is these three things that are expected to abide in and with the Christian and without which his or her Christianity is not merely in jeopardy; it is doubtful.

The surprising conclusion to surveying these sorts of passages is that for Paul, faith is not merely something the believer has or must have, faith is an action word or an activity—it must be exercised to be real or exist. It is thus paradoxically both a gift from God and an activity of humans who respond to God. This is yet another reason why it can be associated so closely with human obedience to God. The chief actions that God requires of human beings is to respond obediently to God's demand that they place their trust in the Almighty.

The eschatological nature of this faith is shown clearly in that it brings benefits (Spirit, eternal life) to the believer that Jews would not normally anticipate receiving before the end of their life or the end of the age. Paul's view is that the Christian faith entails a belief that the future is in part now, because Christ and his grace have already come. They are available to be received and believed in.[100]

We now must consider in some depth the meaning of the phrase "the faith of Jesus Christ." R. B. Hays and M. D. Hooker, among others, have urged that this phrase be taken to mean not "faith in Jesus Christ" but rather Jesus Christ's own faith or faithfulness.[101] In a recent recapitulation of his original argument, Hays says: "The gospel story depicts Jesus as the divinely commissioned protagonist who gives himself up to death on a cross in order to liberate humanity from bondage. . . . His death, in obedience to the will of God, is simultaneously a loving act of faithfulness (*pistis*) to God and the decisive manifestation of God's faithfulness to his covenant promise to Abraham. Paul's use of *pistis 'Iesou Christou* (the faith/fulness of Jesus Christ) and other similar phrases should be understood as summary allusions to this story, referring to Jesus' fidelity in carrying out this mission."[102]

It is quite clear from examples like Rom. 3:3 that "the *pistis* of God" must mean the faithfulness of God, where we have the definite article with the subjective genitive. But in all the examples in Paul where "Christ" is the noun in question, all *lack* the definite article. This is not decisive, however, for in Rom. 4:16 in the phrase *to . . . ek pisteos Abraam* the phrase must refer to the faith of Abraham, where there is a definite article followed by a subjective genitive. What this collateral evidence shows is that it is possible to read *pistis Christou 'Iesou* to mean the faith or faithfulness of Jesus, but the texts in question must be examined to see if they will in fact bear this interpretation (Rom. 3:22, 26; Gal. 2:16, 20; 3:16; and Phil. 3:9). Because Romans gives us the fullest opportunity to judge what this phrase might mean in a larger context, we will turn to it first.

Romans 3:22 clearly enough is speaking about God's righteousness, but the issue is where it is manifested. In v. 24, as in v. 22, we have a *dia* ("through") clause, which at least on the surface of things seems to reveal the vehicle through which this redemptive righteousness is manifested— namely, through "the redemption that is in Christ." If v. 22 is a parallel to this, we may expect the *dia* clause to speak of this vehicle there as well; namely, "through the faithfulness of Jesus Christ," which is a shorthand way of speaking of his obedience unto death (cf. Phil. 2:8). The reference to the ones who benefit because Christ performs this act is also found in v. 22: "unto all those who believe." It was not necessary for Paul to refer twice in the span of eight words to the faith of Christians. What about 3:26 then?

It must be admitted that we have a somewhat different form of expression here: not *dia* but *ek* ("from") is the preposition that precedes *pisteos 'Iesou*. Literally, the sentence in question reads, "in the tolerance of God for proof of God's righteousness in the present time, for God's being righteous and the righter of the one [who lives] from/out of the faith/fulness of Jesus."[103] Hays would have us render the phrase by "justifying the one who *shares* the faith of Jesus," but like the normal translation this also ignores the *ek*.[104] More to the point is the fact that in Gal. 3:7, 9 the phrase *hoi ek pisteos* (those who from faith) seems clearly to refer to believers—those who live from faith, just as Abraham did. Thus it is possible here that the reference is to human faith in Jesus; but in view of the fact that the whole previous discussion is about Christ being the means of right-standing by his offering a propitiatory sacrifice, it seems equally possible to translate here as I have suggested at the beginning of this paragraph. God justifies those who live out of and trust in Christ's faithfulness even unto death, which is, of course, an act of faith, as 3:22c makes evident. This rendering makes good sense in light of Paul's self-professed concern elsewhere "to know nothing but Christ and him crucified" (1 Cor. 2:2), which at the very least shows what he saw as two of the most crucial elements that someone must believe in to be a Christian. Because the Galatians references are in some ways the most controverted, we will save them till last.

In Phil. 3:9 we find a phrase very similar to what we found in Rom. 3:22. We may render this verse somewhat literally as follows: "and be found in him, not having my own righteousness, the [sort that comes] from the law, but the *through* (*dia*) the faith/fulness of Christ, the from (*ek*) God righteousness based upon faith." Here again it seems to me that we do not have to make this an either/or proposition. The last phrase seems clearly enough to refer to human faith, but when Paul wants to talk about the *objective*, not *subjective*, vessel *through* which this righteousness is made available to human beings, he contrasts the righteousness that comes through law on one hand and, on the other hand, the righteousness that comes through the saving acts of Christ, his faithfulness even unto death. As in Rom. 3:22, the *dia* clause speaks of something that happened in and through Jesus' life, not in and through believers. This righteousness is simply bestowed *upon* those who have Christian faith, but the objective means making this possible is Christ's death, not the law. This makes very good sense in light of the larger argument in Philippians, where Paul criticizes his opponents for exalting the law as a means of righteousness or right-standing and thereby becoming "enemies of the cross of Christ" (4:18). He does not say they have become enemies of subjective Christian faith. The issue is the objective basis of right-standing with God, hence the contrast between the cross and the law. For Paul, what it means to gain Christ, or to be found in him, is that he is in one sense incorporated into the story of Christ and so gets the benefits of the death and resurrection of Christ. Paul's life arises out of the story of Christ and the events that made the telling of that gospel possible.

This leaves us with the texts in Galatians. The first two references come closely together in Gal. 2:16 and v. 20. We have already noted how much of what Paul says in this letter arises out of his reading of the story of Abraham and the story of the law,[105] and this cautions us from the outset against treating our present subject as mere abstract ideas without a context in a storied world. This passage shares much in common with the one in Philippians. The issue here again is how one obtains the righteousness, or right-standing, that comes from God; is it by works of the law or *dia pisteos 'Iesou Christou* (2:16)? The very way the matter is put here suggests again something that happens or is made available through Christ. As in two of the previous texts we have examined, Paul goes on to make very clear in 2:16b that this benefit comes to "we who believe in (*eis*) Christ Jesus." As in the two previous examples, this would be quite redundant if in both 2:16a and v. 16b the subject is human faith. Right-standing comes to believers because they appropriate it through the human act of having faith or trust. However, there is a middle term to this equation, and that middle term is Christ, in particular, Christ's faithfulness unto death on the cross, expressed in shorthand by the phrase *dia pisteos 'Iesou Christou*. It is not needful to make this an either/or proposition, any more than was the case in Romans or Philippians.

I would submit that Gal. 2:20 gives powerful confirmation to this view. Paul says quite plainly that he has been crucified with Christ and that it is Christ who lives in him. This means not just that the story of Christ is recapitulated in his own life, but that his own story has somehow also been grafted into Christ's so that he gets the benefit of Christ's death and resurrection. This is not merely a matter of exchange, though there is certainly an element of that, but a matter of substitution. Paul would have been unable to provide his own atonement, but he can benefit from the one provided for him in Christ. Unlike Hays, I do not think it follows that Gal. 2:20 in both parts refers to the faithfulness of Christ on the cross. That is surely the subject in 2:20b: "He gave himself for me." It is as a result of that, that Paul can say that he now lives in or by faith in God's Son. As Longenecker puts it:

> Paul uses *pistis 'Iesou Christou* in his writings to signal the basis for the Christian gospel: that its objective basis is the perfect response of obedience that Jesus rendered to God the Father, both actively in his life and passively in his death. Thus in three places by the use of *pistis 'Iesou Christou* Paul balances out nicely the objective basis for Christian faith ("the faith/faithfulness of Jesus Christ") and [hu]mankind's necessary subjective response ("by faith"): Rom. 3:22 . . . Gal. 3:22 . . . and Phil. 3:9. . . . These are not just redundancies in the Pauline vocabulary, as so

often assumed, but Paul's attempts to set out both the objective and the subjective bases for the Christian life.[106]

What then about Gal. 3:22? The same balancing act between the objective and subjective basis of Christian existence is maintained. Galatians 3:22b refers to what is given to those who believe, and once again the contrast is between the law and the faithfulness of Christ in the first half of the sentence as the objective basis of justification. It does not come "from the law" (*ek nomou*, v. 21), but rather through (*dia*) the faithfulness of Jesus Christ. The Abrahamic promises are conveyable to the believer because of and through the faithfulness of Christ. The issue here, as 3:20 makes clear, is who or what is the objective mediator that conveys the benefits of these promises to God's people. Does it come through the law or through the saving acts of Christ? Clearly Paul believes it is the latter. The Abrahamic benefits are promised to all who believe through and because of Christ's faithfulness. In short, Christian faith is not just in a person, it is in a story about that person who lived a certain life and who performed certain faithful acts that made possible salvation to all through faith alone.

This leads us to some final reflections on another puzzling Pauline phrase that has to do with faith. What is one to make of Rom. 1:17? Here righteousness is said to come *ek pisteos eis pistin*. Cranfield believes, following the Reformation interpretation, that *eis pistin* is probably simply added for emphasis and effectively means that this right-standing comes through faith *alone*.[107] It is assumed that the quotation of Hab. 2:4 confirms that Paul is discussing what comes through faith alone. There are several problems with this view. First, *eis pistin* is a very odd way to express the idea of "alone," if it can be said to be one at all. Here again we are confronted with the problem of redundancy. If, however, we translate the phrase "from (God's) faithfulness unto (human) faith" this shows very nicely the gamut of meaning that Paul elsewhere expresses when he speaks of the faithfulness of Christ in tandem with references to human faith.[108] "The phrase 'from faith to faith' then becomes a rhetorically effective slogan to summarize the gospel message of salvation that originates in God's power and is received trustingly by the beneficiaries of that power."[109] This is so whether or not one takes the quotation of Habbakuk as Hays does to refer to Christ the righteous one and his faithfulness. I think this is unlikely.

The substance of this discussion is that not only is faith a crucial concept for Paul, it is a term, perhaps the key term, by which he links the story of Christ and the story of Christians. Their faith is in the faithful one and in his faithful acts. Because of his faithful act of dying for sin, believers can die to sin; because he was raised, believers can arise to newness of life even before the final resurrection. When one has gained Christ, one has gained

272 "A GOOD LIKENESS": THE STORY OF CHRISTIANS

not only the benefits of the story of his life and death; one has also been grafted into that story in the sense that it is by analogy repeated in the life of the believer, not as an atoning act, but as an experience and a pattern of behavior that transforms and guides the Christian along the path toward greater Christlikeness. We must now examine how Paul relates the subjective side of the story of the Christian life, from new creature to new body, bearing in mind how the career of Christ always stands in the background here.

NEW CREATURES, NEW STORY

Since Bultmann's famous analysis of Paul, the question of the structure of Paul's thought world has been at the forefront of discussion. Bultmann began with Paul's anthropology and moved to christology, with the result that Christ is defined in the kind of human terms that make it difficult to see him as anything more. Although Bultmann is quite right that Paul believes we only know God in God's revelation and in particular in God's special revelation to humankind in the Word and in the Son, not in God's nature, this does not warrant a dismissal of the possibility of knowing something about Christ apart from his human nature, nor does it warrant the starting of the Pauline conversation from the anthropological end of things. Thus, even though now and for a while we will be dealing with Paul's anthropological terms, it is well to bear in mind that we began with the story of Christ that involved both anthropology and theology, and moved to the human story. Of more importance, the Christian's story is to a significant degree modeled on and dependent upon the Christ story. The story of God is much broader than the human story and in Christ incorporates it. To put it more traditionally, theology is properly speaking a discussion that begins with God and moves to its implications for humanity.

E. Käsemann was right to criticize Bultmann's suggestion that human-kind cannot be defined within human limits; rather, humankind is es-chatologically defined in the light of Christ. Paul now looks at humanity with Christian glasses, in regard to humanity both outside of and inside of Christ. He reads the story of Christians with one eye on the story of Christ. Here it may be helpful to include a diagram (Figure 1) showing how Paul conceives the story of Christians within an eschatological framework—surrounded by the story of Christ's two comings and his deeds at each of these comings.

It has often and rightly been argued that Paul's new creation concept is the basis of his anthropology. Paul does not use the Johannine term "born again" or "born from above" when talking about the subjective transfor-

FIG. 1. Pauline Thought within an
Eschatological Framework

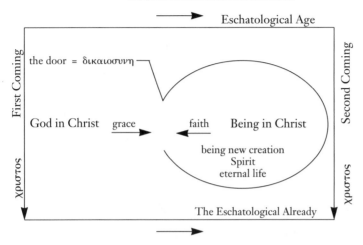

mation of an individual. Instead of this or any talk of a new birth, Paul talks
about a new creation. We have already had some occasion to refer to 2 Cor.
5:16–17 and Gal. 6:15, but here we must consider them in more detail. Is it
new creature, or new creation, or new humanity these texts are talking
about? It is logical to assume that Paul uses the phrase the same way in both
texts, unless there is good evidence to the contrary. On the one hand, the *tis*
in 2 Cor. 5:17 seems to indicate that Paul is talking about what is true of the
individual—he or she is (or possibly there is) for (or in) him *a* (not *the*) *kaine
ktisis.* It seems to make little sense to talk about a new humanity (corporately) when the individual or something that happens to the individual is
in view, as the *tis* makes clear. That leaves us with either the translation
"new creature" or "new creation."

Barrett insists that what Paul means here is a new (act of) creation, a
whole new creation that the individual is grafted into when she or he
becomes a Christian. Bruce also agrees with this view in regard to Gal.
6:15.[110] This would mean that Paul is not using the rabbinic concept of the
proselyte becoming a new creature at conversion. The latter is in fact
implied, however, even if one says, "There is an act of new creation,"
because it is the individual who is acted on and becomes a part of this new
thing. There seems to be an analogy here to the Genesis story: in Adam the

old creation was begun and affected both creatures and the created order thereafter. Thus, here in Christ (the last Adam) a new creation is begun, and this affects believers now and will affect the whole of creation later. It will embrace all of history and nature.

Notice how in Rom. 8:20ff. the creation was affected by the Fall, and it too awaits to be liberated—an event that will transpire when all matter is liberated. When believers experience the resurrection body the earth will also undergo transformation. Its destiny is linked to that of humankind. The fact remains, however, that the material creation has yet to be transformed; only the inner person of believing creatures has thus far been changed. Thus I still favor the translation "new creature" here.

Because Paul is here talking about something that has happened and is happening now,[111] and because vv. 16–17 are parallel here, Paul is saying he no longer looks at Christ or human beings from a fallen human perspective. Now he sees both through the eyes of faith. Does it follow from this that Paul is merely talking about a new perspective on people? This is most unlikely, for Paul is not just talking about knowing "according to the flesh" or by faith, and with spiritual insight. Correct insight is certainly included when he talks about Christ himself, but Paul is also talking about what happens when one becomes in Christ; namely, there is a new act of creation in them, and the individual becomes in one sense a new creature.

Naturally this does not mean a new (resurrection) body, but it does mean a spiritual transformation affecting one's attitudes, thoughts, feelings, commitments, will, and thus one's worldview and orientation toward life in general. There is a new perspective because there is a new person. There is a transformed outlook because the person has been spiritually transformed.

It must be stressed that Paul does not say the old *is* passing away; rather, the old *has* passed away when one enters Christ. What this means is that the Christian is no longer the old person she or he once was. There is no old person/new person coexistent in the believer, though there is still the flesh/spirit tension, for one still has a fallen body and thus experiences old bodily desires. There is also still temptation to act as if one was still the old person and part of the old order of things. The horror of sin for the Christian is that she or he may sometimes *choose* to act like what she or he is no longer—the old person. Bultmann's famous summary of Pauline ethics—"Be what you are"—applies here. Paul is convinced that believers really are recreated in the inner person; therefore, they must no longer act like what they were before. The basis of ethics in the Christian life is not just the story of Christ, but the inner spiritual transformation that happens when one puts faith in that story.

The Galatian passage makes abundantly clear that the distinctions that applied to the old order of things no longer apply or are no longer important. What really counts is not whether you are Jew or Gentile, circumcised or uncircumcised, or even male or female (see Gal. 3:28), but what you are in Christ as a new creature. Galatians 3:28 says literally: "In Christ there is no slave or free, Jew or Greek, no male and female."[112] All are on equal footing insofar as their standing in Christ, the basis by which they get into Christ. This can only be so, not because they have ceased to be these former things, but because these things do not count so far as being saved or one's standing in the eyes of the Lord is concerned. Whereas before, such things did count, they do not any longer, now that the possibility of being something different, a new creature, is here. This allows one to leave behind those aspects of one's ethnic, social, or sexual status that affect one's religious status and apparently also affect one's religious roles.[113]

If all believers are one in Christ, it is appropriate to ask in what sense this is true. Barrett suggests we render the closing clause in Gal. 3:28: "You are all one person in Christ."[114] It is true to say that neither Paul nor Christ was interested in producing just individual new creatures but rather a new community. Paul believes that in one sense a new humanity was begun by the last Adam, by means of his resurrection. Thus, although one becomes a new creature in one's individuality, one is immediately grafted into a new community, the body of Christ; and it is in that context that Christlikeness is expected and assumed to be possible, not through the virtuous striving of isolated individuals.

Similar ideas to the new creature concept can be found in the later Pauline texts. For instance, in Eph. 2:10 it is said that "we are God's workmanship created in Christ." Obviously, this implies that this new creation is an act of God in and for the believer, one he or she cannot cause in himself or herself. Even later, in the Pauline corpus, we find in Titus 3:5 a slightly different idea: "He saved us through the washing of rebirth and renewal by the Spirit." This formulation is rather un-Pauline, but it does not really reflect a different conception than what is found in the earlier and undisputed Pauline letters.

It is precisely because believers are new creatures and thus part of a new humanity and community that they get frustrated with still living in the midst of the old order and groan for the completion of this creation in the redemption of their bodies. In Paul's later letters he speaks more clearly of a corporate new person that all Christians are part of (e.g., Col. 3:9–10). Here we seem to have a corporate recreation of humanity in the Creator's image. In fact, it is Christ they are a part of, he is the new man they have put on. Notice that this putting on involves ongoing renewal (present participle—*anakainoumenon*, "being renewed"; similarly in Rom. 12:2). It is, interestingly enough, the new self that is being renewed in the image of God, and being renewed in his way of thinking in progressive fashion.

The new person Christians are part of (i.e., Christ) is characterized by no social distinctions (Col. 3:11). Ephesians 2:15 makes this more explicit; in Christ is created one new person where formerly there was the distinction of Jew and Gentile. Again, it is the corporate significance that is emphasized. Nonetheless, the corporate is made up of individuals. Thus what is true of the group is also true of the individual: "You have put off the old self and put on the new, by being in Christ" (Col. 3:10). We need now to examine another related concept.

"The inner person or self" (2 Cor. 4:16), despite protests to the contrary, does seem to be talking about a distinction between the person as manifested in her or his body (called the outward self) and the person as she or he is spiritually and inwardly. The renewal believers experience is ongoing day by day and affects not their bodies but their thoughts, emotions, will, attitudes, or in other words, those nonmaterial aspects of their beings. They are strengthened in their inner selves by God's Spirit (cf. Eph. 3:16). Romans 7:22 is problematic but likely supports again the distinction between "self" in all its nonmaterial aspects and all this plus a body. After all, something must be present with the Lord in 2 Corinthians 5, and it can only mean the self of the believer. There is thus a limited anthropological dualism in Paul,[115] and Bultmann's conclusion that one does not have a *soma* (body) but is a *soma* is an inaccurate assessment of Paul's thought.[116]

We have already spoken in some detail about the importance of the *en Christo* (in Christ) formula for Paul, and here we need only summarize a few points as they apply to the believer. It is difficult to maintain the proper understanding of Paul's dialectic between individual identity and union in Christ. As various scholars have pointed out, Paul steers a middle course between crude materialism and overspiritualism. On the one hand, Paul does want to assert a real spiritual union between believers and Christ, and among believers themselves, in Christ's body. First Corinthians 12:13 is about real spiritual transformation and union.

Thus it is not adequate to try to reduce Paul's "participation" language to mere relational terms, as, for instance, Furnish does when he says: "The believers' participation in Christ's death and resurrection is misinterpreted if it is conceived as a 'mystical union' with Christ. The believer . . . belongs to Christ. The categories used to describe the believer's association with Christ are all relational and not mystical categories."[117] On the other hand, Paul is not talking about a quasi-physical union, as Schweitzer held.

This is evident, for instance, from 1 Cor. 6:15–17. Although it is perfectly possible to become one body with a prostitute, when Paul goes on to talk about the union of believers with Christ he distinguishes it from such a physical union by saying in v. 17 that believers become one spirit with the Lord.

When Paul goes on to discuss spiritual union with Christ in the Lord's Supper, he speaks of a sharing in common of Christ's blood (1 Cor 10:16). This is to be contrasted with the sharing in common with demons at their table in pagan temples (v. 20). Now if Paul is talking about any sort of union here with spiritual beings, he cannot be referring to some sort of quasi-physical union or fellowship with demons; yet he uses the same terms to describe both sets of participation. Clearly, *koinonia* is of a real, but nonetheless spiritual, nature. It is precisely not the physical act of eating or the food that bothers Paul, but the spiritual implications and transformations such acts entail.

The language of interpenetration (Christ in the believer and vice versa) can as easily be explained on the assumption of a spiritual union. The language of ownership is easily understood as well: to belong to Christ is not different from being "in him." But if one begins simply with the ownership language and assumes that there is no real spiritual union, it is more than a little difficult to interpret such passages as 2 Cor. 1:5: "For as we share abundantly in Christ's sufferings . . . "; or 2 Cor. 4:10: "always carrying in the body the death of Jesus." It is true that Paul makes clear in 4:11 that this means being given up to death for Christ's sake; but even that suffering, however, has some sort of "life" benefit for Paul's converts (v. 12).

This means on the one hand that Paul did not see his suffering as exactly the same as Christ's, nor indeed as having the same salvific value. It was something done for Jesus. On the other hand, God used it to bring life to Paul's converts, so there was some benefit in and from it, and a likeness to Christ's suffering. Further, these sufferings are "the same sufferings we all suffer." There is a shared experience as a result of being Christ's people, and it is not merely a matter of an apostolic representation of Christ's suffering in Paul's body. It is right to note that Paul only occasionally speaks of suffering with Christ (2 Cor. 1:5; Rom. 8:17). Even in Phil. 3:10–11, perhaps the most vivid text, Paul is careful to say that he wants to take part in the "sharing in common" (*koinonia*) of Christ's sufferings and to share the likeness of his death. There is sharing but not identification involved in this. We see here the justification for the remark that normally suffering merges into dying in Paul. Though we have already discussed "dying in Christ," we affirm again here that in Paul's view every Christian has a Calvary and Easter like Christ's, which is partly a matter of imitating Christ and partly a matter of being transformed by God into Christ's likeness.

Generally, one may say that if one is in Christ and Christ is in that person, one can do things with or for or through Christ (cf. Rom. 1:8; 7:25; 5:1, 21; 1 Cor. 15:27; and 1 Thess. 5:9 on the latter). The "through Christ" phrases stress Christ's mediatorial role and position between believers and the Father, as we have already seen in our discussion of the faithfulness of Jesus. The "with Christ" phrases usually refer to suffering or dying (Gal. 2:20; Rom. 6:4, 8; Phil. 3:10–11). It only makes sense then that the "into Christ" focuses on the transformation that unites one with Christ and his body. The "in Christ" formula, however, is central and by far the most prevalent usage, and, contrary to what some might suggest, it is not difficult to see how the other phrases lead to (eis), depend upon (sun), or presuppose (dia) "being in Christ."

One cannot approach the Father through the Son unless one is "in Christ." Nor can one do something for or with Christ unless one is "in Christ." Theologically and logically this concept is central, and the other concepts converge "in Christ." I would suggest that this is so because Paul believes that the life of Christ goes on, and there is a dynamic union between believers and Christ's ongoing life in heaven, his continuing story. It is of course true that the "in Christ" formula can simply be a phrase attached to all sorts of statements, and sometimes it is intended to enforce the truthfulness or sincerity of the remark, or its Christian content. Sometimes the phrase does refer to something believers have received by being in Christ, or can receive in or from him (cf. Phil. 2:1, 5; Rom. 8:39). Sometimes the formula seems to mean "with him" in the sense of how he reacts to a particular matter (cf. 2 Cor. 1:19, 20). Sometimes the phrase seems to be short for "in the name of the Lord" (see Rom. 16:19). Sometimes it seems to mean "from the Lord's point of view" or "in the Lord's hands" (see 1 Cor. 15:55). Sometimes the phrase is simply a term for "within the Christian fold" or "in the believing community" (cf. 1 Cor. 7:39; Gal. 5:6; 1 Thess. 5:12) or "in a Christian manner" (Phil. 2:29). The core usage, however, has to do with being in Christ and spiritually united to him (cf. 1 Thess. 4:16; Gal. 2:17; 1 Cor. 1:2; 3:1; 15:17 and passim).

The present reality of participation "in Christ" is crucial to Paul, and it is interesting how often he links it to eschatological expectations. The spiritual and eschatological concepts are intimately related. The implications of being in Christ are for Paul quite astounding, for it entails being a new creature, a part of a new community, dead to sin, in possession of the Spirit, and assured of a bodily resurrection, provided one remains "in Christ," walking in the Spirit.[118]

TEMPLE TALK

> Flesh is but the glass, which holds the dust
> That measures all our time; which also shall
> Be crumbled into dust. Mark here below
> How tame these ashes are, how free from lust
> That thou mayst fit thy self against thy fall.
>
> —*George Herbert*
> *"Church Monuments"*[119]

Being part of the body of Christ is virtually equivalent to saying one is in Christ, in Paul's way of thinking. However, the body metaphor for Paul functions in various interesting ways when he is talking about being in Christ, and we must examine them. We have already in part discussed *soma* (body) when we considered the human plight and condition of those outside of Christ.[120]

Let us begin by going back and looking at the new creation from a slightly different angle—namely, dying and rising with Christ. In Romans 6:1ff. Paul does not talk about dying and rising as *one* event in Christ; rather, his progression seems to be union with Christ's death now, new life now, and union with him in his resurrection later. In other words, conversion in itself begins the process of dying and rising, but rising per se, which has to do with one's mortal flesh, comes later. This distinguishes Paul's thought from certain Hellenistic concepts where one could die and rise in the rite of initiation.[121]

The real question is, Does baptism here mean water baptism or spirit baptism or both? It is improbable, in view of 1 Cor. 1:14–17, that Paul saw water baptism as a sacrament that saved people, for he makes quite clear that believing by faith in the preached word, not baptism, is the means of salvation. Elsewhere Paul talks about being baptized by the Spirit into the body of Christ (1 Cor. 12:3), and this is likely in view here. Thus, in v. 3 being baptized into Christ, which may or may not happen coincidentally with water baptism, is just another way of saying "being spiritually united with Christ." Believers have been baptized into his death, buried with him. Verse 5 says literally, "We have grown together with him in his death." This seems to mean in part that when believers are united with Christ the old person has died and been buried. It no longer exists. In Paul's thought, the old self is not to be equated with indwelling sin in the believer. It is the old self, or nature, that has been put off when one becomes "in Christ." Paul uses the language of putting off the old and putting on Christ, drawing on the idea of exchanging clothing. He may have in mind the baptismal ceremony in which one disrobes, is baptized in the nude, and

puts on a new robe symbolizing the new person in Christ. The tension in
the believer is then not old person/new person, but Spirit versus flesh.

✓   The old person was crucified and buried in and with Christ at the point
of conversion, as Rom. 6:6 makes very clear, so that the "body of sin"
might be rendered powerless and believers would no longer be slaves to
sin. The phrase "body of sin" means probably the physical body as it is
controlled by sin (v. 13). The horror of sin in a believer is that, although a
new creature with the old self crucified, he or she sometimes willfully
chooses to act against both what he or she knows and what he or she is. It is
as a new person that believers sin—a new person who is no longer bound to
sin as its slave. Thus the believer cannot place the blame for sin on the old
person, who is dead and buried with Christ (cf. Col. 2:12). On the basis of
this, Paul can give imperatives to avoid sin and be alive to Christ. In other
words, for Paul ethics is grounded not only in the story of Christ, who is to
be seen as an exemplar, but in what God has already accomplished in the
believer's life at and after conversion.

Paul twice uses the body imagery to talk about Christians being in
Christ—once in Rom. 12:4ff. and once in 1 Cor. 12:12ff. By way of
background, notice that at various points Paul says that the whole church is
"in Christ" (1 Thess. 1:1; 2:14; Phil. 1:4). Christ is in essence to be seen as
the place where believers are and salvation is to be found. They are
incorporated into him, and there is some sort of corporate solidarity
assumed in Paul's exhortations to groups of Christians.

At 1 Cor. 12:13 we have a simple description of what is true of the
human body; it is a unity, but is made up of many parts. It has often been
pointed out that for Pauline thought the relation of the one and the many
is a basic problem. Paul solves this without dissolving the many into the
one by speaking of (1) a real spiritual union between one Christ and many
believers, (2) a union between Christ, as head, and his body, and (3) a union
between the various body members as united to each other while still
remaining individuals.

It will be seen that the point of the body metaphor in both 1 Corinthians
12 and Romans 12 is not so much to stress the union of believers with
Christ as with each other. It is used to attack disunity and discord among
Christians, notably in Corinth.[122] What the Spirit has done with believers
is not merely to unite them with Christ, but to "baptize" them into one
body, into union with other believers. The identification of the church is
with Christ's body, *not* with Christ. If the church were simply identified
with Christ, Paul would be quite unable to use Christ as a moral exemplar
for Christian behavior, for one hardly calls for people to imitate themselves. The implications of this for Paul are major: the ultimate God-
revealed unity in the universe is and is in the redeemed community of

Christians. That community is meant to be a paradigm of what God intends for human society, modeling both proper relationships with God and with fellow human beings.

Various pagan philosophers such as the Stoics and also the Gnostics talked about the universe being a body, but not Paul. Paul talks of a unity of persons in Christ, not a unity of all natural things in God (a form of pantheism). When Paul calls Christ the head or Lord over the body, he distinguishes Christ from his body. But when he calls Christ the firstfruits, or the firstborn of many brothers and sisters, or the first of a new humanity, Paul identifies Christ with his followers. One must then see elements of continuity and discontinuity between Christ and his body.

Notice in 1 Cor. 12:13 that the Spirit baptizes one into the body. This takes place at the point of being united to Christ and his people, not later. No Christian is without the Spirit (they are all given the one Spirit to "drink"), and all Christians are united with the body by the Spirit. There is then in Paul's thought world no such thing as (a) a spirit baptism subsequent to conversion or (b) a Christian without the Spirit or without one or more spiritual gifts. In 1 Corinthians 12 Paul stresses the diversity of bodily parts and functions and says they are all necessary and important. He even mentions the genitals as a vital part (v. 23) and says they are treated with special modesty. All the bodily parts (members) are supposed to work together and have equal concern for one another (v. 25) even though some are weaker or less presentable. The unity of the body is such that if one part suffers, all suffer.

Having completed his analogy at v. 26, Paul states boldly at v. 27: "Now you are the body of Christ and individually members of it." In view of the Corinthians' behavior, this is quite a statement. God has given both gifts and functions to the *ekklesia*—both people, and presents to the assembly. Not all have the same function or gift, but all gifts are important, and each is given to build up the body. This is how Paul exhorts a badly divided Christian church in Corinth.

Romans 12:5 adds little to this, and it may be that here, unlike 1 Cor. 12:26, we have just an analogy or simile, not a description, of the *ekklesia* as body. However, Rom. 12:5 suggests a description, and it tells believers that as members of Christ's body, one belongs not only to Christ but to each other. Thus the believer should function so as to serve the body, not sever it from its limbs. The different gifts are to be used to build up the one body and to serve one another, for all belong to each other.

Some of the nuances of this imagery are made more explicit in some of the later Paulines, especially Colossians and Ephesians. Thus, in Col. 1:18 Christ is called head, and the body is said to be the *ekklesia*. Again at 1:24 the *ekklesia* is not just a body; it is Christ's body. At 2:19 for the first time

Paul talks about the body's dependence on the head. In fact, the head is not even mentioned in Romans 12 or 1 Corinthians 12, though we do have a different sort of reference to it at 1 Cor. 11:3: "The head of every man is Christ." At Col. 2:19 it is said that Christ is the source of the sustenance by which the body lives, but also he is the source of unity through which it becomes an organic whole. Believers are one in him and not apart from him. In Colossians it is suggested that each body part is functioning properly only when it is under the direction of the head. Christ supports, nourishes, directs, and binds believers together.

Ephesians 4:16 is very similar at this point. Notice how at 4:15 believers' actions, such as speaking the truth in love, facilitate growing up into him who is their head, Christ. Colossians 2:19b also adds that God causes the body to grow. It is evident from all of the above that Paul and/or the Paulinists believe that they are not just talking about ideas or symbols, but rather ideas that signify a spiritual reality.

Exhibit A of this fact is seen at 1 Cor. 6:15ff. Here Paul is saying that a believer's very body is a member of Christ himself, and thus each one is individually linked to Christ. This is obviously a spiritual union, and Paul in fact says, "We are united with the Lord being one with him in spirit" (i.e., spiritually). He then asks, How can you literally unite the members of Christ with a whore! Obviously Paul believes he is talking about two mutually exclusive but real unions, and the one ought to exclude the other.

Shortly thereafter, at 1 Cor. 6:19 Paul calls the individual body the temple of God. This should be compared to 3:16, where the body of Christ collectively is called God's temple.[123] It is not unheard of for a Hellenistic philosopher to remind his hearers that God's dwelling was in the hearts of human beings, not buildings. In 1 Cor. 3:16, however, Paul is not talking about Christ's dwelling in an individual human heart, but the believing community collectively being the shrine of the Spirit's presence. The point is that a Christian's moral behavior affects not only the individual in question but also the Christian community of which she or he is a part. To borrow a phrase from John Donne, Paul believes that no one is an island entire in oneself. Rather, all are part of *ekklesia*, and thus what they do affects the body. Second Corinthians 6:16 adds little to this except that it stresses that pagan religions and Christianity are incompatible and Christians are the temple of the living God. Elsewhere in passing (1 Cor. 3:9b–10), believers are called God's building being built up and together by grace, and by God's colaborers.

The implications of all this seem to be: (1) temple/building and church/body refer to the people of God and in no case refer to buildings; (2) they are not in Paul's mind mere symbols, for they describe spiritual realities true about the believer's relationship with Christ and with each other; (3) it is God who creates and sustains the body of Christ, which is a living organism, not an organization or club; (4) believers are mutually dependent on each other and on Christ; (5) they all have the Spirit and spiritual fruit and gifts;[124] (6) it is the believers' union and relationship with Christ and each other out of which all of Paul's exhortations and imperatives come. He presupposes these realities when he talks to Christians and argues on the basis of them. We will have more to say about Paul's view of the *ekklesia* as *soma* when we discuss more fully life in this entity.

IN THE SPIRIT OF THINGS

One of the clearest signs that Paul saw himself and the *ekklesia* as living in an eschatological context and age is the presence and work of the Spirit in the whole body of Christ, and in each member of it. It has often been noted how close Christ and the Spirit seem to be in Paul's letter, and we have already had occasion to reflect on the relationship between Christ and Spirit, the latter being the earthly surrogate and agent of Christ.[125] They are clearly distinguishable, however, at certain key points. For instance, the Spirit comes to believers only because Christ is risen and ascended. It is not accidental that it is in a discussion of Jesus' resurrection that we are told that Jesus as last Adam is a life-giving spirit (1 Cor. 15:45). Christ is the one who sends the Spirit, and without his resurrection and exaltation the Spirit would not have come. Romans 1:3–4 indicates that it is through the power of the Spirit that Jesus is enabled to be Son of God in power. The Spirit empowers Jesus, and he sends that power to believers. It is Christ who makes the eschatological age possible, and that age focuses on him. However, this is possible only because the Holy Spirit empowers, illuminates, and enables the believer to have a Christocentric focus and to model himself or herself on Christ.

Let us look now in some detail at the Spirit's functions, thereby preparing the way for discussing the Spirit's gifts and fruit. First Corinthians 2:6–16 enumerates one of the Spirit's primary functions—illumination. The Spirit does not reveal or direct attention to the Spirit's self, but rather reveals the truth about Christ and the wisdom of God manifest in Christ. The Spirit makes believers capable of understanding and properly integrating the Christ, the Christ event, and what God has freely given them in Christ (v. 12). Only the Spirit can comprehend the deep things of God; humans cannot do so by human wisdom.

At v. 14 Paul asserts that a person who does not have the Spirit will not understand or accept God or spiritual truths. This means that having the Spirit is the very *basis* of Christian existence; without the Spirit a believer would not understand salvation or even accept it. Notice how closely allied having the mind of Christ (v. 16b) is with having the Spirit in this context.[126] Various texts, such as 1 Cor. 12:3 and Eph. 1:17–18, suggest that the illumination work of the Spirit is an ongoing activity, not something that happens just once at conversion. It is also by the Spirit that believers receive their adoption as "sons" and "daughters" (Gal. 4:5).

Galatians 4:6 reminds us that what Paul believes characterized Christ's relation to the Father as his Son was the prayer "Abba." So too the Spirit prompts the cry of "Abba" from believers, because having received the Spirit they are now adopted offspring of God and the Spirit is reproducing Christ's life and attitudes and prayer in believers.

Another primary characteristic of the Spirit for Paul is that it is an *arrabon* (cf. 2 Cor. 1:22; 5:5; Eph. 1:14). The word *arrabon* means first installment, or down payment. This points to the eschatological situation (believers have already received the Spirit of the end times); but it also points out the not-yet, for the Spirit is only the first installment. Paul is not referring here to a first installment of the Spirit, as if one got the Spirit in installments; rather, the Spirit *is* the firstfruits of salvation. The Spirit is the one who brings eschatological existence in part to believers now.

As 2 Cor. 5:5 says, the down payment is the earnest, or guarantee, of that which is yet to come. The nature of a down payment is that it implies that later payments will be coming. Ephesians 1:14 says that the Spirit is the down payment guaranteeing to believers their future inheritance until the day of redemption. In this sense the Spirit's presence is an assurance and gives assurance that God is with believers and will finish the divine work in them. Of a similar nature is Rom. 8:23, where we have "the firstfruits of the Spirit," which likely is epexegetical—the firstfruits that consist in the Spirit.[127] In extrabiblical Greek, *aparche* refers to the firstfruits for sacrifice or offering, part of a worshiper's property offered to God. Here we have the converse; it is the firstfruits of something God offers to believers. Firstfruits, which believers have, is contrasted to what they do not yet have—the redemption of their bodies. However great and important the work of the Spirit in the believer is, Paul insists that they must be aware that it is not God's final or ultimate gift to them. The Spirit is the gift, or earnest, in the interim until the redemption of their bodies.

At 1 Thess. 1:5 Paul discusses the full assurance or fullest conviction that the Spirit produces in the believer. The deep inner persuasion of the truth of the gospel is seen as a clear indicator that the Holy Spirit is in one and is working in one's heart. Notice the three-part parallel: the gospel message came to the Thessalonians (1) in power, (2) in the Holy Spirit, (3) in fullest conviction.

All Christians share in common the Holy Spirit. The Spirit's role is not limited to the point of conversion, the uniting of one with the body of

Christ (1 Cor. 12:13). Rather, Christians are also given to drink from the Spirit (1 Cor. 12:13b). Though the giving is a one-time phenomenon, the drinking apparently is to be seen as ongoing. The Spirit is the agent of both the conversion and the renewal in the believer; it is what the believer experiences on an ongoing basis. A person who does not have the Spirit of Christ is not a Christian (Rom. 8:9b). Romans 8:9a indicates that the Spirit of God dwells (*oikei*, present tense) in the believer. Sanday and Headlam call it a present, permanent, penetrating influence in every believer's life. Here we notice the difference between the old covenant and the new. In the Old Testament the Spirit came intermittently, resting on certain individuals, especially in the case of prophets and kings, to equip them for a task. Here the Spirit is a permanent presence in every believer.

If every Christian has the Spirit, what does it mean when the author of Ephesians refers to being filled with the Spirit? Ephesians 5:18b is connected with 5:18a, and v. 19 is likely connected to 5:18b. The phrase in question reads, "be full/filled in spirit," which is an alternative to being drunk with wine. Notice that the verb is an imperfect passive—"let yourselves be filled" (ongoing action). The author does not say "become filled." It is not a matter of receiving the Spirit, or even of receiving a second dose of the Spirit, but being filled with the Spirit, who already indwells the believer. The Spirit then penetrates all of one's being. There is, however, a problem because, as has been noted by grammarians, the use of *pleroo* with *en* to express the content with which a thing is filled is quite without parallel. It is therefore unlikely that we should translate "with the Spirit," but rather "in or through the Spirit." If this is correct, then the Spirit is the means by which the believer is filled, or the context in which one is filled (in the Spirit), but not the *content* of the filling. It is possible that Paul is talking about a spiritual fullness wrought by the Spirit, which leads us to v. 19. When the Spirit fully inspires someone, one is led to sing praises and songs to God, prompted by the Spirit. Elsewhere Paul sees the Spirit of God as that which prompts worship and fills believers with praise (see Phil. 3:3). Thus Paul may be saying here that believers should keep on being filled by the Spirit so they may continue to praise God.[128] This leads us to discuss the gifts and fruit of the Spirit, manifestations that are supposed to characterize the story of the Christian.

The subject of gifts and fruit of the Spirit is a vast one, one we can give only a general orientation to here. It should be noted at the outset that Paul gives us no one definitive list of spiritual *charismata* (gifts). We have, for instance, a list at 1 Cor. 12:8–10, another at 12:28 (cf. vv. 27–30), another at Rom. 12:6–8, and still another and later list at Eph. 4:11. In these lists sometimes Paul is talking about gifts and functions; sometimes he is talking about people or offices. Paul is not trying to give exhaustive lists, only some notable common examples. It is also clear that Paul sees every Christian as having at least one if not several gifts: "To each one the manifestation of the Spirit is given" (1 Cor. 12:7). Paul seems to believe, regarding most if not all these gifts, that they can be used or abused, used selfishly or self-sacrificially, used to build up the body or puff up the individual. A Christian is one who has and must learn how to use such gifts in proper and loving fashion.

We will consider the list in 1 Cor. 12:8–10 first. Verse 8 indicates that the Spirit can give cognitive gifts—wisdom or knowledge—although it is not clear how these are to be distinguished. Knowledge may refer to a gift of instructive discourse; wisdom, to divine insight into the situation or human condition. We have had occasion earlier to refer to special faith,[129] which may refer to miracle-working faith (cf. 1 Cor. 13:2). Notice too the next pair of gifts; the gift of healing is separated from the gift of miraculous powers. Barrett suggests that the latter covers a wider range of supernatural activities (possibly exorcism?). The ability to distinguish between spirits likely refers to the ability to discern when certain phenomena come from the Holy Spirit and when they come from evil spirits, lying spirits. First Corinthians 12:3 may refer to the ecstatic cursing of Jesus under the impetus of an evil spirit or demon.[130] Prophecy, a kind of tongues (*glossai*), and the ability to interpret tongues we will deal with in depth after reviewing the other lists.

The list at 12:28 is a list of persons who have special functions among God's people. To some degree this list simply corresponds to the gifts mentioned in 12:8–10, telling us who exercised these gifts. It will be noted that here as in 12:10 the gift of tongues comes last. This is surely in part because Paul's audience highly overvalued this gift and were in fact using it in various un-Christian ways, apparently causing some to stumble. Paul lists these gifts in order of value to the upbuilding of the community. Essentially, at 12:28 he lists people God has put in the church for its order and instruction. Apostles are listed first.[131] Presumably, the teachers mentioned correspond to the gifts of wisdom and or knowledge. He adds a reference to two previously unmentioned sorts of roles: gifts of support (perhaps here he has benefactors in mind or deacons) and gifts of direction.[132] Some argue that Paul has here in view the administrators who directed congregational life. At this point it is right to note that 1 Corinthians 13 shows the *manner* and context in which all gifts should be exercised. Less likely is the view that love is seen as the ultimate gift, for Paul expects all to have and express love and to exercise their gifts in love. Love "provides the scale by which other gifts may be tested and measured, and also is the means by which the unity of the Body is maintained. At Gal. 5:22 it is mentioned first among the products of the Spirit; here it seems to be distinguished from spiritual gifts in general . . . and all Christians are expected to have it."[133]

At Rom. 12:6–8 we have our third list. Here it appears that God determines who gets what gifts, for it depends on the grace given. However, it appears that one may petition God for more or other gifts (cf. 1 Cor. 12:31). There are certain greater gifts, and Paul makes clear that prophecy is greater than tongues (1 Cor. 14:1), but any gift that builds up the body is to be desired more (1 Cor. 14:12). The list in Romans has crossovers with the lists in 1 Corinthians, but we note the mention of serving, encouraging, contributing, leadership, showing mercy. Some of these gifts are purely miraculous; some may be mainly practical in nature, and some may be related to or an enabling of one's so-called natural talents or one's economic or social situation. Paul does not distinguish between natural and supernatural gifts because he saw all as ultimately coming from the Spirit of God. *Parakalon* means "exhorting," the ability to help and encourage Christians to live out their obedience to Christ. The gift of charity here likely corresponds to what we found at 1 Cor. 12:28. Paul also mentions here *ho proistamenos*, which may be a reference to the presiding ruler or elder over a given congregation, but another possibility is that it is a reference to the overseer of the *ekklesia*'s charitable work. This would explain why it is coupled with contributors and those who have mercy (presumably on the sick or poor or aged). The last three terms seem to refer to the practical work of ministry.

This leaves us with Eph. 4:11, which adds little except to focus on the preaching and teaching; *euangelistais* and *poimenes* are mentioned. The former is the term from which we get the word *evangelist*, and it may mean here those whose gift is to preach to the unconverted (cf. Acts 21:8), perhaps under the guidance or jurisdiction of a missionary apostle. It has been suggested that pastors and teachers refer to local church officials or functions, and this may well be so, as distinguished from some or all of the first part of the list. With this overview let us consider two gifts in more detail—prophecy and tongues, especially as explained in 1 Cor. 12—14.

Is "tongues" in Paul's view an actual language or languages, or is it the use of sounds or words that do not add up to a language but are part of a deep communion with God? On the one hand, Paul draws an analogy in 1 Cor. 14:7–9 that may suggest that tongues is like music; it communicates something but is not cognitive in content. However, it seems from a closer look at v. 9 that the point of this analogy is not that tongues is not a language, but that without interpretation it is unintelligible, undistinguishable, and unclear as to what it means. The point is, as v. 10f. makes clear, that the effect of listening to uninterpreted tongues is like listening to a completely foreign language—there is no understanding. Notice, how-

- ever, that Paul's analogy in vv. 10–11 is to languages. It seems likely, then, that Paul saw tongues as some sort of language, not just babble.

Confirmation may perhaps be found for this view at 1 Cor. 13:1, where Paul talks about speaking in the tongues of humans or angels. Perhaps the reason Paul calls tongues "a kind of tongues" is not because he is referring to a foreign human language miraculously given, but more likely because he is referring to a spiritual, or angelic, language that the Holy Spirit could prompt a Christian to utter. If this is correct, then it is worth noting that Acts 2 is unlike 1 Corinthians 14. There human languages are in view in all likelihood, for it says, "We hear them *speaking in our own languages*" (2:11).[134] First Corinthians 14:15ff. suggests that tongues is the language of prayer (i.e., it is a praying with one's spirit as opposed to praying with one's mind; cf. Rom. 8:16). First Corinthians 14:16 suggests that it is a way of giving thanks to God. It is likely also that 1 Cor. 14:15 refers to singing in tongues. This may also be what is meant in Col. 3:16 and the Ephesians parallel—spiritual songs, songs of one's spirit prompted by the Holy Spirit.

Tongues is unlike prophecy in that in itself it only has value for the individual involved unless it is interpreted. Apparently some Corinthians were so egocentric that all they cared about was self-edification and perhaps self-glorification by showing off their flashy gifts.[135] At 1 Cor. 14:20, having reminded the Corinthians that he, Paul, was also a tongues speaker, he goes on to note its danger to the congregation if uninter-
- preted.[136] It is a poor witness and may cause the non-Christian to conclude that Christians are insane. Prophecy, however, is a sign to the church, a word of conviction, exhortation, application that may also convict, convince, and convert the nonbeliever. Possibly Paul's use of the term "sign" here has an Old Testament background in Isa. 28:11–12, where Israel had spurned God's word in their own tongue, so God spoke to them a word of judgment in a foreign (Assyrian?) tongue. There are, of course, various loose ends here. How does one know there will or will not be interpretation of tongues in a given congregation? Perhaps Paul envisions that the tongues speaker in a local congregation would likely know if anyone had already exhibited the gift of interpreting tongues in that place.

In regard to Christian prophecy, I have dealt with this issue at length elsewhere and must only summarize a few points here.[137] There is no indication in Paul's letters to suggest that he saw it as a phenomenon limited to the apostolic age. From what we have said thus far, it seems likely that for Paul there was simple prophecy and then there was tongues plus interpretation, which could have the same edifying effect as prophecy but is not to be simply identified with it. Clearly, for Paul prophecy is an intelligible utterance. Thus, although tongues are allowed, prophecy is to be sought (v. 39), for Paul puts a premium on intelligibility and order in Christian worship. First Corinthians 14:30 suggests that Paul sees prophecy as a form of revelation, but apparently prophecy is a secondary form of revelation because prophecy must be tested and approved, unlike the Hebrew scriptures. Scripture is fully authoritative and inspired, but Christian prophecy was apparently not in the same category for Paul. It was perhaps like preaching in that it could be authoritative but also fallible. Paul seems to think that one can speak in a way that exceeds one's inspiration; hence the utterance must be weighed and sifted. Christians then should prophesy in proportion to their faith (Rom. 14:6). Prophecy seems to differ from preaching or teaching in that it comes more directly and spontaneously from God on a specific occasion to speak to a specific situation or a specific need of a congregation. In this, too, it seems to differ from scripture, which could have a wider application.

For Paul, even the apostolic tradition and message are more authoritative than the prophecy he is talking about. The authoritative tradition, such as one finds at the beginning of 1 Corinthians 15 or in 11:23, is simply to be believed and passed on, whereas prophecy is to be tested and judged (cf. 1 Cor. 14:29; 1 Thess. 5:20–21). Prophecy was truth telling, forth telling, and 1 Cor. 14:31 suggests that it involves instruction and encouragement.[138] First Corinthians 14:32 suggests that although prophecy is prompted by the Holy Spirit, the human spirit is also involved and the utterance can be controlled by the prophet. It is not merely a mechanical ecstatic utterance, though some Corinthians may have assumed this was the case. Because Rom. 12:6 suggests that one is able to prophesy in proportion to one's faith, this may imply that the point and truth of one's prophecy depend on the state of faith or sanctification of the prophet. Thus imperfections and errors are possible in such prophecy. This is why the ability to distinguish between spirits and to weigh or sift the prophecy is important to Paul.

In short, it appears that for Paul prophecy is a valid and valuable but not infallible gift of the Spirit, not infallible because it involves human cooperation and participation. It *is* a matter of revelation, but it appears to be of lesser inspiration and involves more human contribution than Old Testament prophecy. It was given for a specific limited situation; hence its limited circulation and lesser degree of authority.[139] Tongues is also seen by Paul as a valid and valuable gift, but it must be carefully used lest it cause non-tongues speakers and non-Christians to stumble. It appears that Paul sees it as a prayer language in the main, by the human spirit, prompted by the Holy Spirit, and it may also be sung. With interpretation, it can also aid others and have an equivalent edifying effect to prophecy.

PAUL'S ANTHROPOLOGY:
IN FULL POSSESSION OF ONE'S FACULTIES

> I am a little world made cunningly
> Of elements, and an angelic sprite.
>
> —*John Donne*
> *"Divine Meditations"* 5[140]

Much ink has been spilled on the subject of the fruit of the Spirit, but it is seldom realized that Paul discusses the fruit in the context of his discussion of the tension of flesh against Spirit. Thus we need to understand Paul's anthropological terms, especially *flesh* and *Spirit*, to understand Gal. 5:16–25. First we need to summarize Paul's view of sin.

When Paul discusses sin, he uses the term *hamartia* ("sin") with the full range of meanings its Old Testament equivalents have: (1) to miss the mark or go astray—Rom. 3:23; (2) a blameworthy mistake, that is, one that incurs guilt—Rom. 8:3; (3) rebellion against God—1 Cor. 8:12. Paul discusses sin at length in Rom. 1–3 and Rom. 5. Paul sees the root of the human disorder in the fact that a human being wants to be master of his or her own fate. Thus humankind prefers a religion that does not require them to be a servant or subordinate to anyone. Though human beings were created to have dominion over the earth, they wanted also to be lord over their own lives and destinies. The reason they worship images and things that are less than God is that such things can be manipulated or controlled by humankind. One creates a god that meets the desire to be one's own master, and repudiates a god who mandates a *must* upon them, because this compromises one's self-rule.

Thus, for Paul Adam's primal and primary sin was that essentially he attempted to gain mastery over his own condition and future and indeed even gain control over the one he was called to obey. The promise of the tempter was "You shall be as gods." Ironically, sin, once committed, does not aid one to become one's *own* master, but rather proceeds to become one's master; sin reigns as a lord in the fallen creature. Notice in Rom. 6:6: "enslaved to sin"; and in 6:12: "sin reigns in your mortal bodies"; and again in 6:17: "slaves of sin" (cf. vv. 19–20). Thus, for Paul sin enters the human race with Adam and has been reigning over the fallen ever since. Because it is coextensive with the human race, none are born sinless or innocent; all are under its power, both Jew and Greek (Rom. 3:9). Thus, for Paul human nature as it is, is sinful. Christ, however, is the definition of what a human being *ought* to be. Sin is fundamentally for Paul an act or attitude of idolatry—an attempt to displace or deny God's Lordship over human creatures—and the root of it is pride and self-glorification. If God is the source of life and if sin separates one from God, then sin's consequence is death. Sin, like death, affects the whole person.[141]

In light of the above, Paul's other anthropological terms make sense.[142] *Kardia* ("heart") Paul uses as it is used in the Old Testament. The heart is the seat of thought, will, and affection, and can be either good or bad (Rom. 10:8). In Rom. 1:21 the *kardia* is the seat of thinking and thus often is translated "mind." In 1:24 it is associated with desires or lusts and is often translated "heart." In 2:5 it is said to be hard or impenitent. At 2:29 it is associated in a more metaphorical way with inward piety (i.e., spiritual circumcision is a matter of heart disposition). The heart is the seat of good desires and belief (Rom. 10:1, 10); it is also the place where the Spirit resides (2 Cor. 1:22). It is clear from the flexibility of all this usage that (1) Paul is not talking about the physical organ in the human body, but uses the term in a metaphorical sense; (2) inasmuch as *kardia* is an instrument of one's ego, it can be either good or bad depending on one's condition. Because all are fallen outside of Christ, all experience a "heart that is darkened" (Rom. 1:21).

Nous ("mind") in Paul is very much like *kardia*. It is an instrument or agency of the whole person and can be used by flesh as well as Spirit. Usually it is translated "mind," but we must beware of casting Paul in a purely Hellenistic mold here, because although "mind" can refer to one's reasoning faculty (1 Cor. 14:14, 15, 19) and involves knowledge or ignorance,[143] it is not simply the higher side of human nature that can be contrasted to the flesh. Indeed, the mind itself is called at one point "the mind of his flesh" (i.e., a fleshly mind—Col. 2:18). Paul appears to mean here that the mind can be carnal, in which case he is not talking about the materiality of the mind or brain. He is, however, indicating that he can use the term *sarx* to mean more than physical flesh. Paul also uses the term *phronema* in similar fashion to *nous*. It too should be translated "mind" and can be fleshly; Rom. 8:5 shows where the mind is closely identified with the flesh. Mind (*nous*), however, can on occasion be contrasted to flesh, such as in the case of Rom. 7:23 and 7:25. Here flesh is associated with sin that dwells in one's members as a law or lord, and mind is associated with the self or conscience that attempts to serve the law of God. Notice in v. 22 that *nous* is associated with the inner person. Thus flesh involves the physical being, desires, and a certain carnal orientation that follows these desires, whereas mind involves the inner being, the self, the conscience, and is seen here as a good thing, not carnal or fleshly. It seems here to refer only to one element of human nature. Of course, elsewhere (Rom. 12:2) the renewal of the whole person can be said to be or at least entail the renewal of the mind.

Paul uses the term *pneuma* of the human spirit sparingly. Normally *pneuma* means Holy Spirit in Paul. First Corinthians 14:14 (32?) speaks about "my spirit," and in 14:15 spirit and mind are contrasted. Some have suggested, however, that spirit here refers to something God gives the Christian, not something inherent in human nature (i.e., the spiritual agency that activates gifts). Against this, however, Paul speaks only of the Holy Spirit in these terms, not my "spirit." Further, 2 Cor. 7:1 speaks of defilers of the spirit and of the flesh. It is hard to see how one could defile the Holy Spirit, but the human spirit is another matter. Thus spirit seems to refer to a part of one's being that involves the suprarational or noncognitive aspects of human experience—broadly speaking, that which goes beyond the material and empirical. Paul, however, does *not* seem to see the human "spirit" as a material part of a person. We can only conjecture that he associates it perhaps with something like the *image of God* in humanity, that which makes possible relationships and communion with God, who is Spirit. Elsewhere in 1 Cor. 2:11 Paul parallels the Spirit of God and the spirit of a human being that is "in him." First Corinthians 5:3–5 refers to being present in spirit. Paul goes on to call it "my spirit," for the sinner is said to have "his spirit," and clearly Paul means the human spirit. The Holy Spirit does not need be saved (v. 5). It appears at 1 Cor. 2:12 that Paul uses the term *spirit* in a more metaphorical sense, as we would sometimes refer to the spirit of the age (*Zeitgeist*). This verse presumably refers to the attitude and orientation of the world. Of a similar sort is the usage in Rom. 8:15 ("spirit of slavery"), which refers to a condition or attitude or orientation received from the fallen world. So also at Rom. 11:8, *pneuma* seems to mean an attitude or orientation of stupor.

Paul uses the term *psuche* sparingly as well, and its cognate *psuchikos*. It clearly does not mean soul for Paul. Thus, for instance at Romans 1, quoting the Old Testament, he uses *psuche* in its Old Testament sense of life or self (the Hebrew *nephesh*). So too at Rom. 16:4 Paul speaks of those who risked their "lives" for his life (similarly at Phil. 2:30). In 1 Cor. 15:45 in the Old Testament quotation, Adam is said to become a living being (a living *psuche*). At times then, the term *psuche* is simply synonymous with human being (cf. Rom. 2:9; 13:1), without stress on one's being alive, though that is necessarily implied. First Thessalonians 5:23 has sometimes been used to argue that Paul had a trichotomous view of human nature: body, soul, spirit. Against this, however, *psuche* likely means here the life principle that animates the body. *Psuchikos* as an adjective is used by Paul in its normal sense to mean physical (just the opposite of soul) or natural, or possibly even unspiritual (cf. 1 Cor. 2:14; 15:44, 46). This term describes the natural human being (i.e., a person without the Holy Spirit) over against a person who has the Spirit.[144]

We have seen a certain amount of anthropological dualism in Paul—

spirit versus mind, or spirit versus flesh, or even spirit versus body—that appears inescapable. This raises again the question about the old person/ new person contrast in Paul and its relationship to the inner person/outer person contrast. Let us consider the latter first. At Rom. 7:22–23 we saw the innermost self identified or closely associated with the mind. Paul, it will be noted, does not see the body as the prison house of the soul, nor does he denigrate the body. We know that the contrast between inner person/outer person is characteristic of Hellenism, but Paul uses it in his own way. In 2 Cor. 4:16 we have the phrase "the inner person is being renewed[145] day by day." We are reminded of the language of Rom. 12:2, where we hear about mind being renewed. With R. Gundry we must insist against Bultmann, Furnish, and others that the inner person is not equivalent to the new person in Christ (cf. Col. 3:10; Eph. 4:24). Rather, the inner person refers to the mind and/or human spirit. Gundry is quite right to point out that the phrase "the old person," or even old nature, refers to what the person has crucified or put off in conversion (cf. Rom. 6:6; Col. 3:9; Eph. 4:22).[146]

The outer person then must be seen as simply the physical body subject to decay, hardship, death. The inner person then refers to the nonmaterial aspects or parts of human nature. The human mind, or spirit, or heart, is renewed and revived in conversion (Eph. 3:16), but the new creature, or new creation, is put on (Col. 3:10; Eph. 4:24). This does not lead Paul to an ethical dualism, however, where the body is seen as evil, and the mind or spirit or heart is seen as good. Rather, the body is caught in the middle of a struggle between the inner person and sin reigning in the nonbeliever (Romans 7), and between flesh and Holy Spirit in the believer (Gal. 5:16ff.). The new creation involves the whole person, body and mind/ spirit/heart, but for now it only affects the latter until the day of resurrection. This is why the inner person and new creation are sometimes wrongly confused in Paul. The new creation affects only the inner person, until resurrection day, save in the exceptional cases where physical and miraculous healing touches the body. Notably Paul never stressed such miracles. Rather, he focuses on his suffering for Christ and his body wasting away (2 Cor. 4–5).

This leads us to discuss Paul's use of *soma* and *sarx* (not including the corporate and ecclesiastical use of the former). Quite clearly, Paul can use both of these terms to refer to the individual's physical body or nature. In rapid succession Paul speaks of his members, this body, and his flesh in Rom. 7:23–25. Just as clearly, Paul can use the term *soma* to mean something more than (or other than?) physical flesh—for instance, a principle, proneness, or inclination to evil or sin (cf. Rom. 8:4–13). Again, at Rom. 7:5 flesh cannot merely mean physical flesh, because it implies that the Christian is not any longer living in it. Rather, "living in the flesh" is associated with living according to sinful human passions.[147]

Paul says bluntly at Rom. 8:9: "You are not living in the flesh," by which he means that Christians are not living according to their sinful desires. They are not controlled by carnal passions. Christians are those who do not walk "according to the flesh," but rather according to the spirit (8:4). Living according to the flesh involves the mind and setting one's mind on fleshly things (Rom. 8:5), which involves both death and hostility toward God. The "flesh" is incapable of submitting to God's word or law, and thus those "in the flesh" cannot please God. Thus the physical flesh is not in itself evil; but because the flesh is weak and has physical needs, desires, and urges, it becomes easy prey for sin. The physical flesh in itself cannot resolve to do good (Rom. 7:18); no amount of willpower can accomplish this. Sin is more powerful than either the physical flesh it can control or the human mind/spirit/heart/inner person. Sin can affect and stifle the best intentions and mental plans (Rom. 7:22–23).

There is no doubt that Paul can use the term *soma* of one's physical body with no extra theological connotations (2 Cor. 5:8: "to be absent from the body"; cf. 1 Cor. 15:34–49).[148] But can it be a synonym for the self or the whole person, like *psuche*? Scholars have long debated the matter, but it appears that Gundry is likely correct. Gundry observes that when *soma* is used to refer to a person, it is used by Paul of the physical body exclusively, not with a larger meaning, although it can be used of the *soma* in relation to or in correlation with other facets of the human condition or nature.[149]

Barrett argues that *soma* in 1 Cor. 6:12–20 refers to the whole person. Rather, we must say that Paul is insisting that using one's physical body involves and *affects* the whole person. One cannot radically separate body from personhood and human spirit in this life. Paul is not saying that *soma* *is* the whole person. It is precisely because the physical body *will be* redeemed and raised by God, just as one's spirit/mind/heart has been and is, that what one does with the body matters. The physical body can be dominated by sinful desires; it is the weak link in the human being. Thus, at Col. 2:11 Paul can speak about the body of flesh, that is, a physical body dominated by fleshly desires. That domination or orientation has been circumcised, or cut off, or put off, in Christ.

Though Christians are no longer dominated or ruled by the flesh (i.e., the inclination to sin), they are still affected by that proclivity. Romans 6:6 talks about the body as dominated by sin being destroyed. Notice the progression here. The old self has been crucified, with the purpose that (*hina*), the body of sin, might be destroyed. The former *leads* to the latter, it is not identical to the latter. "Body of sin" must surely mean the body as dominated by sin (Rom. 8:3: "sinful flesh"; 6:6b: "enslaved to sin"). Thus here the destruction of the body of sin is equivalent to the destruction of the domination of a sin orientation over and in the body. Alternately, Rom. 6:6b has been seen to have a future reference, indicating what will happen to the physical body at death/resurrection.[150] So too Rom. 7:24 could be seen as a cry for future bodily resurrection, not present conversion, but this seems less likely.[151] In any case, it is precisely these sorts of texts that make evident that *soma* does not mean self. The speaker in Romans 7 does not want to be delivered from the self, or even probably the body per se, but from the physical body as it is dominated by sin and ultimately subject to both spiritual and physical death. Following Gundry:

> We conclude that in neither the Pauline epistles, nor the literature of the New Testament outside those epistles, nor the LXX, nor extra-Biblical ancient Greek literature does the definition "whole person" find convincing support. This is not to deny that (outside the Platonic tradition) emphasis falls on the unity of [humankind]'s being. But it is a unity of parts, inner and outer, rather than a monadic unity. Ancient writers do not usually treat *soma* in isolation. Rather, apart from its use for a corpse, *soma* refers to the physical body in its proper and intended union with the soul/spirit. The body and its counterpart are portrayed as united but distinct—and separable, though unnaturally and unwantedly separated. The *soma* may *represent* the whole person simply because the *soma* lives in union with the soul/spirit. But *soma* does not *mean* "the whole person," because its use is designed to call attention to the physical object which is the body of the person rather than to the whole personality. Where used of whole people, *soma* directs attention to their bodies, not to the wholeness of their being.[152]

Now finally, we are prepared to examine Gal. 5:16–25. It is clear that the Spirit in Gal. 5:16ff. is the Holy Spirit. We thus do not have a rabbinic tension between good and evil inclination, or human spirit and human flesh. We must ask, however, is the flesh merely the physical flesh or the sinful inclination that guides or goads the flesh? When we look at 5:19 all the works of the flesh are of a negative and immoral sort, which Paul could not say simply of the body. Sanders is perhaps right that flesh here and in other cases means the power that opposes God and enslaves human beings or, more likely, the inclination that gives way to such an urge or power.[153] Flesh then is not just mortal frailty but a perverse inclination. Flesh is willful and sinful human urges that are at enmity with God. The question then becomes, Who is Paul speaking to in Galatians 5? Clearly, the "you" must be Galatian Christians, whereas in Romans 7 the "I" is neither Paul as a Christian, nor Paul as he saw himself when he was a Jew, nor an unregenerate person as he sees himself, but expresses a Christian view of a pre-Christian condition.

There is then in Galatians 5 an eschatological tension extant in the life of the believer between the leading of the Holy Spirit and the urge and inclination that pulls one in another direction and involves, among other things, one's desires for physical gratification. Burton puts it this way: "Does the [person] choose evil, the Spirit opposes him; does the [person] choose good, 'the flesh' hinders him."[154] Literally, the text here reads, "the Spirit desires against the flesh," and vice versa (v. 17). There is then a large difference between Romans 7 and Galatians 5.

> In Rom. 7:7–25 the power of indwelling sin *prevents* the person existing under law from fulfilling the divine law in which his inmost self delights: the "law of sin" in his members wages war against the "law of his mind" (Rom. 7:22f.), and at this stage no mention is made of the Spirit, whereas the conflict in the present text is that between flesh and Spirit.[155]

Galatians 5:16 is properly translated not as in NRSV,[156] but rather, "I say walk by the Spirit and you will not fulfill the desires of the flesh."[157] The stress here is on a means of victory over the fleshly urges for the Christian, though he or she still has that urge. In Romans 7 we hear the cry of one who cannot do what he or she would want to do. In Galatians 5 the battle is not hopeless. If Christians will live and act according to the guidance and urging of the Spirit, they will not be fulfilling fleshly desires. The former activity and lifestyle displaces and supplants the latter. It is, however, implied that the Galatians must actively will the good and do the good. It is they who must choose to "walk by the Spirit," and Paul implies that as Christians they are able to do so.

The new person in Christ must continuously submit to the Spirit. She or he must act in character as a new creation. Obviously, the reason for the exhortation is that it is quite possible for the Christian to act out of character and follow fleshly desires. Submitting to the Spirit repeatedly leads to continual liberation from such desires or inclinations. The believer is able to do and be what God calls her or him to be.

> The believer is not the helpless battleground of two opposing forces. If he [or she] yields to the flesh, he [or she] is enslaved by it, but if he [or she] obeys the prompting of the Spirit, he [or she] is liberated and can make a positive and willing response to the command "Walk by the Spirit" and similar moral imperatives, "doing the will of God from the heart" (as it is put in Eph. 6:6).[158]

The stress on real possibilities and victory is undeniable here. If one, however, allows oneself to vacillate back and forth between Spirit and flesh, this paralyzes one and prevents one from fully doing what God has called one to do.

In Gal. 5:19–23 we have a typical vice-virtue catalog, not unlike what we find elsewhere in Paul (cf. 1 Thess. 4:3–5:1; 1 Cor. 5:9–13; 6:9–11; 2 Cor. 12:20–21; Rom. 13:13; 1:29–31; Col. 3:5–8; Eph. 4:17–19; 5:3–5). It is beyond our purpose to analyze all these at this point; however, it appears that the vice lists have at least two specific functions: (1) they emphasize sins against the common life of the Christian fellowship (i.e., sins that affect the body of Christ, not just isolated individuals); (2) they are listed not merely to remind Christians what they once were, but to reprove Christians who are still acting in such a worldly fashion (see Gal. 5:21a: "I warn you, as I warned you before . . . ").

Clearly, Paul is concerned that in some cases the church is still acting like the world. What is described here is a real threat to Christian individuals and to the body. Galatians 5:21, like 1 Cor. 6:9ff., makes clear that for Paul the kingdom and the believer's inheriting it in the broad sense are essentially in the future.[159] The portion of the kingdom available in the present is the reign of the Spirit in the believer's life, producing fruit and gifts, and the rule of the Spirit in the Christian community, particularly when gathered for worship. It is also possible for those who do not walk according to the Spirit to fail to inherit the kingdom. Although good deeds do not in themselves get one into the kingdom, bad deeds may certainly prevent one from entering or inheriting. This vision of things is not unlike what one finds in M. Sanh. 10:1–3, where the author discusses sins that, if a Jew commits or at least persists in them, leaves him with no portion in the world to come.

Galatians 5:22 lists the fruit of the Spirit. Notice that the operative word is fruit (singular)—*ho karpos.* Although the sins mentioned in vv. 19–21 seem to involve both attitudes and actions, Paul seems to be talking about certain active character traits that manifest themselves in interpersonal behavior (i.e., love, gentleness, patience). That fruit is singular means that Paul expects all these attributes of all Christians. That they are of the Spirit means that he believes that the Spirit creates or at least enables such traits in the believer, which she or he would not be fully capable of without the Spirit. Here then is a description of those who are indwelt by and energized by the Spirit.

It is not by accident that love comes first. What Paul is talking about is very much like what we find in Rom. 5:5: the love of God "poured into our hearts by the Spirit." It is thus a love that is supernatural in origin and nature. It manifests itself in love for God, believers, and all others as well (Gal. 6:10). It is an inclusive, not exclusive, sort of love. The love of Christ is the motivating force in Paul's ministry (2 Cor. 5:14f., 18–20), and I take this phrase to mean Christ's love for Paul, which motivates and directs his energies. First Corinthians 13 could be said to be a portrait of Jesus' own character and behavior. This comports nicely with what we have already discussed about Christ being the ultimate moral exemplar for believers.

Joy for Paul is not something produced by circumstances, nor ephemeral pleasures, but rather is generated by the indwelling Spirit. Indeed, this sort of joy may be manifested often in spite of how one is healthwise or what one's circumstances may be. This joy involves a future-looking attitude. Romans 5:2, 11 indicates that believers can rejoice in the midst of suffering because they know God will consummate God's plan of glory for his Son and for those "in Christ." It is the God of hope and God's future plan that fill Christians with joy and peace (Rom. 15:1). Joy, like peace and righteousness, is of the essence of the kingdom (Rom. 14:17).

To have peace means at least to be at peace with and thus reconciled to God. It may also convey for Paul the fuller sense of shalom—well-being or wholeness. Philippians 4:7 may be referring to the sense of well-being Christians have because they are at peace with God. God not only has made peace through Christ's blood but has given them peace (Col. 3:15). This entails both peace with God and with the believers. It is the polar opposite of a divisive spirit, a spirit of disorder or dissension (Rom. 15:33; 1 Cor. 14:33; Rom. 16:20a; 2 Cor. 13:11; Phil. 4:9; 1 Thess. 5:23). This peace, however, is to exist not only in the Christian congregation but also in the home (1 Cor. 7:15).

Patience involves not being quick to anger or rebuke, but a willingness to bear wrong in love (1 Cor. 13:4) and to bear with those who are difficult to get along with. It involves steadfastness, sympathy, and waiting (1 Thess. 5:14; Col. 1:11; 3:12; Eph. 4:2). God is the model of patience who bears with even sinners and their sin (cf. Rom. 2:4; 9:22), though there clearly is a limit to such patience.

Kindness again is an attribute of God, one the Spirit gives or enables, for again we are not discussing natural skills or dispositions in Galatians 5. Kindness overlaps with mercy (cf. Rom. 11:22). God's kindness is meant to lead sinners to repentance (Rom. 2:4) and to lead Christians to go and be similarly kind (Rom. 11:22). It is love in 1 Cor. 13:4 that is said to be kind. Goodness here seems to mean generosity, doing good to others, and so belongs with the mention of kindness.

Here faithful, not faith, is the next ethical quality. Though it can mean true to God's word (faithful to obey), it can also mean dependable (cf. Gal. 5:22; 2 Cor. 6:15). God is likewise faithful (Rom. 3:30). Another way of viewing this is that *pistos* here means not trust, but trustworthy.

Gentleness and patience are coupled twice in the Pauline letters (Col. 3:12; Eph. 4:2). Aristotle tells us that gentleness is the mean between excessive proneness to anger and incapacity for anger. Paul uses the example of Jesus' gentleness (2 Cor. 10:1),[160] and we remember that the gospel tradition indicates that Jesus was perfectly capable of anger and righteous indignation. Neither in the case of Jesus nor in the case of Christians is meekness or gentleness to rule out righteous indignation.

Finally, *egkrateia* means self-control, not just of anger but of other passions and desires as well. The self-controlled person is not a passive person, devoid of strong feelings, but one who knows how to control and guide and channel passions. Often the word refers to the restraining or controlling of sexual longings (see 1 Cor. 7:9), though it can refer to simple self-discipline (1 Cor. 9:25).

These fruit foster *koinonia,* the sharing in common with fellow believers and the building up of the body's unity, just as the sins noted in vv. 19ff. disrupt it. These qualities go beyond what any law could normally require, and are of course not prohibited by any law. A "vine does not produce grapes by Act of Parliament; they are the fruit of the vine's own life; so the conduct which conforms to the standard of the Kingdom is not produced by any demand, not even God's, but it is the fruit of that divine nature which God gives as the result of what he has done in and by Christ."[161]

In Aristotle (*Pol.* 3.13, 12B4a), the statement "against which there is no law" is used "of persons who surpass their fellows in virtue like gods among [humankind]. They do not need to have their actions regulated by laws; on the contrary, they themselves constitute a law (a standard) for others."[162]

Again and again, when Paul speaks of the fruit of the Spirit throughout his letters he is talking about the life and character of God being replicated on a lesser scale in human lives. Not merely Christ's character but even God's character is set forth as the model, which by analogy the believer is to follow. Here in Galatians 5, Paul is going so far as to say that God is already working in the believer the very character and virtues that the believer then is expected to work out in his or her interpersonal relationships. Thus the Divine is not merely model but modeler of Christians. The story of God in Christ is being replicated in the story of Christians, in the matter of Christian experience, and this is meant to be the basis for replication in Christian behavior. If Christians walk in the Spirit, they will not merely avoid the indulgences of the flesh; they will positively model the character of God in Christ to the world. Theology and ethics are inextricably woven together in Paul's thought, not because Paul wants to blur the creator/creature distinction, but because he believes it possible for believers to be the image of God, the image of Christ upon earth, and he believes that God through the Spirit is actively fashioning and refashioning believers to that end. Paul's narrative thought world begins with the story of God and ends with the story of God, but in between is the story of God's dealings with humankind, especially in the person of Christ and later in the lives of Christians. In such a story it is possible to make distinctions between what God does and what believers do, but one must see the integral and ongoing connections whereby the former action enables, guides, empowers the latter on an ongoing basis by means of the Spirit.

HAVING CHURCH

We have already had occasion to discuss Paul's understanding of entering and being in Christ's body, but we did not then ask the questions: What was life in the community like? What does the term *ekklesia* mean? (Paul uses this term most often to refer to the Christian community.)

The term *ekklesia* has traditionally been translated as "church" or "churches," but this is debatable. The Old Testament word most likely in the background of *ekklesia* is *qahal*, which means assembly and is used of either the assembling or the assembly itself of God's people. This is the meaning not only of *qahal* in the Old Testament but also of *ekklesia* in the LXX, in Philo, and in Josephus.

When we turn to Paul, R. Banks maintains that no passage could not be translated by "assembly," but some in Romans cannot be translated "gathering," because apparently there was no single gathering of all Christians in Rome. In fact, Paul is flexible in his usage and can speak of (1) the assembly of God, by which he means the whole church; (2) the assembly in a particular locality (Thessalonica); (3) the assembly in a particular household; and (4) the assemblies in Galatia or various other regional locations. Paul always uses *ekklesia* to refer to people, God's people, not buildings. This is in part because the early Christian assembly almost always met in homes. We find, for instance, the phrase "the assembly in ____'s house" (cf. 1 Cor. 16:19, Aquila and Priscilla's in Ephesus; Rom. 16:5, Aquila and Priscilla's in Rome; Philemon 2, in Philemon's house in Colossae; Col. 4:15, Nymphia's house in Laodicea). This suggests that Paul uses the phrase "in the house of" to distinguish individual household-based groups from "the whole assembly of that place."

We find at 1 Cor. 14:23 and Rom. 16:23 (cf. 1 Cor. 11:2) references to the whole *ekklesia*. At Gal. 1:13 we have simply the phrase "the assembly of God" (singular) for the assembly everywhere, but this can also be expressed as the assemblies of God (1 Cor. 11:16; 2 Cor. 11:28).[163] Paul can also use the singular to speak of all the assemblies in one place (i.e., the assembly in Jerusalem, 1 Cor. 15:9; Phil. 3:6).[164] More clearly, when we get to Col. 1:18, 24 *ekklesia* is equated with *soma* in the corporate sense and refers to the worldwide assembly of believers.

We thus conclude that for Paul *ekklesia* in the singular can refer to a individual unit of believers meeting in a household, or the assembly in a particular local or regional area, or the assembly corporately worldwide. In the plural it can refer to the latter two, but not to the first. Doubtless this usage reflects Paul's view of the nature of the assembly. As Meeks says, "One peculiar thing about early Christianity was the way in which the intimate close-knit life of the local groups was seen to be simultaneously part of a much larger, indeed ultimately worldwide, movement or entity."[165] We may also conclude that the basic unit of Christianity, the individual household assembly, overlapped with what was seen as the basic unit of society—the household and the family (often extended) that dwelt in it.[166] There is plenty of evidence in Paul and in Acts that one of the main ways, if not the main way, the *ekklesia* grew was by the principle of household inclusion and conversion in the faith.

Perhaps partially because of its meeting in households and the overlap with the household structure, the *ekklesia* early on was called the "household of God," and Christians were seen as a family of brothers and sisters, with Christ as the head of the body, and the Father as head of them all. These factors also in part explain the use of household codes (Col. 3:18–4:1; Eph. 5:21–6:9) for ordering the Christian household, and to some extent the Christian *ekklesia*. The church adapted the structure of the families and applied it to the Christian family and also to a lesser degree to the Christian congregation as family. However, it is not simply the hierarchical scheme of the family that Christianity adopted which structured the Pauline assemblies early on. Spiritual gifts, social and intellectual status, and a host of other factors affected how the *ekklesia* was structured.[167]

Banks argues that the household, or family, is in various places Paul's dominant metaphor for the *ekklesia*, but in fact this is mainly true only in Galatians, Ephesians, and the Pastorals. Paul does make clear that he is talking about the "household of faith" at various points. What we usually have is a coupling of words or ideas, that is, household and family language in various contexts (cf. 1 Cor. 16:15). So far as I can discover, it was not at all common in Judaism to call one's fellow believers brothers or sisters, nor was it common in pagan groups. The prevalence of such language seems to be something distinctive to the Christian assembly. There was apparently a real feeling that Christians were "the household, or the family, of faith." It is notable that Paul often uses the family language (brother, sister) in Galatians and elsewhere especially when he is trying to create or heal the unity between believers.

The "kiss of peace," a common familial form of affection, arises out of household customs, although now it is made into a peace ritual, a sign of reconciliation and unity that has no parallel outside the New Testament (see 2 Cor. 13:12). A related concept is that Paul discusses "fathers" and "mothers" in the faith, terminology that seems to indicate who was the agent or begetter of one's knowledge of Christ and/or the nurturer of that faith in one. Thus, for instance, in Rom. 16:13 "his mother and mine" is not likely a reference to Paul's physical mother. It may mean no more than that she was a hostess or patroness of Paul. However, when Paul calls himself the father (1 Cor. 4:15) or mother (1 Thess. 1:7, 11) of certain Christians and calls them his children (1 Cor. 4:14), he seems to want to imply both a certain family relationship in the Lord but also a certain authority structure and responsibility Paul has over and for those who came to know Christ through him. First Corinthians 4:14 indicates in fact that the term "father" refers exclusively to the agent through whom one is saved. Paul then does not use the term *father* of the minister or local church leader but of the evangelist or apostle through whom one is converted.[168]

This, however, raises these questions: (1) Did Paul see himself as the absolute head of various Christian assemblies and families to whom he wrote as a "father" giving advice, counsel, instruction, as a father would to the children he was responsible for? Clearly, Paul wants his converts to become spiritually mature. (2) Does this mean there is a time when Paul's "fatherhood" would no longer be necessary, or at least it would no longer need to be exercised? Notice how in 1 Cor. 3:1 he talks about converts as infants, and at 4:14 he sees them also as his children. Yet he also calls them brothers (2:1; 3:1), implying a certain equality. Paul also talks about becoming the adopted sons (and daughters) of God. Could the Corinthians outgrow the need for Paul's fatherly direction, while growing up into spiritual adulthood and pressing on to become sons and daughters of God? What patterns of leadership or community development are implied? Could Paul really have not provided for the local leadership of his churches after his death? This seems most unlikely, and it is not surprising that it is almost exclusively in Paul's later letters (Phil. 1:1) that we get any mention of what may be church officers (but cf. Rom 16:1).[169] It appears that the structure and function of Paul's communities were complex and grew gradually, but there is no indication that Paul ever envisioned a time when his communities would be so mature that leadership would prove unnecessary.

It is clear, however, that Paul does not envision some sort of radical clergy/laity distinction. There are several reasons for this. Paul makes clear that all members of the body are given manifestations of the Spirit for the common good (1 Cor. 12:7). Because being "gifted" implies using that gift in the service of the body, it becomes clear that Paul intends that all members of the body be ministers, using their gifts to minister one to another. When Paul discusses gifts and functions in the church in Rom. 12:3ff., Paul is addressing the whole *ekklesia*, not just some ministerial class.

Here also we see a parallel between the grace given to Paul (v. 3), which is the same grace given to believers (v. 6). Thus, how a person ministers in the community (it is not a question of whether) is in part determined by what gifts and graces the Spirit has imparted.

It is then in a sense the Spirit who determines who does what in Paul's communities. Barrett suggests that the reason Paul says so little about the local "ministers" (cf. Acts 14:23) of a church is that believers are *all* called to be ministers. In the Romans 12 list the progression is from gifts to persons, whereas in 1 Corinthians 12 it is the converse. Both of these affect the *ekklesia's* structure. Note how in 1 Cor. 11:21–24 Paul says, "Wait for each other," not wait for the presiding elder to share in the meal that included the Lord's Supper. However, it is also clear from 1 Cor. 12:28 that there are authority figures in and for the community. Paul seems to rank them (in order of authority): (1) apostle, (2) prophet, (3) teacher, (4) miracle workers and others.

Again at Gal. 6:6 a structure is implied. There are local instructors in the word whom the local congregation is not only to heed but to feed. The members are to share all good things with them, which surely implies housing and hospitality. Again in 1 Thess. 5:11–15 the job of exhortation and building up the body is for everyone, but there are obviously some who have specific leadership tasks; they are overseers (*kopiontes*) of the rest of the *ekklesia* and work hard in and for the local assembly.

If these leaders' concern is for the assembly as a whole and its whole oversight, this implies a role (and functions?) not assumed by those who are not "overseers." Notice how in Rom. 12:8 leadership is mentioned separately, though again we are not told specifically what that entails. Were they simply administrators (cf. 1 Cor. 12:28—the seventh person listed)? Yet 1 Cor. 16:15 implies that Stephanus's task is to steer or preside; notice how he and others "devoted themselves" to this task. Thus Paul did not pick or ordain them, it would seem. They are the sort to whom the whole congregation is to submit. At this earlier stage in Paul's ministry, it does not seem that there is any systematically ordered ministry or process of ordination. Some people single themselves out, take the lead, and devote themselves to the work.

In addition, there are, however, numerous functions, such as congregational discipline, that the whole *ekklesia* is to exercise when it meets (cf. 1 Cor. 5:4–5), as well as mutual service and exhortation. It is also clear from 1 Cor. 12–14 that prophecy was a gift of the Spirit that empowered various sorts of people to assume a crucial ministry of the word, and we must note that 1 Cor. 11.5 implies that women were involved in this ministry. This text simply explains how they are to do this.[170] It will be remembered that prophets are ranked by Paul second only to apostles and above teachers.

The evidence suggests that prophets and prophetesses were more than preachers, but 1 Corinthians 14 implies that their words must be weighed and tested. They do not have the absolute authority of an Old Testament prophet, or an apostle, or a word of Jesus. As for the *diakonoi* of Phil. 1:1 (cf. Romans 12), if they were not, as some have suggested, the church's financial officers or treasurers, it appears that their tasks of service were to see to the physical needs of the community (food, shelter, clothing), though perhaps not a place to meet, which seems to have been provided by a well-to-do member or patron or patroness (cf. Rom. 16:23). Because of the elusiveness of this evidence, Meeks has attempted to see if any light comes from exploring contemporary parallels—Jewish or pagan organizations of the day—besides the household. The evidence is largely negative. Thus, when Meeks compares the *ekklesia* to the club organization structures of contemporary pagan society, he concludes that the church did not model itself on the pattern of clubs and their structure, and there is only a minimal amount of shared terminology.[171] Such clubs did have *diakonoi* (which seems to refer to those who waited on tables at feasts).

Paul also uses the term *episkopoi* (Phil. 1:1), overseer, in a similar manner. At Rom. 16:2, *prostatis* may designate an office, and in the contemporary clubs it was a functional designation for a patron or presiding officer (cf. 1 Thess. 5:12).

The most promising candidate for comparison is the synagogue. Besides the obvious elements of theological continuity, Diaspora Jews, like Paul's Christians, saw themselves as both members of a local group, but also part of the larger people of God. However, we should note that although some Diaspora Jews met in households, it appears that in various places, including Corinth, they had a special meetinghouse other than the home—the synagogue itself.[172] In neither early Diaspora Judaism nor early Christian meetings were sacrifices a part of religious devotion, but the *ekklesia* likely shared on the positive side with the synagogue, common meals, prayers and singing, group discipline, a ritual washing, and perhaps also scripture reading. "The Pauline meetings were also marked by prophecy, admonitions, the reading of apostolic letters, and by glossolalia and other phenomena of spirit possession. Whether these things, too, had analogies in the synagogues is impossible to say; in the light of Philo's description of the vigils of the Therapeutae, it would be foolish to deny the possibility."[173]

Though early Christianity took over the Hebrew scriptures and basic parts of its belief systems, norms, and traditions from early Judaism, Christianity seems to have differed in its life in the Spirit, in its expression of spiritual gifts, and in at least some of its rituals. There seems also to have been much that was unique about the *structure* of Pauline groups headed by an itinerant apostle and his coworkers.[174]

The pattern that emerges from all this seems to be the following: (1) apostles; (2) Paul's traveling fellow workers who were over or involved in several congregations (Priscilla, Aquila, Timothy, etc.); (3) local leaders. Presumably other apostles may have also had coworkers. The old distinction Harnack made between local church officials and apostles, prophets, teachers, as those who functioned throughout the church will not stand up to close scrutiny. It is quite obvious that prophets and teachers could be local, but it was also obvious that Paul's coworkers could be peripatetic. What suprachurch authority they had depended in part on their closeness to Paul and their willingness to follow his authoritative word closely. The Pauline coworkers assumed a wide range of functions.[175]

It still remains to ask about the local church leaders and their range of authority and functions. We have already stressed how the Spirit to a certain extent raised up structures and functionaries, though it may be that late in Paul's life he found it necessary to establish and ordain certain officers of the local church (and also those, such as Timothy and Titus, over several churches or areas). First Thessalonians 5:12 does tell us about local congregational functions: laboring, administering verbal discipline, acting as a patron or protector. It is precisely in this latter category that those who were well-to-do or at the higher end of the socioeconomic and educational scale were able to assume positions of importance in the Christian community. These people of higher wealth or status could confer certain benefits on the congregation—place of meeting, financial support, protection, lodging—and this naturally developed into a form of congregational leadership or prominence. First Corinthians 16:19 and the case of Priscilla and Aquila make this clear, as do other examples (Philemon, the household of Stephanas, 1 Cor. 16:15).

In short, we see that certain practical and sociological factors also affected church leadership. Apparently it was particularly in Rome and Corinth that well-to-do people (Erastus?) played prominent roles because of their abilities to host and support the church and its leaders.[176] These functions seem to be mainly practical, but they also appear to be partly pastoral (cf. 1 Cor. 16:15; 1 Thess. 5:12c). This is interesting precisely because Paul, although not abolishing all social or natural distinctions (ethnic, sexual), does use them in service of the *ekklesia*. Previously, such sexual distinctions created religious barriers. Paul tries to use such distinctions and people to build up and knit together the *ekklesia* and provide it a place to exist in safety.

Thus Paul turns the normal use of social distinctions on its head. Instead of being self-serving, they are used to serve others—in particular, the local assembly. For Paul, *diakonia* ("service") is key. It guides how one uses one's wealth, gifts, possessions. Paul requires one to ask, Does this or that activity, behavior, lifestyle, use of money, build up or tear down the community of faith? Thus the community is not purely structured by the Spirit and spiritual gifts, in Paul's way of thinking. It is also structured by whomever Paul or his coworkers appoint and by who is able to host the congregation.[177] One's authority then could come from revelation, from a spiritual gift, from being appointed, from one's closeness to Paul and his dictates, from one's knowledge and use of scripture and authoritative traditions, or from one's experience as one who followed Christ's pattern of death/resurrection. If one embodied Christ and his lifestyle, one should be heeded. In the end, however, all offices/functions/leadership roles functioned in the context of the ministry expected of all Christians everywhere.

WORSHIP RITES

Without question, one of the most important and formative contexts in which a Christian learned and expressed what she or he was in a Pauline community, was in worship. Too often discussions of Paul's views on baptism and the Lord's Supper have been isolated from discussions about worship in the Pauline communities. Yet Meeks is surely right to connect the two and to make clear that such rites intend to deal with the most formative and crucial of Christian experiences—union with Christ and his body, and ongoing communion with the same.

Baptism has to do with entrance and initiation, and thus is a boundary-defining or transference ritual, a rite of passage, whereas the Lord's Supper is an attempt to renew fellowship and communion with the Lord and his people. The Lord's Supper deals with what is of central importance after conversion—remaining in Christ and his body, growing in grace and sanctification, persevering in Christ and with believers, being fully reconciled to both. At the same time, to reaffirm or confirm one's unity with Christ and the believers is also to reaffirm the boundary between oneself and the old life and the world. Paul will insist on certain moral boundaries between Christians and others: "You cannot share in the table of the Lord and the table of demons" (1 Cor. 10:21). Thus both baptism and the Lord's Supper are seen as establishing or reaffirming an exclusive unity and relationship that precludes other ones.[178]

It is clear that viewed from the outside, Christians were seen, like Jesus, as rather peculiar in their religion. They lacked shrines, temples, sacrifices, idols, pilgrimages, and public festivals. A pagan might well wonder what kind of religion they could possibly have without these elements so crucial to the pagan cults. But it is equally clear that at least as early as Pliny (early second century), Christians were seen plainly as a superstitious religious group who met at dawn on a set day to sing praises to Christ as a god.[179] Clearly, he saw them as a religious and ritualistic group. Recent sociological studies of ritual have suggested that the function of ritual is both to inform about a critical reality vital to the community, but also in part to aid in creating that reality. Rituals reflect the fundamental values of a community—what it believes to be of first importance.

How apt a description this is in part is determined by whether you see these rites in Paul as mere signs or as symbols (something that participates in the reality to which it points). It is by no means certain that Paul saw these rites purely as signs (cf. 1 Cor. 10—11). In any event, both baptism and the Lord's Supper do inform us (whether they transform believers or not) about certain key Pauline Christian values. They reflect, in the way Paul interprets them, what he sees as most crucial about the story of Christians: (1) becoming one with Christ and his body; (2) remaining one with Christ and his body in an ongoing relationship; (3) affirming that Christ and his death and resurrection are at the heart of Christianity.

Let us first look at the context of these rituals—Christian worship. It appears, at least in regard to Corinth, that the Lord's Supper was celebrated when the people of God came together in one assembly. The phrase *en ekklesia* (1 Cor. 11:18) seems to mean the people of God assembled. This suggests that the celebration of the Lord's Supper took place when all the household congregations met together in one particular location. If this is so, it shows that the function of this rite was to help bring together and unify the people of God throughout Corinth (cf. 1 Cor. 11:17, 18, 20, 33, 34). It is not clear whether this was a regular worship service or a special meeting that focused on the Lord's Supper but also involved some sort of fellowship meal. The fact that Paul is talking, in 11:1–16, about circumstances in regular worship may suggest that he means that he expects that whenever they came together as a "whole assembly" they would celebrate the Lord's Supper.

Second, it is rather clear that Paul sees the Lord's Supper as part of a larger and longer fellowship meal. First Corinthians 11:20 suggests that some in Corinth were eating before others arrived because they were hungry. Clearly, the Lord's Supper was not seen as a meal to satisfy hunger, but was a ritual meal. Was the problem that some were treating the Lord's Supper as an ordinary meal, or more likely that they did not distinguish between an ordinary meal, following Greco-Roman conventions,[180] and a meal that included the Christian rite? In any event, they were eating without concern for the needs of others, without discerning that this was an act and event of Christ's body, an act of worship. Paul believed that because some had treated this fellowship meal and the Lord's Supper in a sacrilegious way, some had gotten sick and died. Paul seems to think this happened because of divine judgment upon the sacrilegious act, not because the rite itself was magical and could convey blessing or judgment. The latter, however, is not an impossible interpretation of 1 Cor. 11:27ff., which is in any case very difficult.

At this point, Meeks, following G. Theissen's earlier work,[181] helps us understand the situation with some historical background information.

> The divisions in the group (11:18) are primarily between rich and poor. The wealthier members of the church are hosts of the gatherings and probably provide the food for all. Quite in accord with the expectations in many ancient clubs and with the practice often followed at banquets when dependents of a patron were invited, the hosts provide both greater quantity and better quality of food and drink to their social equals than to participants of lower status. The conflict was thus between "different standards of behavior," between "status-specific expectations and the norms of a community of love." Paul's response, Theissen suggests, is a compromise, which asks that the wealthy have their private meal . . . at home, so that in the Lord's Supper . . . the norm of equality can prevail. At the same time, Paul sets the social tensions into a larger symbolic universe by making them part of an "eschatological drama." The sacrament is "a zone under taboo, in which violation of norms has as its consequence incalculable disaster."[182]

The Lord's Supper was seen as a part of worship and thus not just a fellowship meal or ordinary feast. Meeks also contends that 14:23 suggests that all the other functions of worship in Corinth happened at the same corporate gathering—prophecy, singing, tongues, instruction. This conclusion, however, is debatable.[183]

We know from other contexts that it was customary for Paul's letters to be read as part of worship (cf. 1 Thess. 5:27; Col. 4:16). It is also clear simply from Paul's opening greetings (1 Thess. 1:1; 2 Thess. 1:1; 1 Cor. 1:2; 2 Cor. 1:1; Gal. 1:2; Phil. 1:1; Rom. 1:7; Col. 1:2) that he assumes that his letters, which are usually addressed to all the *ekklesia* in that location, will be read to all the assembly or assemblies. Although one special assembly seems to have been common at Corinth, the plural addresses of the Galatian province may suggest that the letter to the Galatians would be read sequentially in various house assemblies. Romans 16 fails to indicate any one central meeting for letter reading, but perhaps 16:23 suggests that the whole *ekklesia* in Ephesus and also Paul met at Gaius's house.

When did such meetings take place? Notice at Acts 20:7 that the meeting is on the first day of the week, and this meeting was for bread breaking (implying perhaps there were other meetings for other purposes). First Corinthians 16:2 may or may not imply the same thing, or were they only going to set aside money in their houses on the first day of the week?[184] It would not be surprising if the Christian communities followed the Jewish pattern of once-a-week meetings. Pliny confirms this for his period and location. Justin Martyr confirms Sunday meetings around A.D. 150, as does Ignatius in his letter to the Magnesians.

We must bear in mind, however, that the combination of Sabbath and Sunday seems to be a phenomenon of the early Middle Ages, not the New Testament period. In fact, Rom. 14:5 suggests that some Christians were regarding seven days, indeed all days, as the Lord's Day, and Paul does not try to correct this idea. Notice, however, how Paul, at Gal. 4:10, condemns going back to the ways of Jewish observance (special days, months, season), and at Col. 2:16 Paul or his disciple says, "Do not let anyone judge you . . . with regard to a religious festival, a new moon celebration, or a sabbath day." These are called mere shadows of the things that have now come in Christ, and this exhortation is in the midst of talking about the canceling by Christ of the written code (Col. 2:14), including day and food regulations (cf. 2:20–22).

Worship in at least some of Paul's communities was filled with songs and hymns. First Corinthians 14:26 indicates that everyone had a "psalm." This was apparently chanted or sung. Colossians 3:16 indicates clearly that psalms and hymns and inspirational songs were sung. The latter may mean songs sung in the Spirit, possibly even singing in tongues. Notice too how Col. 3:16a indicates that singing was a means of teaching and admonishing fellow Christians by all, which Paul encourages. It was not merely a means of stirring up the crowd. This is also the sense of Eph. 5:18–20, which adds the thought that all these are manifestations of the Spirit and are for speaking to each other. Some of these hymns may have followed set or even Jewish models, and some it seems certain, such as what we find in Philippians 2 and Colossians 1, are based on earlier Jewish hymns to or about Wisdom personified.[185] One gets the impression that Christian worship was a time of great praises, but also that worship was aimed by the believers at each other, not just to God. It was to be both inspirational and educational for believers, both doxological and pedagogical. Paul is concerned that worship produce group unity and cohesion, not be an occasion for spiritual exhibitionism or competition, or the exalting of human ability and pride.[186]

How are we to evaluate the use of the Word in worship in Paul's communities? There is nothing explicit about reading the Old Testament and giving a homily, but this may be suggested by all the talk of instruction and teaching, a word of knowledge or of wisdom. Paul's frequent use of scripture implies that he expected his audience to be familiar with a good deal of it (cf. 1 Cor. 10:1ff.; Eph. 2:11–22; 4:8–12; 5:21–33), and at least in the reading of Paul's letters in worship some scripture texts that were incorporated would be read. It cannot be stressed too strongly that instruction and admonition were jobs for the whole congregation (cf. 1 Thess. 4:18; 5:11, 14; 1 Cor. 14:31; Rom. 15:14), though they were likely led or most frequently practiced by certain Christians.[187] In short, instruction was a job for all, males and females, in the worship. Prophecy was a form of instruction that was seen as even higher than teaching and certainly would have been equal to though not the same as preaching. Paul allows women to prophesy, so it is thus unlikely that he would forbid them to preach. This raises the question of what 1 Cor. 14:33b and 1 Tim. 2:8ff. mean, a subject I have addressed at great length elsewhere.[188]

In both cases, Paul and/or the Paulinist is obviously dealing with a specific problem. In Corinth, the problem seems to have been twofold: (1) disorder or chaos, with everyone trying to participate together and at once (14:32ff.); (2) overly liberated women and men who were going beyond what Paul saw as proper (taking off head coverings, etc.). It is clear that Paul, at 1 Corinthians 11 and elsewhere, wants to reaffirm the creation order distinctions in the Christian community, not see them obliterated; however, he also has no desire to quench the Spirit in women or men. The tightrope Paul walks seems to be the following, bearing in mind that in both cases we are dealing with a problem *in worship* in all likelihood: (1) Paul wanted to reaffirm the creation order, though in a way that indicated that in Christ headship and subordination had been transformed according to the model of Christ's own headship and submission (cf. Eph. 5:21ff.). For Paul, "head" did mean authority, but its main connotation was more responsibility, not more privilege—a head servant, not a boss or master concept. (2) This headship pattern is maintained in the family and expressed when the family of faith meets in worship. Nonetheless, if this creation order and its symbols are maintained, women can participate fully with men in the worship. (3) Apparently, in Corinth there were women *and men* who thought that the Spirit had obliterated such distinctions and ordering patterns.[189]

Against this purely pneumatic approach, Paul reasserts the headship pattern in two ways: (1) with the head coverings in 1 Corinthians 11; (2) by a command to silence in 1 Corinthians 14 and an insistence that one direct one's questions to husbands at home. Apparently, the problem was an insubordinate sort or disruptive kind of questioning, perhaps of the prophets (cf. 14:26–32). Some women were insisting on pressing some questions, which was only natural in view of the fact that asking questions of oracles was the regular practice in Greece, whether at Delphi or elsewhere.[190] Paul silences them simply so that activities may be done decently and in order (1 Cor. 14:40). This is certainly not a global prohibition of speaking by women in worship (cf. 1 Cor. 11:5) but an elimination of a particular abuse of a privilege of speaking that Christian women otherwise had. It is true that some scribes moved vv. 34–35 to after v. 40 because they did not see how the verses fit the context, but they are not omitted by any manuscript and so probably should not be seen as an interpolation. The problem corrected here has to do with the time of weighing and sifting of the prophecies, and so 1 Cor. 14:34ff. grows out of the immediately preceding discussion in that chapter.

The problem in 1 Tim. 2:8ff., which comes from a later period in the Pauline communities, seems also to be one of order and propriety. There apparently was some dissension in the congregation (cf. grumbling, v. 8, on the part of the men). Possibly women's clothing as well as their deeds were causing a stir.[191] The writer wants to reestablish the creation order in worship again, and he does so both with a command and a theological rationale to back it up (vv. 13–15). The women are to learn in quietness (a different word than in 1 Corinthians 14—here *hesuchia*) with all submission. Verse 12 is the crux of the matter. Some sort of teaching was apparently being attempted by these women that violated some sort of order. Were they repudiating the creation order and taking opportunities to lord it over the men, now that they were women with the Spirit and power? The key word here is *authentein,* which can mean "to exercise" or "to usurp" authority over someone. Because Paul is dealing with a problem here, it is likely the latter is meant. An in-depth study of this word suggests that it is used to mean "usurp authority" in other similar contexts as well.[192] This view comports well with the example Paul cites in vv. 13–14. Here is a perfect example of one who assumed or usurped an authority to do something that was not rightly hers, and it led to sin. The author then is arguing here against women usurping authority and teaching. He does not rule out their teaching and exercising authority in a proper way. It is the abuse of such power and authority at the expense of the creation order that is the problem. What texts like these show is that even women, unlike in some other ancient religious contexts, were being allowed significant roles in worship, and Paul and/or his disciple is concerned about *how* they exercise such roles, not whether.

Notice how the creation story is used in such passages, either explicitly or by implication. For Paul and his disciples, the story of the Fall must not be reenacted in the Christian community, and certainly not in Christian worship. The story of the new creation is a renewal of the story of God's original design for humankind, and this story has already been reinaugurated by the eschatological Adam, who creates a new humanity that is both inclusive and yet set apart from the world. It is creation and creature in all of their glorious distinctives being redeemed. That fact must be clear in

Christian worship, for especially there Christians are to model what God intended from the beginning for humankind to be—man and woman united with God and with each other in a union that preserves and celebrates the duality of the creator/creature distinction and the dual forms of human creatureliness.

A word in passing may be in order about Gal. 3:28. This text does not *just* mean in God's eyes that these distinctions no longer apply (all are equal in his sight), though that is true enough. Rather, Paul is saying something specific about what is true in Christ's community and among believers. They are all one in Christ. Because this seems to be a baptismal formula, if Gal. 3:28 is primarily about entrance requirements Paul would be saying that no social, ethnic, or sexual distinctions should be used to divide the body of Christ or prohibit one from entering it with status equal to that of all the others. If entrance is on the basis of grace by faith, all stand on equal ground. Gentiles did not have to become Jews to be on equal footing in the community, nor did slaves need to become masters. Notice, however, that Paul says there is "no male *and* female." This harkens back to the Genesis 1 creation story and perhaps its sequel. I have suggested elsewhere that Paul is saying there is no necessary coupling of male and female in Christ. It is acceptable for women to remain single and still have equal status with men in Christ.[193] This is confirmed in 1 Corinthians 7. This allowed some women to assume as their basic life role something other than wife or mother.[194]

What was preaching like in the Pauline communities? Besides exposition of scripture, there is little doubt it included doctrinal statements about Jesus. N. A. Dahl thinks he has found certain patterns of preaching in Paul's letters that he alludes to when he reminds his audience of what he had already said to them: (1) the revelation pattern—a sermon that indicates that what Christians now know about Christ was a secret hidden for ages, but is now revealed; (2) the soteriological pattern—which sets pre-Christian life against life in Christ ("once you were . . . but now you are"); (3) the conforming to Christ pattern—"just as Christ did . . . so must you do" (cf. 2 Cor. 8:9). (4). This was a paraenetic exhortation, which was likely very much like the ethical exhortations we have in Paul's letters.[195] What is interesting about this suggestion is that it means that Paul made it a regular practice not merely to preach on the basis of the story of Jesus, but to urge emulation of it. It also means that the rehearsal of the Christian's own story was a regular part of worship in Pauline communities. Paul and his coworkers were then in the business of intentionally conveying a storied world to their converts.

What was a "typical" worship service like in a Pauline community? Meeks suggests the following:

Joining the meeting in Gaius's overcrowded dining room, we might have heard, along with reminders of our life before baptism and our new life now, revelations of "words of the Lord," prophecies about things to come, admonitions to love each other as Christ loved us, as well as discourses on the *topos* "on marriage," or "on brotherly love." We would have been urged to exercise body and mind for the great contest of life, pressing on to the goal, not fearing the pain or the difficulties, which would prove our character. The Christian prophets and exhorters did not speak only novelties, a "Holy Ghost language." The uninstructed outsider (*idiotes*) who came in off the street to hear this kind of preaching would not think he was hearing the gibberish of some frenzy, but nevertheless he would find something strange, perhaps numinous about it (1 Cor. 14:23–25). What was odd was just the blend of the familiar and the novel.[196]

We have not mentioned prayer, but clearly both spontaneous and glossolalic prayer and orderly prayer according to a preset pattern were used (cf. 1 Cor. 14:13–15). Paul, however, clearly expects even glossolalia to be controlled.[197]

It is possible that there were set ways to begin and end a worship service, especially if Paul's letters, which have such formal introductions and conclusions, were vehicles for worship. We can say no more than that there were likely benedictions, and also the kiss of peace may have closed the service or possibly signaled the transition to the Supper.

WATER RITE AND WATER RIGHTS

> Can sin be drowned in water
> E'en with a flood of tears?
> Or is it rather Spirit
> That grafts the sinner in?
>
> Does parting of the waters
> Make Exodus come true?
> Or is it rather death to sin
> That makes one born anew?
>
> Between the two creations
> Two baptisms confess.
> The one depicts the story
> The other makes one blest.
> Immersion in Christ's story
> Death, burial, new birth,
> Begins the tale of Christians,
> New beings on old earth.
>
> —*Ben Witherington, III*

In this wider context we are now prepared to talk about Paul's view of baptism and the Lord's Supper. Any discussion of Paul's view of baptism must face squarely the implications of 1 Corinthians 1. It is clearly not the most crucial thing to Paul; rather, preaching is. No one who says, "I am thankful that I did not baptize any one of you except . . . ," and adds, "for Christ did not send me to baptize, but to preach . . . " (1 Cor. 1:14–17) could possibly have seen baptism as *the* means or chief means by which one becomes a Christian. In short, this implies a repudiation of a magical view of baptism. First Corinthians 15:29 suggests that some thought that baptizing a surrogate for a dead person was going to have some sort of unexplained benefit (eternal life?) for the dead person.[198]

Paul does not endorse such a view, though he uses it as an ad hoc argument to make his point. Again, surely the point of the analogy in 1 Cor. 10:1–12 is that such rituals as baptism without a proper godly life are no guarantee of salvation or even spiritual well-being. Baptism has no inherent power to convey salvation, regardless of people's lives and commitments. It is noteworthy that baptism is a rite, like the Lord's Supper, of and into the body. Baptism and the Lord's Supper suggest how the one and the many are linked to and in Christ. A great deal of confusion has been caused by assuming that Paul is always talking about the rite of water baptism and its effect when he uses the language of water baptism, such as at Rom. 6:1–14. Dunn's study of this matter has made this very unlikely.[199] At this point, we must simply summarize what seems to be Paul's view of baptism and the role it is meant to play in the story of the Christian and the Christian community.

The primary significance of water baptism for Paul lies in what it symbolizes and the fact that it is a valid and visible word proclaiming and depicting Christ's death and God's judgment on sin, believers' burial with Christ, and God's provision for them through the gift of Spirit baptism, as Rom. 6:1–14 suggests. Although the death-resurrection-Spirit–giving events were the necessary presuppositions for the water rite, it is primarily the first, and only partly the last of these, that is imaged forth in water baptism. Paul does not associate water baptism with the resurrection and thus does not draw on the Hellenistic notion of dying and rising as the substance that the rite depicts.

For Paul, what water baptism symbolizes and means is close to what circumcision meant, and from Colossians 2 it is hard not to believe that Paul saw water baptism as in one sense the Christian circumcision. Though he does not say so, Paul probably saw water baptism as circumcision's replacement rite. It is a more gender-inclusive symbol. Baptism is an act that symbolizes and looks back to Christ's death, symbolizes burial with him in baptism, and points to Spirit baptism, to the act that will convert one from the realm of the dead to the realm of the living. It was a rite for those who wanted to cross the line that circumscribed the new covenant community, or those who had already done so.

Finally, for Paul water baptism was a powerful symbol, the language of which he often used as a metaphor of the Christian experience of salvation history, of the beginnings of the story of the Christian as she or he is integrated into the Christian community. It was an act that he performed in which the baptized was the passive recipient. It was not his main task, however. It was a sign and symbol, not a seal,[200] and a visible word depicting salvation history, not a means of grace in the traditional sense of something that conveyed salvation. It could also serve as a tool to express the faith of a proselyte; in fact, it is part of the faith confessed in Eph. 4:5. As a rite and a powerful symbol of an even greater baptism on the cross and in the believer, it was of some importance to Paul.

But Paul was not led to overestimate baptism, for he in no way wanted to diminish the greater significance of the gift of the Spirit. Paul would never have said of the reception of the Spirit or "Spirit baptism": "I am thankful God did not baptize any of you." That Paul uses the language of water baptism to talk about the reality of Spirit baptism (and spiritual cleansing and the death to sin) shows where his priorities lie. He would not have countenanced the diminishing of the importance of the thing signified for the sake of the sign itself.

If we ask how the ritual was performed, it appears that baptism in a river and immersion were preferred though not mandated in Paul's day.[201] The one being baptized went through a dramatic and stark ritual of derobing and rerobing for baptism, and Paul of course uses the clothing (unclothed, reclothed) language to talk about conversion and its effects. The one being baptized then was likely naked when he or she was baptized. This symbolized putting off the old person and putting on the new creation (once out of the water—rerobing); hence the completeness of the change from one's old life to the new one. This not surprisingly eventually led to the separation of women's and men's baptismal ceremonies.

Paul mentions anointing at 2 Cor. 1:21, but it is not clear whether this refers to baptism, accompanied baptism, or refers to the Spirit's anointment, probably the latter. Possibly Gal. 4:6 and Rom. 8:15f. suggest that the cry "Abba, Father" often accompanied baptism when the baptized had been fully initiated. One of the things Meeks notes rightly about Christian baptism versus pagan or Jewish rites is that in pagan rites washing was often preparatory for initiation (i.e., one had to be pure *in advance* of initiation). Also, in Judaism there was no once-for-all transference from impure to pure. The Pharisees saw the need for continual and ongoing washing and cleansing, whereas for Christians baptism was once and once only. There is no question but that baptism is an initiatory rite for Paul—*not* a confirmation ritual for those long since Christian. It was meant to be performed with or as near to the time of conversion and Spirit baptism into the body of Christ as possible, regardless of one's age, not at some set age.[202]

When Paul alludes to baptism or uses baptismal language, he intends to remind his audience about what happened when the audience first became Christians. It is interesting to note that Paul does see baptism not merely as miming Christ's death, but in total immersion as a picture of Christ's burial as well. Thus baptism symbolizes that the old person is dead, not just dying. If anyone is in Christ, he or she is part of a new creation, not a mixture of old and new.

Romans 6:1–14 makes as clear as it can be made that Paul believes that from the outset of the Christian life one is grafted into the story of Christ, so that at conversion, symbolized by baptism, one is not only "baptized into Christ's death," not only buried with Christ, but given the Holy Spirit to walk in newness of life, just as at the resurrection and exaltation Christ became a life-giving spirit. From day one the Christian's life is hidden in Christ and in Christ's. This experience is seen as the basis for imitation in one's behavior, for as God works the image of Christ into the believer, the believer must work the same out. Paul sees the joining of the Christian community as involving a crisis experience that involves a Copernican revolution not only in one's thinking but also in one's behavior and lifestyle.[203] This is hardly surprising in view of the apostle to the Gentiles' own dramatic change of life. He expects and believes that his converts' stories will in various significant ways be like his own.

AN UNCOMMON MEAL

Love bade me welcome: yet my soul drew back
    Guiltie of dust and sinne.
But quick-ey'd Love, observing me grow slack
    From my first entrance in,
Drew nearer to me, sweetly questioning,
    If I lack'd any thing.

A guest, I answer'd, worthy to be here:
    Love said, You shall be he.
I the unkinde, ungrateful? Ah my deare,
    I cannot look on thee.
Love took my hand, and smiling did reply
    Who made the eyes but I?

> Truth Lord, but I have marr'd them: let my shame
> Go where it doth deserve.
> And know you not, sayes Love, who bore the blame?
> My deare, then I will serve.
> You must sit down, sayes Love, and taste my meat:
> So I did sit and eat.

—*George Herbert*
"Love III"[204]

Our discussion of the Lord's Supper must necessarily be more attenuated because there is less evidence to go on—principally twenty-five verses in 1 Corinthians 10 and 11. We have already suggested that this meal was seen as, or seen as a part of, a fellowship meal. Such meals were common in clubs in pagan antiquity, and some pagans saw the Christian celebration as but one more example.[205] The Corinthians would likely have seen such an occasion in the light of their knowledge of such pagan feasts.

As 1 Cor. 11:17ff. makes clear, the Lord's Supper was an imitation of a part of the Last Supper focusing on two key moments. First was the breaking of bread at the beginning of the supper, accompanied by thanksgiving and an interpretive word—"This is my body." Then later followed the passing of the cup of wine after the meal with an interpretive word—"This is my blood." What this shows is that Paul's community had been taught to live in a storied world. They were meant not only to reflect upon and remember the drama that brought about their redemption, but to act in such a fashion in this Supper so as to show their own participation in and acceptance of the story *and its benefits.* The meal was a memorial meal, remembering Christ's death, and as such may have been seen by the Corinthians as like other memorial meals for dead friends.[206]

The rite alluded to the vicarious nature of Jesus' death; it was "for you." But also there is a stress on the future horizon; believers celebrate it only until he returns. This means that the believer is reminded that there will be an end to the story of redemption and that all such rites are for the present only. Perhaps Paul saw it as foreshadowing the blessings of the conclusion of the story when the messianic banquet will be held. The believer knows that he or she is in the middle of the story, standing between Golgotha and glory, and is expected to both remember and expect.

Both of the sacraments were initiated because Christ has come and died, and they were meant to serve the *ekklesia* until he comes again. Meeks is probably right that the Aramaic *marana tha* (1 Cor. 16:20) were words that were part of the Lord's Supper. In fact, the Didache (10:6) indicates this. The rite thus stresses for the believer "Christ behind us, Christ before us, and Christ in us" when she or he partook of the elements. One could hardly be more immersed in the story of Christ than this. This rite has a past, present, and future referent, though primarily the focus is on Christ's death and how it benefits believers (i.e., because Christ died, he could be everywhere at once, and so present among all his followers).

Clearly, the Lord's Supper is an active rite just for believers, because Paul expects the participant to discern the body of believers when he or she participates (1 Cor. 11:29), which requires active faith. Baptism by contrast is a passive rite. It also signifies the believer's sharing in the benefits of the climax of the Christ story. Only the dead Christ benefits the believer and saves her or him. This is why the believer celebrates Christ's death—an otherwise gruesome idea, one that various pagans took to imply cannibalism—"sharing in someone's body." The function of this rite was to help transform Christians into a unity focusing on Christ and his death, that is, to bring them together around him and what he did for them.

> For Paul and his coworkers, the corollary of unity in the body of Christ is strict exclusion from all other religious connections. That is, group solidarity entails strong boundaries. Consequently Paul uses traditional language from the Supper ritual, which speaks of the bread as "communion of the body of Christ" and the "cup of blessing" as "communion of the body of Christ," to warn that any participation in pagan cultic meals would be idolatry. The single loaf used in the ritual symbolizes the unity of Christ and of the believer with Christ and, consequently, the unity of the community in its participation in Christ (10:17). Just as in 6:12–20 Paul argues that union with the body of Christ excludes union with a prostitute, so here he insists that the unity presented in the Supper is exclusive. "You cannot drink the cup of the Lord and the cup of demons; you cannot share the table of the Lord and the table of demons" (10:21). It is this exclusivity of cult that was perhaps the strangest characteristic of Christianity, as of Judaism, in the eyes of the ordinary pagan. . . . Thus, Paul uses the symbolism of the Supper ritual not only to enhance the internal coherence, unity, and equality of the Christian group, but also to protect its boundaries vis-à-vis other kinds of cultic association.[207]

It would be wrong, however, to suggest that Paul in his discussion of the Lord's Supper was suggesting a withdrawal out of the world altogether. It was rather a giving up of various worldly ways, attitudes, practices, so as to live a Christian life *in* the world. That the boundaries were not always clear between world and *ekklesia*, proper and improper, clean and unclean, is evident in Corinth. All of this raises the question, Did Paul think of baptism or the Lord's Supper as conveying grace, and so as a means of grace? There is no evidence that he did, at least insofar as that might mean a prophylactic against further loss of grace or even of salvation. Yet it is hard to escape the impression that in 1 Corinthians 10 and 11 Paul is saying that at least the Lord's Supper, if not also baptism, has more than symbolic significance; that is, it has some sort of spiritual effect or benefit, helping one to begin or continue one's life in the Spirit. If participated in properly and with faith, the Lord's Supper means being part of Christ and his body. Although Paul certainly gives no hint of transubstantiation,[208] clearly he thinks an improper taking of the elements can lead to harm and judgment, not blessing. It was a means of furthering one's real union and communion with Christ, not merely a means of extracting a dose of grace or blessing from Christ.[209]

What is critical for our purposes is that these rituals show plainly that the Pauline community acted in ways that intentionally reminded the believer that she or he lived not only in an interdependent community called the body of Christ, but that in fact one lived in and by means of Christ and his story, reflecting on the past of that story, invoking the future of that story, gaining benefit from its present reality and vitality. The story of the Christian and the Christian community was to be exegeted out of, indeed to live out of, the story of Christ. These rituals also make clear that the individual Christian was not to think one could live out one's own story or participate in the benefits of Christ's story in isolation. These benefits came and were appropriated in community.

The story of the Christian was not merely the story of life in Christ, but the story of life in and through the body of Christ. The one and the many are united in Christ in such a way that the latter is indispensable to the former without simply absorbing the former. Individual Christians have their own stories, but they must be told, shared, exegeted in community. The goal of such storytelling, as of all spiritual gifts, is the building up of the body of Christ, not the puffing up of the individual. Always standing in the background was the larger story of Christ and his career, which was meant to serve as an exemplar for Christians and the Christian community. We must take this further now, for although the Lord's Supper tells us something about life in Christ, there is more to be considered.

RACING TOWARD THE GOAL

As we conclude our discussion of life in Christ, we would like to look at a few key texts that tell us something about sanctification and the goal of the Christian life. For Paul, sanctification is both a matter of experience and of behavior, the former making possible the latter. It is because God has done something in the believer that one is enabled to do something for God and in accord with God's will. Pauline ethics are then fundamentally grounded in one's experience of the Spirit and the empowering that results therein.

Somewhat late in the Pauline corpus Paul puts it this way: "Work out your salvation with fear and trembling, for it is God who works in you both to will and to do for his good pleasure" (Phil. 2:12). This translation, however, is partially misleading, and due attention must be paid to the context. Paul has just cited the example of Christ's obedience to God, even unto death, in the hymn at 2:5ff. He seeks, as 2:12 indicates, to have the Philippians continue to obey and go further in obedience. This then is advice to those who have been faithful Christians, perhaps for some time. Philippians 2:12b follows this material.

One of the key considerations is that the key verb *katergazesthe* is in the present and is *plural*. This implies continuous action, and this particular verb implies working at something until it is brought to conclusion. That the verb is plural indicates that Paul is not addressing Christians as individuals but as a corporate group—the *ekklesia*.

Another key point is that 2:4 says explicitly, "Each one should *not* look to his own concerns, but to the concerns of the others."[210] Paul's concern is not merely that some Christians are too concerned about themselves and too little concerned about others and the welfare of the body of Christ corporately. Paul is encouraging real self-forgetfulness and focusing on the good of other believers. Thus Christ's example of extreme self-sacrifice and the shunning of self-aggrandizement is all the more to the point. It thus becomes most unlikely that at 2:12 Paul is exhorting the Philippians to be more concerned about their *private* spiritual matters and individual salvation.

Third, the noun *soteria* here could mean spiritual health, so that the Philippians are to work out spiritual health in and for Christ's body, resolving problems, thinking more of others, and the like. More likely, however, it has a more soteriological flavor, for elsewhere in Philippians *soteria* and its cognates always focus on salvation (cf. 1:28: "your salvation"). Paul believes that the working out of *soteria* now has a direct bearing on one's status and standing in the future kingdom, or lack thereof.[211]

Fourth, believers are to do this with "fear and trembling," with a healthy respect for one's fellow believers, but also for God and God's work in the midst of the body. It is after all God who is working in Christ's body.

Fifth, the verb used for God's working is a different verb from that which was used to refer to human effort in this context. Not *katergazesthe*, as in v. 12c, but *energein*, from which the English word *energy* comes.

This verb is a special Pauline word, used eighteen times by the apostle of the twenty times it is found in the NT. It carries within it the idea of working mightily, of working effectively (cf. Matt. 15:2; Gal. 2:8; 3:5;

5:6; Eph. 2:2). The form this new verb takes is a participle used as a noun; thus it becomes another name for God. The Great Energizer, the one who is effectively at work, is God. And God is at work among the Christians . . . at Philippi so as to effect a change in their wills . . . and in turn a change in their conduct.[212]

Notice that God's work in the midst of believers enables them not merely to will the good, but also to do it. They are to do this for the sake of God's good pleasure. Again, the Philippians' focus is to be on pleasing someone *other* than themselves—in this case, the Divine other. Thus this text does *not* promote "enlightened self-interest" or spiritual anxiety about self. It does, however, indicate that it is God's effective work in the body that gives it the ability to work out its salvation. No doubt Paul would have said the same about individuals. It is interesting to note that at the end of the Pauline corpus it is said that scripture, not the Spirit, equips one for every good work (2 Tim. 3:16–17).

For Paul, sanctification did involve holiness. However, it is interesting to see how this holiness works. In 1 Cor. 7:14 we see a dramatic difference from Old Testament holiness. Far from the unbeliever causing the believer to be impure, just the opposite is the case; sanctifying, or cleansing, is what happens to the unbeliever, at least when he or she is in intimate relationship with a believer. Paul is perhaps talking only about the "making clean" of the relationship and the fact that the unbeliever does not defile the believer by marital relationships. So sanctity here does not mean "to save" but has its nonsoteriological sense of "make clean," or "consecrate." Nevertheless, this is still a remarkable statement for someone with the background of Paul to make. He sees Christianity as a world-transforming, not merely a world-denying, religion.[213]

This is most important because it means that Christians do not have to sever relationships with the world to be Christians, to be sanctified and acceptable to God. Indeed, as 7:16 implies, Christians have the possibility of positively affecting others in the world, rather than being defiled by them. Paul here urges detachment from worldly attitudes, not withdrawal from the world. All has been relativized in view of the Christ event, and so Christians should not take worldly affairs and institutions as the be all and end all of existence. They are not to be one's ultimate concern. But precisely because God can work in a person regardless of what condition or social status one finds oneself in, it is not necessary to change one's social status, job, condition (unless it is an immoral one) to please the Lord and be a Christian.

First Corinthians 7:17 must be seen as an urging to "remain as you are." Christians can remain in the world without being of it, especially because the earth is the Lord's and the fullness thereof. True, Paul urges Christians to settle disputes in-house and not go to secular courts (1 Cor. 6:1ff.), but for Paul this does not signal a withdrawal from the world. Not only do Christians not get contaminated by non-Christian marital partners; they do not even need to cease general dealings with immoral or greedy people (1 Cor. 5:9ff.) or cease to have meals with non-Christian friends (1 Cor. 10:27) so long as these activities do not take place in a pagan temple. Apparently they are even expected to invite non-Christians to come to the assembly when it meets for worship (14:23). Gone here altogether is the set of stipulations and Levitical laws that separate Israelites from the world. The boundaries of the Christian community are defined by spiritual experience and Christian morality, not primarily by ritual and not at all by Levitical law or the establishment of an exclusivistic community. Rather, Christianity in Paul's vision is an inclusive religion. Thus Christian sanctification establishes an attitude and a pattern of behavior that does not exclude one from extracommunity relationships of various sorts. The line is drawn only at the necessary point. Christians are not to engage in idolatry or immorality (1 Cor. 10:14ff.); otherwise, they are free to live like other human beings.[214]

Paul does on occasion indicate that God puts attitudes and concerns into the individual Christian heart (2 Cor. 8:16), but by and large Paul addresses the body as a whole when he talks about God's work and the believer's sanctification. His essential perspective is enunciated, for instance, at 1 Cor. 1:7; God equips Christians with whatever spiritual gifts they need and sustains them in the faith, guiltless (cf. 2 Thess. 3:3). Gifts, however, are not given just for personal benefit, but for building up of the body. One grows in grace only in the context of Christ's body. What Christ does in a person, he does not just for the individual's benefit, but for the benefit of the body.

All of this raises the question of the place of good works in Paul's thought world. Surely he thought they were vital or he would not have been constantly exhorting Christians to do them. Good works are in fact so crucial, because they are the tools God uses to bring people to Christ and to build up Christ's body (see 1 Cor. 3:10ff.). Obviously, for Paul the ultimate good work is leading another to Christ. Paul clearly believes that Christians will be rewarded for good works (3:14), especially those that amount to missionary work and the ministry of the Christian body. Thus good works for Paul are both vital because God has chosen to use them and profitable because God rewards those who do them. However, one's justification is not on the basis of good works, but rather Christ's good works (1 Cor. 3:15).

One of the keys to understanding sanctification and ethics in Paul is in seeing how he uses Christ's life, both as a pattern for the Christian to imitate but also as a pattern that is recapitulated in the Christian's experience; that is, Christ's life is recapitulated in a sense in the believer's life. As we have already noted, believers have died to sin, whereas Christ died for sin, and they have been baptized into his death and buried with him, and will be raised just as he was raised. All this describes Christian experience. As a result of that experience, Christians are expected also now to live like Christ; they must consider themselves dead to sin and alive to God in Christ (Rom. 6:10–11). The idea of Christ's life as a pattern for our behavior is brought out well by Meeks:

> In paraenesis, Christ's voluntary submission to death is taken as a model for other-regarding actions and attitudes. Thus, "We who are strong ought to bear with the failings of the weak, and not to please ourselves; let each of us please his neighbor. . . . For Christ did not please himself. . . . " (Rom. 15:1–3, RSV; cf. Gal. 6:2). Christians should "accept one another, as Christ accepted you" (Rom. 15:7); "forgive one another . . . as the Lord forgave you" (Col. 3:13; Eph. 4:32); "walk in love, as Christ also loved us and gave himself up on our behalf as an offering and sacrifice to God" (Eph. 5:2). They are urged to contribute to the collection for the poor in Jerusalem by the reminder of "the grace of our Lord Jesus Christ, who for our sakes became poor, though he was rich, that you by his poverty might become rich" (2 Cor. 8:9). And the whole mythic pattern of Christ's descent from divine to human form, submission to death, and subsequent exaltation and enthronement can be introduced by quoting a hymn or liturgical poem familiar to the readers, as basis for an appeal for unity and mutual regard (Phil. 2:5–11).[215]

Much of Paul's ethic also involves pragmatic advice, such as specific injunctions for problems like marriage and divorce, but the above indicates his fundamental orientation and attitude. Perhaps we should stress that the ethic of love is an overriding and undergirding factor in all Paul's enjoinders, as 1 Corinthians 13 makes clear. It is notable, however, that Paul does not simply tell Christians to obey the Old Testament law, without various qualifications. Yet at points Paul draws on it as valid for direction along with church tradition, the words of Jesus, and his own authoritative exhortations as well as his adaptation of traditional Hellenistic ethical advice. In addition, he points his listeners on occasion to "the law of Christ"—the pattern of Christ's life and teachings circulated in the early preaching and teaching.[216]

The question has been asked, Does Paul envision any progress in sanctification during the Christian life, and are there any goals, such as "perfection," attainable as one pursues one's life in the Spirit? Though Paul reflects no second or third definite work of grace ideas, he constantly implies that he wants Christians to grow in spiritual maturity and fully expects them to do so (cf. 1 Cor. 3:1ff.).

Romans 12:2 is addressed to Christians, and Paul is talking about a present and ongoing renewal of the mind of the believer that involves an openness to God's transforming work in one's life. Clearly, this implies progressive sanctification. Though by grace (v. 3), it is also not without human effort, for Paul is here exhorting Roman Christians, not merely imploring God for a miracle.

There are also goals for Christians: (1) to obtain the glory of Christ (2 Thess. 2:1); (2) to be conformed to the image of the Son (Rom. 8:29); (3) to obtain adoption as sons and daughters, the redemption of our bodies (Rom. 8:23). Obviously this latter is a goal believers will not obtain prior to Christ's return, and (2) is something that, although it begins in this life, is in the end only completed at Christ's return. There is thus some overlap between (2) and (3).

Such texts as 1 Cor. 4:8 suggest that Christians are not filled in this life and do not yet reign in glory. This cannot be deflected by suggesting that Paul is merely mocking immature Corinthian Christians, because 4:8b suggests that Paul did not see himself as yet reigning either. It is significant that only once in the whole Pauline corpus does Paul use the verb *teleioo* ("make perfect"), at Phil. 3:12, and there he uses it as a disclaimer! He says, "not that I have already obtained . . . ." Paul denies even in his later years that he has obtained perfection, as apparently some of his opponents in Philippi were claiming, but he presses on toward it. It is probable from the context that this entails for Paul the resurrection of the body (see v. 10) and full knowledge of Christ, which also elsewhere he associates with the future when the perfect comes (cf. 1 Cor. 13:9–12).

In the meantime, the Christian life is to be seen as a race in which one can make progress toward the goal, and one should press on toward it with all the effort one can muster, drawing on all the grace and aid God gives. This pressing on to the goal is what spiritual maturity amounts to in this life (Phil. 3:12–15), and this implies that the goal is not realized in this life unless Christ returns and transforms one and gives one finally a condition of "entire sanctification." As Paul says, "We do not hope for what we already have," and there is no time in this life when the Christian does not live by faith, with love, and in hope.

Nevertheless, living the Christian life is not seen by Paul as an impossible ideal, but rather one possible by God's grace. Yet when Paul says, "I have strength in all things in him who strengthens me" (Phil. 4:13),[217] Paul is not referring to the ability to accomplish anything in Christ, but the ability to endure anything, as the previous list in 4:12 shows.

Thus Paul's ethics or admonitions are for people who, although not perfect, are nonetheless empowered by the Spirit and the Spirit's grace and gifts to do what God calls believers to do for Christ and his body. His ethics then are not a counsel of perfection, for ethical advice presumably will be unnecessary in heaven; nor does he view his description of Christian experience as an impossible dream. They are a counsel of holiness of heart and life, realized by God's grace. This is what God expects of believers, and this God enables them to be and do. The summary of Bultmann—"be what you already are," or to put it another way, "work out what God has already worked into you as a community"—indicates that the Christian life is a life full of possibilities, with progress and victories over sin as realizable goals. This is because it is God who works in the body both in its willing and doing, and also because believers strive with every fiber of their beings to move closer to what lies ahead. Because of these factors, progress and growth in Christ are possible.

When Paul held himself up as an example of a moral athlete, he believed his example could be followed, for he believed he was just an ordinary person who had had an extraordinary experience of God in Christ. With Christ behind him, Christ before him, Christ in him, Paul believed that Christ enabled him and all believers to be and become increasingly Christlike. The key to understanding Paul's thought world is not to divide it into theology and ethics and then try to decide how the parts are to be parceled out, but to recognize that all of Paul's thought is grounded in a storied world that involves the experiences, words, deeds, and relationships of both human beings and God.[218] That world revolves around the drama of divine redemption.

THE FINISHED PRODUCT—THE TALE'S END

> Manshape . . . death blots black out; nor mark
>   Is any of him at all so stark
> But vastness blurs and time beats level. Enough!
> the Resurrection.
>
> A heart's-clarion! Away grief's gasping, joyless days
> dejection.
> A beacon, an eternal beam. Flesh fade, and mortal trash
> Fall to residuary worm; world's wildfire leave but ash:
>   In a flash, at a trumpet crash,
> I am all at once what Christ is, since he was what I am, and
> This Jack, joke, poor potsherd, patch, matchwood, immortal diamond,
>   Is immortal diamond.
>
> —*Gerard Manley Hopkins*
> *"That Nature Is a Heraclitean Fire"*[219]

We have seen at various points that Paul's view of life is essentially Christocentric and ecclesiocentric. To be "in Christ" means in fact to be "in the body of Christ," and thus experience and ethics coexist in the same context in Paul's storied world.[220] "The whole ethical life of Christians takes place within a social organism, which is not self-contained or self-complete; a community which is a body only because it is Christ's body, depends upon him and serves his ends."[221] Christ and his community are the major players in Paul's storied world, and so it is not surprising that when Paul thinks of the end of the story of Christians he thinks about both the resurrection and the return of Christ and the bearing of these events on the final form of Christian life and the resolution of the story of Christians. We must limit our comments here to matters that pertain to the Christian's resurrection in particular.

We must first return to the extended discussion of resurrection in 1 Corinthians 15. Paul argues that if there is no resurrection, then Christ is not raised, and neither are or will Christians be (cf. 1 Cor. 15:50), for one cannot experience resurrection as one is. We must bear in mind for those raised in a Greek environment often the body was seen as of no great importance, and sometimes it was seen as the prison of the soul. Apparently the Corinthians were arguing that the Christian faith has to do with imperishable, eternal, spiritual things, not perishable, physical things. It is a matter of soul, not body, and so redemption is a spiritual condition. However, the corollary that went along with this was that (a) what one did with or to one's body did not affect one's spiritual life, and (b) thus it did not matter what one did with one's body. Whether one was a glutton, or had sex with a harlot, or was involved in incest, it mattered little or not at all because no such deeds of the body could affect the soul or spiritual life. One cannot read 1 Cor. 5—11 without realizing that somehow at least some Corinthians were contending that their spiritual life was unaffected by what they did with their bodies. Yet it is also clear from 1 Corinthians 15 that some Corinthians were very concerned about their loved ones' dying. First Corinthians 11:30ff. and 1 Cor. 15:29 make clear that they had such a concern. Perhaps they had misunderstood it when (and if) Paul had said, "He who is in Christ, will live forever."[222]

On the whole, then, we may sum up as follows: (1) Paul is arguing against the view that there is no resurrection of the dead and that the future is merely an extension of "life in the Spirit" in the present; (2) it is less likely that he is arguing against the view that the resurrection had already come and gone because of his focus on resurrection being *from the dead*; it is something you cannot experience in flesh and blood. To the question "What about those who have died?" Paul does not respond, "Their souls will be fine in heaven." Rather, he points out that death will be destroyed, although it is the last enemy to be overcome (v. 26).

Thus v. 12 must be taken at face value, and we must see that Paul is insisting that resurrection necessarily entails both a body and rising from the dead. The conclusion that follows from this is that none of the Corinthians could have experienced it, and yet the resurrection body is integral to the essence of new life in Christ. Paul is even able to contend that his audience would not have the Spirit at all were there no resurrection, because "the last Adam became a life-giving Spirit" at his resurrection, not before. In short, if there is no resurrection of Jesus from the dead, then there is no Spirit for the *ekklesia*. Paul, of course, has no desire here to quench the Spirit, but he does want to make perfectly clear that it is the Spirit of the risen Christ they have received.

Here we have, as we do in the Fourth Gospel, the strange paradox that the Spirit could not come to believers unless Christ left them and went to heaven. There is thus a twofold proleptic realization of the end: (1) Christ's resurrection; (2) believers having the Spirit are both pointers and proofs that the resurrection of the body will yet happen to believers. Both of these preliminary incursions of firstfruits presage and promise latter fruits. They have brought the future into the present, making possible, believable, and certain that believers will rise one day.

Verses 12–19 of 1 Corinthians 15 appear in the form of a syllogism. If there is no resurrection, then Christ is not raised and Christian preaching and faith are meaningless. Even worse, Christians have been false witnesses about God, and they are still in their sins. Worst of all, those who have died as Christians have perished! All of this is to refute the contention that there is no resurrection. Paul is saying here that these are the full consequences of such an assertion. If Christ did not in fact rise from the dead, then it was all a very bad joke in very poor taste, deceiving people about God and life. Paul is asserting here: "No risen Christ, no Christian faith, period."

Normally, freedom, or forgiveness, from sins is associated with Christ's death, but here it is made clear that not only Christ's death but his resurrection is necessary for such liberation to happen. To die in one's sins leads to perishing or being destroyed. A. Robertson argues, "The *apoleia* [destruction] is the utter loss consequent upon dying in sin. This meaning is frequent in St. Paul (i. 18, vii. 11; 2 Cor. ii. 25, iv.3; 2 Thess ii. 10). They have surrendered everything in order to have eternal life with Christ at his Coming, and they have died. If they are dead beyond possibility of restoration then death separates us for ever from Christ."[223]

For Paul, eternal life necessarily entails the resurrection, and resurrection necessarily entails the body. There would be no true or eternal life without resurrection, both of Jesus and for the believer. In this conviction Paul is like the Pharisees, who saw resurrection as the form of everlasting life. Verse 19 ends with the hopeless conclusion: "If Christ is not raised, we are not the most enviable, but rather the most pitiable of human beings."

To hope only in this life in Christ is no real hope at all, and yet some Christians were trying to live on the basis of such a hope.[224]

Because we have already dealt with the Adam-Christ typology in vv. 20ff., only a few comments are necessary about this section.[225] Who are the latter fruits—all humanity or all Christians? Verse 23b suggests clearly that Paul is here thinking of the connection between the resurrection of Christ and of Christians—"those who belong to him." Paul does not see Jesus' resurrection as an isolated or isolatable phenomenon, but the first installment of the whole event of eschatological resurrection. This means that the *ekklesia* is in the eschatological age and also that the Christian's future is dependent upon and connected to Christ's past. Christ's history is the believers' destiny in the sense that they are destined to experience what he experienced—a resurrection body.

Notice also that in v. 20 Paul says that Jesus is the firstfruit of those who have "fallen asleep." This phrase does not refer to any doctrine of "soul sleep" or the idea that dying is like lying down to pleasant dreams, of which Paul knows nothing. Nor is it simply the traditional Jewish euphemism for death. Paul may be using sleep here as Jesus did in the Gospel, to mean that death is no more permanent nor potent than a sleep in the hands of God, because by God's power and grace the dead will rise up from it very much alive and renewed (see 1 Thess. 4:15).

We must now examine 1 Cor. 15:35–57. Verse 35 indicates that Paul is discussing the nature of the resurrection body of those who are yet to be raised—believers. It is a reasonable inference, however, that because Paul uses the firstfruits, latter fruits metaphors, that his view of believers' resurrection bodies is not likely to be different from his view of what Christ's resurrection body must have been like. Two further points are in order here: (1) Paul is talking about those who rise from the dead, not those who are yet alive at the resurrection; (2) at 1 Thess. 4:15ff. Paul makes clear the distinction between the two groups. It follows, then, that at vv. 51ff. and not before, Paul begins to discuss the condition of those left alive till the Parousia. Paul draws an analogy between the relation of a seed and the plant that comes from it, to the present physical body in its relationship to a resurrection body. There are elements of both continuity and discontinuity between the old and the new, and we may set these up in a chart:

Elements of Continuity	Elements of Discontinuity	
1. same person	sown	raised
2. a body	perishable	imperishable
3. life in a body is the only	in dishonor	in glory
full-fledged life[226]	in weakness	in power
	natural body	spiritual body

It seems probable at this juncture that Paul is to some degree dependent on his Jewish heritage for the analogy and its meaning. Rabbi Eliezer said:

All the dead will arise at the resurrection of the dead, dressed in their shrouds. Know thou that this is the case. Come and see from (the analogy of) the one who plants (seed) in the earth. He plants naked (seeds) and they arise covered with many coverings; and the people who descend into the earth dressed (with their garments), will they not rise up dressed (with their garments)?[227]

We must do our best not to press the seed/plant analogy too far. For instance, we must not overemphasize either the elements of continuity or discontinuity. Paul is not suggesting that resurrection is a natural process that works itself out by putting human bodies, like seeds, into the ground. Paul sees resurrection as happening to all Christians who are dead at the same time. But both in the case of the seed and the human body, it is believed to be God who gives the new body. Neither the seed itself nor the sower provides these new bodies, and God gives each one the body that is proper to its kind.

The question becomes, Is Paul talking about a replacement of one body with another, or the transformation of the former body into the latter? Paul says clearly, "Flesh and blood [in its present state] cannot inherit the kingdom." To this he adds the idea that God gives the naked grain of wheat a body. Verse 37 says, "When you sow you do not plant the body that will be, but just a seed; rather, God gives it a body." Both of these texts suggest that Paul is talking about sequential replacement, not just tranformation.[228]

Nonetheless, vv. 42–44, which are not part of the analogy, may suggest that Paul is, in the normal course of affairs, discussing transformation of the old body into the new. Paul believed that if there is no old body to transform, God can provide one. By whatever process the resurrection body is constituted, Paul believes that the new body Christians will have will be appropriate to the new age. It will not be subject to decay and death and the physical frailties all now suffer. It will not be a dishonorable body, but a glorious one—nothing to be ashamed of. It will be one that partakes of the qualities of Christ and heaven (i.e., glory, majesty). Paul envisions that believers will be powerful beings, just as the risen Christ was.

At v. 44 we get to the crucial point. As W. D. Davies points out, it is unlikely that Paul, when he talks about a "spiritual body," means an immaterial one.[229] "Natural" body means a body animated and governed by a natural or physical life principle or force. Spiritual body does not mean a body without substance, but a body animated and vivified by God's Spirit. The eternal Spirit will be the force and life source animating this body;

therefore it partakes of the eternal life the Spirit can give. Paul does not likely mean that it is similar to the Holy Spirit in its lack of material form. It is well to observe here that Paul is talking about the raising of individual Christians, not a corporate raising of the body of Christ. Notice, however, that v. 47 connects believers' resurrection as individuals to that of the Man from heaven. They will bear his likeness, just as they have borne Adam's.

Elsewhere, 2 Cor. 3:18 speaks of believers now being transformed into Christ's likeness. Clearly, in this case "likeness" does not mean physical appearance or indeed anything physical, but has likely to do with conformity to Christ's character. In 1 Corinthians 15 Paul refers to a transformation that happens at resurrection when believers will share in resurrection bodies and bear Christ's likeness even physically. Romans 8:29 may refer to believers bearing both a spiritual and a physical conformity to the likeness of Christ. In Paul's mind, redemption is not complete unless it entails a body. Life in heaven without it is decidedly second best and a temporary or interim condition.[230]

Verses 51ff. make clear that both resurrection of the dead and transformation of the living will be instantaneous events "at the last trumpet" when Christ returns. While the dead will be raised imperishable (v. 52), the living will be clothed with immortality. The imagery here is of putting on clothes, presumably over this mortal frame. "*Endusasthai* (aor. of sudden change) is a metaphor which implies that there is a permanent element continuing under new conditions. In a very real sense it is the same being which is first corruptible and then incorruptible."[231]

Moving on to Romans 8, we must note that the believers' resurrection is not an event without connection with the prior history of those believers' lives. For instance, in Romans 8 Paul links the believers' present condition with their future resurrection. In v. 11 the future "giving life to your mortal bodies" is made dependent on the Spirit's current presence and work in the believer. The same point is made in a different way in v. 23. This verse raises the question whether, because Paul calls what believers have of the Spirit "firstfruits," he sees the "redemption of our bodies" as an act of the Spirit or the point at which one receives the fullness of the Spirit. This requires that we take "of the Spirit" as appositive here, or possibly possessive, rather than partitive. The epexegetic sense possibly should be preferred, in which case Paul means that having the Spirit in the present *is* the firstfruits of the eventual harvest that will belong to believers.

In v. 11 we note the clear linking of Christ's and believers' resurrections—or at least their final transformation. A further implication is possible. It is possible that Paul is suggesting that the resurrection body will be numerically and "somatically" identical with the present body. This is not certain, because Paul is addressing the condition of the living. It is in living Christians that the Spirit now dwells. Notice that in v. 11 we are told that it is through the Spirit that *now* dwells in them that life will be given to their mortal bodies. It follows from this that in both vv. 11 and 23 Paul likely is referring to the transformation of the living believers at the Parousia rather than to the resurrection of the dead. This would explain why he speaks of the "redemption of *our* bodies" (v. 23).

Paul seems still to be entertaining the possibility of being alive at the Parousia when he wrote Romans (see 13:11). This may explain why in neither verse does he speak of the believer being raised *ek nekron* (out of the dead). He does not do so because he is addressing what will happen to living believers should Christ soon return. Thus neither of these verses counts against the view that Paul still thought of the exchange of one body for another in the case of dead Christians. Even in Romans 8 we do not read of the resurrection of the flesh of dead believers.[232]

Before moving on to a discussion of glorification, a few parting remarks are in order about resurrection. We have already made clear that Paul views Jesus' resurrection and that of believers not so much as two linked events, but as two episodes of one event or two harvests from one crop—firstfruits and latter fruits. At Col. 1:18 Jesus is called the firstborn from the dead, but notice at 1:15 he is also called the firstborn of all creation. In both cases, firstborn refers not to an order of birth, but an indication of being first, unique, and having a special status and dignity.[233] The concern in Colossians is with Christ's supremacy over the dead, having been one of their number. Christ is supreme in and inaugurator of the resurrection, as 1 Corinthians 15 makes clear, and yet resurrection was an action of God on Jesus' behalf.[234] This passivity of Christ is fundamental to Paul and reflects his identity with the believing dead. Here and at Rom. 8:29 resurrection is used not to prove Christ's divinity, but his identity with and solidarity with Christians.

Taking our hint from 1 Cor. 15:43, it seems clear that for Paul the Christian's glory comes only when he or she receives the resurrection body. In Phil. 3:20–21, Paul suggests that the believers' citizenship is in heaven, by which he does not mean that that will be their permanent dwelling place, but that heaven is their headquarters, and as citizens of heaven, they will in due course experience a heavenly condition. That condition involves Christ changing a Christian's lowly body into a glorious one. Notice that Christ is the change agent at his coming from heaven. This implies that believers do not experience resurrection or glorification until they receive the resurrection body. In short, just as resurrection and exaltation went together for Jesus, so resurrection and glorification go together for Christians.

This is also spoken of in Rom. 8:12–18. The glory believers will have and will see is with Christ after this life. Indeed, v. 23 makes clear that in the full sense believers do not become God's adopted sons and daughters until they receive the redemption of their bodies. Notice again how in Rom. 1:3–4 Jesus did not function as Son of God *in power*, nor was he appointed as such until the resurrection from the dead. This means that only Christ is in any full sense experiencing glory so far (cf. 2 Corinthians 4). Because believers will not receive a body in heaven, but on earth at the resurrection, it follows that life in heaven, in Paul's view, is not really their hope or hope of glory.

Paul can talk about believers being transformed into Christ's likeness and from one degree of glory to another in this life (2 Cor. 3:18), but clearly, this is not where Paul's emphasis lies. It is the eternal weight of glory that Christians prepare for here (2 Cor. 4:17). Obviously, what believers do here is supposed to be for Christ's glory (cf. 2 Cor. 8:19), but such uses of *doxa* refer to his "honor." Sometimes *doxa* is used to mean likeness, as in 1 Cor. 11:7—man is the glory (i.e., likeness) of God. Romans 3:23 may be another example of this usage; humankind sinned and fell short of God's image (or glory).

In Christ, glory and image of God perfectly converge, in human beings the two are at variance. Though humans are in the image, they fall short of the glory, that is, the likeness. Thus, being in Christ not only restores a person's humanity but carries him or her on to his or her proper destiny—glory. Christ obtains what Adam failed to obtain, and Christ gives what Adam could never give. In the meantime, believers rejoice in hoping to share in that future glory (Rom. 5:2). Notice how Rom. 2:7 is phrased: "To those who seek glory, honor, and incorruption, he will give eternal life." Cranfield rightly points out: "It is to be noted that Paul speaks of those who seek . . . glory, honour and incorruption, not of those who deserve them. [These terms] here denote eschatological gifts of God already firmly associated in Jewish thought with the resurrection life of the blessed."[235]

Just as Paul could not conceive of a full life without a body, neither could he conceive of any full-fledged eternal life or glory, or honor or incorruption, without the resurrection body. All this causes us to ask, What then is Paul's view of the so-called interim state, life in heaven?

It has been urged by C.F.D. Moule, C. H. Dodd, and others that between the writing of 1 Corinthians 15 and 2 Corinthians 5 Paul changed his eschatology from one of resurrection of the body to life in heaven, and thus a more spiritual view.[236] Some have maintained that Paul had little or no view of the interim state because he thought the end was necessarily imminent. The arguments about 2 Corinthians 5 have been long and complicated, so one can only hope to summarize the evidence here: (1) it does seem that there is some development in Paul's thinking on this subject; but (2) it is caused not because he gave up the idea either of the possible imminence of the Parousia (something he always seems to have held to) nor the idea of resurrection of the dead, but because he came increasingly to reckon with his own death as preceding the Parousia. This in turn led him to give further reflection to the interim state. A brief survey will bear this view out.

In 1 Thessalonians 4 we have the two categories: (1) Christians who have died; 2) Christians who live till the Parousia. A moment's reflection will show that if one doesn't know the timing of the Parousia, but believes it is *possibly* imminent, the only category one could place oneself in is "we who are living when the Lord returns." Paul could not have said "those of us who will certainly die before Christ returns," for he did not know with certainty the timing of either his death or Christ's return.

If we go to the other end of the Pauline corpus, we have both reflections on departing and being with Christ in heaven (Phil. 1:19ff.), but we also have 3:10–11, the desire to obtain the resurrection of the dead and know the power of the resurrection. It is true that there is no talk of living until the Parousia in Philippians perhaps because Paul faces danger, trials, persecutions, and his death. Thus, whatever we may say about 2 Corinthians 5, it is unlikely to amount to Paul having given up his expectation either of a second coming or a resurrection from the dead. This conclusion is also borne out by a close examination of what Paul says about resurrection in Romans 8, a letter written after 2 Corinthians. What then is the positive significance of the interim state for Paul?

For Paul, death does not mean life without Christ—in some limbo or land of the dead. To leave the flesh, that is, to die, means for the Christian "to depart and be with Christ" (Phil. 1:23) or, as he puts it in 2 Cor. 5:8, the interim state entails being away from the body (hence bodiless) and present (at home) with the Lord. There is no indication of any interval between being absent from the body and present with the Lord; it happens just after death.

Some have seen an apparent contradiction between 2 Corinthians 5 and Philippians 1 because in the latter text Paul calls dying, gaining, but in 2 Corinthians 5 Paul says "not that I want to be unclothed." This apparent contradiction is rather easily resolved when one takes into consideration the point of comparison in each instance. In 2 Cor. 5:4b the comparison is between the interim state and the resurrection state. Obviously, for Paul the latter is preferable. In the former text (Phil. 1:21), the point of comparison is between this earthly existence and being with Christ in heaven. If those are the only two options, Paul would prefer the latter and calls it gain. But if he had his preference, he would prefer living until the Parousia and being transformed, or "further clothed," at that point.

Second Corinthians 5:3 seems to characterize the interim state as one of "nakedness," a condition clearly undesirable as an everlasting condition from a Jewish and early Christian point of view. If one derives from this that Paul seems a bit ambivalent about the interim state, this should not surprise us. It is a good, but it is rather like winning the consolation prize. One may be happy to get it, but it is not what one ultimately longed for.

First Thessalonians 4:13 has sometimes been translated, "are asleep," and been used to suggest that the dead are unconscious until the Parousia, hence not aware of the passing of time until the Parousia. Against this, however, "sleep" is a euphemism for death, not a description of the condition of the Christian dead. In any case, we should likely translate here, "are falling asleep" (i.e., "are dying"). The point Paul is dwelling on at 1 Thess. 4:13 is their deadness, not their condition after dying. G. B. Caird has even gone so far as to argue that Paul's eschatology centers on the idea of sleep, and the concept resolves the problem of the delayed Parousia for Paul. This is highly improbable. The most one could get from 1 Thess. 4:13–16 is that Paul believed that Christians are safe and sound in Christ's hands when they die; they have not experienced eternal death.

Paul characterizes the interim state elsewhere as being "in Christ," or "with the Lord," or an experience of life (Col. 3:1; 2 Cor. 4:4; 5:8; 1 Thess. 4:17; Phil. 1:23). Paul's ideas about the bodiless state are positive not because he held to some Platonic view of the immortality of the soul, or the body as the prison of the soul. Death can be seen in a somewhat positive light only because it means to go and be with Christ in a way one is not and cannot be while living in the earthly body.

It is sometimes argued that Paul could not have held to both resurrection of the body and an intermediate state in heaven at the same time, for they are competing forms of eternal life. However, in light of Jewish apocalyptic documents that combined both of these ideas (1 En. 103:3ff.) and the fact that rabbinic thought sometimes applied the idea of paradise not only to the age to come, but also to those who are dead now, there is plenty enough precedent in Judaism for Paul to have come up with something similar.[237]

Turning to 2 Corinthians 5 in some detail, we note the following: (1) 2 Cor. 4:16–5:10 forms a continuous flow of thought and should be read together. (2) Paul uses the metaphor of clothing to refer to the body. To be unclothed is to be without the body, to be clothed is to have a body, to put on clothes over something refers to transformation at the Parousia for those who live until then. (3) Paul calls the body a tent (*skenos*), indicating the temporary and transitory nature of earthly existence. Elsewhere in 2 Corinthians he refers to the body as an earthen vessel or mortal flesh (4:11; 4:7ff.), or a house or building. These metaphors are interchangeable ways of describing the same phenomenon—the human body. However, it is notable that Paul calls the resurrection body the building (or house), not the tent, perhaps connoting more permanence as a dwelling place than our earthly abode. At 1 Cor. 6:19 the present body is called God's temple, but this is because the issue of personal holiness, not the permanence of the mortal body, is under discussion. Paul was not by any means the only one to call the body a tent. We find it in (a) Wisd. Sol. 9:14 LXX; (b) John 10:14; (c) 2 Peter 1:13ff. It is not found outside the New Testament except in the Wisdom of Solomon, and thus is a biblical image. Plato, however, uses *skenos* to refer to release of the soul from the body.

At 2 Cor. 5:1 the body is referred to as a building or house from and made by God, and thus is not a human product. Thus we must distinguish this idea from what we find in John 14:2—a mansion in heaven. Paul is not talking about a heavenly dwelling place, but a heavenly condition, that is, a heavenly body (cf. 1 Cor. 15:48). The phrase "eternal in the heavens" probably does not speak of the place of the body but its nature; it is a heavenly body, one partaking of a heavenly mode of existence. Often Paul will say that the believer's life, or joy, or body, is hid in heaven, meaning that it is kept safe for them and can be found where Christ is. We should not deduce from "eternal in the heavens" the idea that believers will dwell there bodily forever.

"Eternal" in 2 Cor. 5:1 must be taken to mean everlasting, because it is not talking about a body that always was, but one that always will be once one is given it. This verse is a conditional remark, with *ean* (if) plus the aorist subjunctive, which implies uncertainty as to whether this will happen, but it is certainly a possibility. Verses 2–4 describe the preferred condition—to live until the Parousia and be transformed or further clothed, one's current mortality being swallowed up by life in the form of a new resurrection body. Again, this dwelling is a heavenly one because of its character, but also because it comes to believers from heaven, in the sense that it comes when Christ comes from heaven to make this change.

Against the view that Paul sees believers assuming this heavenly body immediately when they die is the fact that Paul says to be absent from *the* body, not *this* body, in vv. 6ff. These verses mean to be absent from any body and present with the Lord. Paul says that Christians have an eternal heavenly building coming to them, not that they have in heaven an eternal building (body). The verb "have" goes with "building," not with "in heaven." The one thing the believer does not yet have either on earth or in heaven is a resurrection body. When Paul says, "We have this eternal building," the verb is a futuristic present. He means that believers will certainly receive it.

We thus can only conclude that this material cannot be used to suggest that Paul changed his mind about the ultimate form of eternal life, though when he contemplates the possible nearness of his death he gives more emphasis to the interim condition. On closer inspection, 2 Cor. 1:9 and 4:14 still bear witness to the fact that for Paul resurrection of the body connected to Christ, and Christ's resurrection is Paul's primary focus.

The man who was converted by meeting the risen Lord carried with him the idea of his and other believers' resurrection throughout his life as the bedrock of his faith. For him it was the linchpin of all human stories. On the one hand, resurrection was what made possible for Christ to be Son of God in power and send the Holy Spirit, but also it made viable and life-giving the sacrifice he offered on the cross. It was the key to Christ's story. On the other hand, it was likewise the key to Paul's own story; for if Christ was not raised, Paul himself was under a delusion ever since Damascus road, and furthermore his converts would have been laboring under the same deception.

The resurrection turned around both the life of Christ and all those who came to be in him. It is the key to the whole human story in Paul's mind. Otherwise the story of the first Adam, not the last one, prevails upon the earth, and there is no Good News to be told. But Paul did not believe he was laboring under any delusion. In good faith he believed that Christ-likeness was not merely possible, it was the Christian's destiny to be made like Christ, even in the likeness of his resurrection body. Yet Paul realized that there was much still a mystery and many imponderables about the whole human drama and especially about its ending in resurrection, a new creation without disease, decay, death; without suffering, sorrow, or sadness.

Thus he cautioned his converts and all readers of his telling of the tale of human redemption: "For now we see in a mirror dimly; then we will see face to face. Now I know only in part; then I will know fully, even as I have been fully known" (1 Cor. 13:12). The stories Paul tells are not yet over. Though he believes the end is known and the ending seems clear, many of the details are sketchy or are yet to be filled in. The world, Israel, Christ, Christians, all are actors who yet have roles to play in Paul's scripting of the drama, and what may be a foredrawn conclusion in the case of Christ's final role is not so in the case of the other players in the drama. Paul believed in and wrote out of a better world. Who can say with certainty, for all know only in part, that Paul's vision and the stories he told were not true, are not still Good News? I for one believe they are.

I have desired to go,
Where springs not fail,
To fields where flies no sharp and sided hail
And a few lilies blow.

And I have asked to be
Where no storms come,
Where the green swell is in the havens dumb,
And out of the swing of the sea.

—*Gerard Manley Hopkins*
"Heaven-Haven"[238]

20
Synopsis of the Plot
The Story of the Christian

THE story of the Christian is a story that ranges from grace to glory, from new birth to new body. Yet it is a story that does not stand alone; it must be read in the context of the stories of Christ and of the body of Christ. When one is baptized by the Spirit "into Christ," one is in the same act baptized into Christ's body. The story of the one must be seen as an example of the story of the many, though it will have its own individual features. At the same time, the story of the one must be seen as a recapitulation by way of both experience and imitation of the story of the One—the eschatological Adam. The aim of the Christian life is conformity to the image of Christ—in mind, heart, will, and emotions—now through progressive sanctification and ongoing imitation, and in the body later, when Christ returns.

Paul is able to tell this story the way he does because he affirms a limited dualism. A person is not a *soma*; rather, she or he has a *soma*. However, this does not cause Paul to denigrate the body, nor does he conclude that the body plays no part in the redemption of the person. It is the vehicle through which one must strive to act like Christ. Eventually it too will benefit from redemption, though now the believer lives with the tension between flesh and its sinful inclinations and the indwelling Holy Spirit.

When Paul reflects on the drama of his own salvation and that of others, he sees it as encompassing an initial crisis experience involving in the case of Gentiles a turning from idols to the living and true God, and in the case of Jews a moving from being a person under Mosaic law to being a person in Christ. In either case the transvaluation of values is considerable. What the believer becomes in Christ is a new creature, and whatever sort of person one was before is left behind. In the larger sense, the story of Adam

338

is left behind, save for the fact that one continues to live in a fallen body that affects to some degree the whole person. One has the story of Christ recapitulated on a lesser scale in one's own experience involving death to sin, burial with Christ in the Spirit's transforming baptism, and rising to new life so that one can walk in the Spirit and look forward to the redemption of the body. The glory that the believer hopes for is yet to come and goes beyond "Christ in you," which provides the basis of that future hope.

For Paul the Christian story is a story of strenuous effort in striving to press on to the goal of Christlikeness. It is a story in which God takes the initiative, but which requires the believer, in the context of Christ's body, to work out what God has worked in. Christlikeness is not possible without God by the Spirit working in the believer, and in Romans Paul seems to suggest that it is the Spirit who in the end will raise the believer from the dead. But Christlikeness is also not possible without the believer following the moral exemplars set before him or her—chiefly that of Christ, but also Abraham, Paul, and other Christians as well.

Paul believes about Christians that although sinful inclinations remain in the Christian life, due chiefly to having a fallen body that still generates fallen desires, nonetheless sin does not reign in the believer's life. By this Paul means that the believer has a choice about conscious sin, or willful violations of God's revealed will. Further, Paul also believes that although the believer would not be perfect until he or she was perfectly conformed to Christ's image at the resurrection, nonetheless he or she could make progress in the Christian life and have victory over sin by God's enabling grace, as one grows from spiritual infancy to spiritual maturity in Christ.

Yet it must be stressed that Paul does not think this is possible outside the context of the body of Christ. Christians need each other if spiritual growth is to be had. They must build each other up, exhort one another, love each other, and generally exercise and practice the Christian virtues the Spirit is working in them in the context of the *ekklesia*. Believers are and must be dependent on each other, not least because no one Christian has all requisite spiritual gifts to be an independent entity, a body of Christ, on his or her own. For Paul, just as there is no salvation outside of Christ, so too there is no salvation outside of the body of Christ either.

The story of the Christian is then a tale that presupposes and depends upon many other stories—the stories of those saints that have affected the individual and passed on to that person the sacred story of Christ in one way or another. These people are one's spiritual fathers or mothers in the faith. The family of faith is created by sharing the faith resulting in new creatures being born, leading in due course to a set of mutual relationships between brothers and sisters in Christ.

Different things are crucial for different parts of the story. The concept of justification, or faith reckoned as righteousness, is the essential thing one must say about the beginning of the story of a Christian life. It is not, however, the be all and end all of the story; being in Christ and like Christ is the middle and end of the tale. Righteousness through faith comes to the believer because of the faithfulness of Christ, even unto a death on the cross. It is his death and resurrection that makes possible the story of any and every Christian. Without his death, Christians would still be dead in sins; without his resurrection they would have no Holy Spirit and would never walk in newness of life. Christ then stands as the founder of a whole new humanity, the first of many brothers and sisters, the eschatological Adam who blazed a trail that believers must follow. As he was transformed by resurrection, so must they be.

The believer stands between the resurrection and the return of Christ, and so for him or her there is an already and not-yet dimension not only to one's subjective condition, feeling both the desires of the flesh and the leading of the Spirit, but also to the larger cosmic drama of which she or he is a part. If Christ had not come, the believer would not be a believer at all and have the foretastes of glory she or he already has in the Spirit. If, however, Christ does not come again, the goal of conformity to the image of the Son is unattainable. The story of Christ's history is the story of the believer's present experience in part, and the story of his or her destiny when the fullness of the likeness will be put on. Yet even then there will still be the one and the many—the Christ and those individuals who belong to him and by analogy have become like him.

For imitation to be possible there must be both grace and models, both empowerment and memory. Baptism and the Lord's Supper put forth the two most crucial aspects of the Christian story—that one has been joined to the body of Christ in a new spiritual union, and that one experiences ongoing communion with Christ in his body. New nature and ongoing nurture tell the tale of the Christian. Yet what makes the one and the other possible is the Christ event and its retelling, as both baptism and the Lord's Supper depict. The most crucial and formative aspects of the Christ story are reimaged and retold in the sacraments: Christ has died, Christ is risen, and at least in the Lord's Supper, Christ shall come again. The believer as new creature learns to imitate the prayer of Jesus, crying out "Abba, Father" at the Spirit's prompting. But the believer also has another cry as well—"*marana tha*," "Come, Lord." There is both a christological and an ecclesiological already, and a christological and ecclesiological not-yet to be stressed in the Christian story.

The community that cries both "Abba" and "*marana tha*" is at once both inclusive and exclusive. It is inclusive in that neither ethnic, nor sexual, nor social distinctions affect, much less determine, whether one can be in Christ or have equal status in the community once one is in Christ. It is a community of both leaders and followers; yet even the leaders are servants, and headship, if it means anything, is modeled on Christ "who took on the form of a servant."

Yet this community is exclusive as well, for it is a community that believes one must be in Christ to be saved. It is exclusive in that it sets high ethical standards, which are meant to mark it out from a fallen world of sin and sorrow. Without such theological and ethical distinctiveness one loses the sense of one's distinctive identity. One cannot be what one ought to be unless one first knows who one is. The cry "be what you are" presupposes a community of memory who tells the story so all will know who they are, and hence what they may and must be. Thus Paul felt it very necessary to stress that the story of the Christian is a story of passage from darkness to light; from the story of the first Adam to the last; from the story of being an old person, bound in the bondage of sin, to being a new creature in whom the old has passed away in one sense and is passing away in other senses.

Because the believer is indeed called upon to follow the road of the imitation of Christ to the extent that is possible while always still remaining human, the story of the believer in Paul's narrative thought world remains a story yet to be resolved precisely because the story of Christ, in Paul's view, has not yet been fully played out. Golgotha and Easter were in one sense only the beginning of the end of the story, and so believers have only experienced the beginning of the end of their own stories as well. They await the return of the King, with his glorious entourage, whom they will go forth from the earthly city to meet, and then return to earth for the final resolution of all things including final judgment, the death of death, and eternal kingdom.

Until then they live in hope that the story will be finished and turn out well. Until then, they live by faith, their hearts still in pilgrimage. Until then, they set their faces like flint and press on toward their goal. Until then, with one eye on the story of the risen Christ and one eye on their own promised end, they repeat the words of Dylan Thomas, "and death shall have no dominion."

NOTES TO PART 6

"A Good Likeness:" The Story of Christians

1. See, for instance, 2 Cor. 8—9 and my discussion in *Conflict and Community in Corinth: A Socio-Rhetorical Commentary on 1 and 2 Corinthians* (Grand Rapids: Wm. B. Eerdmans, 1994), ad loc.

2. C. S. Lewis, *Poems* (New York: Harcourt, Brace & World, 1964), 110.

3. The next few paragraphs are more fully expounded upon and discussed in a somewhat different form in the introductory section of my *Conflict and Community in Corinth.*

4. For a defense of this traditional summary of the career of Paul, see F. F. Bruce, *Paul: Apostle of the Heart Set Free* (Grand Rapids: Wm. B. Eerdmans, 1977).

5. See M. Hengel, *The Pre-Christian Paul* (Philadelphia: Trinity Press International, 1991), 25ff.

6. Ibid., 30.

7. I believe that Pauline chronology can be figured backward from the date when Paul was likely in Corinth—namely, between A.D. 50–52. See the discussion in the introductory section of my *Conflict and Community in Corinth.* This places Paul's conversion somewhere between A.D. 31 and A.D. 34, perhaps closer to the latter end of that period following Jesus' crucifixion, likely during Passover in A.D. 30. See Hengel, *Pre-Christian Paul*, 63ff.

8. Hengel, *Pre-Christian Paul*, 85.

9. This story may even suggest that Saul took the name in order to aid in the process of converting another Paul, who was a Gentile and a proconsul on Cyprus, Sergius Paulus; cf. Acts 13:7.

10. See the forthcoming collection of essays dealing with such matters, which I am editing for Cambridge University Press. It is titled *The Acts of the Historians.*

11. For example, C. S. Lewis said, when he finally submitted to God, that he was the most reluctant convert in all of Christendom.

12. The Johannine model for conversion uses the language of being "born from above" or being "born of God" by God's Spirit, language that is slightly different from what we find in Paul, who talks about a new creation (cf. 2 Cor. 5:17). The analogy with human birth likewise makes plain that conversion cannot be initiated or caused by mere human will or choosing. One does not make a decision about Christ and then convert oneself; rather, one responds to the grace of God already active in one's life enabling one to repent and believe. In the analogy with birth, the baby does not decide whether and when it will be born; rather, it is an event that happens to one prior to one's conscious choice about the matter. Furthermore, if we may stretch the metaphor, the process of being born can involve a long and arduous labor prior to the birth, or it may happen rather quickly with less difficulty than in some cases. We find these same sort of variables in conversion stories throughout Christian history. The change can be dramatic. Often, however, in the case of those who have grown up in the church and have not willfully strayed from that context, conversion may come simply, without a violent about-face from prior behavior and lifestyle. By recognizing and confirming what God has been doing in one's life for a considerable period of time, one fully accepts and commits oneself to the results of God's work. The crucial thing is the end result, that one be "born of God" or become a "new creation/creature."

13. See pp. 86ff. above.

14. Cf. S. Kim, *The Origins of Paul's Gospel* (Grand Rapids: Wm. B. Eerdmans, 1984); and E. de W. Burton, *A Critical and Exegetical Commentary on the Epistle to the Galatians* (Edinburgh: T. & T. Clark, 1921), 42–43.

15. See A. Segal, *Paul the Convert* (New Haven: Yale Univ. Press, 1990), 117ff.

16. Ibid., 119.

17. G. Lyons, *Pauline Autobiography: Toward a New Understanding* (Atlanta: Scholars Press, 1985), 146, see 146–52.

18. K. L. Schmidt, "*proorizo*," *TDNT* 5 (1967): 456.

19. R. Bultmann, "*ginosko*," *TDNT* 1 (1964): 698.

20. Ibid., 706.

21. Ibid., 715.

22. R. Bultmann, *Theology of the New Testament*, 2 vols. in one (New York: Charles Scribner's Sons, 1951, 1955), 329.

23. See Bultmann, "*ginosko*," 715–16, and the more extensive study in R. T. Forester and V. P. Marston, *God's Strategy in Human History* (Wheaton, Ill.: Tyndale House Publishers, 1973), 178ff.

24. See pp. 57ff. above.

25. W. Sanday and A. C. Headlam, *Romans* (Edinburgh: T. & T. Clark, 1902), 310.

26. J. Murray, *The Epistle to the Romans*, vol. 2 (Grand Rapids: Wm. B. Eerdmans, 1965), 68.

27. See R. N. Longenecker, *Galatians* (Waco, Tex.: Word, 1990), 30.

28. Hengel, *Pre-Christian Paul*, 79.

29. This is also clearly implied in the discussion of the two ministries in 2 Corinthians 3, where Paul stresses that the Mosaic covenant is the old covenant. See my *Conflict and Community in Corinth*, ad loc.

30. Longenecker, *Galatians*, 296.

31. Here "creature" rather than "creation" seems clearly to be a better translation in view of the use of *tis* ("anyone"). See my commentary on this verse in *Conflict and Community in Corinth* on this verse.

32. See Hengel, *Pre-Christian Paul*, 64.

33. Here Segal, *Paul the Convert*, 119ff., misses the mark in suggesting that Paul the convert sees himself as like a Gentile.

34. See my discussion of this term in *Conflict and Community in Corinth*, ad loc.

35. Note the verb tenses in 2 Cor. 5:17. Paul is not saying the old is passing away, but that it has done so.

36. See the discussion above, pp. 142ff.

37. The *houtos kai* means "in this manner we too," indicating the clear parallel between the story of Christ and the story of the Christian—indeed, that the latter is in some sense a representation of the former.

38. See 1 Cor. 1:14–17 and my discussion in *Conflict and Community in Corinth*.

39. See the helpful discussion in J.D.G. Dunn, *Baptism in the Holy Spirit* (London: SCM Press, 1970), 139–46.

40. S. Hafemann, *Suffering and Ministry in the Spirit* (Grand Rapids: Wm. B. Eerdmans, 1990), 58ff. See my *Conflict and Community in Corinth*, ad loc.

41. Notice the use of "Jesus" here, referring to his earthly career.

42. J. T. Fitzgerald, *Cracks in an Earthen Vessel* (Atlanta: Scholars Press, 1988), 179.

43. See the detailed discussion of this in my *Conflict and Community in Corinth*, ad loc., and especially the brilliant treatment of these catalogs in Fitzgerald, *Cracks*.

44. Fitzgerald, *Cracks*, 203ff.

45. On Paul as sage, see my *Jesus the Sage and the Pilgrimage of Wisdom* (Minneapolis: Fortress Press, 1994), chap. 8.

46. Contra Longenecker, *Galatians*, 100–101.

47. *Ta stigmata* means religious tatooing or slave branding; cf. O. Betz, "*stigma*," *TDNT* 7 (1971): 657–64.

48. Longenecker, *Galatians*, 300.

49. But see V. C. Pfitzner, *Paul and the Agon Motif* (Leiden, Neth.: E. J. Brill, 1967).

50. See the discussion in Fitzgerald, *Cracks*, 93ff.

51. Longenecker, *Galatians*, 275–76.

52. A. Malherbe, *Paul and the Popular Philosopher* (Minneapolis: Fortress Press, 1989), 35–48.

53. See my *Conflict and Community in Corinth*, ad loc.

54. T. W. Manson, *The Church's Ministry* (London: SCM Press, 1948), 43–44.

55. See C. K. Barrett, "*Shaliah* and Apostle," in *Donum Gentilicium: New Testament Studies in Honor of David Daube* (Oxford: Oxford University Press, 1978), 88–102.

56. See esp. C. K. Barrett, *The Signs of an Apostle* (London: Epworth Press, 1970).

57. See my *Conflict and Community in Corinth*, ad loc.

58. See E. A. Castelli, *Imitating Paul: A Discourse of Power* (Louisville: Westminster/John Knox Press, 1991), 59ff.

59. See D. B. Martin, *Slavery as Salvation* (New Haven: Yale University Press, 1990).

60. G. M. Styler, "The Basis of Obligation in Paul's Christology and Ethics," in *Christ and Spirit in the New Testament: Studies in Honour of C.F.D. Moule*, ed. B. Lindars and S. S. Smalley (Cambridge: Cambridge University Press, 1973), 175–87, here 186.

61. C. K. Barrett, *From First Adam to Last* (New York: Charles Scribner's Sons, 1962), 105.

62. I. H. Marshall, *Kept by the Power of God* (London: Epworth Press, 1969), 102.

63. See above pp. 227ff.

64. Marshall, *Kept by the Power of God*, 105–6.

65. Ibid.

66. M. Barth, *Ephesians 1–3* (Garden City, N.Y.: Doubleday & Co., 1974), 108. See Barrett, *From First Adam*, 118–19: "The Pauline conception is delicately balanced, and impossible to express in simple and rigid terms. Its delicacy stands out most clearly when it is compared with heavy-handed attempts of later Christian generations to hammer Paul's theology into dogmatics. . . . Predestination becomes a rigid imposition of a numerical class distinction instead of the wrestling of the absolute freedom of God with the limited freedom of [humankind]; eschatology becomes 'the doctrine of the last things' instead of a definition and determination

of the present; the Church and the world begin to glare at each other across an iron curtain. . . . The history of the second century is enough to show how easily and how quickly these perversions and degenerations can take place."

67. See pp. 235ff. above.

68. See S. Fowl, "Some Uses of Story in Moral Discourse: Reflections on Paul's Moral Discourse and Our Own," *Modern Theology* 4, no. 4 (1988): 293–308.

69. Ibid., 296.

70. On "the law of Christ," see above p. 63ff.

71. As the hymn puts it, "Two wonders always I confess; God's great love, my unworthiness."

72. A. Schweitzer, *The Mysticism of Paul the Apostle* (New York: Holt, Rinehart & Winston, 1931), 226.

73. See the discussion above pp. 38ff.

74. See E. P. Sanders, *Paul and Palestinian Judaism* (London: SCM Press, 1977), 453ff.

75. We are not able to engage here in lengthy debate on this matter. For a very helpful discussion of the main proponents of the scholarly debate on "righteousness" in Paul's thought, see S. Westerholm, *Israel's Law and the Church's Faith* (Grand Rapids: Wm. B. Eerdmans, 1988), 70ff.

76. See pp. 163ff. above.

77. Westerholm, *Israel's Law*, 169.

78. Isaiah 5:23, speaking of a human judge; Prov. 17:15, saying God abhors such acquitting of the guilty; Ex. 23:7, where God says, "I will not acquit the guilty."

79. For instance, at Rom. 3:10ff., where Paul quotes Ps. 14:1–3.

80. See Sanders, *Paul*, 434ff.

81. Kim, *The Origins of Paul's Gospel*, 269ff.

82. Here is yet another example of how Paul articulates his storied world in response to varying situations, but those situations have only prompted the articulation, not caused the thoughts.

83. I see no good reason to take the *ek* in *ek pisteos* in any different fashion than the *ek* in *ek Theou*. The believer's faith is being counted as righteousness, and thus in a sense one's righteousness comes from one's faith, rather than from one's works of the law. Cf. Rom. 3:30ff. The *ek* also seems to have a further nuance of "through," as Rom. 3:30 shows.

84. See the discussion in E. Käsemann, *Commentary on Romans* (Grand Rapids: Wm. B. Eerdmans, 1980), 25ff.

85. See pp. 38ff. above.

86. C. K. Barrett, *The Second Epistle to the Corinthians* (New York: Harper & Row, 1973), 180.

87. See pp. 257–58 above.

88. However, it would appear that for Paul right-standing and the new birth happen simultaneously when one first responds to the word with faith.

89. This seems to mean that Christ's righteous life was the prerequisite to his offering an acceptable sacrifice; thus, in one sense the believer is saved by both of these together.

90. C.E.B. Cranfield, *Romans I* (Edinburgh: T. & T. Clark, 1975), 270ff.

91. From *The Harper Book of Christian Poetry*, ed. A. Mercatante (New York: Harper & Row, 1972), 155–56.

92. Bultmann, *Theology of the New Testament*, 330.

93. On this whole passage and its grounding in the stories of Abraham as opposed to the Mosaic covenant, see pp. 54ff. above.

94. Notice the play on words *dia nomou* and *dia nomou pisteos*.

95. Kim, *The Origins of Paul's Gospel*, 270ff.

96. J.D.G. Dunn, *Romans 1–8*, 43.

97. V. P. Furnish, *Theology and Ethics in Paul* (Nashville: Abingdon Press, 1968), 185.

98. Cranfield, *Romans I*, 66.

99. Paul recognizes this, but because having or exercising faith comes from being given the grace to have it or do it, this human response is not seen as meritorious or *the ultimate source of salvation*. It is only the proximate means of salvation.

100. On the above, see P. Minear, *The Obedience of Faith: The Purpose of Paul in the Epistle to the Romans* (London: SCM Press, 1971).

101. R. B. Hays, *The Faith of Jesus Christ* (Chico, Calif.: Scholars Press, 1983); M. D. Hooker, "*Pistis Christou*," in *From Adam to Christ: Essays on Paul* (Cambridge: Cambridge University Press, 1990), 165–86.

102. R. B. Hays, "*PISTIS* and Pauline Christology: What Is at Stake?" *Society of Biblical Literature 1991 Seminar Papers*, 714–29. See also the critique that follows in the same publication by J.D.G. Dunn, "Once More, *PISTIS CHRISTOU*," 730–44.

103. To translate it "the one who has faith in Jesus" ignores the *ek* altogether.

104. Hays, "*PISTIS*," 722.

105. See pp. 52ff. above.

106. Longenecker, *Galatians*, 87–88. He also includes the reference in Gal. 2:16.

107. Cranfield, *Romans I*, 91ff.

108. For this translation, see Dunn, *Romans 1–8*, 44. Unlike some, I have no qualms about believing that for Paul God's faithfulness could be equated with Christ's faithfulness, not only because the former is expressed through the latter's life and death, but also because, as Rom. 9:5 shows, Paul includes Christ in his definition of deity; cf. 1 Cor. 8:6 and pp. 114ff. above.

109. Hays, "*PISTIS*," 718.

110. One may compare their respective commentaries on this point.

111. Notice the verb tenses: the old order "passed away" (aorist); the new "has already come" (perfect tense verb).

112. That is, there is no necessary coupling of the two; cf. my article "Rite and Rights for Women—Gal. 3:28," *New Testament Studies* 27 (1981): 593–604.

113. See the discussion of spiritual gifts below, pp. 285ff.

114. Barrett, From *First Adam*, 110.

115. See my *Jesus, Paul, and the End of the World* (Downers Grove, Ill.: I-V Press, 1992), 184ff.

116. See below, pp. 279ff.

117. Furnish, *Theology and Ethics*, 176.

118. G. Vos, *The Pauline Eschatology*, rpr. (Grand Rapids: Wm. B. Eerdmans, 1972), 46–47.

119. *The Poems of George Herbert* (London: Oxford University Press, 1961), 57.

120. Cf. pp. 23ff. above.

121. Cranfield, *Romans I*, 122.

122. See my extended argument in *Conflict and Community in Corinth*, ad loc.

123. C. K. Barrett, *The First Epistle to the Corinthians*, 151.

124. See pp. 297ff. below.

125. See pp. 116ff. above.

126. On whether Paul believes that there are mysteries of wisdom beyond the basic belief in Christ, which are revealed to the more mature, see my *Jesus the Sage*, chap. 8. The short answer is yes, he does believe such things, as 1 Cor. 15:51 shows.

127. Some still take this as a partitive genitive—the first fruits of the Spirit—implying that the Spirit may be divided up and parceled out. Another possibility would be to take it as a subjective genitive—the Spirit's firstfruits; the present work in the believer is but the firstfruits of salvation. Undoubtedly, the latter makes better sense here than the former, but I think the epexegetical sense makes the best sense.

128. Notice how the Spirit is also the enabler who helps the believer to confess from his or her heart and mean "Jesus is Lord" (1 Cor. 12:3).

129. See pp. 263ff. above.

130. There are other possibilities. See my discussion in *Conflict and Community in Corinth*, ad loc.

131. Barrett, *First Corinthians*, 294.

132. *Kuberneseis* means literally "steerings." Is this administration, or guidance, or counseling?

133. Barrett, *First Corinthians*, 197.

134. The grammatical structure is such that the phrase "in our own languages" qualifies the speaking, not merely the hearing; thus it would seem that this rules out the view that in Acts 2 there were two miracles: (1) speaking in glossolalia; (2) hearing in one's native tongue.

135. There is evidence that having such a gift was seen as a status indicator in antiquity, and there is no doubt that some Corinthians were very status conscious. See D. B. Martin, "Tongues of Angels and Other Status Indicators," *Journal of the American Academy of Religion* 59 (1992): 547–89.

136. It may be a sign of judgment or condemnation to an unbeliever that he or she is not spiritual, not a Christian.

137. See my *Conflict and Community in Corinth* on 1 Corinthians 14.

138. If Acts is any guide, it could also involve foretelling; see Acts 11:27–28.

139. Though it appears we have a few samples of prophetic utterance of the sort Paul is talking about in his letters, in general the New Testament is not peppered with such material. I am skeptical about the arguments of E. Boring and others that a good deal of the gospel logia comes from early Christian prophets. See my *The Christology of Jesus* (Minneapolis: Fortress Press, 1990), 4ff.

140. In John Donne, *The Complete English Poems*, 310.

141. See above pp. 000.

142. On these terms it is still useful to consult R. Jewett, *Paul's Anthropological Terms* (Leiden, Neth.: E. J. Brill, 1971), although the book is marred by now outdated assumptions about Gnosticism in the first century and questionable partitionings of various of Paul's letters. The lengthy discussions by Bultmann in his *Theology of the New Testament* are also still profitable.

143. "God gave them up to a base mind because they refused to acknowledge God" (Rom. 1:28).

144. For a more detailed discussion of this term, see my *Conflict and Community in Corinth* on 1 Corinthians 3; and see B. Pearson, *The Pneumatikos-Psychikos Terminology in 1 Corinthians* (Missoula, Mont.: Society of Biblical Literature, 1973).

145. The verb implies repeatedly, not progressively.

146. R. H. Gundry, *SOMA in Biblical Theology (with Emphasis on Pauline Anthropology* (Cambridge: Cambridge University Press, 1976), 79ff.

147. Ibid., 139.

148. These verses makes quite clear Paul's anthropological dualism. See my *Jesus, Paul, and the End*, 185ff.

149. Gundry, *SOMA*, 156.

150. Ibid., 57.

151. See the discussion of Romans 7, pp. 000 above.

152. Gundry, *SOMA*, 79–80.

153. Sanders, *Paul*, 497ff.

154. Burton, *Galatians*, 302.

155. F. F. Bruce, *Commentary on Galatians* (Grand Rapids: Wm. B. Eerdmans, 1982), 244, emphasis added.

156. "Live by the Spirit and do not gratify the desires of the flesh."

157. See Longenecker, *Galatians*, 244.

158. Bruce, *Galatians*, 245.

159. The "already" dimension of the kingdom that the believer experiences in the present has to do with things like the peace or joy the Holy Spirit can convey to the believer. See my discussion in *Jesus, Paul, and the End*, 59ff.

160. Though with a different Greek word—*epieikeia*.

161. Bruce, *Galatians*, 255.

162. Ibid.

163. Though this may mean all Paul's assemblies.

164. In Phil. 3:6 it may simply mean the corporate entity, the assembly writ large.

165. W. A. Meeks, *The First Urban Christians* (New Haven: Yale University Press, 1983), 75. In what follows we will largely be interacting with this seminal work by Meeks. See also R. Banks, *Paul's Idea of Community: The Early House Churches in Their Historical Setting* (Grand Rapids: Wm. B. Eerdmans, 1980).

166. Meeks, *First Urban Christians*, 75–76.

167. Ibid., 76.

168. Barrett, *First Corinthians*, 115.
169. And of course in the later Paulines: 1 Tim. 3:1ff.; Titus 1:1ff.
170. See my *Women in the Earliest Churches* (Cambridge: Cambridge Univ. Press, 1980), 78ff.
171. Meeks, *First Urban Christians*, 78.
172. Ibid., 80.
173. Ibid.
174. When we get to the latest Pauline letters, the pastorals, it appears an effort was made to firm up a sort of structure that would last beyond the apostolic age. First Timothy 3 speaks of *diakonos* and *episkopos*, but is frustrating because the writer tells us only what sort of persons they should be; the writer does not give a job description. Titus is a bit more helpful. *Presbuteroi* are to be appointed/ ordained in every town. Notice that he does not say in every congregation. Perhaps this role of "elder" is modeled on the elder of the synagogue, but it appears here that he is to be in charge of, or preside over, or oversee more than one *ekklesia* (or was there only one in each town in Crete?). In any case, here as in Acts and at 2 Tim. 1:6 we are told of a process of appointment/ordination that at least at 2 Tim. 1:6 involves a conferring of gifts through the ordination rite. It is also likely that the *presbuteros* of Titus 1:5 is also the *episkopos* of 1:7—the latter verse explaining his function to oversee. We are not told, however, more than what his character must be like and that he must be orthodox and able to encourage with sound doctrine and engage in apologetics. Titus 2:1ff. may suggest that these elders were the older (in age) members of the assembly, at least usually.
175. Ibid., 133–34.
176. See my discussion in *Conflict and Community in Corinth* in the introduction to 1 Corinthians.
177. Meeks, *First Urban Christians*, 136, says: "Instead, I have proposed a simpler and more flexible, tripartite classification of the modes of authority exercised by various people in the local communities: visible manifestations of Spirit-possession, position, and association with apostles and other supra-local persons of authority. These were not mutually exclusive, but tensions and conflicts could arise among them."
178. On boundary markers, see my discussion of 1 Corinthians 5 in *Conflict and Community in Corinth*.
179. See Pliny's famous letter to the Emperor Trajan—10.96.
180. See my discussion on this passage in *Conflict and Community in Corinth*.
181. G. Theissen, *The Social Setting of Pauline Christianity* (Philadelphia: Fortress Press, 1982), 145–74.
182. Meeks, *First Urban Christians*, 159.
183. See my discussions in *Conflict and Community in Corinth*, ad loc.
184. Ibid.
185. See my discussion in *Jesus the Sage*, chap. 7.
186. See Meeks, *First Urban Christians*, 145.
187. Ibid., 146.
188. See my discussions in *Women in the Earliest Churches*, 90ff.

189. See my discussion of 1 Cor. 11—14 in *Conflict and Community in Corinth.*
190. See my excursus on prophecy in 1 Corinthians 14 in *Conflict and Community in Corinth.*
191. Cf. vv. 9–10. Was this merely extravagant dress, or was it worldly dress in a liberated or immoral sense?
192. See my *Women in the Earliest Churches*, 121–22.
193. See my article "Right and Rites for Women," 593–604.
194. These implications were later understood rather well. See the second century Acts of Paul and Thecla.
195. See N. A. Dahl, *Studies in Paul* (Minneapolis: Augsburg Publishing House, 1977), 40ff.
196. Meeks, *First Urban Christians*, 147.
197. Ibid., 149.
198. On this ritual, in light of its Greco-Roman context, see my *Conflict and Community in Corinth*, ad loc.
199. Dunn, *Baptism in the Holy Spirit*, 139–46.
200. A role played by the Holy Spirit, not baptism.
201. Meeks, *First Urban Christians*, 150.
202. Ibid., 153.
203. Ibid., 157.
204. From *The Poems of George Herbert*, 180.
205. See my discussion of 1 Cor. 11:17ff. in *Conflict and Community in Corinth.*
206. Meeks, *First Urban Christians*, 158.
207. Ibid., 159–60.
208. He does not say, "This becomes Christ's body," or on the other end of the spectrum, "This merely symbolizes Christ's body."
209. Meeks, *First Urban Christians*, 163.
210. The *kai* seems clearly to be a later addition and is not even discussed in Metzger's *Textual Commentary*. The word "only" is not in the Greek text at all.
211. G. F. Hawthorne, *Philippians* (Waco, Tex.: Word, 1983), 99.
212. Ibid., 100.
213. Barrett, *First Corinthians*, 165.
214. This is what the apostolic decree in Acts 15 was in essence about as well—a prohibition of idolatry and immorality. See my article "Not So Idle Thoughts About *Eidolothuton*" in the November 1993 issue of *Tyndale Bulletin.*
215. Meeks, *First Urban Christians*, 181.
216. See pp. 81ff. above.
217. This verse does not likely mean that the believer can accomplish anything, but rather that she or he cannot be deflected by circumstances from her or his Christian life and from making progress in it. The power of the Spirit allows the believer to endure whatever the world throws at her or him.
218. See Fowl, "Some Uses of Story," 295: "For the Christian community, the canonical texts provide the church with stories about reality and their place in it. It is in remembering, interpreting and discussing of these stories that we are able to discern what sort of people we ought to be. Our moral discourse then becomes intelligible to the extent to which we order our lives in a manner appropriate to the

identity provided for us by these narratives. Ethical problems, then, are not just questions of decision, but of description and interpretation."

219. From *The Poems of Gerard Manley Hopkins*, ed. W. H. Gardner and N. H. MacKenzie (London: Oxford University Press, 1967), 105–6.

220. See Davidson, "Some Aspects of the OT," 385.

221. C. H. Dodd, *Gospel and Law* (Cambridge: Cambridge University Press, 1951), 36–37.

222. It appears clear that there were several views about resurrection in Corinth. See my discussion of 1 Corinthians 15 in *Conflict and Community in Corinth.*

223. A. Robertson and A. Plummer, *The First Epistle of St. Paul to the Corinthians* (Edinburgh: T. & T. Clark, 1914), 350.

224. Barrett, *First Corinthians*, 350.

225. See pp. 142ff. above.

226. For fuller discussion, see my *Jesus, Paul, and the End*, 196ff.

227. Most conveniently found in W. D. Davies, *Paul and Rabbinic Judaism* (New York: Harper & Row, 1970), 304.

228. F. F. Bruce, *First and Second Corinthians*, 151.

229. Davies, *Paul and Rabbinic Judaism*, 308.

230. Cf. 2 Cor. 4—5 and Rom. 8:23—the redemption of our bodies.

231. Robertson and Plummer, *The First Epistle of St. Paul to the Corinthians*, 377.

232. The last two paragraphs appear in another form in my *Jesus, Paul, and the End*, 209ff.

233. Cf. Ex. 4:22; Ps. 89:27—David as "firstborn," when of course he was not his father's firstborn.

234. Cf. 1 Cor. 15:15 and 1 Cor. 6:14. It was God who raised Jesus from the dead, though see 1 Thess. 4:14.

235. Cranfield, *Romans I*, 147.

236. See my more detailed discussion of the scholarly debate in *Jesus, Paul, and the End*, 203ff.

237. On this whole subject, see A. T. Lincoln, *Paradise Now and Not Yet* (Cambridge: Cambridge Univ. Press, 1981).

238. *The Poems of Gerard Manley Hopkins*, 19.

Epilogue
The Tapestry Complete

PAUL'S storied world is complex and involves many persons and events. There are numerous subplots within the main story lines, although the basic contours of the larger story are reasonably clear. Paul is concerned about the drama of human redemption, and all other stories are mentioned only as they have bearing on this fundamental drama. The story is progressive rather than cyclical; it is also teleological—driving forward toward the goal of the return of Christ, the resurrection of believers, the coming of the kingdom on earth, and thus the new creation. The story is basically about the points of intersection between the story of God and the story of humankind. More particularly, it is about the intervention of God in time and space to create a people redeemed from the darkness of a fallen world.

For Paul, there are certain key figures involved in this drama: Adam, Abraham, Moses, Christ, and those in Christ, including Paul himself. The agent of change, the one who transforms the story twice over, is Christ. His coming, his death, his resurrection and exaltation, and his return trigger the eschatological age's onset (first coming) and completion (second coming). The story of Christ is so critical for Paul that he reads all the other stories in light of it, yet it is also true that he reads the story of Christ in light of the Hebrew scriptures, Christian tradition, and his own personal experiences.

The keys to understanding Paul's reading of the drama of redemption are several: (1) One must recognize that Christ has a role not only in the story of humankind but also in the story of God and thus is able to bring the two stories together in his own person and work. He is the mediator between the two tales. (2) For Paul, the new covenant is the fulfillment of the Abrahamic covenant, with Christ being the ultimate seed of Abraham. This means that the story of Christians, like the story of Abraham, must be a story about faith before faithfulness, grace before grateful response. (3) For Paul, Christ is the eschatological Adam who successfully does what Adam failed to do—obey God, even unto death—and thus is able to be a life-giving Spirit as a result of God's vindication of Christ by means of resurrection. Christ's atoning death is the critical event that allows God to be both just and the justifier of fallen human beings through Christ. (4) In view of (2) and (3), when Paul thinks of the story of Moses he sees the Mosaic covenant as an interim arrangement meant to guard and confine God's people until the coming of Messiah. The Law, though holy, just, and good, could not give life. Indeed, its effect on fallen humankind was death dealing, not life giving. When Christ came, this covenant became obsolete, a glorious anachronism that had had its day and was ceasing to be. When Paul thinks of Adam he thinks of sin; when he thinks of Abraham he thinks of faith; when he thinks of Moses he thinks of Law; and when he thinks of Christ he thinks of grace and redemption.

For the apostle to the Gentiles, the drama of redemption also has cosmic dimensions, not only because of the origins and current dwelling place of Christ, but also because powers and principalities, including especially Satan, have a role to play in the story. To rectify the human situation, Christ must overcome these forces as well as the misdeeds of human beings. In addition, creation as well as creatures must be redeemed, for creation also has felt the effects of the Fall—disease, decay, death. The story of redemption then is a comprehensive one involving the whole material world and all created beings—in particular, angels and human beings.

In Paul's reading of the human story there are dramatic turning points in the story: first with Adam and his sin; then with Abraham and his faith; then with Christ and his death and resurrection; then with believers who by being made new creatures leave behind the story of Adam, and in some cases the story of Moses, and enter the realm where the story of Christ controls and is to be emulated.

The imitation of Christ, both in experience and behavior, is what dictates how Paul tells the story of Christians. They are initially buried with Christ and die to sin, but they eventually will be conformed fully to Christ's image by means of resurrection. In the interim, Christian behavior amounts to walking in the Spirit with one eye on the Christ, and keeping the law of Christ. Both Christian belief and Christlike behavior are expected of Christ's followers. The end result of this is not the deification of the believer but rather his or her glorification, taking on the moral and later the bodily likeness of the risen, glorious Christ. The delay in the completion of being conformed to Christ's likeness until his return means that the believer not only lives in a dark world, but even in himself feels the tension between fallen flesh and fleshly inclinations and the leading of the Holy Spirit.

Paul's letters reflect the fact that for Paul neither the story of Christ nor the story of Christians has yet been completed. There is an already and not-yet dimension to both of these stories, and for that matter the story of the larger world, the form of which is passing away but is not yet gone. This incompletion is not because Paul believes that the story of Christ and the story of Christians is a never-ending story, though that is in one sense true. Nor does the incompletion come from the fact that Paul has doubts about or feels ignorant of how the story of human redemption will end. Paul is quite confident that Christ will complete his role in the drama of redemption.

What finally adds drama to the story for Paul is that because his understanding of election is corporate, it is not known how the story will turn out for individual Christians or non-Christians. Some of the saved may yet apostasize, and some of the lost will yet be saved; thus the individual's response to grace is both critical and necessary. One is not eternally secure until one is securely in eternity. This is why Paul's letters are filled with earnest and sometimes polemical exhortations urging his converts to conform to the positive exemplars whose stories they know and to shun the examples of previous believers whose salvation was incomplete and who ended up outside the "Israel of God" (cf. 1 Corinthians 10).

The script of salvation is clear enough, and the hope of glory has a firm basis for those in Christ; but because life goes on there is always danger for the saved and opportunity for the lost. The door into the community of faith is not a one-way door. In other words, for Paul ethics is not merely grounded in the story and example of Christ; it is the necessary development of that story. Just as Christ's own faithfulness and obedience were required for salvation to be made available to all, so the believer's faithfulness and obedience are required if they are to work out their salvation with fear and trembling and so attain to the resurrection. Imitation of Christ is more than a mere formality; it is required. Initial justification in God's sight is a free gift received through grace, but what one does with that gift thereafter is critical.

Paul's story of redemption, then, is not just about the actions of God. Although the divine initiative and divine grace are clearly the dominant themes in the story, it is also about the responses and responsibilities of human beings. There are for the living still some loose ends in the tapestry, some parts to be played in the drama. The full number of Gentiles and even "all Israel" are yet to be redeemed. This means that there are still stories to be told and lived out. The tapestry of life involves both tragedy and triumph, but for those who are in and remain in Christ this tapestry tells a tale of good news. It is here where the Pauline emphasis rightly lies in the telling of the tale. On the opposite page is a diagram of The Tapestry Complete. We leave the reader with this visual image of the narrative thought world portrayed on this Pauline tapestry.

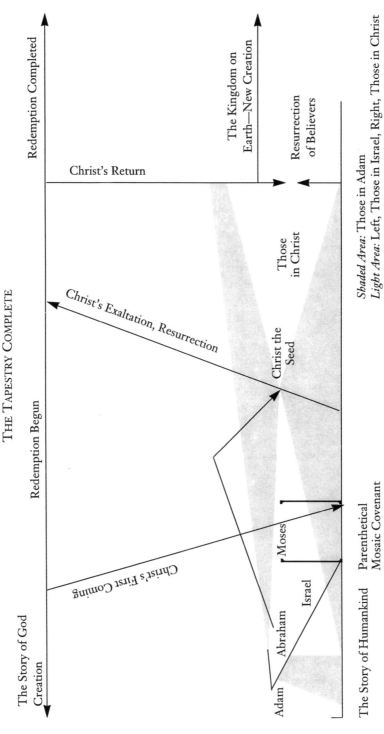

THE TAPESTRY COMPLETE

The Story of God

Creation

Redemption Begun

Redemption Completed

Christ's First Coming

Christ's Exaltation, Resurrection

Christ's Return

The Kingdom on
Earth—New Creation

Resurrection
of Believers

Those
in Christ

Christ the
Seed

Adam

Abraham

Israel

Moses

Parenthetical
Mosaic Covenant

The Story of Humankind

Shaded Area: Those in Adam
Light Area: Left, Those in Israel, Right, Those in Christ

Scripture Index

Old Testament

Genesis

1-3	144
1	312
2	143
2:7	143
3	25
6:1-4	18
9:6-7	46
12	49, 50
12-22	41, 42
12:2-3	41, 48
14	41
15	41, 43, 47, 49, 50, 75 n.7, 76 n.12
15-17	42
15:6	41, 43, 44, 46
16	41
17	41, 46, 47, 49, 50, 75 n.7; 76 n.12
17:6-7	46, 47
17:10ff.	47
18	41
18:19	228
18:25	257
19	41
21:8-21	41
21:12	46
22	41, 42, 49
22:16	41

Exodus

1:8ff.	79 n.61
4:22	351 n.233
7:3, 13-14	79 n.61
8:15, 32	79 n.61
9:7, 12	79
9:27	257
9:34-35	79 n.61
10:20, 27	79 n.61
11:10	79 n.61
12:13	164
14:4, 17	79 n.61
19	188
19:5	68
23:7	345 n.78
23:16, 19	176
24:5-8	164
31:18	53
34	53
34:29	53

Leviticus

4:32	155 n.29
5:6-7, 11	155 n.29
16:3, 5, 9	155 n.29
17:11	167
18:5	48
23:10	176

Numbers

6:16	155 n.29
7:16	155 n.29
16:46ff.	164
18:8, 12	176

Deuteronomy

21:22	87
21:23	48, 133
25:4	63
27:26	48
30:13-14	67
32:21	67

1 Samuel

7:5	70
25:1	70

2 Samuel
7:14   154 n.4

1 Kings
12:1   70

2 Chronicles
12:1   70
29:23-24   155 n.29

Ezra
7:19   188

Job
28   120 n.25

Psalms
2:7   154 n.4
8   95, 141
14:1-3   345 n.79
16:10   175
24:5   257
24:7-10   194
32:1, 2   167
51:4   257
62:12   199
89:27   108, 351 n.233
98:2   257
103:6   257
110   95
139:2   228

Proverbs
1   92, 120 n.25
1:32   92
2:6   92
3   52
3:13-18   92
3:19   92
4:10-27   92
6:6   92
8-9   52
8   75 n.5, 82, 92,
                120 n.25
8:1-5   92
8:4, 31-36   92

8:22-29   92
8:22   92
9   92, 120 n.25
9:1-6   92
11:16   249
17:15   345n.78
24:12   199

Isaiah
2   188
5:23   345 n.78
11:4   196
22:5   188
26:19   172
27:9   71
27:13   194
28:11-12   64, 288
34:8   188
44:9-20   113
45   123 n.48
45:21ff.   103
46:13   257
49:1-6   232
53   100, 133
53:12   174
54:7   175
59:20-21   71

Jeremiah
1:5   228, 232
10:1-16   113
11:16   69
11:20   257
18   58

Daniel
2:47   181
5:23   181
7   155 n.17
7:21-22   195
9:11   70
12:1-3   172

Hosea
1:10   68
2:23   68

14:6   69

Joel
2   188
2:1   194

Amos
3:2   230
4:11   198
5:18   188

Habakkuk
2:4   271

Zephaniah
1:2-3   188
1:15   199
1:18   188, 199
2:2-3   199
3:8   199

Zechariah
7:2   163
8:22   163
9:14   194
14:2   187, 188, 193
14:5   192

Malachi
1:2f.   61
1:9   163
4:5-6   188

New Testament

Matthew
1   139
3:9   61
5:29f.   162
5:38-40   152
10:10   152
10:22   59
12:11   152
12:32   162
15:2   320
18:8f.   162

20:1-16	153	2:11	288		175, 177, 283,	
24	195	2:22-36	89		332	
24:13	59	2:25	227	1:3	87, 134, 183	
24:31	195	2:31	227, 228	1:4	86, 172	
24:43f.	149	2:46	121 n.34	1:5	266, 267	
27:52-53	177	3:13-16	89	1:7	68, 308	
28:41, 46	162	4:10-12	89	1:8	266	
		5:20	121 n.34	1:9	117	
Mark		5:30-32	89	1:16	59, 72, 84, 134	
1:15	148, 149, 153	7:47ff.	121 n.34	1:17	259, 271	
10:45	153	9	218–25	1:17-18	160	
13	195	9:7	223, 224	1:18–3:26	161	
13:13	59	9:15	226	1:18-32	2	
13:32	149	13:7	342 n.9	1:18	21, 195, 278	
14:25	204	13:9	222	1:20	70	
14:26	117	13:46	68	1:21	291	
14:36	153	14:23	303	1:24	291	
		15	350 n.214	1:25	22	
Luke		16:37	216	1:28	348 n.143	
2	139	17:23	113	1:29-31	297	
3:8	61	17:28	216	2-3	25	
4:22	149	18:6	89	2	57	
7:42	153	20:7	308	2:2-3	198	
10:7	152	20:28	121 n.34	2:4	298	
12:39f.	149	21:8	287	2:5-16	202	
14:15-24	204	21:17ff.	221	2:5	197, 198, 291	
15:11-32	153	21:29	227	2:6-8	22	
16:16, 23-25	162	22	218–25	2:6	161	
18:14	152	22:9	223, 224	2:7-10	202	
21	195	22:14	226	2:7	332	
21:28	157 n.56	23:6-8	172	2:8	161	
24:24	79 n.84	23:8	217	2:9	22, 162, 292	
		26	218–25	2:11	161	
John		26:10-11	218	2:12-16	17	
1	83, 95, 96, 97	26:11	218	2:12	22	
1:14	121 n.35	26:14	221, 223	2:13	262	
10:14	335	27:1	221	2:14-15	26, 27	
11:27-28	347 n.138	28:28	89	2:15	22, 34 n.44	
12:31	19			2:16	198	
14:2	335	*Romans*		2:17-24	64	
16:11	19	1-3	290	2:28-29	46	
		1	18, 84, 173	2:29	57, 291	
Acts		1:1	183, 232, 234	3-4	256	
1:23	227	1:2	130	3:1	217	
2	347 n.134	1:3-4	112, 117, 118,	3:2	58	
2:5ff.	121 n.34		128 n.121, 130,	3:3	268	

Romans (Cont.)

3:5   162
3:9   22, 290
3:10-19   64
3:21   70
3:21-24   42, 44, 64
3:22   76 n.13, 268,
       269, 270
3:23-24   43
3:23   22, 29, 153, 290,
       332
3:24   253, 268
3:25-26   259
3:25   44, 163, 164,
       167, 237
3:26   268
3:27ff.   264
3:28-30   42
3:30   298, 345 n.83
4   40, 41, 43, 50, 64,
       258
4:1   76 n.9, 142, 143
4:3   44, 61, 261, 265
4:4   252
4:4-5   44
4:5   265
4:6   61, 233
4:7-8   167
4:8   61
4:11   47, 240
4:11-12   41, 76 n.12
4:11-26   76 n.12
4:13   45
4:16   41, 268
4:17   233
4:18   269
4:19   44
4:23-24   44
4:24   265
4:24-25   172, 177
5   290
5:1-2   253, 264
5:1   278
5:2   166, 298, 332
5:5   297
5:6   250

5:6-8   168
5:8   164, 167
5:9   162, 167
5:10   117, 118
5:11   298
5:12-21   9, 15, 25
5:12   11, 14, 22, 139,
       144, 252
5:15   141
5:17-19   134, 144, 145
5:17   23, 146
5:18   261
5:19   144, 145
5:20-21   253
5:20   161
5:21   23, 278
6:1-14   314, 316
6:1   43, 279
6:2-4   235
6:3-4   266
6:4   278
6:4-9   172, 177, 178
6:6   280, 290, 294, 295
6:8   265, 278
6:10-11   323
6:10   168
6:12   290
6:14ff.   251, 314
6:16   183
6:17   23, 290
6:19   290
6:20   23, 290
6:23   252
7   74, 139, 140,
       155 n.28, 295,
       296, 348 n.143
7:1-4   65
7:4   65, 78 n.43, 172
7:5-6   23, 25
7:5   66, 293
7:6   66
7:7-13   14, 15, 24,
       31 n.10
7:7   78 n.43
7:7, 12   40, 43, 64
7:8-11   14

7:10   43
7:12, 14   52
7:13   34 n.44
7:14-25   15, 22–24, 26,
       29, 34 n.46, 145
7:18   102, 294
7:21   27, 34 n.44, 43,
       64
7:22-23   294
7:22   33 n.43, 276
7:23-25   293
7:23   291, 293
7:24–8:10   27
7:24   295
7:25   28, 278, 291,
       293
8   12, 28, 200
8:1-17   24
8:2   25–27, 64
8:2-9   25
8:3   118, 134, 139,
       140, 290, 294
8:4   140, 294
8:5-15   34 n.46
8:5   117, 291, 294
8:6   346 n.109
8:7   26
8:8, 9   23, 25
8:9   285, 294
8:10   25, 136
8:11   116, 330
8:12-18   332
8:15   115, 117, 153,
       315
8:17   277
8:18-25   171
8:18   194
8:19ff.   29
8:20-22   84
8:20-21   204
8:20ff.   273
8:22   25
8:23-29   179
8:23   176, 284, 324,
       330, 332,
       351 n.230

8:24	118	10:4	54, 56, 65	12:5	281
8:28-30	78 n.59	10:5	40, 48	12:6-8	285, 287
8:29-30	230, 231, 246	10:5-9	67	12:6	252, 289
8:29	101, 118, 173,	10:8	291	12:8	303
	227, 228, 230,	10:9	178, 181, 183,	12:19-21	152
	324, 330, 331		265–267	13	191, 198, 216
8:32	41, 117, 118,	10:10	291	13:1	292
	164, 254	10:11	265	13:1-2	16
8:33-34	262	10:12	248	13:3-4	161
8:33	178	10:14-21	67	13:7	152
8:34	178	10:14	33 n.34, 265	13:8-10	64
8:35-39	232	10:14-15	239	13:9	64
8:38	17, 32 n.25	10:16	265, 267	13:11-14	68, 199, 202
8:39	278	11	59, 60, 217	13:11	157 n.55, 331
9-11	2, 25, 45, 49, 50,	11:1-10	67	13:12	197
	56, 58–60, 66, 72,	11:1-3	230	13:13	297
	76 n.19, 78 n.45,	11:1-2	68	11:15-17	69
	130, 140, 206, 230,	11:1	40, 45	11:19	69
	232, 246	11:2	227	11:24	69
9	41, 42, 43, 57, 66	11:5-7	248, 251	13:4	298
9:1-5	22, 45	11:5	252	13:16	69
9:3	60, 163	11:6	68	14.1ff.	266
9:4	40, 47, 58, 60	11:7	53	14:6	287, 289
9:5	76 n.16, 84,	11:11	58	14:9	178, 183
	111, 112, 134,	11:13	130	14:10-12	201
	346 n.109	11:16-18	45	14:17	116, 153, 298
9:6-15	40, 43, 57, 61	11:21-22	201	15:1-3	323
9:6, 7	38	11:21	232	15:1	298
9:6	248	11:22	298	15:3	123 n.46, 238
9:7	46	11:23	267	15:7	323
9:8	46, 60, 61	11:25-32	70	15:8	133, 238
9:9	47	11:25-26	130, 133	15:9-10	259, 261
9:14	43	11:25	53	15:12	130
9:18	62, 248	11:26	70, 71, 248	15:14	310
9:20-21	58	11:27	71	15:15	252
9:21-24	62	11:28	248	15:16-17	134
9:22-23	161	11:28-29	58	15:16	116
9:22	298	11:30	267	15:18	267
9:24-26	68	12-14	152	15:33	298
9:30	43, 63	12	252, 280, 282, 303,	16:1	302
9:30—10:4	258		304	16:2	304
9:33	265	12:2	20, 25, 276, 291,	16:4	292
10	63		293, 323	16:5	300
10:1-2	66	12:3-7	302	16:19	266, 278
10:1	291	12:3	252	16:20	19, 298
10:3	79 n.63, 264	12.4ff.	280	16:23	300, 304, 308

1 Corinthians
1:2   116, 278, 308
1:4   252
1:7   201, 322
1:8   198–201
1:9   116, 118
1:14-17   279, 314,
                 343 n.38
1:17   135
1:18   327
1:20   20
1:23   133, 135
1:24   82, 111
1:30   52, 111, 238
2:1   302
2:2   269
2:5   266
2:6-16   283
2:11   292
2:12   254, 292
2:14   292
3   148 n.144, 188
3:1-2   241
3:1   136, 278, 302, 323
3:9-10   282
3:10-15   162, 242
3:10   252, 322
3:13   197, 198
3:14   322
3:15   198, 322
3:16   282
4:2   76 n.11, 242
4:4   259
4:8   324
4:9-13   237
4:9   237
4:10   238
4:12   238
4:14   302
4:15   240, 302
4:16   243
4:20   153
5-11   326
5   349 n.178
5:3-5   292
5:4-5   303

5:5   19, 163, 197, 199
5:7   51, 77 n.33, 135,
                       164
5:9-13   297
5:9ff.   322
6.1ff.   322
6:2-3   203
6:3   18, 175
6:4   172
6:9ff.   297
6:11   262
6:12-20   294, 318
6:14   174, 351 n.234
6:15-17   277, 282
6:19   282, 335
6:20   135, 183
7   312
7:1   253
7:5   19, 32 n.22
7:7   252
7:9   299
7:10   151
7:11   327
7:14   321
7:15   298
7:16   321
7:17   321
7:22   183
7:23   135
7:26   194
7:31   9, 84
7:39   278
8:1   113
8:3   113
8:4   113
8:5-6   181, 183
8:5   113
8:6   3, 84, 111, 113,
                    210
8:12   290
8:15   292
9:1   84, 182
9:9   63
9:14   152
9:15-18   243
9:19ff.   216

9:20   55, 64, 235, 239,
                       240
9:21   56
9:22   68
9:24-27   239
9:25   299
9:27   201
10-11   307, 317, 319
10   51, 88, 354
10:1-12   314
10:1-5   2
10:1ff.   310
10:4   3, 51, 81, 111,
                      115
10:6   38
10:9   51
10:11   20, 38
10:12-13   21, 27
10:16   277
10:17   318
10:20-21   18, 84
10:20   277
10:21   306, 318
10:27   322
10:33—11:1   240
11-14   349 n.189
11   310
11:1   214, 239, 243
11:2-16   12
11:2   152, 300
11:3   282
11:5   303, 311
11:7   10, 332
11:8   10, 292
11:10   18
11:12   10
11:16   300
11:17   307, 317
11:18   265, 307, 308
11:20   307
11:21-24   303
11:23-26   164
11:23   141, 151, 289
11:27ff.   308
11:29   318
11:30ff.   326

11:33, 34	307	14:34ff.	311	15:42-44	329
12-14	252, 287, 303	14:37-38	243	15:43	331
12	280, 281–82, 303	14:40	310	15:44-49	142, 143
12:1-3	20	15	12, 82, 107, 135,	15:44	292
12:2	18		144, 170, 172–174,	15:45-49	30 n.5
12:3	87, 181, 183,		177, 193, 197, 199,	15:45	116, 141, 283,
	279, 284, 286,		200, 203, 208, 289,		292
	347 n.128		332, 351 n.222	15:46	292
12:5	279	15:1-11	2	15:47	330
12:7	286	15:1-10	89	15:48	175, 335
12:8-10	285, 286	15:2ff.	265	15:50	163, 326
12:9	263	15:3-8	170	15:51	328, 330,
12.12ff.	280, 281	15:3-5	235		347 n.126
12:13	276, 280, 285	15:3-4	175	15:52	194
12:27-30	285	15:3	132, 133, 151	15:55	278
12:28	285–87, 303	15:4	115, 141	16:13	266
13	243, 297, 323	15:8-9	235	16:15	301, 303, 305
13:1	288	15:8	84	16:17	190
13:2	263, 286	15:9	217, 218, 227,	16:19	39, 300, 305
13:4-7	243		241, 300	16:20	317
13:4	298	15:9-10	87, 259	16:21-22	183
13:9-12	324	15:10	253	16:22-23	181, 184
13:12	336	15:12-19	327		
13:19	116	15:12-17	172, 176	*2 Corinthians*	
14	288, 304, 310, 311,	15:13ff.	3	1	47
	347 n.137	15:15	76 n.11, 115,	1:1	308
14:1	287		351 n.234	1:3-11	183
14:7-9	287	15:17	278	1:5	234, 239, 277
14:10-11	287	15:18	136	1:9ff.	266, 336
14:12	287	15:20-28	2	1:12	251
14:13-15	313	15:20	172, 176	1:14	200
14:14	291, 292	15:21-23	142	1:19	118, 278
14.15ff.	288, 291	15:21-22	11, 25	1:20	38, 47, 278
14:18	243, 253	15:21	30 n.5, 141	1:21	132, 315
14:20	288	15:23	189, 203	1:22	284, 291
14:21	64	15:24-28	115, 203	2:7, 10	167, 254
14:23-25	313	15:24-26	19	2:11	19, 84
14:23	300, 308, 322	15:24	18, 84, 153, 200	2:14-17	237
14:26-32	310	15:26	30 n.5	2:25	327
14:26	90, 309	15:27	141, 278	3-4	129
14:29	289	15:29	164, 314, 326	3	40, 49, 51, 52,
14:30	289	15:32	329		78 n.44, 184
14:31-32	289, 292	15:33	216	3	343 n.29
14:31	310	15:34-39	294	3:4-18	88
14:32ff.	152, 310	15:35-37	328	3:6, 7	52, 55
14:33	298	15:41-48	10	3:7	53

2 Corinthians (Cont.)
3:11   52, 53
3:13   53
3:14   53
3:14-15   53
3:17   116
3:18   330, 332
3:19   332
4-5   35 n.47, 193,
          293, 351 n.230
4:3   22, 327
4:4   15, 19, 21, 83, 334
4:5-6   227
4:7   237, 335
4:10-12   277
4:10-11   178, 237
4:10   238
4:11   335
4:13   263
4:14   172, 336
4:16—5:10   334
4:16   34 n.43, 237,
               276, 293
4:17   332
5   12, 276, 332, 333
5:1   25, 335
5:2-4   335
5:3   76 n.11, 334
5:4   333
5:5   284
5:6ff.   335
5:7   266
5:8   294, 333
5:9-10   191, 201, 203
5:10   162, 188, 241
5:14-20   297
5:14-15   164
5:14-16   153, 154, 165,
                    166
5:15   172
5:16-20   227
5:16-17   273, 274
5:16   87, 153
5:17   25, 136, 234,
     235, 261, 342 n.12,
               343 n.35

5:19   111, 112, 135,
          165, 166, 262
5:21   139, 40,
         164–166, 237,
              260, 261
6:1-9   254
6:1   253
6:2   148
6:4-10   238
6:15   298
6:16   282
6:18   78 n.54, 240
7:1   292
7:6-7   190
7:11   102
8   253
8:2   101
8:9   103, 117, 312, 322
8:16   322
8:23   242
9:4   76 n.11
10:1   241, 298
10:5ff.   267
10:15   266
11:2   11
11:3   9, 14, 30 n.5
11:14   19
11:21-22   217, 235
11:23-29   238, 240,
                    243
11:23-24   218
11:28   300
11:30—12.30   2
11:31   112
12:1   243
12:7   19
12:9   254
12:12   242, 243
12:13   167
12:14-15   240
12:20-21   297
12:20   76 n.11
13:11   298
13:12   301
13:13   115
13:14   116

Galatians
1:2   308
1:4   20
1:6   253
1:7   226
1:10—2.21   227
1:11—2.21   2
1:11-23   86, 225
1:13   217, 218
1:14   25, 64
1:15-16   232
1:16   88, 118, 226, 253
1:18   151
1:22   136
1:23   64, 87
2:8   320
2:9   252
2:11-21   64
2:16   265, 268, 270
2:17   76 n.11, 136, 278
2:19-20   238, 239
2:20-21   250
2:20   117, 136, 268,
               270, 278
2:21   65, 258
3-4   41, 42, 48–50, 54,
       64, 65, 80 n.90, 256
3:1   20, 77 n.27, 238
3:2, 5, 14   267
3:5   320
3:16-18   40
3:6   44, 264, 265
3:7, 9   269
3:8, 9   48
3:8   228
3:10   48
3:10-12   78 n.44,
                 79 n.63
3:11-12   264
3:12   48
3:13   48, 87, 133, 135,
               159, 165
3:15-16   46, 48
3:16   46, 47, 76 n.23,
                    268
3:17   48

3:19-20	16, 32 n.26	6:16	207	*Philippians*		
3:19	48, 54, 55	6:17	239	1		309
3:20	271			1:1	136, 183, 234, 302,	
3:21	48	*Ephesians*			304, 308	
3:22	269–71	1:3-14	248	1:2		134, 136
3:22-23	78 n.43	1:5, 11	246	1:4		280
3:23	48, 54	1:7	167	1:6	190, 198, 200–	
3:24	54	1:14	284		202, 266	
3:25	54	1:17-18	284	1:7		253
3:28	58, 206, 235,	1:20	32 n.31	1:10	101, 198, 201,	
	275, 312,	1:21	18, 32 n.24		202	
	346 n.112	1:22	184	1:13		239
3:29	61	2:2	321	1:19ff.		333
4	51	2:3	162	1:21		333
4:1-3	54	2:10	275	1:23		333
4:3	16, 17	2:11-18	72	1:25		266
4:4	17, 84, 89, 115,	2:11-22	310	1:28		320
	118, 134, 139, 140,	2:12	58	1:29	101, 239, 263, 265	
	149	2:13, 14-18	126–	2	83, 91, 94, 96, 98,	
4:5	135, 140, 284		27 n.100		100, 103, 107, 110,	
4:6	117, 153, 315	2:14-15	88, 226		111, 123 n.52, 182	
4:8-9	16, 17	2:15	64, 276	2:1		278
4:8	113	3:10	18	2.2ff.		214, 240
4:9	17	3:16	276, 293	2:5–3:15		123 n.59
4:13-14	239	4:2	298	2:5-11		323
4:14	32 n.26	4:5	254, 315	2:5-7	99, 103, 116,	
4:21-31	2, 40, 49, 55	4:8f.	254		117	
4:26	80 n.89, 180	4:8-12	310	2:5		278, 320
5:1	55	4:11	285, 287	2:6-11	2, 97, 100, 102,	
5:3	64	4:15-16	282		105, 107, 112,	
5:4	253	4:17-19	297		113	
5:5	262	4:22	293	2:6		83, 168
5:6	278, 321	4:24	293	2:7-8		140
5:16-25	290, 293, 295,	4:32	167, 254, 322	2:7		134
	296, 299	5:2	164	2:8-9		146, 175
5:16	296	5:3-5	297	2:8	145, 239, 268	
5:19-23	296, 299	5:6	162	2:9-11		204
5:19	295	5:18-20	309	2:9		96, 182
5:21	201, 202, 297	5:18	285	2:10-11		183
5:22	286, 297, 298	5:19	90	2:11		178, 181
6:2	68, 240, 323	5:21–6.9	301	2:12	98, 320, 239	
6:6	303	5:21ff.	310	2:15		201
6:10	297	6:6	296	2:16	101, 198, 202,	
6:14	184, 238	6:8	201		232	
6:15-16	58	6:12	18, 31 n.16,	2:24		266
6:15	233, 273		32 n.24	2:25		242

Philippians (cont)
2:29 278
2:30 239, 292
3:3ff. 266, 285
3:4-9 258
3:4-6 217, 227
3:5-6 64
3:6 25, 300, 348 n.164
3:7-10 87
3:7-8 234
3:8-9 102, 136
3:9 123 n.60, 259, 264, 268, 269, 270
3:10-11 101, 102, 277, 278, 333
3:11 233, 239
3:12-16 24, 27
3:12-15 324
3:12 166, 232, 239, 324
3:13-14 239
3:14-17 101
3:16 16, 232
3:17 79 n.84
3:18 136
3:18-19 59
3:20-21 331
3:20 190, 192, 200–202
4:2 184
4:4 116, 184
4:7 298
4:9 298
4:12-13 324

Colossians
1 83, 91, 94, 95, 107, 309
1:2 308
1:6 253
1:11 298
1:13f. 117
1:14 167

1:15-20 83, 90, 105–108, 111, 112, 183, 184
1:15-17 3
1:15 331
1:16 18
1:18 281, 300, 331
1:20 167
1:22 106
1:24 195, 281, 300
2 314
2:5 265
2:6ff. 184, 236
2:8 17
2:9 107, 109, 110, 113, 115, 236
2:10 18, 184
2:11 294
2:12 280
2:13 167, 254
2:14 18, 236, 309
2:15 18, 32 nn.24, 25
2:16 309
2:18 110, 291
2:19 282
2:20-22 309
2:23 17
3:1 58, 175, 334
3:4 116
3:5-8 297
3:6 162
3:9-10 275
3:9 293
3:10 276, 292, 293
3:11 276
3:12 68, 298
3:13 254, 323
3:15 298
3:16 90, 288, 309
3:18–4.1 301
3:25 201
4:15 300
4:16 308

1 Thessalonians
1:1 136, 280, 308

1:4 68
1:5 284
1:6-7 239, 240
1:6 214
1:7 302
1:9-10 172
1:9 18, 213, 225
1:10 77 n.33, 79 n.85, 162
1:11 302
1:14 214
1:28 19
2:7-8 241
2:14-16 58, 59
2:14 214, 234, 240, 280
2:19 190, 192
3.4 194
3:6-11 196
3:11-13 183
3:13 174, 190, 192, 193, 195
4-5 157 n.56, 195, 197
4 333
4:12 334
4:13–5.11 192, 194
4:13-16 334
4:13-18 193
4:13 334
4:14-17 198
4:14-16 173
4:14 199, 265, 351 n.234
4:15 190, 328
4:16 136, 142, 278
4:17 194, 196, 204
4:18 310
5 198
5:2-5 149
5:2 197, 198
5:3 198
5:4 197
5:5 198
5:9 278
5:10 164
5:11 310

5:12   278, 304, 305
5:14   298, 310
5:20-21   289
5:23   174, 190, 195,
              199, 200, 292, 298
5:27   308

2 Thessalonians
1:5-9   59
1:7-9   162
1:7   161, 201
1:12   253
2   157 n.56, 195, 197
2:1-12   196
2:1   190, 196, 324
2:4   113
2:7   216
2:8-12   19
2:8   189, 196
2:8, 9   190, 196
2:9-10   22
2:10   327
2:11-12   265
2:13   16, 68
2:16   253
3.3   322
3:10   152
3:14   152
5-6   17

1 Timothy
1:5, 7   349 n.174
1:15   217
2:8ff.   310
2:13-15   311
2:13-14   142
2:14   31 n.13
3.1ff.   348 n.169,
                 349 n.174
3:16   96, 109,
                 122 n.35
4:14   254
5:6   209 n.9
5:14-15   20
6:9   163
6:12   266

2 Timothy
1:6   254, 349
2:1   254
2:8   154 n.2
2:19   229
3:16-17   321
4:7   266

Titus
1:1ff.   348 n.169
1:1-4   266
2:11   254
2:14   68
3:5-7   254
3:5   275

Philemon
2   300
13   164

Hebrews
1   83, 94
1:2   120 n.23
1:3   96
2:17   140
4:15   140
5:12   16
6:1   16
6:2   16
11:1   266

1 Peter
1:2   227, 229, 231
1:20   227
2:23   238
3:16   136
3:22   136
5:10, 14   136

2 Peter
1:13ff.   335
3:17   227

1 John
4:8   66

Revelation
2:26   59
21   180

**Apocryphal/
Deuterocanonical
Books**

Tobit
4:9-10   199

Wisdom of Solomon
1-6   172
1:1-9   181
1:5   92
1:7   92, 106, 109
1:14   106
2:13   181
2:17   114
3:1-4   172
5-7   99
5:1   100, 105, 110
5:4   100, 105
5:16   99
5:23   106
6:3-4   100
6:12-16   92
6:21-22   106
6:22   106
7-11   52
7   82
7:7-14   92
7:7   92
7:8   106
7:9   75 n.5
7:11   91
7:14   92
7:17-19   31 n.18
7:22ff.   91, 92, 100
7:24, 27   92, 106
7:25-26   53, 92, 106
7:27-28   92
7:29   106
8:1   92
8:2-3   92
8:4-6   92, 114

Wisdom of Solomon (cont.)		48:12	98	50:1-4	172
8:7-9	92	51:13-21	92, 120	54:19	13
9:2	92				
9:4	92, 99, 114	Baruch		1 Enoch	
9:9	92	4:1	92	19	113
9:10-16	92			42:1-3	92
9:14	335	2 Esdras		48:10	154 n.7
9:17-18	92, 96	10:60–12.35	197	52:4	154 n.7
10:1-21	92			99:6-10	113
10:10	113	1 Maccabees		100:4-5	188
11	52	2:51-52	42	103:3ff.	334
11:2-4	81				
11:25	92	2 Maccabees		2 Enoch	
13:10-14	113	4:9	172	20:1	126 n.93
15:3	113	7:10-11	172	65:6-7	172
		12:43-44	172	66:6-11	189
Sirach (Ecclesiasticus)		14:46	172		
1:4, 9-10	92, 120 n.25			Midrash Rabbah	
1:14-20	92	4 Maccabees			
1:25-27	92	12:13	31 n.18	Genesis Rabbah	
3.17ff.	100			14:5	172
4:11-19	92, 120 n.25				
4:17	92	Other Jewish		Exodus Rabbah	
6:18-36	92, 120 n.25	Writings:		41:1	53
6:37	92				
11:1ff.	100	Apocalypse of Baruch		4 Ezra	
14:20–15.8	92,	14:12	199	6:5	199
	120 n.25			7	172
15:1-8	92	Apocalypse of Elijah		7:77	199
15:1	92	4:21	195	8:33, 36	199
16:24–17.7	92				
19:20	92	Apocalypse of Moses		Josephus	
23:1	114	13:3	172		
24	82, 109	41:3	172	Jewish Antiquities	
24:3	92, 126 n.90			3:80, 202-3	189
24:7, 12	92	Assumption of Moses		9:55	189
24:8-12	92	8-9	195	18:261-301	196
24:9	92, 126 n.90	9:1-7	195	18:284	189
24:19-33	92				
24:19-22	92	Babylonian Talmud		Jewish Wars	
24:23	92			2:10:11	172
33:2-3	92	Sanhedrin			
43:26	92, 109	90b	172	Jubilees	
44:19-21	49			23:10	42
46:1	98	2 Baruch		23:23	195
48:1ff.	98	36-40	197		

Mishnah Aboth
1:2   250

Mishnah Sanhedrin
10:1-3   297
10:1   70, 79 n.80,
                     172

Odes/Psalms of
Solomon
16:1-2   90
17-18   133

Philo

Conf.
41   143
62-63   143
146-47   143

De Fug.
109   126 n.90

De Virtu.
62   126 n.90

Leg.
203-346   196

Leg. All.
1:31   143
1:43   126 nn.89, 91

Quod Det.
54   114

Vit. Cont.
28-29   91
68-80   91

Qumran Documents

CD (Convenant of
Damascus)
12:23-24   154 n.7

14:19   154 n.7
19:1011   154 n.7

1 Qap Gen   181

1 Q H
3:13—4.26   195

1 Q Hab
5:7f.   20

1 Q M   197

4 Q Ps Dan Aa 154 n.4

11 Q Ps   91

1 Q Sa
2:11-12   154 n.4

Testaments of the
Twelve Patriarchs

Testament of Benjamin
10:9   172

Testament of Judah
22:27   189
23:3   189

Testament of Levi
3:7-8   126 n.93
4:4   189
8:11   189

Graeco-Roman
Writings

Aristotle

Politics
3:13, 1284a   299

Nicomachean Ethics
5:1129a   257

Cicero

Ad Atticus
8:16:2   194

Euripides

Hipp.
516   154 n.6

Isocrates

Ant.
2,16   32 n.19

Menander

De Hymnodes
1ff.   90

Pliny

Epistles
10:96:7   90

Plutarch

Moralia
875C   31 n.18

Lib. Educ.
16:2   32 n.19

Sib. Oracles
4:176-90   172

Xenophon

Memorabilia
2:1:1

Early Christian Writings

Acts of John
94:1—96:51   90

Didache
10:6   317

Eusebius

Historia Ecclesia
2:17:21ff.   91

Hermas

Similitudes
9:27:3   59

Ignatius

Ephesians
4:1-2   120 n.24
19:2-3   126 n.87

Author Index

Ashton, J., 125 n.80

Baird, W., 190, 210 nn.51, 52
Balchin, J. F., 122 n.39
Banks, R., 300, 301, 348 n.165
Barrett, C. K., 6, 18, 30 n.6, 32 nn.23, 30; 40, 63, 75 nn.4, 6; 77 nn.27, 35; 78 nn.46, 47, 56, 58, 60; 79 nn.64, 65, 72, 74, 78, 80; 128 nn.123, 125, 126; 139, 155 n.25, 156 nn.42–44, 49; 162, 165, 203, 208 n.3, 209 nn.6, 10, 26, 27, 30; 211 nn.68, 70–73; 245, 260, 273, 275, 294, 303, 344 nn.55, 56, 61, 66; 345 n.86, 346 n.114, 347 nn.123, 131, 133; 348 n.168, 350 n.213
Barth, M., 248, 344 n.66
Bassler, J. M., 6
Bauer, W., 164
Beasley-Murray, G. R., 210 n.59
Beker, J. C., 6, 83, 119 nn.5, 6; 170, 171, 177, 209 nn.16, 33
Best, E., 189, 210 n.50
Betz, H. D., 49, 71 n.28
Betz, O., 344 n.47
Brown, R. E., 155 n.24

Bruce, F. F., 78 n.32, 127 n.104, 155 n.23, 210 nn.53, 55; 273, 342 n.4, 348 nn.155, 158, 161, 162; 351 n.228
Bultmann, R., 147, 156 nn.50, 51; 228, 229, 252, 264, 266, 272, 274, 276, 293, 325, 343 nn.19–23
Burkitt, F. C., 112
Burton, E. deWitt, 119 n.14, 342 n.14

Caird, G. B., 200, 210 nn.65, 66; 334
Castelli, E. A., 344 n.58
Charlesworth, J. H., 120 n.27
Cranfield, C.E.B., 23, 25, 26, 31 n.15, 32 n.24, 33 nn.36, 37; 34 n.43, 35 n.47, 62, 63, 71, 76 n.21, 79 nn.62, 79, 82; 124 n.66, 128 nn.126, 128; 155 n.26, 156 n.48, 161, 208 nn.1, 2; 209 n.13, 347 n.121, 351 n.235, 259, 261, 266, 271, 332, 345 n.90, 346 nn. 98, 107
Cullmann, O., 184

Dahl, N. A., 154 n.5, 312, 350 n.195
Davies, W. D., 49, 77 n.31, 171,

209 nn.18, 19; 211 n.69, 329,
351 nn.227, 229
Dodd, C. H., 166, 332, 351 n.221
Dunn, J.D.G., 51, 70, 71, 77 n.37,
79 nn.66, 81, 83; 87, 99, 102–3,
109, 114, 118, 119 n.13, 122 n.45,
123 nn.47, 49; 124 n.66, 126 n.94,
128 nn.118, 126, 127; 139, 144,
155 nn.10, 12, 27; 156 nn.46, 47;
209 n.32, 210 n.63, 316, 343 n.39,
346 nn.96, 102, 109; 350 n.199

Fee, G. D., 156 n.41, 209 n.24
Fitzgerald, J. T., 237, 238, 343 nn.42,
43, 44
Forester, R. T., 343 n.23
Fowl, S., 7 n.11, 44, 76 n.14,
122 nn.39, 44; 123 nn.47, 58;
124 nn.61, 65; 125 nn.88, 97;
126 nn.97, 98; 127 n.101, 251,
345 nn.68, 69; 350 n.218
Furnish, V. P., 77 n.41, 266, 276, 293,
346 nn.97, 117

Georgi, D., 99, 123 n.57
Gese, H., 121, n.30
Glasson, T. F., 99, 123 n.51, 124 n.69,
126 n.90
Grundmann, W., 133, 155 nn.11, 16,
17, 20
Gundry, R., 293, 294, 295,
348 nn.146, 147, 149, 150, 152

Hafemann, S., 237, 343 n.40
Harnack, A. von, 215, 305
Harris, M. J., 76 n.16, 113, 127 n.108,
176, 209 nn.28, 29
Hawthorne, G. F., 100, 103, 124 n.71,
350 nn.211, 212
Hays, R. B., 5, 33 n.32, 38 nn.48, 49;
42, 43, 45, 75 n.3, 76 nn.9, 13, 17;
77 n.39, 268, 269, 270, 271,
346 nn.101, 102, 104, 109
Headlam, A. C., 209 n.12, 210 n.34,
343 n.25
Hengel, M., 95, 117, 120 n.17,

121 nn.32, 33, 155 n.9, 157 n.54,
217, 220, 233, 342 nn. 5, 6, 8, 9;
343 nn.28, 32
Holladay, C. R., 109, 126 n.95
Hooker, M., 268
Hoover, R. W., 103, 122 n.46,
124 n.70
Horsley, R., 113, 127 nn.111, 112,
114
Howard, G., 99, 123 n.55
Hurtado, L. W., 82, 119 n.4, 120 n.29,
122 n.43, 182, 210 n.36

Jeremias, J., 141, 142, 152, 156 nn.32,
37; 157 n.57
Jervell, J., 125 n.79
Jewett, R., 348 n.142
Jonge, M. De, 154 n.7

Kasemann, E., 24, 33 n.38, 35 n.48,
163, 164, 209 n.5, 259, 272,
345 n.84
Kilpatrick, G. D., 189, 210 n.48
Kim, S., 79 n.66, 119 n.14, 155 n.15,
259, 342 n.14, 345 n.81
Kreitzer, L. J., 210 n.64

Lightfoot, J. B., 103, 123 nn.64, 69
Lincoln, A. T., 351 n.237
Longenecker, R. N., 233, 240, 270,
343 nn.27, 30; 344 nn.46, 48, 51;
346 n.106
Lyonnet, S., 31 n.10
Lyons, G., 227, 343 n.17

Machen, J. G., 155 n.24
Macmullen, R., 120 n.18
Malherbe, A., 241, 344 n.52
Manson, T. W., 242, 344 n.54
Marshall, I. H., 78 n.51, 99, 117,
123 n.53, 126 n.94, 128 n.124, 231,
247, 248, 344 nn.62, 63, 64, 65
Marston, V. P., 343 n.23
Martin, D. P., 344 n.59, 347 n.135
Martin, R. P., 96, 122 nn.36–38, 42;
125 n.85, 183, 210 nn.38, 39;
211 n.67

Meeks, W. A., 31 n.17, 301, 304, 306,
308, 315, 317, 323, 348 nn.165–67;
349 nn.171–73, 175, 177, 182, 186,
187; 350 nn.196, 197, 202, 203,
206, 207, 209, 215
Metzger, B. M., 78 n.55, 112, 113,
127 nn.105, 107; 350 n.210
Milligan, G., 209 n.7
Minear, P., 346 n.100
Moore, A. L., 176, 209 n.31
Moule, C.F.D., 122 n.45, 124 n.68,
137, 155 nn.19, 22; 156 n.31, 332
Moulton, J. H., 209 n.7
Munck, J., 59, 78 n.53
Murphy, K. G., 93, 120
Murphy-O'Connor, J., 99, 114,
124 n.67
Murray, J., 230, 343 n.26

Nickelsburg, G. W. E., 172,
209 nn.20, 21
Norden, E., 107, 125 n.84

O'Brien, P. T., 32 n.25, 126 nn.96,
99
O'Neill, J. C., 98, 122 n.41, 125 n.83

Pearson, B., 78 n.52, 348 n.144
Peterson, N. R., 3, 6
Pfitzner, V. C., 344 n.52
Plummer, A., 351 nn.223, 231

Ridderbos, H., 7
Robertson, A. T., 351 nn.231, 233
Robinson, J.A.T., 119 n.12

Sanday, W., 209 n.12, 210 n.34,
343 n.25
Sanders, E. P., 5, 24, 33 n.39, 79 n.70,
295, 345 nn.74, 80
Sanders, J. A., 120 n.21
Sanders, J. T., 123 nn.52, 54;
124 nn.81, 86; 126 n.87
Schmidt, K. L., 228, 343 n.18
Schüssler Fiorenza, E., 96,
121 n.32, 122 n.37

Schweitzer, A., 149, 157 n.53, 255,
276, 345 n.72
Schweizer, E., 106, 120 nn.23, 29;
125 nn.77, 82; 126 n. 91
Segal, A., 227, 342 nn.15, 16; 343 n.33
Stendahl, K., 24, 33 n.40
Strecker, G., 98, 122 n.43
Styler, G. M., 245, 344 n.60

Theissen, G., 308, 349 n.181
Turner, N., 127 n.106

Vermes, G., 75 n.6
Vos, G., 209 n.23, 347 n.118

Wanamaker, C. A., 99, 123 n.50,
125 n.72, 209 n.22
Westerholm, S., 345 nn.75, 77
Whiteley, D.E.H., 7, 209 n.12
Wink, W., 90, 91, 105, 106, 120 n.19,
125 nn.78, 80
Witherington, B., 7, 31 n.11, 32 nn.21,
27, 28; 76 nn.18, 20; 77 nn.29, 30,
34, 40; 78 n.50, 79 n.77, 80 n.88,
119 nn.2, 3, 11; 120 n. 26, 122 n.40,
123 n.56, 127 nn.103, 110, 113;
155 nn.8, 24; 156 nn.38, 40;
157 n.52, 209 nn.15, 17;
210 nn.35, 44, 49, 54, 56, 58, 60;
341 n.1, 342 nn.7, 10; 343 nn.29,
31, 34, 38, 40, 43; 344 n.45,
346 n.115, 347 nn.122, 126, 130,
137, 139; 348 nn.144, 148, 159; 349
nn.170, 176; 178, 180, 183–85,
188–90, 350 nn.192, 193, 205, 214;
351 nn. 222, 226, 232, 236
Wright, N. T., 7, 33 n.41, 75 n.2,
76 nn.19, 23; 79 n.68, 104,
119 nn.7, 9, 11; 121 n.31,
122 nn.45, 48; 124 n.62, 125 nn.71,
76, 78; 127 nn.109, 114–17

Yamauchi, E., 121 n.29

Zeisler, J. A., 31 n.10, 32 n.20, 33 n.42,
44, 76 n.15, 79 n.85, 210 n.41